Metrics and Models for Evaluating the Quality and Effectiveness of ERP Software

Geoffrey Muchiri Muketha
Murang'a University of Technology, Kenya

Elyjoy Muthoni Micheni
Technical University of Kenya, Kenya

A volume in the Advances in
Systems Analysis, Software
Engineering, and High Performance
Computing (ASASEHPC) Book Series

Published in the United States of America by
> IGI Global
> Engineering Science Reference (an imprint of IGI Global)
> 701 E. Chocolate Avenue
> Hershey PA, USA 17033
> Tel: 717-533-8845
> Fax: 717-533-8661
> E-mail: cust@igi-global.com
> Web site: http://www.igi-global.com

Library of Congress Cataloging-in-Publication Data

Names: Muketha, Geoffrey Muchiri, 1970- editor. | Micheni, Elyjoy Muthoni,
   1963- editor.
Title: Metrics and models for evaluating the quality and effectiveness of ERP
   software / Geoffrey Muchiri Muketha and Elyjoy Muthoni Micheni, editors.
Description: Hershey, PA : Engineering Science Reference, an imprint of IGI
   Global, [2019] | Includes bibliographical references and index.
Identifiers: LCCN 2018032615| ISBN 9781522576785 (hardcover) | ISBN
   9781522576792 (ebook)
Subjects: LCSH: Enterprise resource planning--Data processing. |
   Manufacturing resource planning--Data processing. | Computer
   software--Evaluation.
Classification: LCC HD38.5 .M47 2019 | DDC 658.4/012028553--dc23 LC record available at
https://lccn.loc.gov/2018032615

This book is published in the IGI Global book series Advances in Systems Analysis, Software Engineering, and High Performance Computing (ASASEHPC) (ISSN: 2327-3453; eISSN: 2327-3461)

British Cataloguing in Publication Data
A Cataloguing in Publication record for this book is available from the British Library.

For electronic access to this publication, please contact: eresources@igi-global.com.

Advances in Systems Analysis, Software Engineering, and High Performance Computing (ASASEHPC) Book Series

ISSN:2327-3453
EISSN:2327-3461

Editor-in-Chief: Vijayan Sugumaran, Oakland University, USA

MISSION

The theory and practice of computing applications and distributed systems has emerged as one of the key areas of research driving innovations in business, engineering, and science. The fields of software engineering, systems analysis, and high performance computing offer a wide range of applications and solutions in solving computational problems for any modern organization.

The **Advances in Systems Analysis, Software Engineering, and High Performance Computing (ASASEHPC) Book Series** brings together research in the areas of distributed computing, systems and software engineering, high performance computing, and service science. This collection of publications is useful for academics, researchers, and practitioners seeking the latest practices and knowledge in this field.

COVERAGE

- Storage Systems
- Computer Networking
- Human-Computer Interaction
- Metadata and Semantic Web
- Virtual Data Systems
- Enterprise Information Systems
- Distributed Cloud Computing
- Engineering Environments
- Parallel Architectures
- Computer Graphics

IGI Global is currently accepting manuscripts for publication within this series. To submit a proposal for a volume in this series, please contact our Acquisition Editors at Acquisitions@igi-global.com or visit: http://www.igi-global.com/publish/.

Titles in this Series

For a list of additional titles in this series, please visit:
https://www.igi-global.com/book-series/advances-systems-analysis-software-engineering/73689

Interdisciplinary Approaches to Information Systems and Software Engineering
Alok Bhushan Mukherjee (North-Eastern Hill University Shillong, India) and Akhouri
Pramod Krishna (Birla Institute of Technology Mesra, India)
Engineering Science Reference ● ©2019 ● 299pp ● H/C (ISBN: 9781522577843) ● US $215.00

Cyber-Physical Systems for Social Applications
Maya Dimitrova (Bulgarian Academy of Sciences, Bulgaria) and Hiroaki Wagatsuma (Kyushu
Institute of Technology, Japan)
Engineering Science Reference ● ©2019 ● 440pp ● H/C (ISBN: 9781522578796) ● US $265.00

Integrating the Internet of Things Into Software Engineering Practices
D. Jeya Mala (Thiagarajar College of Engineering, India)
Engineering Science Reference ● ©2019 ● 293pp ● H/C (ISBN: 9781522577904) ● US $215.00

Analyzing the Role of Risk Mitigation and Monitoring in Software Development
Rohit Kumar (Chandigarh University, India) Anjali Tayal (Infosys Technologies, India) and
Sargam Kapil (C-DAC, India)
Engineering Science Reference ● ©2018 ● 308pp ● H/C (ISBN: 9781522560296) ● US $225.00

Handbook of Research on Pattern Engineering System Development for Big Data Analytics
Vivek Tiwari (International Institute of Information Technology, India) Ramjeevan Singh
Thakur (Maulana Azad National Institute of Technology, India) Basant Tiwari (Hawassa
University, Ethiopia) and Shailendra Gupta (AISECT University, India)
Engineering Science Reference ● ©2018 ● 396pp ● H/C (ISBN: 9781522538707) ● US $320.00

Incorporating Nature-Inspired Paradigms in Computational Applications
Mehdi Khosrow-Pour, D.B.A. (Information Resources Management Association, USA)
Engineering Science Reference ● ©2018 ● 385pp ● H/C (ISBN: 9781522550204) ● US $195.00

For an entire list of titles in this series, please visit:
https://www.igi-global.com/book-series/advances-systems-analysis-software-engineering/73689

701 East Chocolate Avenue, Hershey, PA 17033, USA
Tel: 717-533-8845 x100 ● Fax: 717-533-8661
E-Mail: cust@igi-global.com ● www.igi-global.com

Editorial Advisory Board

Table of Contents

Section 1
Introduction to ERP Quality and Effectiveness

Section 2
User Perceptions and Usability Evaluation

Section 3
Implementation and Maintenance Evaluation

Detailed Table of Contents

Section 1
Introduction to ERP Quality and Effectiveness

*Majdi Abdellatief Mohammed, Sudan Technological University, Sudan
& Shaqra University, Saudi Arabia*

*Amir Mohamed Talib, Al Imam Mohammad Ibn Saud Islamic University,
Saudi Arabia*

Ibrahim Ahmed Al-Baltah, Sanaa University, Yemen

ERP system provides a central system that integrates most of the core business processes such as human resources, finance, production, and so on. Due to the integration of such complicated functionalities and rapidly evolving customers expectation, ERP systems evaluation has an important impact on organization business success. The aim of this chapter is to understand the evaluation approaches of the ERP systems, and then to map the identified primary studies into a classification scheme to answer the research questions. A systematic mapping study was employed. A total of 36 studies published between the years 2002 and 2018 were collected, analyzed, classified, and discussed. A list of relevant ERP quality attributes that have been measured is identified. Reliability of the metrics methodology and the validity of indicator generated by the metric are two major issues in the current research. It is worth noting that while both the academic and professional literature has shown a great interact in ERP, there does not exist an evaluation approach that is widely accepted.

Over time, the adoption of ERP systems has been wide across many small, medium, and large organizations. An ERP system is supposed to inform the strategic decision making of the organization; therefore, the information drawn from the ERP system is as important as the data stored in it. Poor data quality affects the quality information in it. Data mining is used to discover trends and patterns of an organization. This chapter looks into the way of integrating these data mining into an ERP system. This is conceptualized in three crucial views namely the outer, inner, and the knowledge discovery view. The outer view comprises of the collection of various entry points, the inner view contains the data repository, and the knowledge discovery view offers the data mining component. Since the focus is data mining, the two strategies of supervised and unsupervised are discussed. The chapter then concludes by presenting the probable problems within which each of these two strategies (classification and clustering) can be put into place within the mining process of an ERP system.

Chapter 3

Even though most organizations are using enterprise resource planning applications, very few people understand the underlying interoperability nature within them. Interoperability is the ability of systems to provide services to and accept services from other systems, and to use the services exchanged so as to operate together in a more effective manner. The fact that interoperability can be improved means that the metrics for measuring interoperability can be defined. For the purpose of measuring the interoperability between systems, an interoperability assessment model is required. A comparative analysis among these models is provided to evaluate the similarities and differences in their philosophy and implementation. The analysis yields a set of recommendations for any party that is open to the idea of creating or improving an interoperability assessment model.

Chapter 4

Ramgopal Kashyap, Amity University Chhattisgarh, India

This chapter deals with the security and its structure for the ERP that can be utilized to address all applicable security perspectives inside an association and to guarantee that it shapes a fundamental piece of an ERP framework. The security system is mapped onto the ERP model to give the association an unmistakable comprehension of which security issues must be tended to inside which ERP part. It is clear given the over that security must frame a necessary piece of an ERP framework and that it will be hard to include it once the ERP framework is as of now actualized. In the event that security is included after usage, the ERP framework will experience issues clinging to IT and corporate administration necessities. An ERP framework is additionally an essential piece of the association and can't be dealt with as an autonomous framework without taking the association's approaches and techniques into thought. This chapter furnishes an association with a structure to guarantee that all angles encompassing IT and corporate security are incorporated with an ERP framework.

Chapter 5

Julius Nyerere Odhiambo, Technical University of Kenya, Kenya
Elyjoy Muthoni Micheni, Technical University of Kenya, Kenya
Benard Muma, Technical University of Kenya, Kenya

The quest for sustainable competitive advantage and the urge to adapt to a challenging business environment has made firms around the globe to adopt enterprise resource planning systems so as optimally leverage on the enterprise-wide resources and be more responsive to customer demands. Globally organizations seeking to enhance their competitiveness have utilized Enterprise Resource Planning (ERP) systems to enhance their operational efficiency. The ERP philosophy advocates for the incorporation of personnel, finance, manufacturing, distribution, sales, and marketing modules into a single integrated system and a central database, allowing an organization to efficiently and effectively utilize its resources. The planning and better management of organizational resources, improved business performance, and better integration of business operations can be facilitated by an ERP system to offer an avenue of excellence for a business. Despite the potential benefits an ERP system offers an organization, few studies have explored the ERP reliability in the context of competition driven business imperatives.

Chapter 6

*Stella Nafula Khaemba, Masinde Muliro University of Science and
        Technology, Kenya*

Enterprise resource planning (ERP) systems are increasingly being adopted by many organizations. The cost, time, and effort of the organization need to be reflected in the uptake and use of the system by employees of the organizations in question. ERP system implementation readiness is positively associated with the ERP implementation success. It is therefore important to measure the success of such software in adopting firms which largely influenced by the readiness of the firm for ERPs. Many studies focus on other aspects of readiness leaving out the major players who are employees. This chapter discusses an effort towards extending CREM evaluation model for employee readiness with the aim of highlighting the role of their readiness in the overall success of ERP implementation. Research findings of this study help decision makers of organizations to attain a comprehensive picture about required actions to be accomplished for achieving readiness for implementing an ERP system.

Section 2
User Perceptions and Usability Evaluation

Chapter 7

*Amos Chege Kirongo, Meru University of Science and Technology,
        Kenya
Guyo Sarr Huka, Meru University of Science and Technology, Kenya*

This chapter introduces the service delivery challenges experienced by users of enterprise resource planning systems (ERP) by discussing the user perceptions. The authors administered questionnaires to users of ERP systems and user perception of ERPs was found to affect them in service delivery. Software complexity, software usability, and user resistance were found out as challenges contributing the challenge of service delivery. Attribution theory, diffusion of innovation theory, and compatibility maturity model are discussed; existing theories are discussed in the chapter. Findings are outlined and conclusion made based on the questionnaires addressed to the respondents.

Chapter 8

Kelvin Kabeti Omieno, Kaimosi Friends University College, Kenya

The enterprise resource planning (ERP) system is a complex and comprehensive software that integrates various enterprise functions and resources. Although ERP systems have been depicted as a solution in many organizations, there are many negative reports on ERP success, benefits, and effect on user performance. Previous research noted that there is a lack of knowledge and awareness of ERP systems and their overall value to ERP organizations. ERP systems have been widely studied during the past decade; yet they often fail to deliver the intended benefits originally expected. One notable reason for their failures is the lack of understanding in user requirements. There are many studies conducted to propose software quality models with their quality characteristics. However, there is currently no dedicated software quality model that can describe usability maturity and involve new features of ERP systems. This chapter proposes a framework for evaluating the usability maturity as a quality attribute of ERP systems.

Chapter 9

The technological innovation depends on learnability of the software used in terms of user interface design, program complexity of products that match the end user requirements, program complexity deals with commands used in the given ERP software, and training needs so that the ERP user can learn all required features and commands. Learnability signifies how quickly and comfortably a new user can begin efficient and error-free interaction. The main purpose of this chapter is to evaluate software learnability and performance of ERP software. Primary data was collected using survey through the use of questionnaires. Purposive sampling was used to collect data. The collected data focused on the software complexity, user interfaces analysis, ERP performance, challenges, efficiency, and training needs of ERP. Data analysis was done by inferential and descriptive statistics. The results indicated that there exists a positive and statistically significant relationship between the variables used.

Section 3
Implementation and Maintenance Evaluation

Chapter 10

The world over, higher education institutions have resorted to the use of ERP system to automate operations on a standardized platform in line with their strategic plans. This is because ERP system supports a "do-it-all" approach to organizational management in addition to education managers' quest to improve quality of service to their students and the need to meet regional as well as global standards. In most institutions, operational areas such as student admission, finance, procurement, examination management, staffing, and alumni management can now be done through the ERP system. This chapter examines the issues associated with implementation of ERP system in higher education institutions. After studying this chapter, you should be able to: appreciate the various strategies for ERP system implementation, identify the factors leading to successful implementation of ERP system in higher education institutions, distinguish between the different models for successful ERP system implementation, and understand the metrics for measuring success rate of ERP system implementation.

Chapter 11
Samwel Mungai Mbuguah, Kibabii University, Kenya
Franklin Wabwoba, Kibabii University, Kenya
Chrispus Kimingichi Wanjala, Kibabii University, Kenya

Most institution of higher learning are implementing enterprise resource planning (ERP) in automating various activities. The architecture of most of the ERP is based on the service-oriented architecture (SOA) where each module can be called as service. In most of the contracts signed between the vendor and the university, payment is tied to the level of implementation. The question is how to then measure the level of implementation. This chapter proposes a metric that could be used. The metric was derived based on an acceptance test on each of functionality of module as per terms of reference. The result of a test was rated as a fail; the result was then coded such that a fail was assigned a zero (0), pass one (1), and query a half (½), from which a metric was derived which measures the level implementation.

Chapter 12
Elyjoy Muthoni Micheni, Technical University of Kenya, Kenya

This chapter will explain ERP software maintenance and the effort required to locate and fix errors in the ERP software. Software maintenance is defined as the totality of activities required to provide cost-effective support to a software system. The purpose of software maintenance is to modify and update software application after delivery to correct faults and to improve performance. The chapter will highlight activities performed during the pre-delivery stage, including planning for post-delivery operations, supportability, and logistics determination, and also activities performed during the post-delivery stage, including software modification, training, and operating a help desk. The chapter will discuss the types of maintenance and highlight the ERP process support activities and the ERP system maintainability framework. The chapter will explain the maintenance of ERP software and will also discuss the ISO/IEC 9126 and IEEE Standard 1219-1998 for software maintenance. Issues in ERP software maintenance are also presented and discussed.

Julius Murumba, Technical University of Kenya, Kenya
Jackson Kipchirchir Machii, Technical University of Kenya, Kenya

The role of software inspections, product reviews, walk-troughs, and audits in ERP software is analyzed in this chapter. Software inspections are a disciplined engineering practice for detecting and correcting defects in software artifacts with the aim of correcting them. Walkthroughs involve software peer review mechanism in which a programmer leads peers through a software product, in a process in which participants ask questions and make comments about possible errors, violation of development standards, and other problems. This chapter also discusses ERP systems audit and control risks and seeks to help understand key risks and control issues surrounding ERP systems.

Preface

Enterprise resource planning (ERP) is a class of integrated software that uses software technologies to implement real-time management of business processes in an organization. ERPs normally cut across organizations, making them large and complex. Researchers have long established that high complexity has a negative effect on software quality and effectiveness. Researchers have also over the years proposed novel metrics and models that have been used for evaluating and therefore controlling software quality.

Metrics and Models for Evaluating the Quality and Effectiveness of ERP Software is a book that has been written so that it carefully documents the theory and current state ERP software from a user perspective. The book covers quality themes such as interoperability, security, reliability, user perception, implementation, maintenance, software inspections, and audits, among others. Interesting case studies from selected institutions of higher learning are also covered. The objectives of this book are: 1) to create awareness of quality among ERP users and managers; 2) to help improve decision making in organizations that have embraced ERPs; 3) to improve the efficiency and effectiveness of users as they interact with their institutional ERPs; and 4) to improve their return on investments (ROI). The book is essential for ERP users and managers, software developers, researchers, academicians, and information security professionals.

The book is divided into three logical parts, which together contain thirteen chapters as elaborated below.

Section 1 presents a general introduction to ERP quality and effectiveness and contains the first six chapters as follows: 1) Metrics and Models for Evaluating the Quality of ERP Software: Systematic Mapping Review; 2) Quality and Effectiveness of ERP Software: Data Mining Perspective; 3) Interoperability of ERP Software; 4) Security Framework for Enterprise Resource Planning; 5) Understanding Enterprise Resource Planning Reliability for Operational Excellence: Components of a Reliable Enterprise Resource Planning System; and 6) Evaluation of Employee Readiness for ERP Systems: A Case of Kitale National Polytechnic.

Section 2 presents user perceptions and usability evaluation and contains the next three chapters as follows: 7) ERP User Perceptions and Service Delivery Challenges: User Perceptions and Service Delivery Challenges; 8) Evaluating the Usability Maturity of Enterprise Resource Planning Systems; and 9) Evaluating the Learnability of ERP Software: A Case Study of Kabarak University, Kenya.

Section 3 presents implementation and maintenance evaluation issues and contains the last four chapters as follows: 10) Enterprise Resource Planning System Implementation in Higher Education Institutions: A Theoretical Review; 11) Implementation Evaluation Metrics for ERP Solution: A Case of Kibabii University; 12) ERP Software Maintenance; and 13) ERP Software Inspections and Audits.

The experiences and challenges encountered by ERP users and managers while trying to execute their institutional business processes in real time are both difficult and interesting. In response to this scenario, researchers and practitioners have shown dedication to developing new methods of evaluation that will help control ERP software quality in the long run. This book is a good step in that direction.

Geoffrey Muchiri Muketha
Murang'a University of Technology, Kenya

Elyjoy Muthoni Micheni
Technical University of Kenya, Kenya

Acknowledgment

This book would not have been possible without the cooperation and assistance of many people. The editors would like to thank Ms. Josephine Dadeboe and the many other dedicated team at IGI Global for their expertise in guiding this project. We thank all the authors who contributed to this book, without their willingness to share their knowledge, this project would not have been possible. We also that our reviewers, many of whom doubled up as authors of other chapters. We would like to thank the book's Advisory Board for support and valuable suggestions. We also acknowledge our respective institutions for supporting us for this project. Finally, the editors wish to acknowledge their families for their understanding.

Section 1
Introduction to ERP Quality and Effectiveness

Chapter 1
Metrics and Models for Evaluating the Quality of ERP Software:
Systematic Mapping Review

Majdi Abdellatief Mohammed
Sudan Technological University, Sudan & Shaqra University, Saudi Arabia

Amir Mohamed Talib
Al Imam Mohammad Ibn Saud Islamic University, Saudi Arabia

Ibrahim Ahmed Al-Baltah
Sanaa University, Yemen

ABSTRACT

ERP system provides a central system that integrates most of the core business processes such as human resources, finance, production, and so on. Due to the integration of such complicated functionalities and rapidly evolving customers expectation, ERP systems evaluation has an important impact on organization business success. The aim of this chapter is to understand the evaluation approaches of the ERP systems, and then to map the identified primary studies into a classification scheme to answer the research questions. A systematic mapping study was employed. A total of 36 studies published between the years 2002 and 2018 were collected, analyzed, classified, and discussed. A list of relevant ERP quality attributes that have been measured is identified. Reliability of the metrics methodology and the validity of indicator generated by the metric are two major issues in the current research. It is worth noting that while both the academic and professional literature has shown a great interact in ERP, there does not exist an evaluation approach that is widely accepted.

DOI: 10.4018/978-1-5225-7678-5.ch001

INTRODUCTION

Enterprise resource planning (ERP) software is playing an increasing role in the software industry and is considered to be the new engine to sustain the high growth of data and information technology. Huge investments are being made by organizations with great expectations for the gains to be made through ERP systems. The claim is that ERP systems allow the reduction of cost and time through the reuse of such systems in different enterprise environments. Generally, ERP system is designed to fit the needs of all organization requirements, but it could be useless or even harmful if the system does not adequately fit specific organization needs. In most cases, ERP system might be ill-fitting with the organization requirements for the following reasons:

- ERP systems implement package software rather than software written for or by one customer.
- ERP systems operate on organization's internal and external operations, and affect its business and strategy
- ERP system provide central systems that have a variety of associated stakeholders and the relationships between them.
- Different organizations may implement the same ERP system using different development methodologies.

Evaluation model and metric are two different but closely related concepts. This is because both metrics and evaluation models are used to determine or predict the quality of the product or process. They differ in their aims and results. The goal of the evaluation is to determine if a software product, process or project passes assessment and achieves minimum requirements. Evaluation model outcomes are descriptive and do not have to be quantitative. On the other hand, the goal of the metric is to obtain objective and quantifiable measurement of some attribute of a software product or process. Metrics are convenient and easily understandable evaluation methods. In some cases, evaluation models employees' metrics composed of multiple measures to overcome the descriptive results.

Having the right metric is the first step toward delivering high-quality product. Metrics can explore, but does not solve, the problem. In order to control the quality of ERP systems, many kinds of metrics and evaluation models exist, but not all of them are meaningful in the specific context of an organization. Therefore, defining the right metrics in the proper context is very important. To make sure that the metric is defined in a meaningful way, the author of metric should clearly describe these five elements: 1) Measured Element: which element of an ERP system are being measured? 2) Purpose: why are we measuring the element? 3) Focus: what characteristic or attribute of the element are we interested in? 4) Viewpoint: who is the primary target? 5) Environment: in which context is the element measured? Covering these five elements in the metric definition process guarantees that the metric is a reliable and valid indicator. Reliability means that a metric system generates consistent outcomes in replication. Validity concerns whether the evaluation is properly conducted.

The objectives of this study is to understand, classify and analyze existing metrics for measuring the quality of ERP software and direct future research. This review is important and useful for practitioners as an indication of maturity in the selection of an existing metric and to remain up-to-date. Moreover, a new and an enhanced metrics can be proposed based on this extend literature. After reading this paper, the readers will be able to answer the following questions: how much activity was there in the last 16 years to evaluate ERP software? Which techniques, methods, metrics, models and tools were developed to evaluate ERP systems in the literature? Were there limitations on the current research of ERP Metrics and Evaluation models? To answer the aforementioned questions, a systematic mapping review is used as a research method for this study. Compared to a traditional literature review, a mapping review has many advantages such as: a well-defined methodology that reduces bias and a wider context that allows for a general conclusion. To do this, the next section of the paper discusses related works. Then, the authors present the research method, followed by the primary study background. After that, we discuss the results. Finally, we conclude the paper.

RELATED WORKS

In a recent study, Valdebenito and Quelopana (2018) investigated the adoption of ERP system in the last 14 years (2003 -2017) based on publication from web of science. The distribution of researches is analyzed based on publication years, county, and citation analysis. They collected 150 papers from 31 countries, the total number of citation was 2405, and 50% of the papers was published in 2015 and 2016. Another survey conducted by Ömüral and Demirörs (2017) analyzed three ERP effort estimation approaches, which based on function points. These approaches are COSMIC-EPC, COSMIC-FFP and ERP service effort estimation strategies. Both COSMIC-FFP and COSMIC-EPC methods use function point for size measure and then converts it to effort estimation. While, ERP services effort estimation strategies approach uses a matrix that integrate different strategies likes resource, topics and situation. Deshmukh, Thampi, & Kalamkar (2015) have investigated the effects of top management's support, training, project management and hardware and software on ERP quality aspects. They collected data from 95

Indian enterprises and analyzed the effect of each factor on ERP quality aspects using regression model. The results showed the positive significant of hardware and software, training, project management and top management support on quality aspects. Garefalakis, Mantalis, Vourgourakis, Spinthiropoulos, and Lemonakis, (2016) also have discussed the adoption of ERP systems in healthcare sector, and how can be used to improve the quality of their functionality. They argue that the adoption process of ERP system is not standard due to many factors. To overcome this issue, they proposed a methodology for adoption ERP system in healthcare organization. The findings revealed that the right adoption increase the quality and productivity significantly.

RESEARCH METHOD

Considering the research questions stated in the next section, the authors performed a systematic mapping study (SMS) to identify and classify an existing ERP metrics and evaluation models. SMS is a methodology that offers a visual map of the area to identify research gap and to direct future research. This study is performed in six steps outlined as follows: I) protocol development II) research questions formulation and justifications, III) identification of articles, IV) inclusion and exclusion criteria, V) data extraction, and VI) synthesis and reporting. In the following sections, the researcher detailed each process used according to the guidelines published by (Kitchenham, 2004; Kitchenham et al., 2009, 2010). The execution of the overall process involved refinement, consultation and iterations of the defined process as a result of the researcher's experience in systematic literature review(Abdellatief, Sultan, Ghani, & Jabar, 2013).

Protocol Development

Pre-defined protocol describes how the review will be conducted to reduce bias (Kitchenham, 2004). An initial scoping study can help determine an appropriate strategy for completing the research in a proper way.

Research Questions

The SMS aims to show trends and differences by identifying and classifying the research on ERP software metrics. To achieve this goal, the researcher addresses the following four dimensions:

- The timeline of publications (When),
- The evaluated quality attributes (What),
- The measurement produced (How),
- The application context (Where).

Then, to study the prospective of ERP evaluation methods in a more comprehensive perspective, the researcher performed a brainstorming process and formulated the following research questions:

RQ 1: How much activity was there in the last 16 years to evaluate ERP software?

RQ2: What did ERP system evaluation research produce? In other words, the question is, which techniques, methods, metrics, models and tools were developed to evaluate ERP systems in the literature? The aim of this question is to identify which type of evaluation strategy was employed, and to understand the current state-of-the-art ERP evaluation approaches.

RQ 3: Were there limitations on the current research? The aim of this question is to identify gaps in the current research and to direct future research.

Identification of Primary Studies

A general overview of procedures used to identify the primary studies related to the research question is shown in Figure 1. The search strategy is conducted in three phases: An automatic search, reference checking and author search. Such a combined approach should identify a wider range of primary study than would be

Figure 1. Identification of primary studies

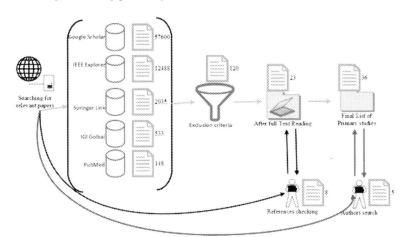

5

possible with one approach, resulting in an unbiased search strategy, and reducing the missing relevant literature.

An Automated Search

An automated search was conducted on the following databases: Google Scholar, IEEE Explore, Springer Link, IGI global, ISI Web of Science and PubMed. These databases were selected because they were accessible to the researcher. To make the search precise and comprehensive, librarians were consulted. The search process was conducted using the following defined search strings:

- "ERP"OR "Enterprise Recourse Planning" AND ("Metrics" OR "Measurement" OR "Measure" OR "Evaluation" OR "Model" OR "Tool")

First, the authors start the search process using Google Scholar. It is considered a powerful and a useful search engine that indexes many journals. However, not all publishers make their journals available via Google Scholar. Using the above search strings in Google Scholar, 57600 results were found. Second, another automatic search was conducted using IEEE explorer. Unfortunately, IEEE database did not allow the use of the above-defined search strings. Therefore, the search strings were modified according to the syntax of used search engines. Using IEEE database, 12488 results were found, which consisted of (10,848) conferences, (1465) journal & magazines, (50) books, (50) standards, (50) courses and (69) early access articles. Third, again simplified search strings were used in Springer link. Out of 2035 results, only 743 were related to computer science, which consisted of 377 conference papers, 130 articles, and 227 chapters. Fourth, only 533 results were found in IGI global. Fifth, using (ERP Metrics [Title/Abstract]) OR ERP Evaluation Models [Title/Abstract] as search string 148 results were identified from PubMed. To handle the search results such as storage of full-text papers, identifying duplicates, managing exclusion and inclusion criteria, and bibliography generation, the authors used the reference management tool Zotero[1].

Reference Checking

Reference checking was conducted after an exclusion and inclusion step. The value of reference checking was to increase the reliability of the search strategy and minimize retrieval bias.

Author Search

Author search is an extended search technique used to find articles that may have been missed during search strategy. It may be useful to carry out an author search to see whether the authors have published other relevant material that is not identified in the electronic search.

Exclusion and Inclusion Criteria

In fact, search results included a huge unworkable number of relevant and irrelevant papers. The inclusion and exclusion criteria allowed the selection of appropriate papers. The exclusion criteria adopted were:

- Irrelevant studies or papers that lie outside the field of ERP software metrics based on title, abstract, and keywords of those candidate primary studies.
- Duplicate research of the same work.
- Books and Lecture note

On the other hand, the researcher included:

- Only studies that proposed metrics, model or method for evaluation of ERP software.
- Whether the studies were proposed metrics to evaluate ERP process or ERP product
- Only studies related to themes of ERP software measures in their title or abstract or keywords.
- Papers published between Jan 1st 2002 and Dec 30th 2018.The year 2002 was chosen as a starting date for the search because ERP technology was growing fast during 2000s (Xu, Rahmati, & Lee, 2008).

During the exclusion and inclusion step, the author read the title of papers, abstracts, and keywords, and, when needed, looked over the concepts that reflected the contribution of the paper. Thus, after applying the defined inclusion and exclusion criteria, 31 related papers were selected.

Data Extraction and Analysis Strategy

After reading the full text of all primary studies, the authors tried to find common grounds in all papers where each paper could answer the research questions. This step resulted in the classification scheme shown in Table 1. The classification scheme is

Table 1. Primary study background

No	Ref	Type of Source	Application Context	Evaluation Perspective	Research Method	Measured Attributed	Contribution
S1	(Esteves, Pastor-Collado, & Casanovas, 2002)	Journal, 2002	Organization	Project Manager and Their Team	Proposal	Sustained management support	Metrics based on GQM
S2	(Aversano, Pennino, & Tortorella, 2010)	Conference, 2010	Open Source ERP System	Software engineer	The applicability of the framework was described through Anecdotal case study	Framework for Quality Model	Quality Model
S3	(Huifen & Chiang, 2010)	Conference, 2010	ERP Software Process	organizations	Proposal	Performance	Theory of institutional
S4	(S. Parthasarathy & Anbazhagan, 2006)	Conference, 2006	ERP Software Process	Project team	Proposal	Requirement Stability, Schedule Slippage, Age of problem	Software Metrics Plan (SMP)
S5	(AlGhamdi & Muzaffar, 2011)	Conference, 2011	ERP implementation and Development	Developer (Practitioners)	Proposal	Productivity (*efficiency*)	Metrics for Requirement Volatility index, Defect Removal Efficiency
S6	(De Carvalho & Monnerat, 2008)	Journal, 2008	Software process and software product	Manger and Developer	Proposal	Customization and Maintenance	Development Tool

continued on following page

Table 1. Continued

No	Ref	Type of Source	Application Context	Evaluation Perspective	Research Method	Measured Attributed	Contribution
S7	(Kwak, Park, Chung, & Ghosh, 2012)	Journal, 2011	ERP implementation	User prospective	3000 questionnaires were distributed online and off-line in UK and Korea. The repose rate was 10%	User acceptance	Extended Technology Acceptance Model (TAM)
S8	(Anil Kumar, Tadayoni, & Sorensen, 2015)	Conference, 2015	Educational ERP system	User	Proposal	Usability	Fuzzy Logic Model
S9	(J. J. A. Baig & Fadel, 2017)	Conference, 2017	ERP Requirement collection	Developer	Interview with 17 ERP consultants working on 4 different ERP projects.	Reusability	- Amount of reuse - Cot benefit metrics
S10	(Selmeci, Orosz, Györök, & Orosz, 2012)	Conference, 2012	Organization	Company	An example is provided to motivate the usefulness of the proposal	Performance	KPI collector
S11	(Chen, Law, & Yang, 2009)	Journal, 2009	ERP implementation	Management	Within 15 months 8 directors of California-based multinational company are interviewed three times.	Failure	Road map for project success

continued on following page

Table 1. Continued

No	Ref	Type of Source	Application Context	Evaluation Perspective	Research Method	Measured Attributed	Contribution
S12	(Jawad Javed Akbar Baig, Shah, & Sajjad, 2017)	Conference, 2017	ERP implementation	Developer (Practitioners)	23 professionals from six organizations are interviewed	Complexity	Agile method for ERP quality control
S13	(Dittrich, Vaucouleur, & Giff, 2009)	Journal, 2009	ERP Software Product	Software Engineer	Different data collection methods are combined	Customization	Highlight challenges for ERP Customization
S14	(Bansal & Negi, 2008)	Journal, 2008	ERP implementation	Project Management	Sales and order process of SAP is provided as example to motivate the usefulness of the proposal	Complexity	Information Flow Metrics
S15	(Capaldo & Rippa, 2008)	Conference, 2008	ERP implementation	Company perspective	A simulation is carried out human resource information system of Telecom Italia	Feasibility	Methodology for assessing feasibility
S16	(Luo & Strong, 2004)	Journal, 2004	ERP implementation	Managers perspective	The applicability of the framework in a private university is provided	Customization	A Framework for Evaluating ERP Customization

continued on following page

Table 1. Continued

No	Ref	Type of Source	Application Context	Evaluation Perspective	Research Method	Measured Attributed	Contribution
S17	(Al-Rawashdeh, Al'azzeh, & Al-Qatawneh, 2014)	Journal, 2014	ERP implementation	Company perspective	Proposal	Quality Model	ERPSQM Quality Model
S18	(Alrawashdeh, Muhairat, & Althunibat, 2013)	Journal, 2013		Company perspective	Proposal	Quality Model	Framework for evaluating the quality of education institutions'
S19	(S. Parthasarathy & Anbazhagan, 2007)	Journal 2007	ERP implementation	Project Manager	The applicability of the framework is provided	Customization	framework for evaluating ERP Customization
S20	(Gleghorn, 2005)	Journal 2005	Organization	Project Manager	Proposal	Integration	Guideline for ERP integration
S21	(Hossain, Rashid, & Patrick, 2002)	Book chapter 2002	ERP implementation	Project Manager	SWOT analysis of five Australian ERP Venders is provided	Functionality	SWOT framework
S22	(Sudhaman Parthasarathy & Sharma, 2016)	Journal 2016	ERP implementation	Developers and the consultants	Case study is conducted on 12 ERP systems developed for education institution	Efficiency of customized ERP package	Methodology for assessing efficiency of ERP packages

continued on following page

11

Table 1. Continued

No	Ref	Type of Source	Application Context	Evaluation Perspective	Research Method	Measured Attributed	Contribution
S23	(Hwang, Han, Jun, & Park, 2014)	Journal, 2014	Manufacture	-	Proposal	performance	SCOR model metrics related with RFID technology
S24	(Sabau, Munten, Bologa, Bologa, & Surcel, 2009a)	Journal, 2009	Higher Education		The proposed framework was applied to four Romanian Universities		Framework for Evaluation of educational ERP
S25	(Surendro & Olivia, 2016)	Journal, 2016	Education	Management	The proposed model was applied to evaluate the quality of an Indonesian academic cloud ERP system	Quality Model	an assessment model for Cloud ERP system
S26	(Koch, 2007)	Conference, 2006	ERP implementation		43 Questionnaire were distributed to Austrian ERP companies	Effort and cost estimation	Effort (Person-Years) Cost for Software Cost for Hardware Cost for Consultant
S27	(Firouzabadi & Mehrizi, 2015)	Journal, 2014	ERP implementation	organizations	A questionnaire was distributed to unknown number of experts	Evaluation of ERP	Fuzzy VIKOR for ranking ERP systems

continued on following page

Table 1. Continued

No	Ref	Type of Source	Application Context	Evaluation Perspective	Research Method	Measured Attributed	Contribution
S28	(Sudhaman Parthasarathy & Sharma, 2017)	Journal, 2016	ERP implementation	developers (Implementation team)	105 questionnaires were distributed to IT professional in three countries through email. The response rate was of 81% with 85 responses	customization	A software quality framework for ERP customization.
S29	(Leite, de Carvalho, & Gonçalves Filho, 1899)	Conference, 2009	ERP Products	Customers	862 questionnaires were sent to organizations that had maintenance contracts with software company called Alpha. Only 684 users was found to be valid response.	Customer satisfaction	Investigation of the European Customer Satisfaction Index (ECSI) model in Brazilian Software Companies.
S30	(Bouwers & Vis, 2009)	Journal, 2009	ERP development ERP implementation and Development	developers and manager	An example is provided to motivate the important of the software monitoring	Software Monitor	The requirements for a Software Monitoring System
S31	(Aversano & Tortorella, 2013)	Journal, 2013	Software process and software product	Software	Case Study	Functionality	Quality model for the evaluation of Open Source Software

continued on following page

Table 1. Continued

No	Ref	Type of Source	Application Context	Evaluation Perspective	Research Method	Measured Attributed	Contribution
S32	(Stoilov & Stoilova, 2008)	Conference, 2009	ERP implementation	End user	Three open source ERPs are compared	Functionality	An analysis of the general functions of ERP
S33	(Daneva, 2008)	Conference, 2008	ERP Development	Project Mangers	Data was collected from 13 SAP projects.	Cost	Cost estimation using combination of three existing approaches
S34	(Singh & Wesson, 2009)	Conference, 2009	ERP Products	Designers	Proposal	Usability	The study proposed a set of ERP usability heuristics
S35	(Scholtz, Cilliers, & Calitz, 2010)	Conference, 2010	ERP Products	Designers	The applicability of the proposed technique was described through Anecdotal case study	Usability	triangulation technique
S36	(Johansson & de Carvalho, 2010)	Conference, 2010	ERP Development	Developer	Proposal	Understandability of requirements	Tool for requirement management

consisted of reference of each paper, type of source (whether it is a journal, article, conference or other), the context in which the metric was defined, and the element was measured. The answer of the first research question was extracted from the first two columns. Evaluation perspective identify who is the primary target. For example, evaluation can be performed from persons engaged in ERP development (i.e. developers Ali, Abdellatief, Elfaki, & Wahaballa (2018), programmer, designer and project manager). The literature shows that an evaluation perspective is very important to justify the extent to which the metrics is empirically validated. This strategy offers an efficient approach to understanding and assessing the different sets of existing metrics (Abdellatief, Sultan, Jabar, & Abdullah, 2010).The fifth column, research method, presents the specific procedures or techniques used to validate the proposed metric. The answer of the third research question is extracted from the research methodology applied and the quality assessment question. The sixth column, measured attribute, identify the focus of the metric: what characteristics or attributes of the element we are interested in. The last column, study contribution is used to answer the second research question (what are the main outcomes of ERP software metrics researchers).

RESULTS AND DISCUSSION

36 primary studies are comprehensively analyzed and necessary data is extracted using a data extraction from. The results of quality assessment and results against each question are discussed in the following subsections.

Primary Study Background

By categorizing the primary study according to the data extraction method, the following summary data was generated. In Table 1, looking at the research method used in the primary studies, 33% (12 articles) result from research studies that are still in progress. Although these papers proposed a solution that could be useful, the validation of the proposed solution has not been implemented yet. Another 28% (10 articles) evaluated the applicability of the proposed solution using anecdotal evidence to motivate the usefulness and the importance of their work. 39% (14 articles) investigated their work using different methodologies such as case study, interview, survey and simulation. However, no research paper had achieved an industrial level validation. This achieves the reliability and validity of the metrics methodology which are the two major issue causing debates.

An organization and its implementation team evaluate ERP product and its applicability, whereas a developer, designer and project manager evaluates an ERP development processes and projects. Looking at the context in which the metrics or the models would be applied and /or the point in the process when the measure would be employed, 58% (21 studies) assume that the proposed solution can be applied in the context of ERP implementation. Of the 36 papers that were identified to be primary studies, six articles were targeted to ERP process evaluation, while four were directed towards the evaluation of ERP product. The reset of the papers has addressed different contexts such as educational ERP, manufacture, and organization context.

The field of software metrics has different stakeholders. Software developers, for example, can use metrics to measure the program size or to confirm requirement completeness. Software managers can use metrics to control the project cost and schedule. End users, in turn, can use metrics to verify if the final product satisfies the needed requirements. As the ISO explicitly states, it is important to identify the target users of the proposed metric. Investigating the primary studies, four target users are identified: project managers, ERP developers, ERP end users, and organizations that need to evaluate the ERP.

RQ 1: How Much Activity Was There to Evaluate ERP Software in the Last 16 Years?

The primary studies were published in the period between Jan 2002 and Dec 2018. Figure 2, presents the number of primary studies with respect to the year of publications. The results are consistent with the results reported by (Tahir, Rasool, & Noman, 2018), who found that 35 studies are proposed a measurement in SME. When analyzing the number of primary studies that were published in 2-year intervals,

Figure 2. Distribution of publication per year

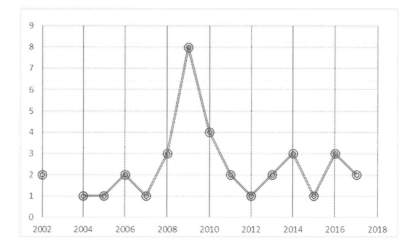

Figure 3. The distribution of publication types

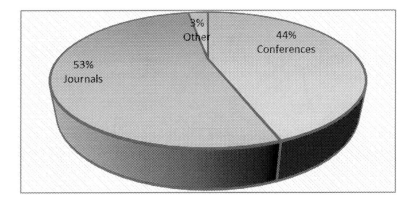

on average three papers were found to have been published in these timeframes until 2008. This shows that the focus regarding the evaluation of ERP software was rather low during this time. However, the number of studies has increased with a maximum annual rate of 8 studies published in 2009. Between 2009 and 2018, 26 papers were published, which is three times as many as was published between 2002 and 2008. This means that there was an emerging trend related to the research on ERP software metrics after 2009. However, after 2009, the trend declines to an average of two papers per year, and it is hard to assess why, since the interest in ERP seems to grow in general.

With respect to where the ERP software metrics researches were published, Figure 4 shows that the majority were published in journals 53% (19 studies) while 44% (16 studies) were in the conference proceeding. Journal paper more strongly contributes to building a knowledge basis, whereas conference paper mostly proposes new or innovative ideas. While journal paper is a complete and mature research, the conference paper is a snapshot of the work, presenting the essence of the contribution and might further be extended in a journal. For example, in the search process, we found that one of the conference articles (Aversano et al., 2010) is extended in another journal article (Aversano & Tortorella, 2013). However, both conference and journal papers are considered equally important in computer science (Montesi & Owen, 2008).

RQ 2: What Does ERP System Evaluation Research Produce?

The authors provided an overview on the set of quality attributes being evaluated using mind map technique. The 36 primary studies are refered as S1 to S36 as shown in Table 1. As shown in Figure 4, researchers have evaluated the attributes of ERP

Figure 4.

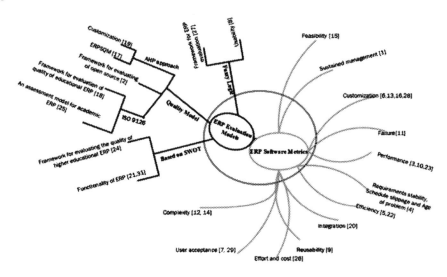

software using various methods and techniques. S17 and S19 used AHP approach to propose a quality model for ERP and a framework for customizing ERP respectivly. They utilize AHP approach to evalute and rank the attributes and characteristics of proposed ERP model. However, Karthikeyan, Venkatesan, and Chandrasekar (2016) have discussed some unsovled limitations of AHP approach. S8 and S27 utilized fuzzy logic techqnique to propose a framework for evlaution of ERP systems. These proposals attempt to define appopriate quality characteristics, attributes and metrics with respect to the particular features of ERP software. Although some researchers think that fuzzy logic is not a perfect solution of quality evaluation, but it remains a flexible and an efficient tool for making otimal decisions under uncertainty like a quality measurment (Ertuğrul & Güneş, 2007).

Some attention has been put into an acadimeric ERP systems evaluation (A. Kumar, Tadayoni, & Sorensen, 2015; Sabau, Munten, Bologa, Bologa, & Surcel, 2009b; Surendro & Olivia, 2016). The cliam is that acadimeric ERP systems store very important historical data and implement most complex technology, and hence, become more challenging to mange and control. In this regard, S18 extended the ISO9126 to fit the need of academic ERP requirments. However, this approach does not adress all specific features of ERP such as customization of ERP. Using SWOT analysis, S24 and 25 disscussed the quality requirements that have to comply with both academic ERP and cloud attributes. S24 applied the proposed framework to evalute the quality of an Indonesian academic ERP system, while the framework proposed by S25 was applied to evalute and compare the quality of four Romanian Universities.

The most investigated attribute of the ERP system is customization. An ERP customization refers to the configuration of system components to meet the organization's requirements that are not matched. This includes customization of data, process, operation and package functionality, for example, changing existing reports (invoice, order and so on) or hiding some of the filed or table in database. Moreover, the ERP source code may require modification. Therefore, size and complexity of customization are also investigated. This indicates that, regardless of whether an ERP system is bought or developed, organizations are facing some difficulties in ERP customization. S28 investigates the effect of module, database and source code customization on four software quality characteristics (functionality, reliability, usability and maintainability). The results show that source code and database customization significantly affects functionality, usability and maintainability of ERP, but not reliability. In contrast, module customization does not affect functionality, usability, maintainability and reliability. Another researcher S16, proposed a framework for evaluating ERP customization considering process and technical customization options. They assume that both technical and process capabilities of organization could evolve over time. However, the case study provided is not a full validation of the proposed framework, rather it is only describing the applicability of the framework.

S14 have adopted a more sophisticated approach for introducing a metric to measure the complexity of ERP system. They utilized the well-known information flow analysis to quantify the flow of information within and among function and process. According to their analysis, the control flow complexity is defined in terms of number of joins and splits modules. In this context, it is difficult to measure the information flow in the entire process. Therefore, the accuracy and the interpretation of the metrics is questionable. Moreover, the proposed metric does not relate to any external quality attribute.

S26 argue that traditional metrics such as function-point or line-of-code are not easily applicable to ERP systems. Using a data set of 39 projects from Austrian companies, the Data Envelopment Analysis (DEA) technique has been applied for effort and cost estimation of ERP projects. This technique is also used by S22 to study the efficiency of customized ERP software.

The attributes illustrated using mind map in Figure 4, are not the only important attributes in ERP implementation. Other attributes such as changeability, understandability and management support are equally important.

RQ 3: Are There Limitations on the Current Research?

Although the set of metrics and models included in the primary studies are indeed useful for the characterization of the ERP software, the above results clearly provide a judgement regarding the following:

- Insufficient information such as non-stated hypotheses and inadequate contexts provided by the primary studies(Al-Rawashdeh et al., 2014; Alrawashdeh et al., 2013; Capaldo & Rippa, 2008, 2008; S. Parthasarathy & Anbazhagan, 2007). This is because metrics are not defined within the scope of the requirements of a particular quality model. To avoid such a problem, authors must justify the need for their metrics and clearly state the aims and what problems the metrics are intended to solve.

- Ambiguity in the metric definition and lack of appropriate mathematical properties that can abuse metrics quality (AlGhamdi & Muzaffar, 2011; Al-Rawashdeh et al., 2014; Alrawashdeh et al., 2013; J. J. A. Baig & Fadel, 2017; S. Parthasarathy & Anbazhagan, 2006). This is because most of the metrics definitions were derived in an ad-hoc fashion, rather than meeting requirements of the elements of ERP software. An ambiguous definition of the metrics affects understanding of the metrics, makes reliable metric data collection very hard, and leads to an incorrect interpretation of the metrics results (Abdellatief et al., 2013; Kitchenham, Pfleeger, & Fenton, 1995).

- A software metrics involve not only the defining appropriate metrics for quality attributes but also the extent to which they empirically validate the proposed metric. Thus, datasets and data collection are an important step in metrics validation process. For example, PROMISE (NASA)[2], Jazz[3] and tera-PROMISE[4] are samples of publicly available datasets, which are created mainly for object- oriented metrics. Unfortunately, no datasets were found for the ERP software metrics in all primary studies to be a platform for study replication and cross-studies. In fact, without standard datasets, the replication of the metric might obtain different values and interpretations (Kitchenham et al., 1995).

- Lack of metrics that provide a reliable method to measure the quality attribute of ERP software. This is because most of the proposed metrics and quality models are not validated (Al-Rawashdeh et al., 2014; Alrawashdeh et al., 2013; J. J. A. Baig & Fadel, 2017; Bansal & Negi, 2008; Esteves et al., 2002, 2002; Huifen & Chiang, 2010; Hwang et al., 2014; Woodings & Bundell, 2001). Instead, only the applicability of the proposed metric is tested, limiting the generalization of the results (Luo & Strong, 2004). Unfortunately, an independent validation and an industrial level validation have not been achieved yet. This might be due to the difficulties in experiment replication.

- In addition, there are no tools to collect metrics from ERP system representations. This may cause misleading results,and provides evidence that current metrics might not meet the practitioner's expectations. However, this is not a major issue because if a measure is supported by a tool, its computation might not correspond to what practitioners want (Nuñez-Varela, Pérez-Gonzalez, Martínez-Perez, & Soubervielle-Montalvo, 2017).
- Relatively large number of studies relate only to discussion the requirements of specific ERP metrics.

CONCLUSION

There are many ERP system metrics and models available in literature to predict and control ERP system quality. However, literature lacks a comprehensive study to evaluate and compare various proposed methodologies so that quality practitioners may select an appropriate technique. The authors have mapped and classified 36 studies. The mapping process leads to a number of insights into the derivation of ERP software measurement models and definition of appropriate metrics. Between 2009 and 2018, 26 papers were published, which is three times as many as those published between 2002 and 2008. Overall, ten studies were proposed software metrics and fifteen studies were proposed specific ERP quality models. Other eight studies discussed the requirements of ERP metrics, and aimed at establishing a roadmap for both researchers and practitioners. Out of 36 studies, only three studies have discussed the need for metrics tools. This study also shows the different perspectives of proposed metrics, the contribution, and the context where the metrics will be applied. Common problems on current approaches to ERP system evaluation are identified. Although a number of metrics were proposed for measuring the ERP software quality attributes, the metrics field is still young in comparison with other software theories. Therefore, considering the current state of ERP software, further research will be needed to optimize ERP software metrics strategy. This paper helps the practitioners and researchers towards a better selection of ERP software metrics based on the context.

REFERENCES

Abdellatief, M., Sultan, A. B. M., Ghani, A. A. A., & Jabar, M. A. (2013). A mapping study to investigate component-based software system metrics. *Journal of Systems and Software, 86*(3), 587–603. doi:10.1016/j.jss.2012.10.001

Abdellatief, M., Sultan, A. B. M., Jabar, M. A., & Abdullah, R. (2010). Developing General View of Quality Models for E-learning from Developers Perspective (F. Baharom, M. Mahmuddin, Y. Yusof, W. H. W. Ishak, & M. A. Saip, Eds.). Sintok: Univ Utari Malaysia-Uum.

Al-Rawashdeh, T. A., Al'azzeh, F. M., & Al-Qatawneh, S. M. (2014). Evaluation of ERP systems quality model using analytic hierarchy process (AHP) technique. *Journal of Software Engineering and Applications, 7*(04), 225–232. doi:10.4236/jsea.2014.74024

AlGhamdi, J. S., & Muzaffar, Z. (2011). Metric suite for assuring the quality of ERP implementation and development. *13th International Conference on Advanced Communication Technology (ICACT2011)*, 1348–1352.

Ali, S., Abdellatief, M., Elfaki, M. A., & Wahaballa, A. (2018). Complexity Metrics for Component-based Software Systems: Developer Perspective. *Indian Journal of Science and Technology, 11*(32). doi:10.17485/ijst/2018/v11i32/123093

Alrawashdeh, T. A., Muhairat, M., & Althunibat, A. (2013). Evaluating the quality of software in ERP systems using the ISO 9126 model. *International Journal of Ambient Systems and Applications, 1*(1), 1–9.

Aversano, L., Pennino, I., & Tortorella, M. (2010). Evaluating the Quality of Free/Open Source ERP Systems. *ICEIS*, (1), 75–83.

Aversano, L., & Tortorella, M. (2013). Quality evaluation of floss projects: Application to ERP systems. *Information and Software Technology, 55*(7), 1260–1276. doi:10.1016/j.infsof.2013.01.007

Baig, J. J. A., Shah, A., & Sajjad, F. (2017). Evaluation of agile methods for quality assurance and quality control in ERP implementation. Intelligent Computing and Information Systems (ICICIS). In *2017 Eighth International Conference On*, (pp. 252–257). IEEE.

Baig, J. J. A., & Fadel, M. A. A. (2017). Measuring reusability during requirement engineering of an ERP implementation. *2017 Eighth International Conference on Intelligent Computing and Information Systems (ICICIS)*, 258–262. 10.1109/INTELCIS.2017.8260056

Bansal, V., & Negi, T. (2008). A metric for ERP complexity. *International Conference on Business Information Systems*, 369–379. 10.1007/978-3-540-79396-0_32

Bouwers, E., & Vis, R. (2009). Multidimensional software monitoring applied to erp. *Electronic Notes in Theoretical Computer Science*, *233*, 161–173. doi:10.1016/j.entcs.2009.02.067

Capaldo, G., & Rippa, P. (2008). A Methodological Proposal to Assess the Feasibility of ERP Systems Implementation Strategies. *Proceedings of the 41st Annual Hawaii International Conference on System Sciences (HICSS 2008)*, 401–401. 10.1109/HICSS.2008.30

Chen, C. C., Law, C. C., & Yang, S. C. (2009). Managing ERP implementation failure: A project management perspective. *IEEE Transactions on Engineering Management*, *56*(1), 157–170. doi:10.1109/TEM.2008.2009802

Daneva, M. (2008). Complementing approaches in ERP effort estimation practice: an industrial study. *Proceedings of the 4th International Workshop on Predictor Models in Software Engineering*, 87–92. 10.1145/1370788.1370808

De Carvalho, R. A., & Monnerat, R. M. (2008). Development support tools for enterprise resource planning. *IT Professional*, *10*(5), 39–45. doi:10.1109/MITP.2008.100

Deshmukh, P. D., Thampi, G. T., & Kalamkar, V. R. (2015). Investigation of quality benefits of ERP implementation in Indian SMEs. *Procedia Computer Science*, *49*, 220–228. doi:10.1016/j.procs.2015.04.247

Dittrich, Y., Vaucouleur, S., & Giff, S. (2009). ERP customization as software engineering: Knowledge sharing and cooperation. *IEEE Software*, *26*(6), 41–47. doi:10.1109/MS.2009.173

Ertuğrul, I., & Güneş, M. (2007). The Usage of Fuzzy Quality Control Charts to Evaluate Product Quality and an Application. In P. Melin, O. Castillo, E. G. Ramírez, J. Kacprzyk, & W. Pedrycz (Eds.), Analysis and Design of Intelligent Systems using Soft Computing Techniques (pp. 660–673). doi:10.1007/978-3-540-72432-2_67

Esteves, J., Pastor-Collado, J., & Casanovas, J. (2002). Measuring sustained management support in ERP implementation projects: a GQM approach. *AMCIS 2002 Proceedings*, 190.

Firouzabadi, S., & Mehrizi, S. (2015). ERP software quality assessment using fuzzy VIKOR. *Uncertain Supply Chain Management*, *3*(2), 189–196. doi:10.5267/j.uscm.2014.12.001

Garefalakis, A., Mantalis, G., Vourgourakis, E., Spinthiropoulos, K., & Lemonakis, C. (2016). Healthcare Firms and the ERP Systems. *Journal of Engineering Science & Technology Review*, *9*(1), 139–144. doi:10.25103/jestr.091.021

Gleghorn, R. (2005). Enterprise application integration: A manager's perspective. *IT Professional*, *7*(6), 17–23. doi:10.1109/MITP.2005.143

Hossain, L., Rashid, M. A., & Patrick, J. D. (2002). A Framework for Assessing ERP Systems Functionality for the SMEs in Australia. In Enterprise Resource Planning: Solutions and Management (pp. 182–208). IGI Global.

Huifen, W., & Chiang, D. (2010). Evaluation ERP II Application Performance from Institutional Theory View. *Software Engineering (WCSE), 2010 Second World Congress On*, *1*, 89–93. 10.1109/WCSE.2010.83

Hwang, G., Han, S., Jun, S., & Park, J. (2014). Operational Performance Metrics in Manufacturing Process: Based on SCOR Model and RFID Technology. *International Journal of Innovation, Management and Technology*, *5*(1). doi:10.7763/IJIMT.2014. V5.485

Johansson, B., & de Carvalho, R. A. (2010). Software tools for requirements management in an ERP system context. *Proceedings of the 2010 ACM Symposium on Applied Computing*, 169–170. 10.1145/1774088.1774123

Karthikeyan, R., Venkatesan, K. G. S., & Chandrasekar, A. (2016). A Comparison of Strengths and Weaknesses for Analytical Hierarchy Process. *Journal of Chemical and Pharmaceutical Sciences*, *9*(3), 4.

Kitchenham, B. (2004). Procedures for performing systematic reviews. Keele, UK: Keele University.

Kitchenham, B., Brereton, O. P., Budgen, D., Turner, M., Bailey, J., & Linkman, S. (2009). Systematic literature reviews in software engineering–a systematic literature review. *Information and Software Technology*, *51*(1), 7–15. doi:10.1016/j. infsof.2008.09.009

Kitchenham, B., Pfleeger, S. L., & Fenton, N. (1995). Towards a framework for software measurement validation. *IEEE Transactions on Software Engineering*, *21*(12), 929–944. doi:10.1109/32.489070

Kitchenham, B., Pretorius, R., Budgen, D., Brereton, O. P., Turner, M., Niazi, M., & Linkman, S. (2010). Systematic literature reviews in software engineering–a tertiary study. *Information and Software Technology*, *52*(8), 792–805. doi:10.1016/j. infsof.2010.03.006

Koch, S. (2007). ERP implementation effort estimation using data envelopment analysis. In *Technologies for business information systems* (pp. 121–132). Springer. doi:10.1007/1-4020-5634-6_11

Kumar, A., Tadayoni, R., & Sorensen, L. T. (2015). Metric based efficiency analysis of educational ERP system usability-using fuzzy model. *Image Information Processing (ICIIP), 2015 Third International Conference On*, 382–386.

Kumar, A., Tadayoni, R., & Sorensen, L. T. (2015). Metric based efficiency analysis of educational ERP system usability-using fuzzy model. *2015 Third International Conference on Image Information Processing (ICIIP)*, 382–386. 10.1109/ICIIP.2015.7414801

Kwak, Y. H., Park, J., Chung, B. Y., & Ghosh, S. (2012). Understanding end-users' acceptance of enterprise resource planning (ERP) system in project-based sectors. *IEEE Transactions on Engineering Management, 59*(2), 266–277. doi:10.1109/TEM.2011.2111456

Leite, R. S., de Carvalho, R. B., & Gonçalves Filho, C. (1899). Measuring Perceived Quality and Satisfaction of ERP Systems: an Empirical Study with Customers of a Brazilian Software Company. Hicss, 1–8.

Luo, W., & Strong, D. M. (2004). A framework for evaluating ERP implementation choices. *IEEE Transactions on Engineering Management, 51*(3), 322–333. doi:10.1109/TEM.2004.830862

Montesi, M., & Owen, J. M. (2008). From conference to journal publication: How conference papers in software engineering are extended for publication in journals. *Journal of the American Society for Information Science and Technology, 59*(5), 816–829. doi:10.1002/asi.20805

Nuñez-Varela, A. S., Pérez-Gonzalez, H. G., Martínez-Perez, F. E., & Soubervielle-Montalvo, C. (2017). Source code metrics: A systematic mapping study. *Journal of Systems and Software, 128*, 164–197. doi:10.1016/j.jss.2017.03.044

Ömüral, N. K., & Demirörs, O. (2017). Effort estimation methods for ERP projects based on function points: a case study. *Proceedings of the 27th International Workshop on Software Measurement and 12th International Conference on Software Process and Product Measurement*, 199–206. 10.1145/3143434.3143464

Parthasarathy, S., & Anbazhagan, N. (2006). Significance of Software Metrics in ERP Projects. *2006 Annual IEEE India Conference*, 1–4. 10.1109/INDCON.2006.302776

Parthasarathy, S., & Anbazhagan, N. (2007). Evaluating ERP implementation choices using AHP. *International Journal of Enterprise Information Systems*, *3*(3), 52–65. doi:10.4018/jeis.2007070104

Parthasarathy, S., & Sharma, S. (2016). Efficiency analysis of ERP packages—A customization perspective. *Computers in Industry*, *82*, 19–27. doi:10.1016/j.compind.2016.05.004

Parthasarathy, S., & Sharma, S. (2017). Impact of customization over software quality in ERP projects: An empirical study. *Software Quality Journal*, *25*(2), 581–598. doi:10.100711219-016-9314-x

Sabau, G., Munten, M., Bologa, A.-R., Bologa, R., & Surcel, T. (2009a). An evaluation framework for higher education ERP systems. *WSEAS Transactions on Computers*, *8*(11), 1790–1799.

Sabau, G., Munten, M., Bologa, A.-R., Bologa, R., & Surcel, T. (2009b). An evaluation framework for higher education ERP Systems. *WSEAS Transactions on Computers*, *8*(11), 1790–1799.

Scholtz, B., Cilliers, C., & Calitz, A. (2010). Qualitative techniques for evaluating enterprise resource planning (ERP) user interfaces. *Proceedings of the 2010 Annual Research Conference of the South African Institute of Computer Scientists and Information Technologists*, 284–293. 10.1145/1899503.1899535

Selmeci, A., Orosz, I., Györök, G., & Orosz, T. (2012). Key Performance Indicators used in ERP performance measurement applications. *Intelligent Systems and Informatics (SISY), 2012 IEEE 10th Jubilee International Symposium On*, 43–48. 10.1109/SISY.2012.6339583

Singh, A., & Wesson, J. (2009). Evaluation Criteria for Assessing the Usability of ERP Systems. *Proceedings of the 2009 Annual Research Conference of the South African Institute of Computer Scientists and Information Technologists*, 87–95. 10.1145/1632149.1632162

Stoilov, T., & Stoilova, K. (2008). Functional Analysis of Enterprise Resource Planning Systems. *Proceedings of the 9th International Conference on Computer Systems and Technologies and Workshop for PhD Students in Computing, 43*, 8–43. 10.1145/1500879.1500927

Surendro, K., & Olivia, O. (2016). Academic Cloud ERP Quality Assessment Model. *Iranian Journal of Electrical and Computer Engineering*, *6*(3), 1038–1047.

Tahir, T., Rasool, G., & Noman, M. (2018). A Systematic Mapping Study on Software Measurement Programs in SMEs. E-*Informatica Software Engineering Journal, 12*(1).

Valdebenito, J., & Quelopana, A. (2018). Understanding the landscape of research in Enterprise Resource Planning (ERP) systems adoption. *Proceedings of the 2018 International Conference on Computers in Management and Business*, 35–39. 10.1145/3232174.3232178

Woodings, T. L., & Bundell, G. A. (2001). A framework for software project metrics. *Proc. 12th European Conference on Software Control and Metrics (ESCOM'01).*

Xu, Y., Rahmati, N., & Lee, V. C. (2008). A review of literature on Enterprise Resource Planning systems. *Service Systems and Service Management, 2008 International Conference On*, 1–6. 10.1109/ICSSSM.2008.4598481

ENDNOTES

[1]   https://www.zotero.org/
[2]   http://promise.site.uottawa.ca/SERepository/
[3]   https://jazz.net/
[4]   http://openscience.us/repo/index.html

Chapter 2
Quality and Effectiveness of ERP Software:
Data Mining Perspective

Stephen Makau Mutua
Meru University of Science and Technology, Kenya

Raphael Angulu
Masinde Muliro University of Science and Technology, Kenya

ABSTRACT

Over time, the adoption of ERP systems has been wide across many small, medium, and large organizations. An ERP system is supposed to inform the strategic decision making of the organization; therefore, the information drawn from the ERP system is as important as the data stored in it. Poor data quality affects the quality information in it. Data mining is used to discover trends and patterns of an organization. This chapter looks into the way of integrating these data mining into an ERP system. This is conceptualized in three crucial views namely the outer, inner, and the knowledge discovery view. The outer view comprises of the collection of various entry points, the inner view contains the data repository, and the knowledge discovery view offers the data mining component. Since the focus is data mining, the two strategies of supervised and unsupervised are discussed. The chapter then concludes by presenting the probable problems within which each of these two strategies (classification and clustering) can be put into place within the mining process of an ERP system.

DOI: 10.4018/978-1-5225-7678-5.ch002

OBJECTIVES

At the end of this chapter, the reader is expected to;

1. Explain the value and place of data in an ERP system
2. Describe the metrics of data quality desirable in an ERP system
3. Explain the importance of data quality in ensuring the quality and effectiveness of an ERP System
4. Understand the various ways in which data mining can be integrated into an ERP System
5. Understand the different approaches to extract information from the data collected in an ERP system

INTRODUCTION

Enterprise Resource Planning (ERP) is a software which an organization uses to integrate all its data and processes into one single system. This has several implications. Since all the data is centralized, it is much easier to draw data insights from multiple business processes at once. Similarly, new mechanisms are required to analyze and understand the data in order to draw some intelligence from them. Given their myriad advantages, ERP adoption rates have been constantly on the increase since their inception. Even though they were initially viewed as majorly applicable in only large organizations; the narrative has since changed and their adoption has been witnessed in both small and medium organizations including learning institutions, non-governmental organizations and even health facilities. This in effect has proliferated the demand for ERP systems across the various domains in which they are expected to operate while meeting their anticipated expectations. Whereas it is greatly acceptable and desirable for an organization to streamline information flow and control, reduce labor and operations costs, and enhance efficiency; the success of an ERP system is greatly reliant on the quality of its data and its interaction with the various organization's data points.

Like any other software system, an ERP will automatically fall victim to the computer adage of "Garbage in Garbage Out". This is so because, in its design and implementation, an ERP software is typically an integrated collection of applications that collect, process, store, manage and interpret data from multiple points spread across the organization. This data is centrally stored in a database or a repository from which each of the business applications draws its lifeline. Consequently, in its salient nature, the effectiveness of an ERP system can greatly be measured by the collective efficiency of individual applications which in turn rely on the quality of data collected.

This chapter discusses in detail the value of data quality in an ERP system and the various metrics that measure it. The importance of integrating data mining approaches into the design and implementation of an ERP system are then discussed. To further elaborate the integration, a number of these specific approaches that can be amalgamated into the system are discussed in detail.

Data Quality

The goal of an ERP system is to ensure all the processes access and share data appropriately without having multiple independent applications. Consequently, the quality of data in the system is defined within organization-based values to determine whether it is fit for the intended purposes and especially in providing the desired business intelligence for decision-making. Organizations therefore must be guided by certain principles in underscoring the vitality of ensuring data quality (Pipino, Lee, & Wang, 2002). However, this matter has been complicated by the emergence of Big Data whose volume and velocity may not be fully supported by data profiling algorithms (Cai, Zhou, Yang, Yang, & Wang, n.d.; Saha & Srivastava, 2014).

Nevertheless, it is the responsibility of the organization to ensure that all data that's entered into the ERP is of high quality. To achieve this, the business entity must have a set of practices aimed at maintaining high quality commonly referred to as *data quality management (DQM)*. It entails proper oversight from the data acquisition processes to analysis leading to actionable accurate insights from the information. Unfortunately, the quality of data can best be judged based on the information harnessed at the tail end. However, DQM asserts that data quality can be enforced through people, data profiling, matching, reporting and repairing.

People play a very crucial role in data quality. Even though technology has advanced immensely over the years, the human role has not become obsolete yet. To ensure the desired quality, people provide the oversight role at different levels such as defining the metadata, quality constraints and monitoring the data entry points. Additionally, experts can ensure an ERP system provides necessary functionalities that perform data profiling. Data profiling allows the analysis of sample data to detect data quality issues. This can be integrated with data matching which compares and merges related data to avoid unnecessary duplication across various data sets. Through this process, any detected data issues can be reported and appropriate repairs and enforcements made.

To achieve this, measuring the quality of data can be defined using various metrics as outlined next.

Metrics of Data Quality

Determination of data quality is anchored on the six metrics of *completeness, consistency, conformity, timeliness, integrity,* and *accuracy* (3CTIA), which provide both subjective and objective assessment dimensions (Y. Lee, Pipino, Funk, & Wang, 2006). We briefly define each of these dimensions with reference to software data, but a more detailed discussion shall be provided in the chapter.

Completeness defines the extent to which data is not missing in depth and breadth relative to the system expectation. To avoid the generality of this definition, this metric demand additional user defines dimensions in order to explicitly define the data set rules bearing the varying levels of data constraints. It is worth noting that data completeness can be evaluated from three main perspectives of schema completeness, column completeness, and population completeness all which affect the overall data quality. An incomplete record in an ERP would most probably mislead a number of departments hence having an impact on the end product (Pipino et al., 2002; Wang, Kon, & Madnick, 1993).

Consistency offers a more inclusive data quality measure. From the database perspective, it demands that any data written must be in accordance with the laid down constraints, rules, cascades, triggers and any combination thereof. This reinforces the need to have similar data representation across all storage units without any level of variance pointing to the same item. This synchronization of data is very crucial in an ERP system given its multiple sources of data and diverse data manipulation points (Askham et al., 2013).

Conformity defines the validity of data in accordance with the desired formats including the data types and size, and ranges. Ensuring conformity of data enhances its believability since it is within the user's expectation levels (Even & Shankaranarayanan, 2007). For instance, a field in the ERP database is expected to store the date of birth of the employees. By default, any employer is expected to be within the legal age of the implementation country. If for instance, the age is 18 years, it would be greatly misleading to pull a record of an underage among the salary recipients of the organization.

Timeliness presents the expectation for the availability and accessibility of data within the system. It mirrors how up-to-date the data is with respect to the task it is intended for. In an ERP system, timeliness plays a very crucial role given the real-timeliness of the system. Further, this immensely influences the performance of the system with respect to its effectiveness in service delivery to its customers. Timeliness thus can be viewed from a multi-thronged perspective encompassing currency of data which is a computed metric; data volatility which defines the length of time which data remains valid; delivery time to the user; input time into the system; and age-defining how old the data was when it was first received by the system (Askham et al., 2013; Pipino et al., 2002).

Integrity is an overall goal that is realized by ensuring the accuracy and consistency of the data. It offers the assurance that the data stored is only from authorized sources, all the data modifications are by only the accredited users and that at any given time in the existence of the system, the data shall be true with no unsanctioned alterations. Given its importance, integrity is a vital element in the analysis, design, implementation, and maintenance of the ERP system (Batini & Scannapieco, 2006).

Accuracy is the degree to which data correctly reflects the real world entities or events which they model (Olson, 2003). This implies that any data item captured and stored must be the right value and represented in a consistent and unambiguous form. The data capturing devices must therefore be audited before integration into the ERP system to ensure the correctness. In addition, a mechanism needs to be in place to detect the inaccurate figures before they are committed into the database.

Importance of Quality Data

Data quality assurance is a very crucial factor in any type of information system because it guarantees the extraction of reliable and quality information. This is no exception for ERP systems as well. This not only concerns the accuracy and integrity of the data but also its completeness, timeliness and how it can be improved. Maintaining clean data in an organization brings along a myriad of benefits (Xu, 2006). These include but not limited to reduced records reconciliation, reduced costs, increased efficiency, informed and reliable decision-making, and improved service delivery. However, poor data management leads to huge losses, misinformed decisions and ultimately failure. As a result of this potential detriment of data quality mismanagement, the total data quality management (TDQM) was developed (Wang, 1998).

TDQM cycle consists of key stages of defining, measuring, analyzing and improving data quality through multiple, continuous improvement cycles towards ensuring quality data is delivered to the end user. The TDQM, therefore, enforces the importance of data in any information system. This is in line with the core stages of the data mining process as illustrated in Figure 1. However, this chapter will not focus much on the TDQM and the user is encouraged to further study using the provided literature sources. Depending on the size of the organization, data may be emanating from varied sources and information systems which are either centralized within the company or that are distributed across different physical locations. All

Figure 1. Phases of the data mining process

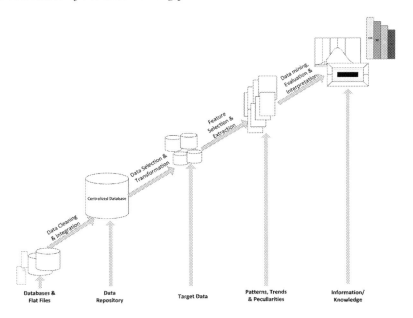

these data is crucial to the strategic decision-making of the organization. It is crucial therefore to integrate the data from different databases into a warehouse or centralized database where the data mining processes can be able to extract knowledge from the raw facts. However, this data cannot be used in its raw form and pre-processing becomes crucial to ensure the quality of data that is to be used in the final decision-making process of the organization. Data mining can thus be defined as the *process of extracting knowledge from vast volumes of data also known as Knowledge Discovery from Data (KDD)* (Jiawei & Micheline, 2006). Figure 1 illustrates the various stages of the data mining process.

Each of these phases is crucial in the end product of the knowledge or information that is extracted from the system. The process of knowledge discovery is iterative in nature and the phases are dependent on each other as explained in each of the following steps;

1. **Data Cleaning and Integration:** As earlier noted, an ERP system contains multiple data entry points which are either distributed or centralized. Much of this data is related but is bound to be coupled with inconsistent values, missing values or noise such as errors and outliers. To ensure quality, these need to be cleaned and integrated together into a shared repository. However, cleaning and integration are two related but distinct phases within the data mining discipline with equally distinct methods. For instance, missing values

can be resolved by ignoring the record or replacing the value with the mean or median of the attribute among other approaches. Noise can be fixed using smoothing methods such as binning, regression and clustering. On the other side, data integration entails merging data from the multiple sources while enforcing data integrity through controlled redundancy. Since this involves comparing multiple data values from different sources, well known statistical methods such as the chi-square (Dutta & Bhattacharya, 2010) and Pearson's Correlation Analysis (Ma et al., 2015) are used.

2. **Data Selection and Transformation:** Not all data in the repository is used for data mining, rather, depending on the desired knowledge, a subsection of the data is extracted from the main repository. Selection means retrieval of only the relevant clean data from the data repository hence reducing on its size and volume. Reduction is however a complex and delicate task because it aims to provide a subset of the data that's manageable yet representative. To achieve this, data mining makes use of data discretization mechanisms (Dimitrova, Licona, McGee, & Laubenbacher, 2010; Jin, Breitbart, & Muoh, 2009; Ramírez-Gallego et al., 2016), dimensionality reduction techniques (Leskovec, Rajaraman, & Ullman, 2014; Nylen, Wallisch, Nylen, & Wallisch, 2017)and data cube aggregation methods (Jiawei & Micheline, 2006) which are either supervised or unsupervised depending on whether the problem at hand is for classification or clustering respectively. Once this is achieved, the data is transformed into the *target data* in conformance to the desired data mining format.

3. **Feature Extraction and Selection:** Since data mining entails extraction of relevant information from data, it is guided by the features of the data. Retrieving these features from the data set is referred to as *feature extraction*. However, not all extracted features are relevant for the final decision-making while others have a lesser weight to the final extracted knowledge. The determination and extraction of the crucial features to arrive relevant to the task at hand is known as *feature selection*. Well-known methods such as the support vector machines (SVMs)are commonly used in this phase (Abe, 2010; Scholkopf, Smola, & Muller, 2012; Yin, Ng, & Abbott, 2012). As this process continues, data is mined into unique *patterns* and the business *trends* identified. Unusual activities are also flagged and presented for further interpretation.

4. **Evaluation and Interpretation:** Mass data contains a mass of patterns and trends which may be interesting or not. A pattern can be viewed as a series of data values that organize themselves in recognizable ways, whereas trends present the overall direction of data values for a specified time period which can either be upward, downwards or horizontal. Patterns can either be seasonal or cyclic. Seasonal patterns are influenced by seasonal occurrences such as

festive seasons. For instance, it may be obvious that sales surge during Christmas festivities. Since this may occur every year, such a pattern is considered seasonal or sometimes called *periodic* occurrence since its pattern is regular. Such events are easily predictable in nature. On the contrary, *cyclic* patterns exist in an irregular manner and are hard to predict. An occurrence is considered cyclic if it exists in a long-term period usually exceeding one year (García & Rodríguez, 2013; Seemann, Hua, McCauley, & Gunaratne, 2012). However, in data mining, each trend and pattern must be *evaluated* and *interpreted* in order to identify what is truly interesting based on a defined measure. The chosen pattern is thus considered interesting is it is valid, novel, actionable and understandable (Jiawei & Micheline, 2006). Once this is achieved, the output can be considered as *knowledge* or *information* that can be relied upon by an organization in it's planning and decision-making processes.

Phases 1, 2 and 3 comprise the pre-processing stages of knowledge discovery and mainly are key in enforcing the quality of data. Since the data mining core step as elaborated in phase 4 is entirely dependent on the previous stages, it therefore follows that if a repository contains quality data the decision-making process will result in timely, reliable and progressive decisions for an organization. This simply enforces the need for an organization to ensure that in implementing its ERP system, the data sources are accurate and reliable for the success of the organization. However, the entry point is as important as the endpoint. Employing the wrong data mining would definitely lead to skewed, misleading and outrageous knowledge. To overcome this, it is crucial for any organization seeking to implement an ERP system to employ qualified staff who can determine the data mining requirements of the system. This would entail the data quality enforcement and integration of the ERP system with the necessary data mining techniques. In the next section, we discuss how data mining can seamlessly be integrated with an ERP system for quality decision-making.

Integrating Data Mining and ERP System

It is worth noting that the effectiveness of an ERP system will be judged by the ability to draw crucial and critical decisions in a timely manner and based on factual quality data. This is often provided for by the integration of data warehouses and business intelligence solutions which often provide a dashboard for all levels of decision-making at any given point in time. By providing this, an ERP system enables the decision makers to gain an appropriate intuition into their organizations, markets and competitors' environment for faster and better decision-making. In order to achieve this, a business intelligence system needs to be integrated into the data repository.

To avoid any confusion, *business intelligence* is a term used to define the data-driven decision-making approach of generating, aggregating, analyzing and visualizing data. Loosely, a business intelligence system is the support system engine that analyzes, visualizes and reports on the data with the goal of enhancing the quality of the management's decision-making. However, this is entirely dependent on the quality of the data stored in the repository. Consequently, ensuring the quality of data being stored is akin to assuring the quality of information presented for decision-making. This is made possible by integrating data mining techniques into the ERP system in form of business intelligence. Figure 2 presents a layered structure of integrating data mining techniques (business intelligence) and the ERP system herein referred to as the outer view, inner view and the business intelligence (or knowledge discovery) view.

Figure 2. The outer, inner and knowledge discovery views of an ERP

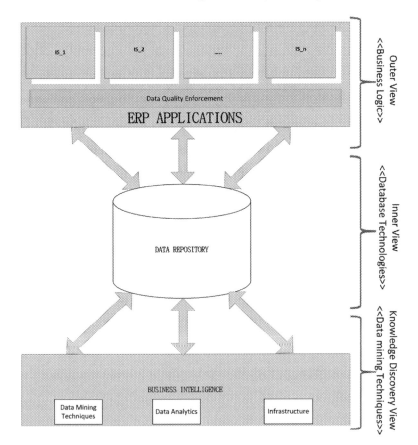

The outer view refers to the various collective points from which data enters into the data repository of the ERP system. An organizational ERP system will contain a number of Information Systems (IS) that are working independently but in synergy to achieve a collective objective. In Figure 2, these are represented as *IS_1*, *IS_2* all the way to *IS_n* where *n* is the total number of the applications in the organization's ERP system. These may include such systems as the payroll module, human resource management system, sales and marketing system, customer relationship management system and the procurement system. Each of these systems implements the business logic of its own department. The business logic will dictate how various objects interact with each other, data flows from the application to the database and the rules that govern the data itself. Since the business logic implementation is ideally independent, it is at this level where data quality can be enforced before it is stored in the data repository as outlined in the sub-section covering *Data Quality Enforcement*.

The inner view comprises the data repository which may be implemented database technologies or NOSQL (Bhogal & Choksi, 2015; Hauck, 2014) mechanisms depending on the format of the data. This justifies the use of the repository over database which has been commonly inwards relational databases. Despite having been enforced at the business logic, this level of the system employs appropriate mechanisms that assure the quality of the data to be stored in the repository. Databases are relatively a matured field spanning over three decades now. The readers are therefore advised to educate themselves on these mechanisms as this chapter is not focused on databases rather data mining. Finally, the knowledge discovery view presents the role of data mining in the core of the decision-making module of the ERP system as discussed in the section of *Business Intelligence*.

Data Quality Enforcement

The focus of this chapter is on how quality and effectiveness of an ERP can be enforced with the goal of ensuring qualitative data mining. As can be observed in Figure 2, the data plays a central role to both the end-user application and the drawn business intelligence for decision-making. To enforce the data quality thus requires unique and specialized methods that can be analyzed and responsively realize any potential violations such as out of range cases, outliers, noise, and missing values. This subsection briefly describes some of these methods;

- **MIN or Max Operations:** These are basic but crucial data quality enforcers at the data entry point. The acceptable range of data values can be defined manually within the application setup or automatically within the functionality logic. Any values outside the minimum and maximum allowed values should be captured before the transaction is committed.

- **Simple Ratios:** As Pilipino and others note, simple ratio evaluates the result of the desired outcomes versus the actual outcomes (Pipino et al., 2002). The data is normalized between 0 and 1 with 1 representing the most desirable and 0 the least. This can be useful in enforcing the quality metric of completeness and correctness. If a vector of data contains all the desired values, it will automatically be assigned a value of 1, otherwise a value less than 1. The difference between the two explains the level of completeness in a set of data.
- **Weighted Average:** This is a variant of the min operator for multivariate case which entails assigning weighting factors of between zero and one. It is an appropriate way of ensuring believability of the data since each variable has an assigned weight based on its importance. However, this is dependent on the organizations understanding of its business operations, their criticality and contribution towards the decision-making process (Cappiello, Francalanci, & Pernici, 2004).

These and many other database technologies ensure the data quality through the referential, integral or key constraints. There are other emerging approaches such the self-organizing maps (SOMs) to match up with Big Data and deep learning trends which are quickly gaining acceptance in business.

Business Intelligence

As indicated in Figure 2, business intelligence (BI) entails a number of infrastructural requirements, data mining techniques and data visual analytics. The term was coined by the Gartner Group (Nedelcu, 2012) and defines business intelligence as;

An umbrella term that includes the applications, infrastructure and tools, and best practices that enable access to and analysis of information to improve and optimize decisions and performance. (Hostmann, Rayner, & Friedman, 2006)

From this definition, it is clear that BI is a buzz word that captures the two broad goals of data mining namely the descriptive and predictive roles.in utilizing the data warehouses and repositories, BI utilizes data mining techniques to provide predictions and analysis. By incorporating the infrastructural support as indicated in Figure 2, BI enables real-time data analysis based on operational data and alerts using the appropriate media such as mobile phones. Data and visual analytics provide the much-needed reporting ability to the business. This involves dashboards, scorecards and insights into decision-making towards gaining competitive advantage.

Consequently, we can conclude that the main engine of BI is data mining. Data mining approaches are broadly utilized in ensuring real-time decision-making and can broadly be categorized into two as earlier noted. Descriptive data mining seeks to explain the existing characteristics of the data and its behavior as captured historically. On the side, predictive data mining makes use of both historical and operational data to forecasts the future possibilities. To achieve these functionalities, it is imperative that data mining is integrated into an ERP system. However, though theoretically simplistic, integrating data mining into ERP systems remains a challenge for most organizations. This is so because data mining is data intensive and therefore relies on the massive collection (which can only be realized over time) to sift through while identifying trends and patterns in the data to establish new, novel and intuitive information. This information transforms raw data into crucial nuggets useful in offering the organization a competitive advantage. The next section discusses various data mining approaches that an ERP system can adopt into its business intelligence for improved decision-making and competitive approach.

Data Mining Approaches

Oracle company (Oracle, 2011) defines data mining as;

The practice of automatically searching large stores of data to discover patterns and trends that go beyond simple analysis. Data mining uses sophisticated mathematical algorithms to segment the data and evaluate the probability of future events. Data mining is also known as Knowledge Discovery in Data (KDD).

From this definition, data mining can be viewed to comprise of three critical components namely data availability, algorithms, and knowledge discovery. Earlier in the chapter, the importance of data was emphasized and the value of knowledge discovery as enshrined in business intelligence. Consequently, it is imperative in the design of an ERP system appropriate algorithms to be integrated be based on the nature of the data that an organization deals with. This is crucial because algorithms designed for geospatial data analysis may not necessarily work for time series data and vice versa. It is also important to determine the nature of the data mining problem at hand which can be considered as either classification or clustering.

In data mining, two steps are fundamental in establishing the accuracy, reliability, and effectiveness of any technique. Any given data set is broken into two sets. The first is considered to be the training data set which 'teaches' the method how to arrive at certain decisions. The second is the testing set which evaluates the performance of the method in drawing decisions from previously unmet data. In this case, a technique has to be first trained using known number of class label and then used to classify future values. If this is the case, then this is referred to as *classification* or *supervised learning*. It is supervised because it banks on the training of existing and known labels. For instance, a research institute may be seeking to classify tumors as either benign or malignant. Using pre-existing data the researchers can train a technique using the measured features showing what leads to benign tumors and vice versa. In this scenario, the existing data will contain a labeled class guiding the data mining approach. After training, the technique can now be subjected to unclassified data to determine its accuracy. It therefore has what is known as prior knowledge (Jiawei & Micheline, 2006).

In the same scenario of the researcher, now let's consider that a new research fellow has been hired and has developed a data mining technique to mine the same data. Since he is new, he has access to feature values but doesn't exactly know which of these are benign or malignant. Since he lacks the prior knowledge, his is an exploration of the data seeking to come up with some classes. The work may entail clustering together the various data values into closely related sets based on defined metrics such as distance or correlation. This way the technique is finally able to give the two classes that were there before. If this method is used, then this considered to be *clustering* or *unsupervised learning*. This section will discuss some commonly used data mining approaches based on these two broad categories

Unsupervised Approaches

Unsupervised machine learning approaches are used for data that has no labels. The objective of an unsupervised learning technique is to explore data and determine the hidden structure in the data. These approaches are mostly used for data dimensionality reduction, density estimation, visualization of data, information extraction, and outlier detection among other functions. Traditional unsupervised learning techniques include principal component analysis (PCA), Independent component analysis (ICA), k-means clustering, self-organizing maps (SOM), manifold learning models (MLM), kernel density estimation, support data description, deep learning among others. This chapter will briefly describe each of these methods for the readers to explore them.

Principal Component Analysis

Principal component analysis (PCA) is a statistical technique that transforms a set of correlated variables into linearly uncorrelated variables referred to as *principal components* (Jolliffe, 2005). The number of principal components is always less than the number of the original variables. The transformation of variables is done such that the first principal component has the highest variance given that it is orthogonal to the preceding components. Principal components are uncorrelated and do not influence each other which improves its efficiency in data analytics. Principal component analysis is commonly used for reducing data dimensionality without losing data generality. High dimensional uncorrelated data (mined from some warehouse) can be reduced through dimensionality reduction using PCA. This makes further data analytics much easier and efficient. PCA can also be used for outlier detection, abnormality detection or novelty detection, which are common applications in data mining.

Independent Component Analysis

Independent component analysis (ICA) (Li & Wang, 2002) is a technique that was proposed for handling blind source separation problem (Hyvärinen & Oja, 2000). ICA is used for finding independent latent components from measured variables. It uses optimization algorithms to recover real components from observed variables. The main difference between ICA and PCA is that ICA seeks to find latent components that are non-Gaussian and statistically independent making it able to reveal more meaningful information in non-Gaussian data compared to PCA. Like PCA, ICA can be used for dimensionality reduction, extraction of non-Gaussian information from data warehouses, data visualization among other applications.

K-Means Clustering

Originally developed for signal processing, K-means (Lloyd, 1982) is a clustering technique used for vector quantization. K-means is commonly used for cluster data analysis. The objective of K-means technique is to partition data into k clusters, where each data element belongs to the cluster with the closest mean. A warehouse may contain a wide range of data samples. K-means can be used to cluster data in a data warehouse depending on data similarity. These clusters could be indexed and this increases searching and data mining process, which further improves data analytics efficiency.

Kernel Density Estimation

Kernel density estimation (KDE) is a non-parametric technique that estimates the probability density function of a random variable. Given a finite number of training data samples, KDE can generate inferences about a population, which could be non-Gaussian (Wand & Jones, 1995). This technique can be used in estimating the distribution of data in a data warehouse, monitoring statistics in a data warehouse or other quantities which can be handy in describing the nature of a process under study.

Self-Organization Maps

Self-organizing maps (SOM) is a type of artificial neural network that produces low-dimensional, discretized representation of the data (Kohonen, 1982). Just like neural networks, SOMs consist of nodes and each node is associated with a weight vector. Each weight vector has similar dimensions as the input data and a location in the map. SOM can be used for visualization and dimensionality reduction of mined data.

Gaussian Mixture Model

Gaussian mixture model (GMM) is a probabilistic model that represents sub-populations in a population, without necessarily requiring that the observed data identifies the sub-population to which it belongs (C M Bishop, 1995). GMM can be used to learn patterns in data with highly non-linear correlations or data that is non-Gaussian. In these cases, GMM is used as a data local linearization or local Gaussianity tools for describing data. GMM can also be used for data clustering and cluster analysis, data visualization and dimensionality reduction

Manifold Learning Methods

High-dimensional data requires more than two or three dimensions to represent. This makes it impractical to interpret the data. To simplify high dimensional data, one may assume that the data lie on an embedded nonlinear manifold within high dimensional space (J. A. Lee & Verleysen, 2007). Traditionally used manifold learning techniques are principal curves, Gaussian process latent variable model, diffusion maps, locality preserving projections (LPP), neighborhood preserving embedding, generative topographic mapping among others.

Support Vector Data Description

Support vector data description (SVDD) is similar to one-class support vector machine. With one-class support vector machine, the boundary of the data can be used to detect innovative data or outlier (Tax & Duin, 2004). SVDD finds a spherical shaped boundary in a data pool, which defines a space for describing normal data. Kernels can be used with SVDD to describe nonlinear data. SVDD can be used to detect novel data in a data pool, outlier detection, data abnormality among others.

Supervised Learning

As noted in the definition of terms, supervised learning is inclined to only classification data mining problems. In classification, the problem at hand is modeled using the existing historical data. Consequently, the goal is to predict the target class for each record in new data that is non-existent. It works therefore by taking the existing data and passing its values to the data mining technique and the result also passed in. this implies that at the training stage, two data sets are used namely the input values $(I_1, I_2, I_3, ..., I_n)$ and the matching output values $(O_1, O_2, O_3, ..., O_n)$. Since each input vector has a matching expected output, the relations between the two are calculated and stored as a model which can be used to evaluate new data.

In an ERP system, classification can be used in customer profiling, credit worthiness as well as supplier reliability. For instance, a financial company may use the existing data to study the loan repayment credentials of their customers using their income, employment sector, gender, marital status, spending habits, and many other factors to determine those who are likely to default or otherwise. Any new entrants into the system can be evaluated using the model to determine their credit worthiness and arrive at a decision of the amount the customer can be advanced. Commonly used methods in classification employ regression approaches and dimensionality reduction techniques such as the Principal Component Regression (PCR), Partial Least Squares (PLS), Support Vector Machines (SVM), Artificial Neural Networks (ANNs), Fisher Discriminant Analysis (FDA) among others. Each of these is briefly discussed without providing the technical details but rather to guide any organization to understand the underlying building blocks of these methods which can guide in ascertaining the appropriateness of an ERP system based on the data mining techniques it embraces to provide business intelligence. However, most established ERP systems such as Oracle (Saran, 2007) and SAP (Board, 2017)provide a mixture of these hence offering the desired flexibility.

Principal Component Regression

Principal component regression (PCR) is a regression technique based on principal component analysis (PCA). In PCR, principal components returned by principal component analysis are used in regression instead of applying regression of actual data. PCR is used to overcome the problem of multi-linearity problem of data (Vigneau, Devaux, Qannari, & Robert, 1997). Principal component analysis is first applied to data to obtain the principal components. A regression model is learned on the principal components to learn the underlying pattern of data. However, instead of utilizing the actual data, the identified principal components are then regressed.

Partial Least Squares

Partial least squares (PLS) is a statistical modeling technique that learns a linear regression model by simultaneously projecting predicted variable and observed variables to latent variables. The latent variable forms the connection between predicted variables and observed variables. Like PCR, partial least squares extends the concept of the PCA and multiple linear regression. However, whereas PCA just performs data reduction without considering the correlation, PLS performs the real correlation function between the dependent and independent variables (Mou et al., 2017; Yan, 2008). The pair of variables (dependent and independent) are picked in a manner to ensure that the relationship between any two successive scores is as strong as possible hence providing a mechanism for redundancy analysis (Tobias, 1995).

Fisher Discriminant Analysis

Fisher discriminant analysis (FDA) is a dimensionality reduction technique designed for the classification of data. FDA focus on obtaining a transformation matrix that minimizes within-class scatter matrix and maximize between-class scatter matrix (McLachlan, 2004). This ensures that data that belong to the same class cluster together more than data in different classes.

Artificial Neural Networks

Artificial neural networks are inspired by biological information processing in the human central nervous system (C M Bishop, 1995; Christopher M Bishop, 2006). The network consists of neurons connected to each with each neuron having numeric weights that tuned based on experience to make them adaptive to input. Neural networks are capable of solving a wide variety of tasks in different application domains.

Support Vector Machines

Developed by Vapnik (Cortes & Vapnik, 1995), support vector machine (SVM) is a machine learning technique used for regression and classification of data. Given training data, SVM learns a model that separates one class of data from the other class where classes are separated by support vectors. SVM achieves this data separation by creating planes, or hyper-planes in high dimensional space that separate between classes. If the data is continuous, a regression model can be learned to predict unobserved data based on the pattern of the observed data. It is best suited for sparse data and has been widely used in recognizing handwritten characters, image analysis and bioinformatics.

Nearest Neighbors

This is a non-parametric technique that can be used for both regression and classification. The input is made up of k-nearest neighbors (KNN) in the training data space. In classification, the output is a class label that a particular data member belongs to. A continuous output is given for regression. The value for a particular data is found by averaging values of its k-nearest neighbors. Most KNN approaches use distance based methods to ascertain the 'nearness' between any pair of vectors or values (Anava & Levy, 2016; Laaksonen & Oja, 1996). Despite being an old approach, it is one of the most used techniques in data mining.

These and many other approaches comprise both the supervised and unsupervised data mining techniques that can be integrated into an ERP system to reap the benefits of data mining. However, it is crucial to understand when an organization can use classification and/or clustering for its type of data. This can be largely guided by the problem at hand and the desired output from the existing data. In the next section, the authors discuss the broad application areas of the two data mining learning strategies.

Gaussian Process Regression

This is an infinite dimensional statistical process that can be used to generalize multivariate Gaussian (normal) distributions. In this technique, each point in the input space is mapped with a normally distributed random variable. The joint distribution of all the random variables forms a Gaussian distribution (Rasmussen, 2006). Gaussian process regression is the technique of inferencing continuous values with a Gaussian process prior where the Gaussian process is used as a prior probability distribution in Bayesian inference. Therefore, given some data values, the distribution can be inferred using the Bayesian process to provide posterior of the distribution.

Bayesian Networks

A Bayesian network is a probabilistic model for representing variables and their relationships (Heckerman, 1995; Nielsen & Jensen, 2009). The nodes of this network are discrete or continuous random variables and directed edges as the relationship between the nodes. Each network variable can be an input to another variable.

Information Extraction

To acknowledge the value of integrating data mining techniques into an ERP system, it is crucial for the organization to understand its needs first. This guides the developers or providers of the ERP system to know exactly what to include and what not to. Besides, including all the techniques is not only cumbersome and time-consuming but also not advisable and impacts on the system performance. This determines whether the ERP will address classification or clustering problems.

Classification is best suited for problems whose target outcome is well known. A good example is the one discussed earlier of determining the customer's credit worthiness. Additionally, whereas regression addresses classification problems, this is determined by the type of data at hand. Mainly, regression will work best when dealing with numerical data values. Classification can further be used in an ERP system to detect anomalies within the organization's data. For instance, utilizing the same financial institution, the unusual spending habits of customers can be detected as fraud and stopped immediately. Similarly, demographic data can be used to detect unlikely withdrawal points to identify stolen cards.

On the other side, clustering techniques are mainly in association problems or feature extraction and selection challenges. In association, the commonly used scenario is market basket analysis (Jiawei & Micheline, 2006) which seeks to predict the likelihood of having a combination of goods in a basket. It uses association rules and confidence levels to draw conclusions. These can be used by an organization to create targeted advertisements, promotions as well as personalizing the shopping experience of customers. In feature extraction, a collection of data features are used to characterize a pattern. For instance, an organization can use monthly inflation rate, consumer spending habits and annual events to determine the restocking levels of their products. The advantage of feature extraction can also serve as dimensionality reduction techniques as they comprise a number of data points and are crucial in making predictions.

SUMMARY

This chapter has discussed the value and the place of quality data in an ERP system. However, data quality is a metric that is multifaceted and can be looked into based on factors such as *completeness, consistency, conformity, timeliness, integrity,* and *accuracy* (3CTIA). Each of these was explained and their importance in ensuring the quality and effectiveness of an ERP system emphasized. However, determining whether the data is of quality or not requires certain computations such as the use of the *Min/Max* operations which enforce the data points to be within the acceptable ranges. The use of *simple ratios* which are good measures of measuring the completeness of a vector of data values and finally the *weighted averages* which are a variant of the *min* operation but for a multivariate data sets.

Additionally, the chapter looked into the way of integrating data mining into an ERP system. The three crucial views were discussed encompassing the outer view, inner view and the knowledge discovery view. The *outer view* comprises of the collection of various entry points of an ERP system which entails the information systems implementing the core business processes such as finance, accounting, and customer relationship management systems among others. The *inner view* refers to the repository where the information systems at the outer view deposit their data. However, before the data is permanently stored in the repository, the data quality needs to be enforced to warrant its integrity as well as the quality of decision-making. Finally, the *knowledge discovery view* comprising of the data mining component, data visualization, and infrastructural components are discussed.

Since the focus of the chapter was data mining, the two strategies of supervised and unsupervised were discussed. Supervised techniques are guided by well-known training data sets which require an input vector accompanied by the accompanying expected output values. Due to their nature, supervised data mining techniques are appropriate for resolving *classification* problems. Such methods entail dimension reduction or regression techniques such as the Principal Component Regression (PCR), Partial Least Squares (PLS), Support Vector Machines (SVM), Artificial Neural Networks (ANNs) and the Fisher Discriminant Analysis (FDA). In unsupervised data mining strategies, the methods employed must explore and learn on the go and hence appropriate for anomaly detection, feature extraction, and prediction. Such methods include principal component analysis (PCA), Independent component analysis (ICA), k-means clustering, self-organizing maps (SOMs), Manifold learning models (MLM) and kernel density estimation. Ultimately, the chapter concluded by presenting the probable problems within which each of these two strategies can be put into place.

REFERENCES

Abe, S. (2010). *Feature Selection and Extraction*. Support Vector Machines for Pattern Classification. Advances in Pattern Recognition; doi:10.1007/978-1-84996-098-4_7

Anava, O., & Levy, K. (2016). k*-Nearest Neighbors: From Global to Local. *Advances In Neural Information Processing Systems, 29*, 4916–4924. Retrieved from http://papers.nips.cc/paper/6373-k-nearest-neighbors-from-global-to-local.pdf

Askham, N., Cook, D., Doyle, M., Fereday, H., Gibson, M., & Landbeck, U. … Schwarzenbach, J. (2013). *The Six Primary Dimensions for Data Quality Assessment. Group, DAMA UK Working*. Retrieved from https://www.dqglobal.com/wp-content/uploads/2013/11/DAMA-UK-DQ-Dimensions-White-Paper-R37.pdf

Batini, C., & Scannapieco, M. (2006). Data Quality. *Quality, 262*. doi:10.1007/3-540-33173-5

Bhogal, J., & Choksi, I. (2015). Handling Big Data Using NoSQL. In *Proceedings - IEEE 29th International Conference on Advanced Information Networking and Applications Workshops, WAINA 2015* (pp. 393–398). IEEE. 10.1109/WAINA.2015.19

Bishop, C. M. (1995). Neural networks for pattern recognition. *Journal of the American Statistical Association, 92*, 482. doi:10.2307/2965437

Bishop, C. M. (2006). Pattern Recognition and Machine Learning. In Pattern Recognition (Vol. 4, p. 738). Springer. doi:10.1117/1.2819119

Board, E. (2017). SAP SE (NYSE: SAP). *Global Journal of Enterprise Information System, 9*(1), 136. doi:10.18311/gjeis/2017/15884

Cai, S.-M., Zhou, P.-L., Yang, H.-J., Yang, C.-X., & Wang, B.-H. (n.d.). Diffusion entropy analysis on the scaling behavior of financial markets. *Physica A, 367*, 337–344.

Cappiello, C., Francalanci, C., & Pernici, B. (2004). *Data Quality Assessment From the User's Perspective*. IQIS.

Cortes, C., & Vapnik, V. (1995). Support-Vector Networks. *Machine Learning, 20*(3), 273–297. doi:10.1007/BF00994018

Dimitrova, E. S., Licona, M. P. V., McGee, J., & Laubenbacher, R. (2010). Discretization of Time Series Data. *Journal of Computational Biology, 17*(6), 853–868. doi:10.1089/cmb.2008.0023 PMID:20583929

Dutta, S., & Bhattacharya, A. (2010). Most significant substring mining based on chi-square measure. In Lecture Notes in Computer Science (Vol. 6118, pp. 319–327). Springer. doi:10.1007/978-3-642-13657-3_35

Even, A., & Shankaranarayanan, G. (2007). Utility-Driven Assessment of Data Quality. *The Data Base for Advances in Information Systems*, *38*(2), 75–93. doi:10.1145/1240616.1240623

García, M. A., & Rodríguez, F. (2013). Analysis of MODIS NDVI time series using quasi-periodic components. In *Proceedings of SPIE - The International Society for Optical Engineering* (Vol. 8795). 10.1117/12.2027170

Hauck, M. (2014). NoSQL Databases Explained. *MongoDB*. Retrieved from http://www.mongodb.com/nosql-explained

Heckerman, D. (1995). A tutorial on learning with Bayesian networks. *Tutorial*. Retrieved from http://citeseerx.ist.psu.edu/viewdoc/summary?doi=10.1.1.56.1431

Hostmann, B., Rayner, N., & Friedman, T. (2006). Gartner's Business Intelligence and Performance Management Framework. *Business (Atlanta, Ga.)*.

Hyvärinen, A., & Oja, E. (2000). Independent component analysis: Algorithms and applications. *Neural Networks*, *13*(4-5), 411–430. doi:10.1016/S0893-6080(00)00026-5 PMID:10946390

Jiawei, H., & Micheline, K. (2006). *Data Mining: Concepts and Techniques* (2nd ed.). Morgan Kauffman.

Jin, R., Breitbart, Y., & Muoh, C. (2009). Data discretization unification. *Knowledge and Information Systems*, *19*(1), 1–29. doi:10.100710115-008-0142-6

Jolliffe, I. T. (2005). Principal component analysis. *Applied Optics*, *44*(May), 6486. doi:10.1007/SpringerReference_205537 PMID:16252661

Kohonen, T. (1982). Self-organized formation of topologically correct feature maps. *Biological Cybernetics*, *43*(1), 59–69. doi:10.1007/BF00337288

Laaksonen, J., & Oja, E. (1996). Classification with learning k-nearest neighbors. *ICNN 96. The 1996 IEEE International Conference on Neural Networks, 3*, 1480–1483. 10.1109/ICNN.1996.549118

Lee, J. A., & Verleysen, M. (2007). Nonlinear dimensionality reduction. Advances in Neural Information Processing Systems, 5. doi:10.1007/978-0-387-39351-3

Lee, Y., Pipino, L., Funk, J., & Wang, R. (2006). *Journey to data quality. Computer* (Vol. 1). Retrieved from http://141.105.33.55/~lomov/??????????/bigdvd/dvd44/Lee.pdf

Leskovec, J., Rajaraman, A., & Ullman, J. (2014). Dimensionality reduction. *Mining of Massive Datasets*, 405–437. Retrieved from http://www.mmds.org/

Li, R. F., & Wang, X. Z. (2002). Dimension reduction of process dynamic trends using independent component analysis. *Computers & Chemical Engineering*, *26*(3), 467–473. doi:10.1016/S0098-1354(01)00773-6

Lloyd, S. P. (1982). Least Squares Quantization in PCM. *IEEE Transactions on Information Theory*, *28*(2), 129–137. doi:10.1109/TIT.1982.1056489

Ma, R., Zhou, X., Peng, Z., Liu, D., Xu, H., Wang, J., & Wang, X. (2015). Data mining on correlation feature of load characteristics statistical indexes considering temperature. *Zhongguo Dianji Gongcheng Xuebao. Zhongguo Dianji Gongcheng Xuebao*, *35*(1), 43–51. doi:10.13334/j.0258-8013.pcsee.2015.01.006

McLachlan, G. J. (2004). *Discriminant analysis and statistical pattern recognition. Wiley series in probability and statistics.* doi:10.1002/0471725293

Mou, Y., Zhou, L., You, X., Lu, Y., Chen, W., & Zhao, X. (2017). Multiview partial least squares. *Chemometrics and Intelligent Laboratory Systems*, *160*, 13–21. doi:10.1016/j.chemolab.2016.10.013

Nedelcu, B. (2012). Business Intelligence Systems. *Database Systems Journal*, *4*, 12–20. Retrieved from http://www.dbjournal.ro/archive/14/14_2.pdf

Nielsen, T. D., & Jensen, F. V. (2009). *Bayesian Network and Decision Graph.* Springer Science & Business Media; doi:10.1007/978-0-387-68282-2

Nylen, E. L., Wallisch, P., Nylen, E. L., & Wallisch, P. (2017). Dimensionality Reduction. In Neural Data Science (pp. 223–248). Academic Press. doi:10.1016/B978-0-12-804043-0.00008-8

Olson, J. E. (2003). *Data Quality: The Accuracy Dimension. Data Quality: The Accuracy Dimension.* doi:10.1016/B978-1-55860-891-7.X5000-8

Oracle. (2011). *What Is Data Mining.* Retrieved from https://docs.oracle.com/cd/B28359_01/datamine.111/b28129/process.htm#CHDFGCIJ

Pipino, L. L., Lee, Y. W., & Wang, R. Y. (2002). Data quality assessment. *Communications of the ACM*, *45*(4), 211. doi:10.1145/505248.506010

Ramírez-Gallego, S., García, S., Mouriño-Talín, H., Martínez-Rego, D., Bolón-Canedo, V., & Alonso-Betanzos, A., … Herrera, F. (2016). Data discretization: Taxonomy and big data challenge. *Wiley Interdisciplinary Reviews. Data Mining and Knowledge Discovery*. doi:10.1002/widm.1173

Rasmussen, C. E. (2006). Gaussian processes for machine learning. *International Journal of Neural Systems*, *14*(2), 69–106. doi:10.1142/S0129065704001899 PMID:15112367

Saha, B., & Srivastava, D. (2014). Data quality: The other face of Big Data. In *Proceedings - International Conference on Data Engineering* (pp. 1294–1297). Academic Press. 10.1109/ICDE.2014.6816764

Saran, C. (2007). Oracle extends sector specific ERP for SMEs. *Computer Weekly*, *16*. Retrieved from http://search.ebscohost.com/login.aspx?direct=true&db=bth&AN=26259654&site=ehost-live

Scholkopf, B., Smola, A. J., & Muller, K. R. (2012). Kernel Principal Component Analysis. *Computer Vision And Mathematical Methods In Medical And Biomedical Image Analysis*, *1327*, 583–588. doi:10.1162/089976698300017467

Seemann, L., Hua, J.-C., McCauley, J. L., & Gunaratne, G. H. (2012). Ensemble vs. time averages in financial time series analysis. *Physica A*, *391*(23), 6024–6032. doi:10.1016/j.physa.2012.06.054

Tax, D. M. J., & Duin, R. P. W. (2004). Support vector data description. *Machine Learning*, *54*(1), 45–66. doi:10.1023/B:MACH.0000008084.60811.49

Tobias, R. D. (1995). An Introduction to Partial Least Squares Regression. In *Proceedings of the Twentieth Annual SAS Users Group International Conference* (pp. 1250–1257). Cary, NC: SAS Institute Inc;

Vigneau, E., Devaux, M. F., Qannari, E. M., & Robert, P. (1997). Principal component regression, ridge regression and ridge principal component regression in spectroscopy calibration. *Journal of Chemometrics*, *11*(3), 239–249. doi:10.1002/(SICI)1099-128X(199705)11:3<239::AID-CEM470>3.0.CO;2-A

Wand, M. P., & Jones, M. C. (1995). Kernel Smoothing. Encyclopedia of Statistics in Behavioral Science, 60(60), 212. doi:10.2307/1268906

Wang, R. Y. (1998). Total Data Quality Management. *Communications of the ACM*, *41*(2), 58–65. doi:10.1145/269012.269022

Wang, R. Y., Kon, H. B., & Madnick, S. E. (1993). Data Quality Requirements Analysis and Modeling. *Data Engineering*, *8*(April), 670–677. doi:10.1109/ICDE.1993.344012

Xu, H. (2006). The Importance of Data Quality for SAP Implementation in Medium-sized Organizations. *Issues in Information Systems*, *VII*(2), 88–91. Retrieved from https://digitalcommons.butler.edu/cgi/viewcontent.cgi?article=1082&context=cob_papers

Yan, S. M. (2008). Principle Component Analysis and Partial Least Square: Two Dimension Reduction Techniques for Regression. *Casualty Actuarial Society*, 79–90. Retrieved from https://www.casact.org/pubs/dpp/dpp08/08dpp76.pdf

Yin, X., Ng, B. W.-H., & Abbott, D. (2012). Feature Extraction and Selection. In *Terahertz Imaging for Biomedical Applications* (pp. 95–118). Academic Press. doi:10.1007/978-1-4614-1821-4_7

KEY TERMS AND DEFINITIONS

Business Intelligence: A term used to refer to collective technologies, infrastructure, algorithms and visualization techniques that are used in collecting, organizing, and storing data, knowledge extraction, and presentation of information for business strategic decision-making process.

Classification: A data mining category of data mining challenges that seek to group data into already known sets (classes); hence, the training of the algorithms is considered to have been supervised before the actual task is executed.

Clustering: A closely related term to classification. However, unlike classification whose probable data sets are known prior to the actual execution, clustering is blind and learns from the provided data sets without any knowledge; hence, training is unsupervised.

Data Mining: Refers to the process of extracting patterns, trends, and knowledge from a pool of an organization's data using algorithms.

Data Quality: Refers to the feature that data can be relied upon for accurate decision-making process, planning, and projections.

Effectiveness: The extent to which a system functions as intended offering the expected results.

Enterprise Resource Planning (ERP): An integrated software system comprising of all the organization's core processes and backed up by an appropriate information and communication technologies (ICT).

Chapter 3
Interoperability of ERP Software

Elyjoy Muthoni Micheni
Technical University of Kenya, Kenya

Geoffrey Muchiri Muketha
Murang'a University of Technology, Kenya

Evance Ogolla Onyango
Technical University of Kenya, Kenya

ABSTRACT

Even though most organizations are using enterprise resource planning applications, very few people understand the underlying interoperability nature within them. Interoperability is the ability of systems to provide services to and accept services from other systems, and to use the services exchanged so as to operate together in a more effective manner. The fact that interoperability can be improved means that the metrics for measuring interoperability can be defined. For the purpose of measuring the interoperability between systems, an interoperability assessment model is required. A comparative analysis among these models is provided to evaluate the similarities and differences in their philosophy and implementation. The analysis yields a set of recommendations for any party that is open to the idea of creating or improving an interoperability assessment model.

DOI: 10.4018/978-1-5225-7678-5.ch003

INTRODUCTION

The quest for sustainable competitive advantage has made firms around the globe to adopt Enterprise Resource Planning (ERP) systems so as optimally leverage on the enterprise - wide resources and be more responsive to customer demands. Globally organizations seeking to enhance their competitiveness have utilized ERP systems to enhance their operational efficiency (Verville, Palanisamy, Bernadas, & Halingten, 2007). This has been exacerbated by ERP internet extended functionalities, stakeholders demand to bridge speed with value.

ERPs are universally accepted by the industry as a practical solution to achieve integrated enterprise information systems (Davenport, 2000; Moon, 2007). These systems need to be continuously reviewed and enhanced to meet new user requirements (Peng & Nunes, 2009). Hence, these systems have evolved over time thanks to ERP developers, who have identified and developed new functionalities for them. In some cases, these changes have been made to include new business processes in the ERP, while in others; they have been driven to connect ERP functionalities with legacy systems in the organisation or other in systems beyond the organisation. Thus, proposals about the integration of new functionalities and new interoperability requirements produce new developments in ERP systems.

Interoperability is central to any form of collaboration between organizations, as it enables information and knowledge sharing by cooperating entities within and across organizational boundaries. Interoperability is particularly important in the public sector where collaboration between public agencies is necessary to realize the notions of seamless services and one-stop government (Sanchez et al., 2008).

According to Hadil and Dieter (2017), interoperability can be defined as the ability of computer systems to communicate with each other and how they make use of certain information. In most cases, these computers can either be connected via a network system or through some distributed or grid technology. However, though grid technology only offers a single resource to multiple sets of clients within the network architecture.

A significant development in computing within the Nineteen Nineties has been the move toward additional distributed computer systems through network communication facilities. David (2013) highlights that, rather than viewing computers as individual devices, users wish to integrate these connected resources into one procedure setting. Both hardware and software package vendors square measure developing means that support distributed computing at each system and program level.

Xihui and Hua (2010) reveals that, deeper understanding of interoperability schema requires a three to four tire process in order to be progressive; this includes the computer hardware, software, human user and/ or the internet. Although many

ERP software are stand-alone web or desktop applications, their completeness and usefulness require the above four mentioned aspects. Finally, ERP interoperability becomes significant as we begin to look at the different tasks that ERP software can perform simultaneously.

This chapter gives a detailed background of interoperability and its various forms, ERP software, Software Metrics, ERP interoperability, Significance of ERP programs, Methods to measure ERP programs and concludes by discussing the ERP Interoperability Metrics.

BACKGROUND INFORMATION

What Is Enterprise Resource Planning (ERP)?

ERP can be defined as an enterprise - wide information system that collates and controls all the business processes within an organization onto a single computer system so as to serve organization's needs. ERP as an information technology (IT) resource seeks to reliably integrate, synchronize and centralize organizational data strategically along its value chain (Kilic, Zaim, & Delen, 2014). Holland et al (1999) defines ERP systems as integrated enterprise-wide information systems that automate the business processes.

According to Yi and Ben (2011), many people did not know about ERPs until the 1990s, as described by the Gartner institute of research. The term was initially called the Material Resources planning (MRP) in the 1960s that was used to refer to the inventory management techniques by that time. Software developers came up with MRPs to monitor inventories, balance books of accounts and report on certain project statuses. With time and over the years, these systems have advanced to include human resource management, accounting, supply chain and procurement and finally employee management. In addition, the term material was later changed to enterprise to include not only the manufacturing bit of ERPS but now that all businesses could now work with ERPs to monitor and manage other departments as well. It is clear now the interoperability nature of ERPs, we also bear in mind that ERPs are built with multiple/several departments in mind even though they can still handle a single function at a time. Currently there are other technologies that are coming to graft into ERP such as cloud solutions that offer real time solutions to ERP applications and systems.

What is Interoperability?

Interoperability has been defined in a number of ways by different scholars. According to IEEE (1990), Rukanova (2006) and Lebreton (2007), interoperability is the ability of two or more systems or components to exchange information and to use the information exchanged. Miller (2000) defines interoperability as an on-going process of ensuring that systems, procedures and cultures of an organization are managed in such a way as to maximize opportunities for exchange and reuse of information. The European Commission, IDABC (2004), views interoperability as the ability of ICT systems and the business processes they support to exchange data and share information and knowledge. According to the Australian Ministry of Finance and Deregulation (2005), interoperability is the ability to transfer and use information in a uniform and efficient manner across multiple organizations and information technology systems. The New Zealand Government perceives interoperability as the ability of Government organizations to share and integrate information and business by using common standards (State Services Commission, 2006). Interoperability has also been defined as the ability of Government organizations to share and integrate information and business by using common standards, Heubusch (2006). Interoperability is the ability of two or more systems or applications to exchange information and to mutually use the information that has been exchanged, Jack and Suri (2010). Interoperability is the ability of independent systems to exchange meaningful information and initiate actions from each other, in order to operate together to mutual benefit. In particular, it envisages the ability for loosely coupled independent systems to be able to collaborate and communicate, Jenkins (2008) and ISO/IEC 21000-6. Interoperability has also been defined as being able to accomplish end-user applications using different types of computer systems, operating systems and application software, interconnected by different types of local and wide area networks, Thea and Terry (2001). Other definitions of interoperability include a solution that enables two or more software applications to exchange data and achieve a common objective, even if the two applications were not originally intended to cooperate. However, interoperability can take place at different governance levels; i.e. from the exchange of simple data items, to structured documents (e.g., a purchase order), to business process cooperation where different organizations are enabled by interoperable software applications to achieve a common objective (O'Brien & Makaras, 2010). The definition of interoperability in this chapter conforms to Jenkins (2008) and ISO/IEC 21000-6 definition of interoperability, the ability of two or more systems or components of systems to exchange meaningful information electronically, securely, accurately and verifiably, when and where needed. In particular, it envisages the ability for loosely coupled independent systems to be able to collaborate and communicate.

TYPES OF INTEROPERABILITY

Kasunic and Anderson (2004) interoperability is a function of operational concepts and scenarios, policies, processes, and procedures in heterogeneous domains. Organizational entities that manage data are autonomous in adopting the architecture, design and communication technology etc. Architecture and design autonomy give them leverage to adopt any architecture/design suitable for holding the data across the organization. Communication autonomy comes into existence when organization is willing to share data with different architectures, vendors or solutions. According to Sheth P. Amit (1998), in interoperability, element of associative autonomy has to be there to control autonomy at different level of data sharing across the organization for inter/intra communication and exchange of information. Interoperability is categorized into many different types (Gradman, 2008; Rowlands, 2009; Lueders, 2005). Based on this studies interoperability can be categorized into the following categories.

Technical Interoperability

Technical interoperability, also known as system interoperability deals with the machine level communication. It makes heterogeneous systems of systems a reality (Hamilton & Murtagh, 2000). Technical interoperability entails addressing the technical issues (hardware, software, telecommunications) involved in interconnecting computer systems and services, including key elements such as open interfaces, interconnection services, integration of data and middleware, presentation and exchange of data, accessibility and security services (Sanchez et al., 2008). A communication protocol and infrastructure are needed exists for exchanging data between participating systems (Veer H. & Wiles A., 2008). On this level, a communication infrastructure is established allowing systems to exchange bits and bytes, and the underlying networks and protocols are unambiguously defined. Various middle ware technologies like CORBA, RMI, and DCOM contributed towards system interoperability. Technical interoperability is concerned with the technicalities associated with connecting computers for the purpose of exchanging information; it includes the standards & specifications needed for such association and enablement of coherent exchange of information (Lallana Emmanuel, 2008). Scope of technical interoperability is limited.

Structural Interoperability or Conceptual Interoperability

Structural Interoperability, also known as conceptual interoperability tackles heterogeneity at modeling/architectural level for data representation. Conceptual models for interoperability are needed to bridge the gap between technical and conceptual design (Tolk & Muguira, 2003). Many new technologies are there to structure the information on the web which helps in achieving structural interoperability. Structural interoperability describes the level of agreement on the data format and focusing on each separate data string (e.g. date format). Structural interoperability is achieved through data models for specifying semantic schemas in a way that they can be shared (Woodley, 2001). Metadata description languages are developed to achieve structural interoperability. One of the most popular is a Dublin Core metadata initiative which is used by many countries to achieve interoperable solutions.

Syntactic Interoperability

Syntactic Interoperability deals with the data representation in machine readable form and usually associated with data formats. Intent is to identify elements, rules for structuring the elements, mapping, bridging, and crosswalks between equivalent elements (Veltman, 2001). Syntactic interoperability helps in making two or more systems capable of communicating and exchanging data. It specifies data formats, communication protocols, GIF (Government Interoperability Framework) Structure or arrangement of words eventually leads to meaning.

Semantic Interoperability or Information Interoperability

Semantic Interoperability, also known as information interoperability deals with the meaning of terms and expression hence it is the ability to automatically interpret the information exchanged meaningfully and accurately in order to produce useful results as defined by the end users of both systems. Semantic interoperability is must to ensure only relevant information can be exchanged or shared. It will support high level, context sensitive information request over heterogeneous information resources, hiding system, syntax and structural heterogeneity (Sheth P. Amit, 1998).

To achieve semantic interoperability, both sides must refer to a common information exchange reference model. Different layers of semantic interoperability are acceptable to scientific fields but in e-governance solutions, locally or nationally customized semantics of metadata are more favoured (Veltman, 2001). The semantic challenge is of enabling each system to appropriately understand the information that is being shared related to the logical aspect of using and sharing data based on their intended meaning (Papazoglou & Ribbers, 2009). A semantic concern involves how information is used differently by other organizations. Two core elements that need to support semantic interoperability are meta-data and ontology. Where metadata describes Meta information about the resources, ontology is used to define the knowledge and is meant to be stable over time. Ontology serves as the reference model of entities and interactions in some particular domain of application and knowledge. Inter-mediation, semantic mapping and context sensitivity are three main elements in solutions that exhibit semantic interoperability (Pollock, 2004). Semantic interoperability is also called information interoperability (Lallana Emmanuel, 2008).

Data Interoperability

Data Interoperability means single data definition for all systems. Interoperability at the data level requires involvement in the development of standards for data descriptions (catalogues and reference data), data access (database interfaces), and data transport (representation and protocols), (Kasunic & Anderson, 2004). The basic idea is that shared data is stored only once and maintained by the producer. In this way, data in use should be up to date and no redundant versions need to be stored (Winter, 2002). When a single set of definitions is mandated for all applications, definitions are no longer locally optimal, and therefore the successful implementation of such mandates, centralized agreeable initiative is needed. Following approaches may be used to achieve data interoperability

Organizational Interoperability

Organizational Interoperability, also known as operational interoperability depends on successful implementation of technical, syntactical and semantic interoperability (Veer & Wiles, 2008). Because organization interoperability is the function of technical, syntactical and semantic interoperability, it may not be considered the standalone type of interoperability. It is more related to the behaviours of organization to effectively communicate and transfer (meaningful) data (information) even though they may be using a variety of different information systems over widely different infrastructures, possibly across different geographic regions and cultures.

Veer and Wiles (2008) consider organizational interoperability as the one of many types of interoperability. Organizational interoperability can also be named as operational interoperability due its dependency on the same elements as that of organizational interoperability (Kasunic & Anderson, 2004). This dimension of interoperability is concerned with defining business goals, modelling business processes and bringing about the collaboration of administrations that wish to exchange information and may have different internal structures and processes.

Semiotic Interoperability

Semiotic Interoperability, also known as Pragmatic Interoperability or Dynamic Interoperability is one level higher than semantic interoperability; it works at contextual level to deal with the heterogeneity. This level is reached when the interoperating systems are aware of the methods and procedures that each system is employing. In other words, the use of the data - or the context of its application - is understood by the participating systems; the context in which the information is exchanged is unambiguously defined. This layer puts the (word) meaning into context. Semiotic Interoperability is also needed as the State of the system will change as a system operates on data over time, and this includes the various assumptions and constraints that affect its data interchange. If systems have attained semiotic Interoperability, systems are able to comprehend the state changes that occur, during system operation and they are able to take advantage of those changes. Ontology Inference Layer (OIL) and OWL Web Ontology Language are two tools used to achieve this objective.

SOFTWARE METRICS

According to Hilda (2003) quality software refers *to* software which is reasonably bug or defect free, is delivered in time and within the specified budget, meets the requirements and/or expectations, and is maintainable ". This is in-turn divided into 4 major categories:

- **Software Functional Quality**: Shows how much software meets a specific design given a few functional requirements and specifications.
- **Software Structural Quality**: Deals with the handling of the non-functional requirements and the degree to which the software was produced.
- **Software Quality Control**: Software Quality Control (SQC)is a set of activities to ensure the quality in software products. These activities focus on determining the defects in the actual products produced. It involves product-focus and education

The Software Quality Challenge

Product Complexity

It is the number of operational modes the product permits. Normally, an industrial product allows only less than a few thousand modes of operation with different combinations of its machine settings. However, software packages allow millions of operational possibilities. Hence, assuring of all these operational possibilities correctly is a major challenge to the software industry.

Product Visibility Since the industrial products are visible, most of its defects can be detected during the manufacturing process. Also the absence of a part in an industrial product can be easily detected in the product. However, the defects in software products which are stored on diskettes or CDs are invisible.

Software Quality Factors

Several models of software quality factors and their categorization have been suggested over the years. The classic model of software quality factors, suggested by McCall, consists of 11 factors (McCall et al., 1977). Similarly, models consisting of 12 to 15 factors, were suggested by Deutsch and Willis (1988) and by Evans and Marciniak (1987)

McCall's Factor Model

This model classifies all software requirements into 11 software quality factors. The 11 factors are grouped into three categories –product operation, product revision, and product transition factors. Product operation factors: Correctness, Reliability, Efficiency, Integrity, Usability. Product revision factors: Maintainability, Flexibility, Testability. Product transition factors: Portability, Reusability, Interoperability.

Product Operation Software Quality Factors

According to McCall's model, product operation category includes five software quality factors, which deal with the requirements that directly affect the daily operation of the software. They areas follows:

- Correctness these requirements deal with the correctness of the output of the software system. They include:

Output Mission

The required accuracy of output that can be negatively affected by inaccurate data or inaccurate calculations. The completeness of the output information, which can be affected by incomplete data. The up-to-datedness of the information defined as the time between the event and the response by the software system.

Reliability

Reliability requirements deal with service failure. They determine the maximum allowed failure rate of the software system and can refer to the entire system or to one or more of its separate functions.

Efficiency

It deals with the hardware resources needed to perform the different functions of the software system. It includes processing capabilities (given in MHz), its storage capacity (given in MB or GB) and the data communication capability (given in MBPS or GBPS). It also deals with the time between recharging of the system's portable units, such as, information system units located in portable computers, or meteorological units placed outdoors.

Integrity

This factor deals with the software system security, that is, to prevent access to unauthorized persons, also to distinguish between the group of people to be given read as well as write permit.

Usability

Usability requirements deal with the staff resources needed to train a new employee and to operate the software system.

The Standards for Coding and Documenting the Software System

Reliability

Reliability requirements deal with service failure. They determine the maximum allowed failure rate of the software system and can refer to the entire system or to one or more of its separate functions.

Efficiency

It deals with the hardware resources needed to perform the different functions of the software system. It includes processing capabilities (given in MHz), its storage capacity (given in MB or GB) and the data communication capability (given in MBPS or GBPS). It also deals with the time between recharging of the system's portable units, such as, information system units located in portable computers, or meteorological units placed outdoors.

Integrity

This factor deals with the software system security, that is, to prevent access to unauthorized persons, also to distinguish between the group of people to be given read as well as write permit.

Usability

Usability requirements deal with the staff resources needed to train a new employee and to operate the software system. Product Revision Quality Factors According to McCall's model, three software quality factors are included in the product revision category. These factors are as follows:

- **Maintainability:** This factor considers the efforts that will be needed by users and maintenance personnel to identify the reasons for software failures, to correct the failures, and to verify the success of the corrections.
- **Flexibility:** This factor deals with the capabilities and efforts required to support adaptive maintenance activities of the software. These include adapting the current software to additional circumstances and customers without changing the software. This factor's requirements also support

perfective maintenance activities, such as changes and additions to the software in order to improve its service and to adapt it to changes in the firm's technical or commercial environment.

- **Testability:** Testability requirements deal with the testing of the software system as well as with its operation. It includes predefined intermediate results, log files, and also the automatic diagnostics performed by the software system prior to starting the system, to find out whether all components of the system are in working order and to obtain a report about the detected faults Another type of these requirements deals with automatic diagnostic checks applied by the maintenance technicians to detect the causes of software failures. Product Transition Software Quality Factor According to McCall's model, three software quality factors are included in the product transition category that deals with the adaptation of software to the environments and its interaction with other software systems. These factors are as follows:

- **Portability:** Portability requirements tend to the adaptation of a software system to other environments consisting of different hardware, different operating systems, and so forth. The software should be possible to continue using the same basic software in diverse situations.

- **Reusability:** This factor deals with the use of software modules originally designed for one project in a new software project currently being developed. They may also enable future projects to make use of a given module or a group of modules of the currently developed software. The reuse of software is expected to save development resources, shorten the development period, and provide higher quality modules.

- **Interoperability:** Interoperability requirements focus on creating interfaces with other software systems or with other equipment firmware. For example, the firmware of the production machinery and testing equipment interfaces with the production control software.

ERP INTEROPERABILITY

According to Hilda (2003), enterprise resource planning applications are not built as stand-alone programs. Usually, the developers of these applications begin by doing/ conducting a thorough need/ feasibility assessment analysis, just as it is the requirement with any other software program. This stage is referred to as the software development life cycle (SDLC). A team of experienced system stakeholders design the project and write down the project deliverables. This team is usually composed of:

- **Systems Analyst**: Gathers all the requirements (both technical and hardware based) to achieve the project needs required.
- **The Clients**: In most cases are the also the financiers of these projects. In view to ERPs, clients could be the potential or the already existing organizations that are using these ERPS.
- **System Designers**: Draw the mockup designs and prototypes of these applications.
- **Programmers**: Skilled with computer programming languages such as PHP, Java, C++ or Python to develop the actual ERP applications. In most cases, extra skills in database implementations such as MySQL or Oracle is needed of these people.
- **Vendors**: Once the ERP software has been developed, the vendors through the appropriate licenses sell the applications to end users. An end user license agreement (UELA) is usually a license with terms and conditions giving the final user of the ERP application the appropriate rights to use the program under the agreed terms.

The ERP development life cycle process is composed of five major important stages as indicated in Figure 1.

However, as per the standards of good and quality software, such should be able to accommodate the varied and ever demanding needs of the market. Ever since the 1990s, consumers of ERP applications have occasionally raised the need to have an application that will reduce costs, give a return on investment (R.O.I), engage more clients and reduce the unnecessary management efforts. Finally, all these should

Figure 1. SDLC process

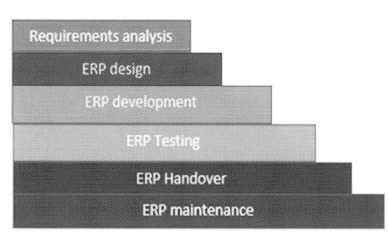

be channeled towards ensuring that all the three levels of management have the appropriate decision-making support tools (ERPs).

Consequently, the designers of these applications hence had to adopt systems that could accommodate multiple departments, hardware/software platforms and versions and finally offer multiple support options to the different users. Hence therefore, ERP interoperability can be discussed in three major levels:

1. Organizational/Departmental interoperability
2. Hardware/ Software interoperability
3. Functional/Use interoperability

Organizational/ Departmental Interoperability

Within an organization/company, there are various departments. These departments include Supply chain and procumbent, Transport and logistics, finance, human resource, Marketing and sales and finally accounting. So when we talk about the departmental nature of ERPs, what this means is that an organization/corporation adopts an application that will be able to integrate all the functions of the company on a single user interface. This was the primary need for ERP developments as outlined by the Gartner research institute way back in 1990.

The top management were looking for a uniform, simpler and quicker method to managing organizational departments in various locations without themselves being in those multiple locations at the same department. Factors such as the tight schedule of mangers and the complexity of organizational processes together with the tedious nature of seeking reports from junior employees were some of the reasons why organizational ERPs were widely adopted.

Suppose a CEO is in the headquarters and would want to know what is happening at one of its branches in a particular region; he simply logs into the ERP system and at the click of a button gets information on the accounting, finance, HR and any other information together with reports on the specific branch without necessarily travelling there in person. Think about it, isn't that useful? However, it is also worthwhile noting that organizational ERPs are only as useful to the extent to which they are used as we shall see later at the end of this chapter. What this means is that, with the costly nature of ERPs, it would not be advisable to adopt an ERP program when the business itself only operates within a small geographical location and has fewer say less than 10 employees top run the application.

The two figures above (Figures 2 and 3) describe two situations of the ERP implementation process. In the first diagram, a large organization adopts an ERP system for use in its entire system including those of its outer branches. The various operations of the company can be viewed and accessed by the managers at the

Figure 2. Single ERP for the organization

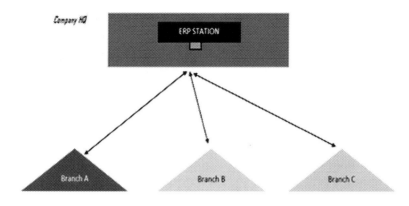

Figure 3. Functions of the ERP application

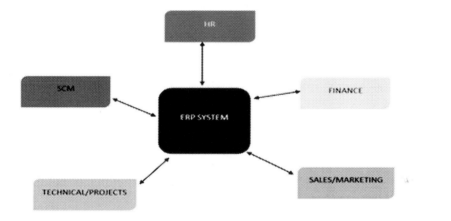

central stations. This has managed to work well for most of the banking sectors, where the branch manager in location C can send reports to the central ERP at the headquarters. At the same time, the general manager at the headquarters can view any activity at any of the bank's branches.

As is discussed in the chapters ahead, this method that the ERP uses in the above Figure 4 is most important for security reasons. A junior employee say at the bank outlet is supposed to view the bank records, but not edit records of a client database details. This action within the ERP can only be performed by a senior employee within the company with assigned privileges. This helps in ERP auditing and accounting. It is also worthwhile noting that even though, only senior employees are assigned these privileges, abuse or breach of access can still occur within the system. There are two privilege access levels when it comes to ERP access.

Figure 4. Privilege level access

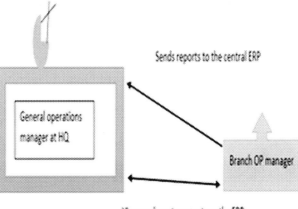

- Horizontal access
- Vertical access

Horizontal

Users within the same department/ staff level have passwords and login credentials to the same ERP system. This could be an accounting department where say four chief accountants have same username and passwords to access a given segment of the ERP system. Take a look below. The four accountants have the same privilege level access to the ERP accounting module. The user rights given to them are the same. This is why we refer to this kind of an access as the horizontal privilege level access. However, we must note that in case of breach or abuse of security access within the same level, it will be referred to as the horizontal abuse.

This can happen when one of the staff members in another accounting department steals the login credentials of another staff in the other accounting department and uses those details to access his/her module without their knowledge. In most cases, this happens for malicious intentions. It may still be difficult to ascertain exactly who authorized the transaction process since an audit will not reveal exactly who performed these processes. This challenge can be overcome by assigning biometric authentication programs to this levels such as finger print sign in. Moreover, having multiple authentication procedures also would go ahead into sealing this loop hole. It is done by letting the user pass through at least two or three authentication stages before they get into the system. In a typical organizational scenario, apart from just username and password, an extra short message authentication process can be added to the method.

Vertical

Happens when junior employees pass information to their seniors and d vice versa within the ERP system. The scenario in Figure 5 clearly depicts. Also, an abuse of privilege access at this level is referred to as vertical abuse.

Hardware/Software Interoperability

Most ERPs have the capability to support different computer hardware and software platforms. This happens because organizations are very dynamic and have different preferences when it comes to hardware and software materials. The computer hardware consists of the CPUs, Mouse, Monitor, Keyboard and the speakers. There are two types of ERP software:

- Online ERPs
- Desktop ERPs

Online ERPs are web based and are built to run online. Usually, the application is created and hosted securely in some server, assigned a domain for access and then the management can interact with it anywhere. On the other hand, since, ERPs are meant for internal organizational use, it is preferable to make these online ERPs as

Figure 5. Horizontal level access

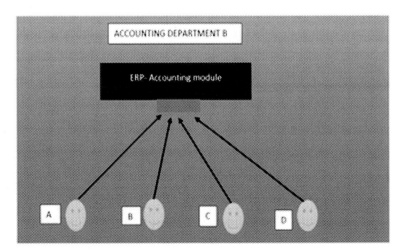

intranets (Only members of the originations with rights can access them). This is done by assigning a range of specific IPs to this domain. Any other IP outside the network will not get access to this site.

Desktop ERPs are developed to run on most of the common operating systems such as Windows, Mac and Linux. A good number of organizations use the Windows operating systems; a product of Microsoft. However certain individuals would still prefer to use the Mac and Linux OS. Unlike the Linux and Mac OS that could be very difficult to use for a good number of people; the windows OS is much user friendly. This is the reason why most developers have come together to build interactive ERPs that can be downloaded and installed on any OS. Usually, this requires an ample disk space, RAM and the right processor on.

Whereas there are open source ERP programs that are freely available in the internet, most organizations prefer to purchase their own ERP programs. Much still, organizations would still want to build their own in house ERP programs. Finally, when discussing the interoperability nature of ERPs in terms of their hardware and software capability, we are looking at an ERP program that will work comfortably on any computer hardware or software program dedicated to it.

Functional/ Use Interoperability

Given the vast nature of organizations and the numerous departments that they support, managers would want to use as minimal time as they can while increasing their income revenue. A typical ERP program should support more than one functional department as it cuts across the whole enterprise. Some of these functions include Accounting, HR, Finance, Sales and Logistics. A manager somewhere should be able to log in to the ERP program and view the number of employees currently in the company, what their roles are, how much they are earning, their leave days and performance trends. Moreover, if the manager watches to the sales module for instance, a detailed report should be available on how much revenue the company is earning, what are the most selling products of the company together with the customer trends and behavior? This is the primary use of ERP programs.

SIGNIFICANCE OF ERP PROGRAMS

So why do most organizations prefer to use these ERP systems? The value of ERP programs can be attributed to cost efficiency, decision support tool, time management and transparency within the various levels of the organization.

Cost Efficiencies

In order to reduce losses incurred during errors in stock and inventory controls, unnoticed depreciating assets and travelling packages by supervisors, ERP programs come in to streamline these processes. All the above activities can be done within the ERP program at the click of a button.

Decision Support Tool

The capability of managers to know how well their departments are performing is of great importance. For instance, the sales and manager using the data acquired in the field can view analyzed data on the sales trend, market position of their products and the consumer behavior of the different products available in the market. This acts as a great decision support tool in helping the managers to make decisions that will enhance company performance.

Time Management

Gone are the days when supervisors would travel to different offices to observe what employees were doing and whether they were doing the right thing. The whole process was tedious and too engaging for these supervisors, in the long run a lot of time is wasted that could have been used by the supervisors by doing something else for the company. This is where ERP programs came in. It supervisee sand reports every employee in the organization.

Transparency

The fact that we can be able to assign tasks within the ERP system and track their progress brings a lot of transparency to the ERP program. Furthermore, for purposes of auditing, a detailed statement of activities available within the ERP can easily be compared to the necessary books of accounts and effective action taken where the two contradict.

METHODS TO MEASURE PERFROMANCE

System developers and researchers have been trying to come up with methods and ways to measure ERP performance for over two decades now. Most of these methods developed in this chapter are formed on the basis of industry and corporate professionals who cite them on the basis of their area of career and professional

Figure 6. The ECOGRAI method

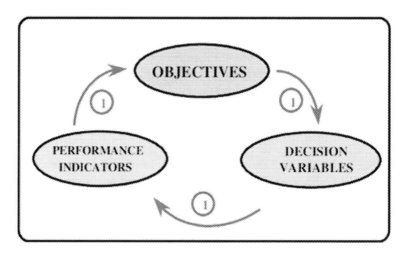

Figure 7. The balanced score card method

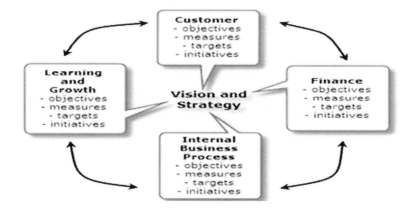

experiences. They include accountants, managerial consultants, computer experts and engineers. Some of them include, performance score cards (Kaplan, 1996), the performance prism (Neely, 1992), ECOGRAI (Ducq, 2005), QPMS, (Bitici, 1997) and IDPMS (Ghalayini, 1997).

The ECOGRAI Method

Ducq et al, (2005) outlines the ECOGRAI as a method to design and develop performance indicators for different organizations. It relies wholesomely on the decisions of the top management. Moreover, it has two major steps involved. This includes the design phase and the implementation phase. During the design phase, a lot is revealed concerning the expected system parameters such as intra-componence and the performance indicators of the particular system.

Features of the ECOGRAI Methods

- **A Logical Process of Analysis:** Which takes a top-bottom approach allowing objectives to flow from the top decision makes to the bottom operatives.
- **Tools and Graphics:** These include actograms, splitting diagrams, coherence panels and specification sheets.

A uniform distribution of performance indicators covering the various decisions and the various decision levels.

The Balanced Score Card

The main principle in this method is to employ the whole strategy throughout the whole organization/enterprise. Different departments within the organization are taken into account such as Research and development (R&D), Finance and Innovation. The main focus here is to use a model of business process and a strategy map in order to achieve full organizational needs both in the short term and long term. The BSC unlike the ECOGRAI method covers the whole enterprise as a unit without necessarily studying the smaller components such as the performance indicators in the various levels of the organization, hence it becomes somewhat difficult to have a very detailed understanding of the performance and of the control of the performance.

The Performance Prism

Developed by Neely (2002), tries to discover the impact that the different stakeholders of the enterprise/ organization. These stakeholders include investors, customers, employees, suppliers, regulators and communities. Once one has determined the different stakeholders in play, five key areas are then followed. These include:

- Stakeholder expectations
- Strategy to implement to achieve these expectations
- Which business process to implement in order to achieve these innovations
- The capabilities expected to be sued to achieve these business process
- What returns are expected from stakeholders

Figure 8. The performance prism method

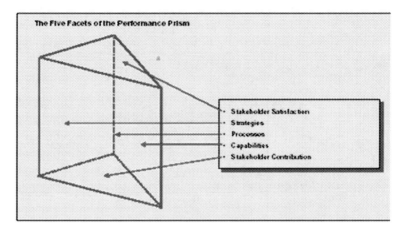

Figure 9. QMPMS method

Factor	Direct effect
Fixed cost per unit	0.500
Variable cost per unit	0.500
Fixed cost	0.137
Volume	0.205
Material and supplies cost per unit	0.072
People related cost per unit	0.365
% Labour utilisation	0.006
Overtime	0.359

The most significant advantage of this process is that it allows a connection between the external enterprise stakeholders and the internal players of the enterprise.

Quantitative Model for Performance Measurement System (QMPMS)

This method was developed by Bitici in 1997 to help enterprises understand the relationship between quantitative elements of the organization. It has three major steps that include; identification of performance factors using cognitive tools and maps, building of cause and effect diagrams and finally the analytical hierarchical process (AHP), which is used to quantify processes and factors.

Figure 10. The IDMPS method

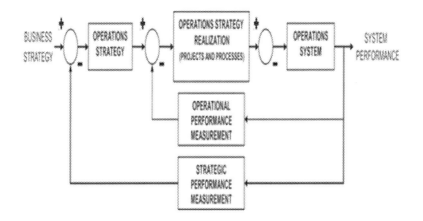

Integrated Domain Measurement Performance System (IDMPS)

This method takes into consideration three main domains of system measurement.

- **The Management Domain:** Measurement of the managerial functions of the organization such as managers and head of departments and functions.
- **Continuous Improvement Teams:** These are teams that manage the different entities of the ERP system. They can be designers, developers or systems reliability engineers.
- **Workshop Teams:** The measurements of performance of technical teams who roll their sleeves and get their hands dirty to do the actual work.

Interoperability Measurement

Since interoperability is scalable and can continuously be improved, there also exists methods of measurement that allow us to measure it in actuality. However, in order to measure it fully, three major types of measurement are highlighted in this chapter.

- Interoperability potential
- Interoperability compatibility
- Interoperability operational performance

Interoperability Potential

The IP focusses on a particular set of characteristics of the system that that reveals its ability to deliver the expected functions. During the process, potential barriers to system performance are also identified and worked on before the system is handed over to third parties. The main goal of measuring interoperability potential is to identify both internal and internal attributes of the system that makes it able to meet industry and general use requirements. In addition, IP capability has the ability to address obstacles likely to be faced by the end users of the ERP applications.

Interoperability Compatibility

According to Athena (2007), the compatibility aspect has to be performed during the systems engineering stage as discussed in the first topic of this chapter. This is equally possible when the different stakeholders of the cycle are totally included in the development process. This way, hardware, software, user and even network compatibility are very likely to be addressed. Duclin et al (2006), proposes three major questions that should be asked when analyzing the system interoperability compatibility. They include:

- Conceptual compatibility
- Can the information to be passed expressed in the same *syntax*? (Syntactic)
- Can the information to be exchanged have the same meaning? (Semantic)
- Organizational compatibility. Are the IT platforms compatible? (Platforms)

Interoperability Performance

Athena (2007) outlines that the performance should be measured during system run time. At this point, the system is able to clearly reveal to us strengths and weaknesses and performance factors such as cost, delay and quality are analyzed. A table with specific coefficient values can then be assigned to compare the performance of these aspects.

ERP INTEROPRABILITY METRICS

The Models

The need for quality software has been on the rise with more and more and more organizations streamlining their processes in order to conform to quality standards

Figure 11. The MC call model

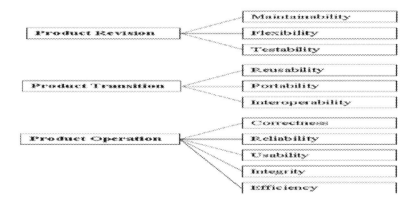

Figure 12. The Boehm model

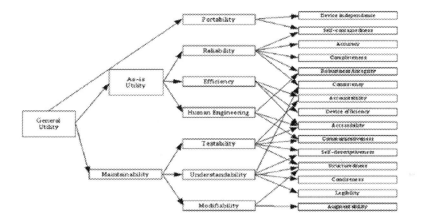

(Athena, 2007). The IEEE defines software quality as the degree to which the software application together with its components meets the required end user needs. Quality software means that organizations will spend less on bug fixes and manage programs effectively.

However, how do we determine the quality of a software program given the zillions of ERP programs out there? The metrics and models discussed below will help us to understand how we can measure the quality of ERP programs as much as interoperability is concerned. The models illustrated below look at the characteristics of the interoperability nature of ERPs and how this conforms to the ERP quality standards.

Figure 13. The Dromey model

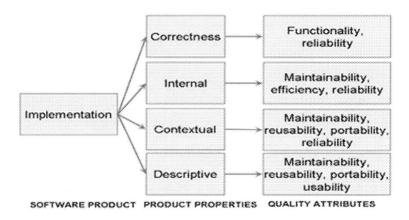

Figure 14. ISO 9126 model

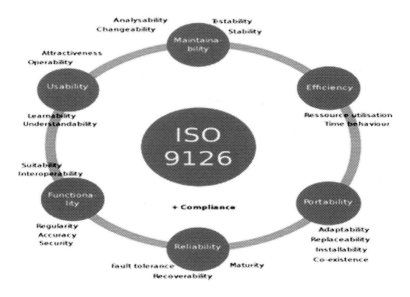

The Mc Call Model

This model identifies software quality through three main important features grouped as:

- Product review (maintenance, flexibility and testing)
- Product operation (correct, reliable, efficient, integrity and usability)
- Product transition (Portability and reusability)

The Major significance of this model is that it has been used to compare the ERP quality characteristics against the metrics provided. However, its limitations is in its inability to accurately measure software quality as most of its responses are based on mere YES or NO decisions.

Boehm Model

Is made of different characteristics that expand from the Mc Call's model adding various improvement to the software at the preceding levels. Major factors considered under this model include maintainability, testability and under stability of the ERP program.

The Dromey Model

The major focus under this model is the product quality. An emphasis is put on the detailed product elements and not just the program as a whole.

ISO 9126 Model

This model is based on the composition of the Boehm model and the Mc Call models. Under this model, software is evaluated based on its internal attributes together with its external attributes. The internal quality of the software is evaluated during program exception and run time, while its external features are evaluated when the final end users are using the program; some of the factors to look out here for include security and usability of the application.

CONCLUSION

What informs a good ERP software is its ability to offer multi-platform support. This should consider the organizational, functional and user abilities. On the other hand, quality of ERP systems cannot be overlooked and there are approved standard models that developers together with corporations can use to integrate quality programs into their business processes. When this is done, sales revenues will shoot high, proper and efficient business processes will flow and finally, the management task will become easier.

REFERENCES

ATHENA. (2007). *Guidelines and best practices for applying the ATHENA Interoperability Framework to support SME participation in Digital Ecosystems.* Deliverable DA8.2, ATHENA IP.

Australian Ministry of Finance and Deregulation. (2005). *Department of Finance (Finance) Governance Arrangements for Australian Government Bodies (Governance policy document).* Author.

Bititci, U. S., Carrie, A. S., & Mcdevitt, L. (1997). Integrated performance measurement system: A development guide –. *International Journal of Operations & Production Management, 17*(5-6), 522–534. doi:10.1108/01443579710167230

C4ISR. (1998). *Architecture working group (AWG), Levels of information systems interoperability (LISI).* C4ISR.

Chen, D., & Daclin, N. (2007), Barrier driven methodology for enterprise interoperability, PROVE2007. *Proc. Establishing The foundation of Collaborative Networks,* 453-460.

Clark, T., & Jones, R. (1999). Organisational Interoperability Maturity Model for C2. *Command and Control Research and Technology Symposium.* Retrieved March 7, 2011, from http://www.dodccrp.org/events/1999_CCRTS/pdf_files/track_5/049clark.pdf

Clark & Jones. (2011). *Organisational Interoperability Maturity Model for C2.* Academic Press.

Ducq, Y., & Vallespir, B. (2005). Definition and aggregation of a Performance Measurement System in three Aeronautical workshops using the ECOGRAI Method. *International Journal of Production Planning and Control, 16*(2), 163-177.

European Communities. (2004). European Interoperability Framework for Pan-European eGovernment Services. Luxembourg: Office for Official Publications of the European Communities.

Ghalayini, A. M., Noble, J. S., & Crowe, T. J. (1997). An integrated dynamic performance measurement system for improving manufacturing competitiveness –. *International Journal of Production Economics, 48*(3), 1997. doi:10.1016/S0925-5273(96)00093-X

Gradmann, S. (2008). *Interoperability: A key concept for large scale, persistent digital libraries.* Available: http://www.digitalpreservationeurope.eu/publications

Hamilton & Murtagh. (2000). *Enabling Interoperability Via Software Architecture.* Technical Reports, AD Number: ADA458021. Retrieved from http://www.dtic.mil/dtic

Heubusch, K. (2006, January). Interoperability: What it Means, Why it Matters. *Journal of American Health Information Management Association, 77*(1), 26–30. PMID:16475733

IEEE. (1990). *IEEE Standard Computer Dictionary: A Compilation of IEEE Standard Computer Glossaries.* New York, NY: Institute of Electrical and Electronics Engineers.

ISO/IEC 21000-6 RDD Registration Authority. (n.d.). Retrieved from http://www.iso21000-6.net

Jack, W., & Suri, T. (2010). *Monetary Theory and Electronic Money: Reflections on the Kenyan Experience.* Retrieved from http://www.mobilemoneyexchange.org/Files/8e31752b

Jenkins, B. (2008). *Developing Mobile Money Ecosystems.* Washington, DC: IFC and the Harvard Kennedy School. Retrieved from http://www.hks.harvard.edu/m-rcbg/CSRI/publications/report_30_MOBILEMONEY.pdf

Kaplan, R.S., & Norton, D.P. (1996). *The Balanced Scorecard.* Harvard Business School Press.

Kasunic, M., & Anderson, W. (2004). *Measuring Systems Interoperability: Challenges and Opportunities, Software Engineering Measurement and Analysis Initiative.* Technical Note CMU/SEI-2004-TN-003. Retrieved from http://www.sei.cmu.edu/library

Kilic, H. S., Zaim, S., & Delen, D. (2014). Development of a hybrid methodology for ERP system selection: The case of Turkish Airlines. *Decision Support Systems, 66*, 82–92. doi:10.1016/j.dss.2014.06.011

Lallana Emmanuel, C. (2008). *eGovernment Interoperability.* UNDP. Retrieved from http://www.apdip.net/projects/gif/gifeprimer

Lebreton, B., & Legner, C. (2007). Interoperability Impact Assessment Model: An Overview. In R. J. Gonçalves, J. P. Müller, K. Mertins & M. Zelm (Eds.), *Enterprise Interoperability II - New Challenges and Approaches* (pp. 725-728). Springer London. Retrieved from http://www.xml.coverpages.org/Comptia-ISC-OpenStandards.pdf

Matsuda, M., & Wang, Q. (2010). Software Interoperability Tools. *Standardized Capability-Profiling Methodology, ISO16100.* doi:10.1007/978-3-642-15509-3_13

Miller, P. (2000). Interoperability: what is it and why should I want it. *Ariadne, 23*.

Moon, Y. B. (2007). *Enterprise Resource Planning (ERP): a review of the literature*. Intern.

Neely, A., Adams, C., & Kennerley, M. (2002). The performance Prism – The scorecard for measuring and managing Business Success. Prentice Hall.

O'Brien & Marakas. (2010). *Management Information Systems* (10th ed.). McGraw-Hill. Retrieved from http://getcollegecredit.com/assets/pdf/dsst_fact_sheets/DSST_ManagementInformationSystems.pdf

Papazoglou & Ribbers. (2009). e-Business: Organisation and Technical Foundation. Wiley India Pvt, Ltd.

Peng, G. C., & Nunes, M. B. (2009). Surfacing ERP exploitation risks through a risk ontology. *Industrial Management & Data Systems*, *109*(7), 926–942. doi:10.1108/02635570910982283

Pollock, J. (2004). Adaptive Information: Improving Business through Semantic Interoperability, Grid Computing, and Enterprise Integration. John Wiley & Sons.

Rowlands. (2009). *Beyond Interoperability: A new policy framework for e-Government*. Available: http://www.cstransform.com/white_papers/BeyondInteropV1.0.pdf

Rukanova, B. D., Van Slooten, K., & Stegwee, R. A. (2006). Business Process Requirements, Modeling Technique and Standard: how to Identify Interoperability Gaps on a Process Level. In D. Konstantas, J.-P. Bourrières, M. Léonard, & N. Boudjlida (Eds.), *Interoperability of Enterprise Software and Applications* (pp. 13–23). London: Springer-Verlag. doi:10.1007/1-84628-152-0_2

Sanchez. (2008). *Enterprise Architectures - Enabling Interoperability Between Organizations*. Academic Press.

Sheth, P. A. (1998). *Changing Focus on Interoperability in Information Systems from system, syntax, structure to semantics*. Interoperability Geographic Information System. Retrieved from http://lsdis.cs.uga.edu/library/download/S98-changing.pdf

Tolk, A., & Muguira, J. A. (2003). *The Levels of Conceptual Interoperability Model*. Virginia Modeling Analysis & Simulation Centre (VMASC), College of Engineering and Technology. Retrieved from http://www.Psu.edu

Veer, H., & Wiles, A. (2008). *Achieving Technical Interoperabilty – the ETSI approach*. European Telecommunications Standards Institute. Retrieved from http://www.etsi.org

Veltman, K. H. (2001). Syntatic and semantic interoperability: New approaches to knowledge and the semantic web. *New Reviews of Information Networking*, *7*(1), 159–183. doi:10.1080/13614570109516975

Verville, J., Palanisamy, R., Bernadas, C., & Halingten, A. (2007). ERP acquisition planning: A critical dimension for making the right choice. *Long Range Planning*, *40*(1), 45–63. doi:10.1016/j.lrp.2007.02.002

Winter. (2002). *Chapter on Interoperability*. European Territorial Management Information Infrastructure (ETeMII). Retrieved from http://www.ec-gis.org/etemii/reports/chapter3.pdf

Woodley. (2001). *Dublin Core Metadata Initiative, Glossary*. Retrieved from http://dublincore.org/documents/2001/04/12/usageguide/glossary.shtml#S

KEY TERMS AND DEFINITIONS

Enterprise: A business unit running the ERP software.

ERP: Enterprise resource planning software that runs organizational activities.

Interoperability: The ability of an ERP to serve more than one function.

Interoperability of Business: When all business processes are streamlined to work in achieving a common objective. This includes all the departments such as finance, accounting, or human resources and the overall management process.

Interoperability of Data: The ability of different data models to coordinate to achieve a particular task. These models include hierarchical and relational. Data from different databases can equally respond to queries conducted across the databases management systems.

Interoperability of Processes: The main objective is to make the different process work together. A single CPU can assign an algorithm to certain tasks that end up becoming processes that can only be shared within the ERP applications.

Interoperability of Services: Identification of the various functions that applications render; these services are designed and implemented by the systems independently.

Model: A means of measuring ERP software quality.

Chapter 4
Security Framework for Enterprise Resource Planning

Ramgopal Kashyap

(iD) https://orcid.org/0000-0002-5352-1286
Amity University Chhattisgarh, India

ABSTRACT

This chapter deals with the security and its structure for the ERP that can be utilized to address all applicable security perspectives inside an association and to guarantee that it shapes a fundamental piece of an ERP framework. The security system is mapped onto the ERP model to give the association an unmistakable comprehension of which security issues must be tended to inside which ERP part. It is clear given the over that security must frame a necessary piece of an ERP framework and that it will be hard to include it once the ERP framework is as of now actualized. In the event that security is included after usage, the ERP framework will experience issues clinging to IT and corporate administration necessities. An ERP framework is additionally an essential piece of the association and can't be dealt with as an autonomous framework without taking the association's approaches and techniques into thought. This chapter furnishes an association with a structure to guarantee that all angles encompassing IT and corporate security are incorporated with an ERP framework.

INTRODUCTION

Enterprise Resource Planning (ERP) is data framework programming that incorporates divisions and capacities over an association into one PC framework. It keeps running off a single database, empowering different divisions to share data, what's more,

DOI: 10.4018/978-1-5225-7678-5.ch004

speak with each other. Incorporation is a critical part of ERP. Davenport asserts that "ERP is an undertaking wide data framework, which encourages the stream of data and organizes all assets and exercises inside the association." An ERP framework is a bundled business programming framework that enables an organization to A.) Automate and coordinate the more significant part of its business forms; B.) Share regular information and practices over the whole venture; C.) (Hoch & Dulebohn, 2013). ERP's principle objective is to incorporate information and procedures from all zones of an association and bring together it for simple access and the stream of work. It expects to enhance and streamline personal business forms, which regularly requires reengineering of current business forms. As indicated the characterized ERP from four viewpoints:

1) Business Process Perspective: ERP framework as instruments for empowering endeavors to oversee and streamline business forms, through crosses practical or a cross-authoritative combination. 2) Technological/Technical Perspective: ERP framework as configurable, online ongoing intelligent programming bundle, which contains various modules or applications to help data handling capacity over the entire undertakings, through single database also, uniform working stage (Zare & Ravasan, 2014). 3) Communication Perspective: an ERP framework as undertaking broad data framework that incorporates all data streams and gives access to consistent data. 4) Functionality Perspective: ERP frameworks as a coordinated set of projects that provide robotizations of different business methodology

ERP SYSTEMS IN EDUCATION

ERP is a business administration framework that incorporates all part of the business the stream of data among all business capacities. An expansive number of business associations and advanced education organizations abroad have embraced ERP. Numerous best western Universities are running their grounds organization through ERP frameworks. Colleges are generally unique about business associations in their choice making forms. With regards to choosing and embracing an ERP framework for colleges, we have to guarantee that it deals with various points of view relating to understudies, instructors, staff, organization, guardians and graduated class. All the information is overseen in a period touchy way alongside the principles and approaches relevant around then, so at whatever point required, the correct data can be re-delivered (Badewi, Shehab, Zeng & Mohamad, 2018). Various capacities including various grounds prerequisites, Human Resources and Financials ought to be coordinated.

As of late, numerous advanced education organizations need to take focal points of ERP frameworks. They contribute a large number of dollars in ERP ventures.

Figure 1. Components of an ERP system

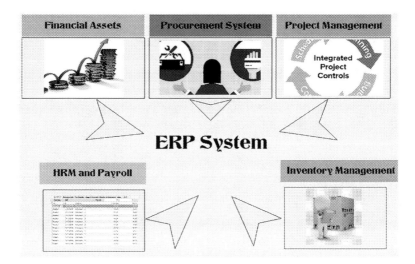

For instance, the investigation directed previously six years disclose to us George town University in U.S.A spent about $60 million on a grounds extensive ERP. The College of Minnesota had a comparative affair when anticipated expenses of $38 million, at last, came to $60 million. The interest in ERP frameworks speaks to the most significant investment in ICT (Information Communication Technology) for advanced education foundations. The best reasons organizations are embracing ERP arrangements to supplant heritage frameworks, enhance client benefit, change undertaking forms, enhance organization, and look after aggressiveness, increment working effectiveness (Ouyang, Herzmann, Zhou & Sommer, 2011). The fundamental points of interest of ERP for advanced education foundations are, as indicated by ECAR association (EDUCAUSE Center for Applied Research) is the accompanying: a) improved data access for arranging and dealing with the foundation. b) Improved administrations for the staff, understudies, and representatives. c) Lower business dangers. d) Increased pay and diminished costs due to enhanced proficiency. Key information segments of an ERP framework are exhibited in Figure 1 underneath.

Reasons for the necessary disappointments of ERP framework viability lies in various reasons including inadequate change administration systems. Different causes incorporate non-accessibility of a structure for ERP usage, so the venture supervisors will do what they believe is the best along these lines neglect to execute the ERP frameworks appropriately. All the more scientifically, the "ERP execution Framework" feature the means that must take after when the vehicle organization needs to actualize its cloud-based ERP effectively.

Figure 2. Cloud mobile ERP system components

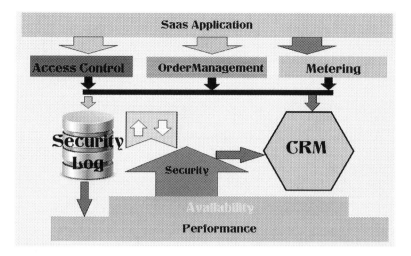

It is whereby a free merchant on the cloud facilitates the information and programming given in Figure 2. The above structure is a general system and is more reasonable to assembling industry and not appropriate for the transport area. Diverse ERP sellers give ERP frameworks some level of claim to fame; however, the center modules are nearly the same for every one of them. A portion of the center ERP modules found in the fruitful ERP frameworks are the accompanying (Bjelland & Haddara, 2018):

- Accounting administration
- Sales and conveyance administration
- Financial administration
- Human assets administration
- Manufacturing administration
- Supply chain administration
- Production administration
- Customer relationship administration
- Transportation administration
- E-Business using some of the previously mentioned modules, Figure 3 outlines how these modules interconnected through an ERP framework.

Figure 3. ERP systems concept

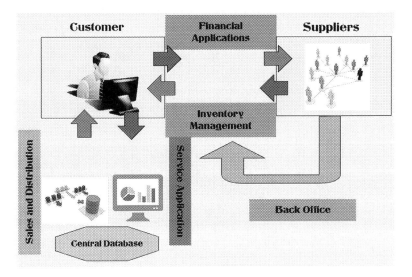

FAILURES OF ENTERPRISE RESOURCE PLANNING

ERP framework is a coordinated programming arrangement, which is regularly offered by a seller as a bundle. The bundle provides consistent reconciliation of all the data that moves through the venture. The data likewise reflect the business procedure in the experiment, for example, money related, bookkeeping, HR, production network, and client. As depicted ERP framework as an venture comprehensive arrangement of administration headings that balances request and supply, coordinates the clients and providers into a total inventory network, utilizes demonstrated business forms for essential leadership, and gives high degrees of cross-practical combination among business forms, i.e. stock/coordination's, fabricating, deals, fund, building, promoting, client bolster, and HR. In this manner, an ERP framework empowers an undertaking to maintain its business with an abnormal state of profitability and client benefit, and all the while bring down expenses and inventories (Pavel & Evelyn, 2017). As ERP framework plays an essential part in business, the related issues and significant variables of the users have examined in the past examinations.

There have been numerous reports of unsuccessful ERP usage inside the business, counting the powerlessness of Hershey to deliver treat at Halloween, Nike losing shoe requests, and FoxMeyer's inability to process orders. It revealed that 70% of ERP executions did not accomplish the assessed benefits. In different examinations, the disappointments of ERP usage run from 40% to 60% or higher. Further, the frustrations of ERP framework usage ventures have referred to prompt issues as genuine as authoritative liquidation. Consequently, various examinations have been

Figure 4. ERP success frameworks

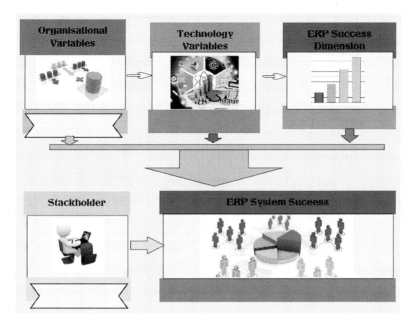

explored to decide the essential disappointments factor for actualizing ERP (Zare & Ravasan, 2014).

The structure (Figure 4) features the effect of the possible factors on the reliant variable that is the ERP frameworks achievement. The spotted lines are utilized to isolate the natural settings, i.e., outside and inside. The broken line bolt demonstrates the effect of possibilities in the extreme condition on ERP achievement. The measurements of ERP achievement and viewpoint of the evaluator appear in Figure 4. Imperatively, we separated hierarchical factors in two sections: authoritative and innovation (IT issues), since it is likely that more bits of knowledge will rise out of such an approach. Scientists, including push that ERP activities have both innovative and business suggestions and would illuminate if saw in that light (Nordin & Adegoke, 2015). So also, contend that reviews utilizing the possibility hypothesis or approach ought to not just consider the business-related possibilities, for example, size, culture, et cetera: a more profound comprehension of the effect of options on authoritative execution for our situation ERP achievement may arise when scientists "value the communications of the different parts of MIS". Next, we talk about every part of the examination structure and the related earlier hypothetical base and systems that educated its improvement.

Figure 5. Key contrasts amongst WFMS and ERP frameworks

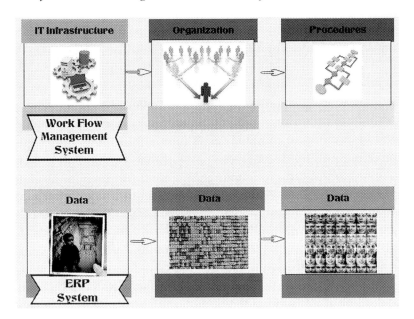

WORKFLOW MANAGEMENT SYSTEM AND ERP

When we contrast the workflow management system (WFM) frameworks with ERP frameworks all the more nearly, we see that while the two frameworks center on business forms, the approach taken by every framework in particular. A WFMS, as, utilizes a work process demonstrate, which is at that point altered to suit particular business process structures. ERP frameworks actualized around pre-assembled applications (Tong, Zhang, Xu & Qi, 2014). ERP makers create applications for specific parts of the business. Associations obtain the applications as per their necessities. The work process demonstrates she installed in these applications. It implies numerous applications have bits of the procedure display "hard-coded" in the product. The ERP programming applications are worked with parameters to permit some adaptability in designing business forms. Every application incorporates the rationale important to control hierarchical procedures from an information and data perspective. Applications regularly should be custom fitted by setting a considerable number of parameters.

Utilizing a work process definition and model, the framework implementers can create applications to help the stream of work depicted in the work process show (see Figure 5). These applications cooperate to shape a WFMS. Work process framework is process-driven, concentrating on the administration of stream rationale. For ERP frameworks, the work process demonstrate is usually implanted in application

Figure 6. ERP qualities regrouped under three measurements

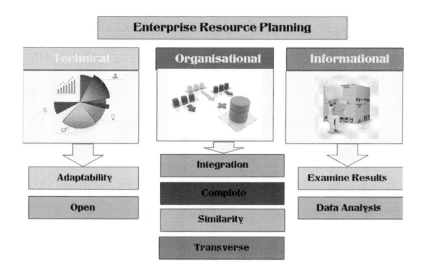

programming (see Figure 5). Framework implementers work at designing the structure by setting parameters that are gotten to by the applications. Following qualities (see Figure 6) ERP frameworks are broadly acknowledged under three measurements. The first measurement is specialized which alludes to abilities and offices of ERP framework contrasted with common frameworks (Pavel & Evelyn, 2017). Authoritative viewpoint identified with the arrangement of the structure in the association. The third measurement is enlightening which alludes to quality and value of data which the ERP framework gives to the association.

THE ERP FRAMEWORK

The ERP structure plan for poly system universities and the essential parts of the system are portrayed in Figure 6 as demonstrated as follows. Customer The customer quality incorporates distinctive hubs, for example, working framework, network imperative, GUI (Graphical UI) and division of duty. The working framework incorporates the sort of working framework bolstered by customer programming. The network imperatives check the sorts of systems that can associate customers to application servers. A Web Service is a product framework intended to help interoperable machine-to-machine interaction over a system, what's more; those administrations are self-ruling parts that procedure all around characterized XML messages. It adjusts the accompanying standard. Extensible Markup Language (XML): is the essential building square of web administrations (Bukhari & Liu, 2018).

ERP MODULE INTEGRATION TECHNIQUES

The structure contains an essential module, for example, Fund, Department, Registrar, Human Resource and Store. There are two sorts of module incorporation method utilizing web benefit remote façade and massage specialist.

Message Broker

Message agent is a segment that goes about as a delegate between the coordinating modules. Every module does not straightforwardly conjure each other but rather discuss just with the message merchant. With each correspondence, message merchant furnished with the coherent recognizable proof of the goal module where the message merchant conveys the message to that assigned recipient. In a commonplace execution, all modules need to get enlisted with the message merchant before activity (Karpiuk, 2016). The disadvantage of message agent module incorporation is the presentation of a single purpose of disappointment the framework will stop working the whole module around the message representative will stop correspondence.

Interface

The interface comprises of three parts, for example, Reconciliation standard, part interface convention and reconciliation strategy that permits coordinating the ERP framework with the outer condition. This recorded interface write comprises sub-part, for example, the combination standard contains XML, part interface convention as per this structure it utilizes web administration and combination strategy included either utilizing message dealer or web benefit remote veneer (Wang & Tsai, 2014).

Database Availability

The Database availability contains distinctive segments, for example, JDBC, OLBE and ADO.NET. Every one of availability varies from each other relying upon the Database Administration System (DBMS) utilized. For example, the ERP structure will utilize ADO.NET information base availability to get to the SQL server.

Security

It comprises of the accompanying segments: - 1) Identification and confirmation – The first duty of data security inside an ERP framework is to guarantee that real and approved client access the ERP framework. 2) Authorization – One of the most basic viewpoints to consider inside ERP security is to confine the entrance rights and activities of the clients inside the ERP framework. The entrance privileges of a client controlled by the expert appointed to the client ID 3) Confidentiality – Protecting the privacy of information suggests the confirmation that exclusive approved individuals are ready to see particular informational collections. 4) Integrity – Integrity implies that lone approved clients can adjust the information of the ERP framework. Adjustment alludes to the refresh, cancellation, and formation of information inside the ERP framework (Hustad, Haddara & Kalvenes, 2016).

THE CLOUD BASED ERP FRAMEWORK

The structure has got principle parts which incorporate present situation analysis, problem and business process detection, developing a new process, information system incorporation, organizing system training, application, process improvement and ERP system delivery. Each stage comprises of individual, corporate and Strategic issues which ought to be set up keeping in mind the end goal to fruitful execute cloud-based ERP framework (A. Al-Johani & E. Youssef, 2013).

Security Issues

A compelling cloud-based Enterprise Resource Planning framework reception needs fitting official inclusions. The cloud-based ERP framework usage system will address various zones which add to impacting transport business segment to accomplish elite. The transport industry is the center of all business exercises so if the vehicle framework is great all different business capacities will perform well in this way accomplishes elite. The cloud-based ERP framework usage system should enable the administration to comprehend the necessities and help the venture group to get administration trust, duty, and support. Duty and support three issues should tend to individual, corporate and procedure issues (Michelberger & Horváth, 2017). These issues will be clarified in detail as takes after Technique Issues Executive and also Non-Executive administration ought to give assets to the fruitful usage of the cloud-based Enterprise Resource Planning framework, inability to get their trust, responsibility and subsidizing, the association will neglect to effective receive new framework. All the required assets gave by the best administration and additionally the authority for the cloud-based ERP usage. Top administration is there to give clear heading on ERP execution, staff advancement, and their part conceal to the post-reception period of the structure. A clear procedure for cloud-based Enterprise Resource Planning framework reception and solid goals ought to be set up. Techniques ought to be noticeably upgraded ahead of time, and the execution approach must be in arrangement, majority of the work compel produced, and the changeover methodology ought to be in the way that enables the organization to spare time and cash. When putting your information on the cloud, there is need clear techniques and set up fitting security systems to ensure the information (Webb, Richter & Bonsper, 2010). Training and staff improvement concerning the cloud-based ERP framework should begin toward the beginning of the appropriation to the lion's share of the workforce and staff advancement ought to incorporate into what way the ERP will utilize and how the business procedure will change because of the execution of cloud-based ERP framework. Framework manuals must be accessible for clients to have perspective when looked with challenges (Zafar, 2013). Worker and additionally clients and providers individual data must ensure. As the information relocated to the cloud, there is have to legitimately to level with the goal that every client will approach data applicable to his or her line of obligations to keep away from irreconcilable situation and licking of delicate data. Proper review trails ought to be set up keeping in mind the end goal to have the capacity to follow who gotten to what, when, how and for what reason?

Corporate Issues

Project group ought to be set up toward the start of the undertaking and the venture director ought to be the best worker, with a superior comprehension of what should accomplish and a reputation experience and information of good accomplishments. The venture group must be given duty and have a characterized venture design. It is noted that cloud-based ERP framework will bring about the reengineering of corporate methodology, so the corporate strategies ought to be investigated to distinguish the likely changes required for reengineering. The worker ought to be enabled, get representative contribution in preparing and training that will help in changing the culture of the association. The levels of leadership and correspondence ought to be taken after all through the phases of the structure. To fruitful usage of the cloud-based ERP framework there is need important qualified and experienced representatives because both the Information Technology and PC abilities are useful for cloud-based ERP framework execution (Zeng & Skibniewski, 2013).

Recommendations

The accompanying distinguished as the proposals for tending to difficulties and issues in the execution of ERP:

- Adequate time ought to distributed to the task administration group for ERP framework usage.

- Enough assets ought to be given to permit great execution of the ERP framework.
- Management of progress ought to be going by the undertaking administration group.

Discovering Recommendation Time Constraints

There is have to distribute enough time for the ERP framework usage there is have to draw in individuals with proper capabilities to assume responsibility of the cloud-based ERP framework venture. Absence of best administration bolsters top administration must be locked in at the beginning periods and should frame some portion of the resolve to lead the undertaking. Include top administration from the earliest starting point. Give them a chance to give their sources of info with the goal that they will trust and bolster the undertaking. Resource allotment issues the issue of asset portion is dependably an issue if the best administration isn't supporting the venture, for the most part, they will attempt to constrain the assets since they won't confide in the vision (Saunders, 2014).

BENEFITS OF ERP EXECUTION

"What are the advantages of ERP frameworks?" is the issue that shows up in any talk on the usage of ERP framework. The utilization of ERP framework can be as per the following:

LIMITATIONS OF ERP FRAMEWORK

Lack of limits made by ERP framework in a vehicle association can cause issues of who assumes the fault, lines of obligation and worker inspiration. A few people may have the data on the off chance that they get data that not expected for them. The establishment of the ERP framework is expensive. ERP advisors are exceptionally costly to take roughly 60% of the financial plan.

- The achievement relies upon the abilities and experience of the workforce, including instruction and how to influence the framework to function appropriately.
- Resistance in sharing personal data between divisions can lessen the productivity of the product. • The frames can be hard to utilize (Zare & Ravasan, 2014)

Table 1. The utilization of ERP framework

Task Preparation	Prerequisites of the organization	Higher capacity to send new data frameworks usefulness	Improve client adaptability
Business Outline	Execute business	Improved the execution of the vehicle business	Talent administration examination
Acknowledgment Final	Prerequisites based on the Business Plan	Improve the data precision/speed/quality/ and accessibility	Real-time information access over various locales
Readiness	Finish the planning for go Live	General data combination	Generate item separation
Go Live and Support	Slice over to live creation	Improve the collaboration between specialty units	Increase the mix between association with clients
Give beginning	Activity and constant bolster	Improve basic leadership capacity	Reduce process duration of creation
Arranging and readiness for your ERP venture	Improve worker execution administration	Better asset administration	Financial data precision and speedier essential leadership capacity
Reports the business process Better creation arranging planning	Improve getting the hang of, preparing and advancement	Facilitate business learning	Centralize the managerial exercises

- Change of staff; organizations can use heads that are not prepared to deal with the ERP arrangement of the utilizing organization, proposing changes in business hones that not synchronized with the framework.

- Having an ERP framework has numerous points of interest, yet does not ensure the aggregate achievement of the organization. Authoritative culture, know how to include staff and foresee changes that will endure the association utilizing this arrangement of organization, are critical components for the finishing of the usage.

- The adequacy of the ERP framework may diminish if there is protection from share data between specialty units or divisions. Because of substantial changes that execution of the ERP framework gets the way of life of work, there might be ineffectively prepared or impartial in making utilization of similar staff.

- The advantages of having an ERP framework are not given the execution of the product quickly; they will be apparent long after the structure is running (Oh, Han, Shin, Kim & Kim, 2015)

- The zenith of the execution relies upon the capacity and ability of the workforce, additionally includes instruction and preparing, to make the framework is effectively connected.

Principle capacities and qualities of ERP Systems ERP frameworks cover a large portion of present-day organizations' useful territories, including monetary bookkeeping, HR, fabricating, arrange handling, inventory network administration, venture administration, and client relationship administration. For most market-driving ERP frameworks, a separation in business modules had built up — the distinctive modules, which frequently show the bureaus of a business association. As of late, the fringes between these modules are getting to be obscured, as ERP venture approaches tend to be more process situated. In any case, by the by, ERP venture groups are as yet set up and composed because of this characterization. This arrangement likewise has significance for the definition which ERP ventures have fit the bill for the observational study on the achievement of ERP usage. To be affirmed for the example, the ERP venture at any rate needed to incorporate the center modules Finance, Materials Management (MM) and Sales and Distribution (SD).

ERP programming institutionalizes data inside the association and furthermore streamlines the information stream between various divisions of the organization. The ERP frameworks as 'programming bundles made out of a few modules, for example, HR, deals, back, and generation, giving cross-association coordination of information through inserted business processes.' Four key qualities of ERP frameworks can depict with terms multinational, reference models, incorporated data and flexibility. ERP frameworks can be considered as multinational frameworks since they reflect national laws and controls from particular nation situations. Furthermore, ERP frameworks involve reference models that reflect favored plans of action as far as best practices, information utilized and authoritative structure. Besides, ERP frameworks' coordinate all business forms inside an association, empowering ongoing access to similar data. Lastly, ERP frameworks give adaptability, enabling associations to tweak the framework to satisfy particular situations and conditions (Orougi, 2015). The ERP showcase is as yet developing an extremely productive, so there are great reasons why endeavors choose for ERP systems. The main advantages and explanations behind organizations which receive ERP:

- Integrating money related data
- Integrating client arrange data
- Standardizing and accelerate fabricating forms
- Reducing stock
- Standardizing HR data

During the most recent decade, ERP gives product engineering, as well as offers process formats that incorporate enterprises 'best practices', which are sets of reference forms for each branch. This approach, for the most part, makes ERP usage less demanding and empowers organizations to take an interest from demonstrated procedures and arrangements. As said previously, a productive and successful data stream all through the entire undertaking suggests huge focal points. A division of viable advantages into five viewpoints. It audits ERP advantage from other points of view, and endeavors to clarify why ERP frameworks are exceptionally engaging for ventures of each size.

ADVANTAGES OF ERP

1. Operational benefits by robotizing business forms and empowering process transform, they can offer advantages as far as cost diminishment, cycle term decrease, efficiency change, quality change, and enhanced client benefit (Gassel, 2010).
2. Administrative benefits with brought together a database and implicit information examination abilities, they can enable an association to accomplish better asset administration, enhanced basic leadership and arranging, and execution change.
3. Key benefits with vast scale business inclusion and inward/outer coordination abilities, they can aid business development, the organization together, advancement, cost, separation, and outside linkages.
4. IT foundation benefits with coordinated and standard application design, they bolster business adaptability, lessened IT cost and minor cost of specialty units' IT, and expanded capacity for rapid execution of new applications.
5. Hierarchical benefits they influence the development of hierarchical abilities by supporting association structure change, encouraging representative picking up, engaging laborers, and building essential dreams (Azevedo, Romão & Rebelo, 2012). Various ERP venture examples of overcoming adversity recorded in broadened contemplate around the world, depicting benefits incorporate cost diminishments, better cost administration and product conveying.

PROGRAMMING AS-A-SERVICE QUALITY ASSESSMENT

The nature of a Software-as-a-Service (SaaS) application identified with its item quality and administration quality. Item quality defined with the functionalities of the app itself. Then again, benefit quality set with the rate of consistency and administrations gave by the distributed computing suppliers (Peng, 2012). These two

Figure 7. Programming quality evaluations and measurement

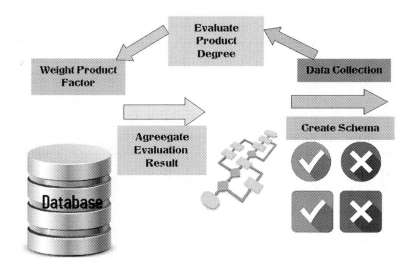

kinds of value should be met by scholarly cloud ERP framework, as this framework requires not just academic ERP utilitarian abilities, yet also advantages of distributed computing administrations.

The goals described refined by breaking down relevant reports to get more data. From that point forward, list exercises amongst partner and the framework that is expected to come to the objectives (Venkadasalam, 2015). Quality objectives characterized by investigating practices, organizing, and settling on how profound is each movement going to be bolstered by the framework. The following stage is to distinguish curios identified with every quality objectives, the effect from the frame, and pick the substances to assessed from every ancient rarity. Material investigation can be utilized to get item factor from every element. Characterized item factors are rechecked and included or deducted if necessary. At long last, quality prerequisites can determine.

Programming Quality Evaluation and Measurement

After the quality necessities characterized, the subsequent stage to do is to assess and measure the framework's satisfaction of every product quality necessity. The required advances appear in Figure 7.

Information gathered for every item factor from quality arranging. At that point, the level of presence for every item factor assessed from the information gathered. Every item factor given a weight number, based on its effect on the item quality. At that point, the assessment result is collected with the weight so that we can get the quality estimation. From that point forward, we have to build up an understanding outline, keeping in mind the end goal to have the capacity to translate the estimation result, is it a decent or awful number (GAO, 2009). Information gathered for every item factor from quality arranging. At that point, the level of presence for every item factor assessed from the information gathered. Every item factor given a weight number, based on its effect on the item quality.

DIFFICULTIES IN ERP SYSTEM

ERP frameworks center on the coordination of the hidden sub-frameworks using a focal information vault an RDBMS regularly. ERP frameworks enable its clients to take a shot at a LAN or then again electronic situations. Besides, the client gets to benefits are not constrained to any sub-framework rather get to benefits are characterized according to the obligations allotted to representatives; hence the ERP frameworks are presented to a number of security and different difficulties, for example, 'absence of progress administration', 'information possession', 'anchoring custom assembled modules', 'complexities in overseeing parts', 'unapproved data access' and 'hacking' (Horowitz-Kraus, 2015). The difficulties in ERP frameworks ordered into two gatherings, in particular, the 'nonspecific difficulties' and 'particular item difficulties.' Item particular difficulties/issues are talked about in detail by concentrating on two driving industry items: SAP R/3 and Oracle E-Business Suite. The bland difficulties found in all ERP items.

Internal Threats vs. Outside Threats

The security dangers from inside the undertaking are possibly, and they have a higher likelihood of an event. There is a need for appropriate controls executed inside the association. We firmly prescribe the view that associations must take after the security structures inside the association.

Application Development Architectures

Stages give us various approaches to create and send endeavor applications; new administration situated structures utilize web administrations to create independent, measured applications that can be interfaced effectively to make dynamic, once in a while transitory, applications. These composite applications are stage and dialect autonomous. However, they open associations to security dangers and all the more critically they may not be good with security designs.

Problems Because of Third Party Tools

ERP sellers frequently offer a 'coordinated arrangement' that made out of the seller's ERP modules and an arrangement of third-party items that inside and out make a total coherent framework; sadly, in some cases the resultant 'mix' does not function admirably, especially when it comes to keeping up security (Ching, 2010).

Lack of Change Management

Absence of progress administration is a noteworthy issue found in ERP items, which conceivably impacts security. The way changes done to the projects, and the designs should be legitimately signed all together empowers heads to determine security-related issues. Successful isolation amongst improvement and generation conditions, the procedures of testing, quality affirmation furthermore, movement ought to be evaluated by the reviewer.

Challenges Due to Extensive Interfacing

ERP frameworks need to send/get information from different frameworks through a coordination middleware; an interface has the potential to wind up a weak point that can trade off security. Review investigation of interfaces is one of the vital parts of ERP security audits.

Challenges to the Privacy

ERP frameworks are such an extensive archive of various types of information that they can hugely affect security issues. Most ERP frameworks have an HR and faculty module, and such modules handle a ton of information about the representatives of the organization. The ERP can likewise hold data about clients, providers, and accomplices (Mazurczyk & Caviglione, 2015).

Problems Out of Hand of ERP Software

If an ERP is utilizing the incorporated validation conspire, the security of clients' passwords and different certifications is the obligation of the OS or the index administrations running. Dangers caused by the poor system foundation, exchanging and steering plans, ill-advised setup of the firewalls or other security gadgets/programming; infections, spyware or different projects with related diseases may likewise make substantial harms the ERP frameworks.

Figure 8. Standard model front end and OS security layer

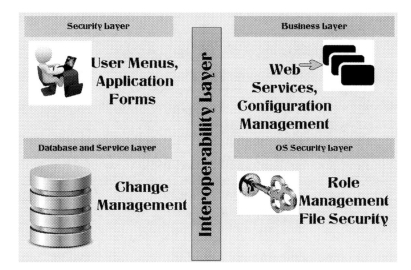

STANDARD FRAMEWORK

This area displays the system that evacuates peculiarities found in the at presently accessible ERP frameworks.

Frontend/Application Layer

This layer particularly handles the undertakings like: I. Arrangement of the frontend for broadened customers, e.g., web, versatile or work area customers. ii. Arrangement of menus to clients given their benefits. iii. Menu avoidance records.

This chart gives the structure of the Frontend/Application Layer; there exists a 'Frontend/Application Level Security Layer' as shown in Figure 8, which stores the whole security settings particular to the frontend and application, for instance:

Menu Generation According to Privileges

The frontend exhibited to the client must create the menu as characterized in the client's lord record. Suggestions: All ERP frameworks ought to have simple to configure office to characterize menus for ERP clients. More critically, such rundown ought to anchor from unapproved changes, and any progressions must be traceable. Presently the ERP frameworks don't bolster following changes in such objects.

Menu Exclusion List

This rundown contains the rundown of choices to be prohibited from a specific client menu. Proposals: All ERP frameworks should bolster menu prohibition records, and these rundowns ought to anchor from unapproved changes, and any progressions must be traceable (Jain, 2011). Presently the ERP frameworks don't bolster following changes in such protests.

Digital Signature Usage

Advanced marks are utilized to demonstrate personality while transmitting touchy data inside ERP framework. Suggestions: Users must give the arrangement to utilize advanced mark at whatever point exchanging basic data (Caprioli, 2014).

Failure Status

A portion of the terrible programming procedures uncovers source code to the end clients when some blunder happens. Suggestions: This is regularly done deliberately in the advancement conditions yet when the item prepared for the organization it ought to altogether assess for such defects.

Ensuring Continuous Improvement of the Security

Security typically viewed as a one-time venture, and associations don't allow spending plan for security constantly. Suggestions: Top level administration ought to be resolved to make persistent enhancements to the security of ERP framework.

BUSINESS LOGIC COMPONENTS LAYER

The mind-boggling applications running in ERP include three-layer engineering, in particular, the frontend, business rationale, and the backend layer; the 'Business Logic Layer' particularly handles the errands like I. Enrolling the parts for ERP framework II. Dealing with the execution benefits III. Coordination administrations, e.g., web administrations. There is a 'business rationale level security layer' that contains whole security settings particular to the business rationale segments, e.g., execution benefits. The substance of this layer regularly incorporates the accompanying.

Execution Security of Built-In and Custom Parts

As of now, accessible ERP frameworks don't give a simple approach to anchor the execution of custom form objects. Suggestions: Recommend the utilization of profiles to be related with each protest that characterizes its get to restrictions to the database and different administrations (Morgan, 2004).

Security-Aware Development

Generally, the product designers are not the security specialists; subsequently one can't expect security mindful programming improvement practices to be effortlessly received. Proposals: The security mindfulness ought to be compulsory at all levels of an ERP framework.

Code Security of Built-In and Custom Components

There are potential outcomes of code infusions or other comparable dangers in the ERP framework. Proposals: Recommend the hashing strategy to be received to guarantee that there is no code infusion or any other comparative assault.

Change Management in Security Objects

The adjustments in the security object not logged which prompts significant issues in review and traceability. Suggestions: We prescribe a change administration segment to be the piece of security system to keep tracks of every single such change (Miller & Stuart Wells, 2007).

Limiting the Execution of Concurrent Programs

Clients can run foundation programs/reports while working on different applications regularly which may prompt execution issues. Proposals: The asset utilization confined for clients; ERP frameworks must have an element to confine CPU, memory and other asset utilization. Staying away from framework disappointment is important.

Secure Programming Procedures

Secure programming improvement hones exist yet the vast majority of the associations don't take after such practices while creating programming. Proposals: ERP engineers prepared for secure programming advancement techniques.

Application Configuration

Each application may have its particular settings that need to be put away inside the ERP framework. Suggestions: As examined in prior, the application modules must have a profile related with them to store all settings of a specific module.

Data Types and Formats

The applications here and there confront issues if legitimate information sorts and configurations not chosen. Suggestions: Programmers should take mind in the choice of information writes, and should know about support flood issues and should forestall such circumstances to happen.

Security of Custom Components

Custom fabricated parts are typically not anchored as a matter of course in a large portion of the current ERP frameworks. Proposals: As examined in prior, all the segments must have a related profile to store all settings identified with its setup, security and so on.

Ensuring Continuous Improvement to the Security

Security ordinarily viewed as a one-time venture, and associations don't apportion spending plan for security constantly. Suggestions: A program to constantly make strides of security should exist in the association.

DATABASE AND SERVICES LAYER

ERP ordinarily gets to the database and different administrations being kept running in an endeavor. This layer particularly handles the undertakings like:

1. Access to the database and different administrations.
2. A mix of heterogeneous information sources.
3. Access to alternate administrations, e.g., validation administrations.
4. Taking care of clients' lord records
5. Change administration: It suggested that there ought to be a Change Control Board to assess the effect of each change and the progressions ought to be legitimately archived and controlled.

6.   The task of a part of one client to another if there should arise an occurrence of leave: Strongly recommends that the leave administration ought to incorporate with the assignments of parts in an ERP framework.

There is a 'database and administrations level security layer' which stores data particular to the security of databases and administrations being gotten to by the ERP framework (Geum, Kim & Lee, 2017).

The normal data put away incorporates the following.

Maintaining the Logs and Tracing

Logs are essential to be kept up to empower traceability and inspecting. Suggestions: Almost all database motors bolster logging; notwithstanding, it suggested that the security of the logged information must be guaranteed (Bhattacharya, Van Stavern & Madhavan, 2010).

Securing Users' Master Records

Client ace record is a standout amongst the most basic segments of ERP framework; RDBMS basic the ERP framework is in charge of putting away this record. Proposals: The progressions to the clients' lord records must be traceable, and change administration controls must be actualized.

Enforcing Strong Password Policies

Now and again the ERP frameworks permit weak passwords consequently making the framework helpless against the danger of secret word burglary or being assaulted by animal power. Suggestions: If the ERP is utilizing the validation administration of database, solid watchword strategies must be implemented and maturing, and secret key history highlights must be empowered (Sutton, 2018).

Encryption of Sensitive Data

Touchy information scrambled while it remains to put away in the database Suggestions: Encryption must be sufficiently solid to secure information for a base characterized day and age regardless of whether a bruit drive appends it.

Ensuring the Integrity of the Data

Unapproved people ought not to make any changes in the information. Suggestions: Access control component ought to be used to guarantee to control. Line level locking instruments are accessible in RDBMS frameworks now a day.

Third Party Services

At times the ERP used outsider administrations. Suggestions: If the ERP includes the outsider administrations programming modules or others used at that point the accompanying security review contemplations are to include: Risk Assessment, Risk Treatment, and Risk Alleviation.

Limiting Concurrent Requests Made by a Single Client

The client may demand to run parallel questions consequently devouring heaps of assets.

Validation of Data

Information approval performed at the front end, business rationale or back end layer Proposals: Data approval rules must be characterized at the backend level as various applications are getting too similar information, and it would be very unfeasible to approve information at the front end or business rationale layer. Consequently, it prescribed that all the approval made at the database level (McLaughlin, 2015).

Change Management

It is essential to have a legal change administration framework that controls, records and assesses all the changes. Suggestions: Change Control Board should exist in the ERP framework to play out every single such undertaking.

Roles and Rights Management

Database motors give highlights to make parts and allow benefits to these parts given the activity portrayal of the general population. Suggestions: Database directors ought to build up parts according to the prerequisites.

Ensuring Continuous Improvement to the Security

Security ordinarily viewed as a onetime venture, and associations don't apportion spending plan for security persistently. Proposals: Continuous security improvement is important to guarantee up to check security.

OPERATING SYSTEM LAYER

This layer particularly handles the errands like I. Capacity administrations ii. Client accounts administration

Our structure has an 'OS level security layer' that contains security-related data particular to the practical framework level; the run of the mill data put away incorporates:

Definition of Roles, Groups, and Group Policies

Each venture working framework enables us to characterize client records, gatherings and gathering approaches separated from these OS likewise enable us to characterize Access Control Lists (ACL) to execute security. Proposals: Security highlights of OS must be legitimately used to guarantee security at end clients' machines.

File System Level Security

All endeavor level working frameworks enable directs to characterize get to benefits to be characterized on a document or organizer level. Suggestions: The OS can make the first commitment to the security by anchoring the critical records at the grass root level, as everything is put away in documents. Subsequently, the document security lies at the center of the security worldview (Murikipudi, Prakash & Vigneswaran, 2015).

Protection Against Viruses, Worms, Trojans

Dangers like infections, worms, Trojans, code infusions, cushion over streams, and execution of the information fragments are common dangers to the working framework that can influence the execution of any ERP framework. Proposals: Being the least layer in the system, the OS must be given the primary need while the security activities are to taken in any ERP System.

Protection Against Spyware

Spyware assaults the protection of the client (privacy) like key lumberjacks, typically such assaults propelled by changing interfere. Proposals: The engineering of the working framework ought to be sufficiently solid to counteract such dangers.

Enforcing Strong Password Policies

Once in a while, the OS strategies permit weak passwords henceforth making the framework defenseless against the risk of secret key robbery or assaulted by a savage power. Proposals: If the ERP is utilizing the verification administration of OS or registry server, at that point solid secret word strategies must be upheld and maturing, and watchword history highlights must be empowered (Maclachlan, 2011).

Limiting Resource Usage to Avoid System Failure

The client may demand to run parallel projects consequently devouring many assets. Suggestions: It prescribed that asset use must be restricted to a degree so the framework never crashes and can react to all clients.

Applying Patches to Remove Vulnerabilities

OS sellers give customary fixes and administration packs to keep framework from various dangers. Suggestions: There ought to be the approach to refresh all the working frameworks, it prescribed that the patches ought to be naturally connected to every one of the machines being some portion of the venture and should be controlled by a focal framework organization (Meghanathan, 2013).

Ensuring Continuous Improvement to the Security

Security regularly viewed as a one-time venture, and associations don't dispense spending plan for security consistently. Suggestions: Top level administration ought to be resolved to make consistent upgrades to the security of ERP framework.

NETWORK INFRASTRUCTURE LAYER

This layer particularly handles the assignments like I. Arrangement of correspondence framework. ii. Enabling clients to get to the ERP utilizing excellent methods of correspondence, e.g., Mobile gadgets, Remote sessions. iii. Arrangement of security in various methods of correspondence. System Infrastructure Layer has data about the requirements on the stream of activity over the system, e.g., for basic applications it is compulsory to utilize secure channel of correspondence while they are gotten too remotely.The security-related errands performed by this layer talked.

Basic Information to Flow in Encrypted Mode

In some ERP frameworks the secret word and other basic qualifications stream in plaintext mode, bundle sniffers can discover these qualifications and make potential harms to the ERP. Suggestions: Policies must be characterized to guarantee that each method of correspondence utilizes encryption to transmit passwords and other basic data.

Messaging (Email) System Security

Dangers like spamming can diminish the execution of the ERP informing framework or work process servers; phishing assault is additionally a potential danger to the clients. Suggestions: Up-to-date measures for informing security ought to embrace. Security strategies ought to record.

Authenticating Clients in Light of Their IP Addresses

A few administrations are just open from the PCs being the piece of associations LAN; thus, PCs are regularly verified utilizing their IP addresses. Proposals: The PCs are verified utilizing their IP addresses (González, Dueñas-Osorio, Sánchez-Silva & Medaglia, 2015).

Handling Certificate Based Security

Central servers and customers utilize the computerized declarations to guarantee secure correspondence. Proposals: Certificates ought to be acquired based on the association's strategy; legitimacy of the declarations is likewise a critical issue.

Limiting Resource Usage to Avoid System Failure

A portion of the system Trojans and worms send a large measure of bundles to irregular or indicated goals and diminish the system and henceforth the ERP's execution. Suggestions: Proper system safety efforts ought to taken and applications ought to be permitted to get to the system administrations in light of their mark; the mark of noxious projects ought to add to the confined program list.

Generating Logs

Logs assume an important part of following the exercises of various clients signed on to the OS. Proposals: Logs ought to empowered according to the security prerequisites of the ERP.

Data Encryption

Information encryption highlights are accessible in present-day working frameworks. Suggestions: The clients of ERP should know how to encode the basic information, so the secrecy and respectability of the information are guaranteed.

Ensuring Continuous Improvement to the Security

Security regularly viewed as one-time speculation and associations don't dispense spending plan for security constantly. Suggestions: Top level administration ought to be resolved to make persistent upgrades to the security of ERP framework.

INTEROPERABILITY LAYER

Because of expansive scale incorporation, it is probably going to happen that ERP comprises of the different OS, equipment, database, applications, and different stages; this layer particularly handles the undertakings like I. Interoperability among the administrations and applications having a place with various stages/merchants. ii. Reconciliation administrations (e.g., web administrations). This layer additionally stores the security data particular to the interoperability. Since ERPs are huge scale frameworks, they use the administrations of mixture stages and merchants. ERP sellers additionally offer bundled items that contain outsider items; association may likewise obtain outsider programming additional items to utilize with their ERP frameworks (Chavan & Nighot, 2016). Suggestions: All such items/administrations must completely experience the Change Control Board previously their usage.

Managing Security Issues Because of Interoperability

As examined over, the ERP frameworks use outsider programming/benefits; subsequently, it likewise uncovered the ERP framework to the new security vulnerabilities because of outsider association.

Disaster Aversion Because of Interoperability

Contrary qualities and irregularities may prompt inaccessibility or much debacle of the framework. Suggestions: The administrations or items ought to try for the similarity and consistency before being incorporated.

Continuous Improvement

Strategies and procedures for the interoperability need to be constantly checked and refreshed inside the association. Suggestions: Continuous security improvement is important to guarantee up to stamp security.

SUGGESTION FOR FUTURE RESEARCH

There is still a requirement for future research because there are different measurements that should investigate, even though this examination accomplished its destinations. The procedure needs to contemplate every one of the components that contribute to the survival of the association among the business intensity. The field of data innovation is dynamic to the point that things are changing each day. So future research can address the speed of getting to information put away on the cloud and the capacity limit of the cloud. Cloud put away information encryption is another zone for future research; tool the cloud put away information encoded and unscrambled. The structure can additionally be altered to consolidate the issue of information encryption ideas.

CONCLUSION

The cloud-based ERP Framework was produced to help transport association in executing cloud-based ERP frameworks. Cloud-based ERP frameworks assist associations with cutting expenses in wording equipment, programming, and redesigns and additionally lessen in advance costs. With cloud-based ERP frameworks the association will enhance availability, portability, and ease of use. Moving into the cloud-based ERP framework is exceptionally helpful and enhanced framework accessibility and fiasco recuperation. ERP is a data framework that incorporates divisions and capacities over an association into one PC framework. It keeps running off a single database, empowering different offices to share data, what's more, speak with each other. In this chapter the survey most existing ERP structure utilized Service-Oriented Design for module combination it permits the ERP framework incorporates all data of various units utilizing extraordinary stages into one focal database. The advantages of this approach incorporate cost investment funds, enhanced business nimbleness by diminishing time to convey comes about, and improved joint effort, what's more, sharing of the asset. The researcher has a plan ERP system for Poly Technique schools given the current general Service Situated Architecture ERP system. Since Service-Oriented Engineering based ERP system comprises extraordinary segments, for example, we benefit, Common Object Request Representative Architecture and Enterprise Java Beans. This ERP system configuration center on Service Oriented engineering utilizing web benefit by the utilization of Simple Object Access convention over Hyper Text Transfer Protocol and incorporate the inward bureau of poly Technique College through web benefit remote façade. As a future work ERP system configuration can be stretched out to help incorporation with other outside association, customization in light of the business needs of poly strategy universities and include distinctive module modules.

Security is a bit of hindsight in the more significant part of ERP framework usage that prompts a few issues. A great deal of work in the territory of security has just done, and the partners of ERP framework require exhaustive comprehension of security needs at various levels as delineated by the structure. Furthermore, the responsibility of proper administration to actualize and support security activities matters a considerable measure. There is a misconception that the area of security is just constrained to a specific gathering inside a venture. On the off chance that we altogether consider every security sub-layer we can without much of a stretch make an inference that security mindfulness is a necessary prerequisite for each representative of an endeavor. We unequivocally prescribe the persistent change to be accomplished in each sub-layer to guarantee that ERP is secure and can safeguard any new test. This investigation has a security structure, especially for ERP applications. This structure has created preventive measures that would utilize as a part of future advancement of ERP applications. The main point is to secure the layers of the ERP application that incorporates a database layer, business layer, and introduction layer. The utilization of academic ERP framework in the instructive foundation is exceptionally indispensable. In any case, some instructive organizations can't execute the structure given need in spending plan or assets, and other instructive organizations require more versatile scholarly ERP framework to adjust with their advancing business. Academic cloud ERP framework empowers these highlights and rapidly turns into an answer.

What's more, as the execution of cloud ERP expands, issues emerge on the best way to assess this framework. Along these lines, this chapter gives the appraisal display for scholarly cloud ERP quality assessment, to help extend supervisors in settling on a choice on actualizing cloud-based scholastic ERP framework. The appraisal demonstrates it created given academic cloud ERP prerequisites, programming item quality estimation, and Software-as-a-Service assessment. The appraisal angles are centered on the attributes of the scholastic cloud ERP framework as an item and as an administration. The weighing for these angles is resolved on how vital these angles are in influencing ERP execution.

REFERENCES

Al-Johani, A., & Youssef, A. (2013). A Framework for ERP Systems in SME Based on Cloud Computing Technology. *International Journal On Cloud Computing: Services And Architecture*, *3*(3), 1–14. doi:10.5121/ijccsa.2013.3301

Azevedo, P., Romão, M., & Rebelo, E. (2012). Advantages, Limitations, and Solutions in the Use of ERP Systems (Enterprise Resource Planning) – A Case Study in the Hospitality Industry. *Procedia Technology*, *5*, 264–272. doi:10.1016/j.protcy.2012.09.029

Badewi, A., Shehab, E., Zeng, J., & Mohamad, M. (2018). ERP benefits capability framework: Orchestration theory perspective. *Business Process Management Journal*, *24*(1), 266–294. doi:10.1108/BPMJ-11-2015-0162

Bhattacharya, P., Van Stavern, R., & Madhavan, R. (2010). Automated Data Mining: An Innovative and Efficient Web-Based Approach to Maintaining Resident Case Logs. *Journal of Graduate Medical Education*, *2*(4), 566–570. doi:10.4300/JGME-D-10-00025.1 PMID:22132279

Bjelland, E., & Haddara, M. (2018). Evolution of ERP Systems in the Cloud: A Study on System Updates. *Systems*, *6*(2), 22. doi:10.3390ystems6020022

Bukhari, A., & Liu, X. (2018). A Web service search engine for large-scale Web service discovery based on the probabilistic topic modeling and clustering. *Service Oriented Computing and Applications*, *12*(2), 169–182. doi:10.100711761-018-0232-6

Caprioli, E. (2014). Commentary on digital evidence and electronic signature of a consumer credit contract in France. *Digital Evidence And Electronic Signature Law Review*, *11*(0). doi:10.14296/deeslr.v11i0.2160

Chavan, A., & Nighot, M. (2016). Secure and Cost-effective Application Layer Protocol with Authentication Interoperability for IOT. *Procedia Computer Science*, *78*, 646–651. doi:10.1016/j.procs.2016.02.112

Ching, L. (2010). New Governance, Old Problems: Explaining the Appeal of Third-Party Tools. *Asia Pacific Journal Of Public Administration*, *32*(2), 187–197. doi:1 0.1080/23276665.2010.10779374

Gao, S. (2009). Manufacturing Resource Planning Technology Based on Genetic Programming Simulation. *Chinese Journal of Mechanical Engineering*, *22*(02), 177. doi:10.3901/CJME.2009.02.177

Gassel, F. (2010). Robotizing housing and design. *Gerontechnology (Valkenswaard)*, *9*(2). doi:10.4017/gt.2010.09.02.128.00

Geum, Y., Kim, M., & Lee, S. (2017). Service Technology: Definition and Characteristics Based on a Patent Database. *Service Science*, *9*(2), 147–166. doi:10.1287erv.2016.0170

González, A., Dueñas-Osorio, L., Sánchez-Silva, M., & Medaglia, A. (2015). The Interdependent Network Design Problem for Optimal Infrastructure System Restoration. *Computer-Aided Civil and Infrastructure Engineering*, *31*(5), 334–350. doi:10.1111/mice.12171

Hoch, J., & Dulebohn, J. (2013). Shared leadership in enterprise resource planning and human resource management system implementation. *Human Resource Management Review*, *23*(1), 114–125. doi:10.1016/j.hrmr.2012.06.007

Horowitz-Kraus, T. (2015). Improvement in non-linguistic executive functions following reading acceleration training in children with reading difficulties: An ERP study. *Trends in Neuroscience and Education*, *4*(3), 77–86. doi:10.1016/j.tine.2015.06.002

Hustad, E., Haddara, M., & Kalvenes, B. (2016). ERP and Organizational Misfits: An ERP Customization Journey. *Procedia Computer Science*, *100*, 429–439. doi:10.1016/j.procs.2016.09.179

Jain, A. (2011). Approach for reducing menu access time by enabling bidirectional cursor movement within the nested menu(s). *Software Engineering Notes*, *36*(5), 1. doi:10.1145/2020976.2020986

Karpiuk, M. (2016). Bill of materials as a part of CAD and ERP integration. *Mechanik*, (12), 1874-1875. doi:10.17814/mechanik.2016.12.531

Maclachlan, G. (2011). Scandal, Spyware, and Trust. *Infosecurity*, *8*(5), 45. doi:10.1016/S1754-4548(11)70071-7

Mazurczyk, W., & Caviglione, L. (2015). Information Hiding as a Challenge for Malware Detection. *IEEE Security and Privacy*, *13*(2), 89–93. doi:10.1109/MSP.2015.33

McLaughlin, D. (2015). Assessing the fit of biotic ligand model validation data in a risk management decision context. *Integrated Environmental Assessment and Management*, *11*(4), 610–617. doi:10.1002/ieam.1634 PMID:25779880

Meghanathan, N. (2013). Source Code Analysis to Remove Security Vulnerabilities in Java Socket Programs: A Case Study. *International Journal Of Network Security & Its Applications*, *5*(1), 1–16. doi:10.5121/ijnsa.2013.5101

Michelberger, P., & Horváth, Z. (2017). Security aspects of process resource planning. *Polish Journal Of Management Studies*, *16*(1), 142–153. doi:10.17512/pjms.2017.16.1.12

Miller, C., & Stuart Wells, F. (2007). Balancing Security and Privacy in the Digital Workplace. *Journal of Change Management*, *7*(3-4), 315–328. doi:10.1080/14697010701779181

Morgan, D. (2004). Network security and custom Web applications. *Network Security*, *2004*(4), 15–17. doi:10.1016/S1353-4858(04)00068-6

Murikipudi, A., Prakash, V., & Vigneswaran, T. (2015). Performance Analysis of Real Time Operating System with General Purpose Operating System for Mobile Robotic System. *Indian Journal of Science and Technology*, *8*(19). doi:10.17485/ijst/2015/v8i19/77017

Nordin, N., & Adegoke, O. (2015). Learning from ERP Implementation: A Case Study of Issues and Challenges in Technology Management. *Jurnal Teknologi*, *74*(1). doi:10.11113/jt.v74.3369

Oh, Y., Han, H., Shin, D., Kim, D., & Kim, N. (2015). The Framework for Adaptive ERP Systems Using the Ontology Model of a Manufacturing Supply Chain. *Journal Of Korean Institute Of Industrial Engineers*, *41*(4), 344–351. doi:10.7232/JKIIE.2015.41.4.344

Orougi, S. (2015). Recent advances in enterprise resource planning. *Accounting*, 37-42. doi:10.5267/j.ac.2015.11.004

Ouyang, G., Herzmann, G., Zhou, C., & Sommer, W. (2011). Residue iteration decomposition (RIDE): A new method to separate ERP components on the basis of latency variability in single trials. *Psychophysiology*, *48*(12), 1631–1647. doi:10.1111/j.1469-8986.2011.01269.x PMID:21895682

Pavel, J., & Evelyn, T. (2017). An Illustrative Case Study of the Integration of Enterprise Resource Planning System. *Journal of Enterprise Resource Planning Studies*, 1-9. doi:10.5171/2017.176215

Peng, X. (2012). Efficient Construction Scheme of Software Service Outsourcing Industry. *Journal of Software*, 7(11). doi:10.4304/jsw.7.11.2583-2590

Saunders, L. (2014). Linking Resource Decisions to Planning. *New Directions for Community Colleges*, 2014(168), 65–75. doi:10.1002/cc.20121

Sutton, H. (2018). Scaling up PLA requires strong policies, planning backend processes. *The Successful Registrar*, 18(2), 1–5. doi:10.1002/tsr.30454

Terminanto, A. (2014). Forecast to Plan Cycle in Oracle E Business Suite (Case Study Automotive Company). *Advanced Science Letters*, 20(1), 203–208. doi:10.1166/asl.2014.5279

Tong, X., Zhang, X., Xu, X., & Qi, J. (2014). Improving Workflow Management System Implementation with Workflow Localization Method. *Applied Mechanics And Materials, 513-517*, 3859-3863. Retrieved from www.scientific.net/amm.513-517.3859

Venkadasalam, S. (2015). Linear Programming: An Alternative Enterprise Resource Planning (ERP) in Higher Learning Institution. *Journal Of Business And Economics*, 6(9), 1633–1637. doi:10.15341/jbe(2155-7950)/09.06.2015/010

Wang, C., & Tsai, W. (2014). Elucidating How Interface Design and Cognitive Function Affect Learning Performance in the Enterprise Resource Planning (ERP) Software System. *Journal of Testing and Evaluation*, 44(1), 20140044. doi:10.1520/JTE20140044

Webb, N., Richter, A., & Bonsper, D. (2010). Linking Defense Planning and Resource Decisions: A Return to Systems Thinking. *Defense & Security Analysis*, 26(4), 387–400. doi:10.1080/14751798.2010.534647

Zafar, H. (2013). Human resource information systems: Information security concerns for organizations. *Human Resource Management Review*, 23(1), 105–113. doi:10.1016/j.hrmr.2012.06.010

Zare, A., & Ravasan, A. (2014). An Extended Framework for ERP Post-Implementation Success Assessment. *Information Resources Management Journal*, 27(4), 45–65. doi:10.4018/irmj.2014100103

Zare, A., & Ravasan, A. (2014). An Extended Framework for ERP Post-Implementation Success Assessment. *Information Resources Management Journal*, 27(4), 45–65. doi:10.4018/irmj.2014100103

Zeng, Y., & Skibniewski, M. (2013). Risk assessment for enterprise resource planning (ERP) system implementations: A fault tree analysis approach. *Enterprise Information Systems*, 7(3), 332–353. doi:10.1080/17517575.2012.690049

Chapter 5

Understanding Enterprise Resource Planning Reliability for Operational Excellence:
Towards Understanding the Components of a Reliable Enterprise Resource Planning System

Julius Nyerere Odhiambo
Technical University of Kenya, Kenya

Elyjoy Muthoni Micheni
Technical University of Kenya, Kenya

Benard Muma
Technical University of Kenya, Kenya

ABSTRACT

The quest for sustainable competitive advantage and the urge to adapt to a challenging business environment has made firms around the globe to adopt enterprise resource planning systems so as optimally leverage on the enterprise-wide resources and be more responsive to customer demands. Globally organizations seeking to enhance their competitiveness have utilized Enterprise Resource Planning (ERP) systems to enhance their operational efficiency. The ERP philosophy advocates for the incorporation of personnel, finance, manufacturing, distribution, sales, and marketing modules into a single integrated system and a central database, allowing an organization to efficiently and effectively utilize its resources. The planning and better management of organizational resources, improved business performance, and better integration of business operations can be facilitated by an ERP system to offer an avenue of excellence for a business. Despite the potential benefits an ERP system offers an organization, few studies have explored the ERP reliability in the context of competition driven business imperatives.

DOI: 10.4018/978-1-5225-7678-5.ch005

Table 1. ERP success or failure

Top Five Reasons for ERP Success	Top Five Reasons for ERP Failure
User involvement	Lack of user input
Executive management support	Incomplete requirements and specifications
Clear statement of requirements	Changing requirements and specification
Proper planning	Lack of executive support
Realistic expectations	Technological incompetence

Figure 1. Making an order before ERP

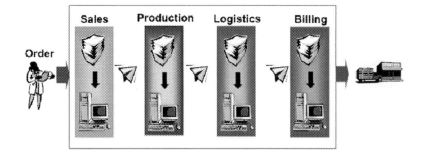

INTRODUCTION

The quest for sustainable competitive advantage and the urge to adopt to a challenging has made firms around the globe to adopt Enterprise Resource Planning (ERP) systems so as optimally leverage on the enterprise – wide resources and be more responsive to customer demands. Globally organizations seeking to enhance their competitiveness have utilized ERP systems to enhance their operational efficiency (Verville, Palanisamy, Bernadas, & Halingten, 2007). This has been exacerbated by ERP internet extended functionalities, stakeholder's demands to bridge speed with value.

Meaning of ERP

ERP can be defined as an enterprise - wide information system that collates and controls all the business processes within an organization onto a single computer system so as to serve organization's needs. ERP as an information technology (IT) resource seeks to reliably integrate, synchronize and centralize organizational data strategically along its value chain (Kilic, Zaim, & Delen, 2014). Holland et al (1999) defines ERP systems as integrated enterprise-wide information systems that automates the business processes.

Understanding ERP Reliability

The ERP philosophy advocates for the incorporation of personnel, finance, manufacturing, distribution, sales and marketing modules into a single integrated system and a central database, allowing an organization to efficiently and effectively utilize its resources (Momoh, Roy, & Shehab, 2010; Rerup Schlichter & Kraemmergaard, 2010).

The planning and better management of organizational resources, improved business performance and better integration of business operations can be facilitated by an ERP system to offer an avenue of excellence for a business. Despite the potential benefits an ERP system offers an organization, few studies have explored the ERP reliability in the context of competition driven business imperatives. This chapter seeks to explore the different aspects of harnessing RP operational and functional reliability in the business organization.

An organization comprises of many function departments, such as HR, finance, purchasing, logistics and manufacturing. Before the advent of ERP systems, each functional department had its own computing system optimized for the departments particular procedures. ERP combined the key procedures from each independent department into a single, integrated software program that run off a single database in a way that enables the various departments to share an information and communication platform.

Impact of ERP Reliability

A reliable ERP system is one that can be dependable in the long run within the business environment, so as to 'extensively' leverage on the business procedures. Accurate data is essential for any business operation as it enhances optimal decision making. ERP facilitates the integration of the information demands, business functions and procedures into a single software solution that is able to seamlessly service/address the functional needs of the business. This in turn reduces data redundancy by ensuring that the information is reliable, accurate and available to all stakeholders in need of making the decisions. As a business strategy, it reliably builds on its stakeholders' value by enabling and optimizing the enterprise and inter-enterprise collaborative operational and financial processes (Huang & Yasuda, 2016). Through the collation all the information needs of an organization to a centralized location, reliable access at any given time period is accorded to key system stakeholders.

Figure 2. ERP in a modern business environment

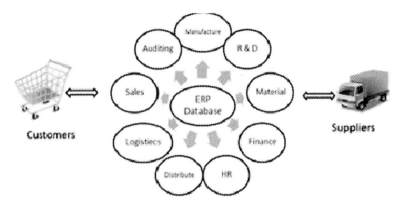

The competitiveness and dynamic nature of the current business environment requires proper management of information if organizational performance is to be enhanced (Yaghubi et al., 2014). Due to ever-increasing globalization, the level of competition among firms has increased, and it is for this reason that organizations are recognizing the need to invest highly in information systems in an attempt to integrate and coordinate their activities to achieve efficiency and effectiveness. A number of companies have and will continue to benefit from ERP utilization, and the witness the following impacts.

Company Growth and Sustainability

In the era of globalization coupled with an advancing economic landscape, enhanced profitability is inevitable for an organization seeking to stay afloat. According to Rajan and Baral (2015), ERP assists many companies in integrating their information flow as well as business processes and essentially, they support various departments and other functions within the organization through the use of a single database. The latter makes it possible to collect and store data in real time. Growth and sustainability is realized because a successful implementation ensures that there are faster information transactions, enhanced financial management, and reduced cycle times among others (Yaghubi et al., 2014).

Example

KenAfric Industry Ltd, is a Kenyan company that has adopted the use of i360 that is built on System Application and Product (SAP) business intelligence solutions and had made it possible for the company to gain access to predictive analysis tools. These tools assist in examining the business trends and provide the management with meaningful business decisions because such are based on the aggregated data. The benefit that ERP system produces at Kenafric Industries is increased flexibility in information generation, good quality reports as well as improved ways of integrating accounts applications.

Company Competiveness

Studies have established that firms that adopt the use of ERP systems often have a competitive edge over their rivals in the industry (Yaghubi et al., 2014). This is because; ERP helps in cutting operational costs by increasing flexibility as well as boosting the overall business efficiency. Accordingly, very effective ERP systems improve client interactions (Njuguna, 2011). It is from this perspective that manufacturing companies gain their competitive advantage in the industry. This notwithstanding, ERP can also help in streamlining every aspect of the business. It is for this reason that firms need to understand the implementation of the ERP from the perspective of the user so as to prepare employees to go about the new challenges that might arise (Rajan & Baral, 2015). This enables organizations to make good use of the available technology solution and reap substantial benefits to the company.

Example

Kenya Revenue Authority (KRA) has implemented ERP systems for efficient management of its internal and external resources. KRA consulted Alliance Technologies in Kenya to provide it with A1 Enterprise Resource Planning for the Public Sector. The resulting benefits include reduced paper work and efficient operations both of which have transformed key business operations. Such benefits have enabled the organization to be honored for its contributions to the implementation of an efficient ERP system through the use of the Free Open Source System (FOSS). Among the departments that have shown tremendous improvement following the adoption of ERP system are summarized in the following table:

Dynamism of ERP Reliability

The dynamism of an ERP system is drawn from its effective and efficient utilization and not from the system itself and entails having a strong alignment between technical and organizational imperatives (Erturk & Arora, 2017; Moon, 2007). ERP systems quite often understood on the premise of their transactional capability, as they are utilized in large and middle – sized institution worldwide to influence automation

Table 2. Current progress on finance components

Modules	% Completed
Budget: RPF, LPO Funds Commitment, Booking Actual Expenditure, Reports	43%
Cash Office: RTGS Payments, Cheques, Petty Cash, Receipting, Cash Books, Reports	40%
General Ledger: Invoicing, Payroll Link, Link to accounting centre, Customer Reports, GL Reports	67%
Expenditure: Imprest Payments, Imprest Surrenders, Supplier Payments, Staff Payments, Reimbursements, medical Payments, Reports	37%
Overall Percentage Completion: 46%	

Table 3. Current progress on procurement and supplies components

Components	% Completed
Annual Procurement Planning	50%
Supplier Selection	50%
Request for Purchase (RFP)	100%
Procurement Method (Tender, RFP Proposals, RF Quotation) and Thresholds	68%
Bid Evaluation	100%
Local Purchase/Service Orders	100%
Award of Contracts (Procurement/Tender Committee)	100%
Delivery, Receipt and Inventory Management	50%
Stock Management/Quarterly Stock Take	100%
Disposal of Disused/Surplus Stores	0%
Overall Percentage Completion: 51.5%	

Source: Kenya Revenue Authority, FOSS ERP Business Process Analysis, 2010

and spur the business agility. Cloud based ERP systems utilization is an emerging trend expected to arise on account of growing innovation in the technological world, providing avenues for organizations to collaborate with key partners at minimal costs for timely and more informed decisions. Thus a dynamic ERP system would allow for better co-ordination and collaboration between core business functionalities by undertaking a given task with low variation on the expected output.

One of the fundamental points worth noting is that during implementation ERP systems, utilizing a specific approach and/or methodology of development is vital. The dynamism of ERP reliability can best be understood in terms of key characteristics of the system and they include the following.

Functionality

This refers to the capability of the ERP system to provide functions or services that meet the needs of the users as specified. Functionality of the ERP system is measured based on accuracy, interoperability, functionality compliance, suitability and security among others (Kumar et al. 2009). The other one relates to the reliability of ERP systems, and according to Gupta et al. (2014), it is the ability of ERP to keep its performance level under specific conditions. The metrics of this attribute include fault tolerance, reliability compliance, maturity as well as recoverability (Fahmy et al. 2012).

Usability

ERP usability is another attribute that can be used to qualify the dynamism of an ERP software. This is best understood in terms of learnability, attractiveness, understandability and operability of the ERP system. Either way, any ERP system adopted by an organization must be understood, learned, and well executed under certain conditions. With the ever growing global competition and increasing demand of goods and services, many firms across the world are now moving towards adoption of enterprise resource planning systems as a means through which they gain competitive advantage (Matende et al., 2015).

Example

Different organizations have managed to implement ERP systems in Kenya as a way of enhancing their business operation strategies and consumer satisfaction level. This entails the optimization of supply chain, inventory management, enhanced business forecasting and minimization of costs so as to reap the benefits. Symphony Ltd has enabled many of Kenyan companies integrate ERP into their daily business routine e.g. The Kenya Seed Company, Cadbury Kenya, Kenya Wine Agencies Ltd. (KWAL), and General Motors East Africa Ltd

Table 4 gives a diverse dynamism of ERP reliability as utilized in these companies. A specific reference is made to Deacons Kenya Ltd that committed about Kshs. 36 million to implement new ERP systems to allow the company's management

Table 4. ERP application to enhance usability

Company	ERP application
Kenya Seed Company	ERP systems have been implemented to automate and create a seamless workflow between different departmental applications to address the challenge of lack of centralized coordination and management of ICT services.
Cadbury Kenya	ERP systems boost the key operational activities such as procurement, sales and distribution as well as inventory management.
General Motors East Africa Ltd	ERP aids in functional integration of core business areas such as accounting, sales and marketing. Sales and marketing function is also aligned with production through information system.
Kenya Wine Agencies Ltd (KWAL)	ERP system enables easy tracking of purchasing, transportation, requisitions, workflow, and expenses. ERP also assists in optimization of all administrative duties and/or operations.

to monitor or control the inventory levels. Additionally, it is also from the ERP attributes already mentioned that enable the above organizations to consolidate their financial reporting. This is a clear indication that the significance of ERP systems is continuously being recognized across different companies that invested highly in information systems in the Kenyan economy.

Information Visibility

Successful implementation of ERP systems results in greater benefits to the organizations that uses information gathered to make critical decisions. The measurability of ERP reliability can be made possible through improved information visibility, increased financial management, reduced risks to the business as well as enhanced alignment of various business operations provided that the system is adopted properly (Kronbichler et al., 2010). In Kenya, the companies that have developed and adopted ERP systems in order to regularize and improve their business activities have at some point faced varied challenges including poor management (Gupta et al., 2014). This notwithstanding, a balanced scorecard (BSC) can also be ideal in ensuring that the performance of an ERP systems is closely monitored and checked against the goals of the company. The reason for using a balanced scorecard to measure the effectiveness and reliability of the software is to supplement the traditional financial measures with other perspectives (i.e. the customer perspective, the internal business process perspective and the learning and growth perspective) (Kronbichler et al., 2010). As a metric tool, a balance scorecard is preferred since it is useful in controlling how the system is used across the functional units within an organization. The figure 3 shows the ERP operation balance scorecard.

COMPONENTS OF A RELIABLE ERP SYSTEM

Enterprise resource planning systems can be used to streamline and improve operational efficiency within an organization. In its course of implementing key ERP procedures, an organization will need to automate and standardize its operational routines so as to eliminate unnecessary manual effort and save time. Prior to the implementation of an ERP system a company needs to select/streamline various components that is often pegged upon its specific processes.

Consider Thika Motors Ltd - an automobile assembling company in Kenya. It has a huge target market as it services the whole of East Africa i.e. Uganda, Rwanda, Burundi and South Sudan. By its very nature the company will need to combat manufacturing, inventory, supply chain and distribution functions that its ERP system must address.

Figure 3. The ERP operation Balanced Scorecard
Source: (Kronbichler et al., 2010)

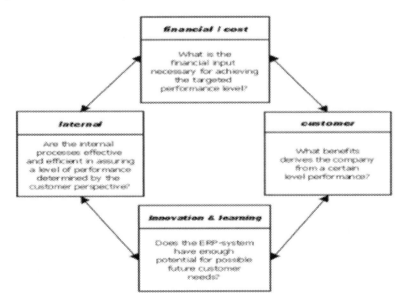

Despite the variability manifested for different companies, the following components should be considered prior to the implementation of an ERP system

Management Support

Management support is an integral component in ERP implementation (Costa, Ferreira, Bento, & Aparicio, 2016) The provision of leadership and critical resources is an important ingredient towards a reliable ERP system (Shatat, 2015). Additionally, the leadership of an organization can enhance the reliability of an ERP system by establishing reasonable objectives for the system, understanding its capabilities, limitations, exhibiting commitment and communicating the corporate strategy to employees and stakeholders (Badewi & Shehab, 2016; Muinde, Lewa, & Kamau, 2016). Thus the top management should continuously provide support and monitor the direction and progress of the ERP system.

Case: Management Information System

Management information systems are integral supporting key managerial decision-making within an organization. The management information system is tasked with availing information products that supports many critical decision-making needs of managers. Reports, responses, and other feedback generated by information systems provide essential information for the management to reliably meet their information needs. Thus satisfying the information needs at the operational and tactical levels of the organization tasked with more structured decision making situations

Case Study: Enterprise Portals

Major changes and expansion are taking place in the management support environment. Tools have been advanced to avail information and modeling needs essential for managers to undertake their decision making routines. These changes are best understood in the following contexts.

- Extensive growth of corporate intranets, extranets, as well as web-enabled portals, has accelerated the development and utilization of diverse information delivery and decision support software tools by lower levels of management and by individuals and teams of business professionals.
- Dramatic expansion of ERP has opened avenues for the utilization and collaboration of agile e-business tools for suppliers, customers, and other business stakeholders of a company for customer relationship management,

supply chain management, and other e-business applications enhancing the overall business reliability
- The dynamic nature of business coupled with massive rapid developments in end user computing and networking; Internet, and the explosion of e-commerce activity.

Information Portals

Enterprise information portals (EIP) are being integrated by organizations as a way to providing the critical web-enabled information, timely knowledge, and critical decision support to organizations management, employees, customers, suppliers, and other business stakeholders.

- *Enterprise information portals* can be described as the customized, personalized and web-based interface for the organization's intranets. It accords its users access to diverse internal and external business applications, services and databases.

Knowledge Portals

Enterprise information portal is the entry to organization's intranets that serve as the primary knowledge management systems. Knowledge management systems utilizes information technology to effectively gather, organize, and share key business insights within an organization. The knowledge portals accord the managerial end users with information products that supports the day to day decision making of the organization's needs. Managers are thus placed in a position to generate information they need for the more unstructured types of decisions in an interactive, computer-based information system. The knowledge portals use decision models and specialized databases procedures to enable a seamless decision-making processes of managerial end users.

- They play a major role in helping an organization utilize its intranets as knowledge management systems to share and disseminate knowledge in support of its business decision-making.

Business Plan and Vision

The complexity of ERP implementation demands an effective strategy to oversee its implementation. A reliable ERP is pegged on a clear and concise vision of the organization. The ERP goals should be categorically stated and its key functions conceptually and operationally defined (Rajan & Baral, 2015). The expectations of all stakeholders also should be clearly demarcated in line with the business plan and vision. Resistance should be managed by the project champion during the operationalization of the ERP system (Erturk & Arora, 2017). The effectiveness of the ERP implementation demands to link all the core functions of the chain seamlessly to propel the business plan and vision.

Business Process Re-Engineering

Reengineering has been considered as an enabling factor in ERP implementation. It is important to fully understand the core functionalities of the organization (Erturk & Arora, 2017). According to (Capaldo & Rippa, 2015), organization can customize their functionalities to fit ERP software specifications.

Teamwork

Teamwork is an important component of organizations seeking to advance in operational efficiency. Organizations in the modern environment are increasingly becoming unstable and dynamic, necessitating the integration of all functional units within the organization in a cooperate way extends to all stakeholders within the business environment.

A team consists of two or more individuals working cohesively together but undertaking interdependent tasks. For this to work out effectively team members should possess the right attitude, requisite knowledge and skills to accord the team a positive working disposition.

Given the interdisciplinary nature of the tasks within an organization, a huge effort should be geared towards ensuring that team members/individuals stay together on course, for the shared goal.

ERP reliability is thus not an automatic consequence of collating people, functions or procedures together. Reliability is sustained by the shared commitment and ambition of individual team members rather than the mandated assignments undertaken.

ERP reliability can thus be enhanced by having the right people with knowledge and skills perform the core business procedures synergistically. Efforts and cooperation between the technical and business experts within the organization should be leveraged to reliably improve on the ERP system.

User Involvement

User involvement enhances ERP acceptance and satisfaction by developing realistic expectations about system capabilities. User involvement is essential because it improves perceived control through participating the whole project plan. According to Zhang et al (2002), there are two areas for user involvement when the company decides to implement an ERP system: user involvement in the stage of definition of the organization's ERP system needs, and user participates in the implementation of ERP systems. The implementation of an effective Enterprise Resource Planning system is such a complicated IT-related phenomenon characterized by an extensive body of knowledge (Njuguna, 2011). Besides, a successful implementation of an ERP system is characterized by huge expenditures, lengthy duration as well as organizational commitment (Mungai, 2016). It is from this perspective that any firm wishing to adopt the use of ERP system must be subjected to information, people, technological and business process challenges (Matende et al., 2015).

ERP implementation is hierarchical and is likely to affect users at different departments performing diverse functions within the organization because all the functional units are affected in one way or the other. Again, the users range from low level management to top level management across the firm since they are the people using the system to facilitate their routinely operations. Al-Fawaz et al. (2008) indicate that user involvement or participation is one of the critical success factors as far as ERP implementation is concerned. Many researchers are interested in establishing why user involvement is such an important factor when ERP is being implemented. User participation is an area that that has been mostly cited as the crucial success factor in enterprise resource planning implementation projects (Musyimi & Odongo, 2015). The reason why users are held with high esteem is that they are welcomed to take part in an information system development process so that they can share the rich application domain knowledge via a prolonged period of exposure to their line of duty (Matende et al., 2015). Again, user involvement is recommended to ensure that users' needs and viewpoints are factored in and eventually create a better information system for the company. Additionally, Harris and Weistroffer (2008) provide that user involvement ensure information system quality, expanded knowledge of the system, increased commitment as well as user acceptance among others.

In East Africa, firms that already use ERP systems have at some point involved users drawn from all the functional units. A study by Nyagah (2006) on the critical success factors that are ideal for successful implementation of ERP in Kenyan companies revealed that teamwork and positive communication among the implementation partners encourage user participation. This is because; partnership trust among the team members ensures that they work in harmony to accomplish the objective.

On the other hand, Kutswa (2011) did investigate the challenges associated with the implementation of ERP systems at Kenya Electricity Generating Company (KenGen) and discovered that resistance to change and poor communication associated with lack of user involvement were among the factors. At KenGen, lack of user involvement at the initial stages of ERP implementation resulted in resistance to change. Withal, Kutswa (2011) posits that KenGen managed to overcome this hurdle by identifying change agents that were selected from all the functional units within the company. With open communication from the top management, the users from all the departments were convinced by the benefits of adopting the use of ERP systems and welcomed the change idea as well-intended. It is for this reason that all stakeholders must be involved to create change ownership and user buy in. Previously we elaborated the effect of user involvement in ERP reliability at Kenya Revenue Authority also confirm that it is such an important factor for a successful implementation of ERP. At HACO Industries, user involvement played a major role in ensuring that ERP is properly implemented (Kang'ethe, 2007; Matende et al., 2015). In all these instances, it is possible to assert that user participation in ERP reliability is critical and should never be overlooked at all cost. Mungai (2016) investigated if stakeholders in Mombasa International Airport participated in the ERP implementation process. In his findings, he established that about 58% of the respondents attested to the fact that stakeholders are involved in the implementation process. His findings are as summarized as shown below.

Business Plan and Vision on ERP Reliability

Sufficient knowledge attained through training increases expertise and knowledge levels for ERP system user within an organization. Empowered decision makers are important in ensuring the reliability of an ERP system (Wanyoike, 2017). Proper planning for ERP implementation provides an ideal environment for timely reporting. This makes the system adoptable to providing measurable value to the firm. Studies have managed to identify a number of ERP projects throughout the world, and have noted the challenges thereof (Yaghubi et al., 2014). It is from this perspective that companies are seeing the need to create a vision for ERP reliability. Since ERP systems are quite comprehensive, developing viable business plans that integrate all business functions as well as organizational process to give a holistic view of the firm and its business activities from central information architecture is ideal (Matende et al., 2015). Having a clear vision regarding the implementation and use of ERP system is sensible. However, customizable and standard application of ERP often helps in giving the state-of-the-art information system infrastructure that ameliorates the flow of information within the organization (Kang'ethe, 2007). Proper business plan and vision for ERP reliability, core business practices including manufacturing, marketing, finance, supply chain, and human resources can be improved significantly.

Many organizations do rely on ERP solution providers to improve their business activities. The design and the implementation plan of ERP are made in such a way that the software meets the needs of the company. As such, the management is likely to experience very high win rates, enhanced employee utilization, and streamlined business management (Matende et al., 2015). In all these cases, companies end up gaining incredible visibility and practical insights to maintain profitability. In other words, a convincing business plan and vision makes the firm to be quite smarter in dealing with its day-to-day operational activities. Clear vision gives a complete visibility into the opportunities across the organization. Besides, the management can use the information generated by ERP software when making business decisions for further improvements (Yaghubi et al., 2014). For example, plans help in ensuring proper budgeting and scheduling and therefore, the ERP software should be adjusted towards this dimension.

CASE STUDY

Enterprise Resource Planning for Product-Oriented Companies

Supply Chain

Trends in business dictates for ERP systems to accommodate not only its internal operations but also inco-operate the supply chain operations of business partners and suppliers involved in its production eco-system. This enhances an organizations visibility into both its internal and external engineering and manufacturing processes. This is beneficial to for organizations or business partners that constantly review their product design and configurations. ERP system can then track different product versions with the help of modules that store information at every stage of product design and subsequent configuration.

Distribution

ERP distribution systems can employ automation systems to sync the organizations customers' quotations and orders directly into its inventory, fulfillment and accounting management system. This enables orders to be comprehensively processed in a timely manner to meet the organization's distribution requirements, especially for its multiple warehouse locations. Thus an organization has the ability to track the movements of their products across the various locations and reassign inventory as needed between the locations.

Inventory System

This system will optimize the organization's inventory stocking and consumption initiatives and provide a platform for forecasting. Routine reports can also be availed to aid the management in its decision making process. Linking the inventory system into logistics and billing systems would also enable the organization to optimize on its daily transaction time.

ERP RELIABILITY ANALYSIS (ERA)

Reliability of any software revolves around; freeness from error, fault and failure. ERP reliability is therefore the extent to which an ERP system is able to operate within the intended environment without fault, error, failure or defect (Nwankpa & Roumani, 2014). ERP reliability analysis involves measuring and assessing ERP reliability scores and quantifying the consistencies and inconsistencies in observed scores so as to establish the extent to which an ERP system can operate as intended in the intended environment (Rajan & Baral, 2015). Among other tools, Generalizability Theory and Weibull Reliability Model are the popularly used tools in ERP reliability analysis.

Generalizability Theory (GT) of ERP Analysis

Generalizability Theory (G Theory) was proposed by Clayson and Miller (2017). The theory provides algorithm for flexible and multidimensional approach in analysis of ERP reliability. G theory can be used through ERP analysis toolbox (open-sourced, matlab software) to measure contributions of multiple trials in an ERP system. The purpose of ERP analysis toolbox is to characterize dependability of ERP scores and use the scores to estimate ERP reliability based on study-by-study estimates. The toolbox determines the minimum number of trials needed to give a reliable ERP reliability score. The toolbox can measure the impact of group and event type reliability as well as measure psychometric features of an ERP system. The ERP data is stratified based on ERP systems groups and conditions so as to allow users compare ERP systems' reliability. Based on the conditions, some groups may require more trials than others to achieve acceptable reliability level.

Advantages of Generalizability Theory

1. The theory does not need parallel forms of equal means, variances, and covariance to measure ERP reliability
2. The theory can handle can be used to analyze ERP reliability in areas of unbalanced designs
3. The theory can be singly be used in ERP reliability analysis for designs with multiple sources of error
4. The theory can be used to analyze newly developed ERP systems

Weibull Reliability Model for System Analysis

Weibull Reliability Model analyses ERP reliability based on three factors; probability of operating without failure over specified time period, time interval between failures, if any within a specified time period and the number of defects in an infinite time period. Weibull Reliability Model considers ERP reliability as he ability of an ERP system to perform its required functions under stated conditions for a specified period of time (Livaja, Fertalj, & Urem, 2011).

Assumptions of Weibull Reliability Model

1. The occurrence of software failures follows an non-homogeneous Poisson process
2. There can be software failure during execution attributed to faults in the software
3. Software failure detection rate at any time is proportional to the number of remaining faults in the software at that time
4. When a software failure occurs, a debugging effort removes the faults immediately
5. For each debugging effort, some new faults may be introduced into the software system, regardless of the debugging outcome
6. The environment affects the unit failure detection rate

CONCLUSION

The implementation of a reliable ERP system enhances the core functional and operational requirements of a business. The reliability of ERP systems is adequately perceptible from the fact that they facilitate an organizations principal procedures. However, successful implementation of an ERP system has been a challenge for many organizations seeking to be competitive as it spans diverse business functions and different type of end users. Thus this chapter proposes to explore the impact, components and measures of reliability within business decision making environment. Is important to realize that information technology and information systems can be mismanaged and misapplied so that they create both technological and business failure.

REFERENCES

Al-Fawaz, K., Al-Salti, Z., & Eldabi, T. (2008). *Critical Success Factors in ERP Implementation: A Review.* European and Mediterranean Conference on Information Systems 2008 (EMCIS2008), Dubai, UAE.

Badewi, A., & Shehab, E. (2016). The impact of organizational project benefits management governance on ERP project success: Neo-institutional theory perspective. *International Journal of Project Management, 34*(3), 412–428.

Capaldo, G., & Rippa, P. (2015). Awareness of organisational readiness in ERP implementation process. *International Journal of Information Systems and Change Management, 7*(3), 224–241.

Capital, F. M. (2013). Kenafric Industries adopts SAP ERP Platform. *Capital News.* Retrieved from https://www.capitalfm.co.ke/business/2013/12/kenafric-industries-adopts-sap-erp-platform/

Costa, C. J., Ferreira, E., Bento, F., & Aparicio, M. (2016). Enterprise resource planning adoption and satisfaction determinants. *Computers in Human Behavior, 63,* 659–671.

Davenport, T. H., & Harris, J. G. (2007). *Competing on analytics: The new science of winning.* Harvard Business Press.

Erturk, E., & Arora, J. K. (2017). *An Exploratory Study on the Implementation and Adoption of ERP Solutions for Businesses.* arXiv preprint arXiv:1701.08329

Gupta, H., Aye, K. T., Balakrishnan, R., Rajagopal, S., & Nguwi, Y. Y. (2014). A Study of Key Critical Success Factors (CSFs) for Enterprise Resource Planning (ERP) Systems. *International Journal of Computer and Information Technology, 3*(4).

Harris, M. A., & Weistroffer, H. R. (2008). Does User Participation Lead to System Success? *Proceedings of the Southern Association for Information Systems Conference*, Richmond, VA.

Huang, T., & Yasuda, K. (2016). Comprehensive review of literature survey articles on ERP. *Business Process Management Journal, 22*(1), 2–32.

Kang'ethe, P. N. N. (2007). *An Evaluation of the Successful Implementation Of Enterprise Resource Planning System at HACO Industries.* Research Paper School of Business University of Nairobi.

Kilic, H. S., Zaim, S., & Delen, D. (2014). Development of a hybrid methodology for ERP system selection: The case of Turkish Airlines. *Decision Support Systems, 66*, 82–92.

Kutswa, C. E. (2011). *Challenges of Implementing Enterprise Resource Planning Strategy At The Kenya Electricity Generating Company.* Research Paper School of Business University of Nairobi.

Lotfy, M. A., & Halawi, L. (2015). A conceptual model to measure ERP user-value. *Issues in Information Systems, 16*(3), 54.

Matende, S., Ogao, P., & Nabukenya, J. (2015). User participation in ERP Implementation: A Case-based Study. *International Journal of Computer Applications Technology and Research, 4*(1), 24–29.

Momoh, A., Roy, R., & Shehab, E. (2010). Challenges in enterprise resource planning implementation: State-of-the-art. *Business Process Management Journal, 16*(4), 537–565.

Moon, Y. B. (2007). Enterprise Resource Planning (ERP): A review of the literature. *International Journal of Management and Enterprise Development, 4*(3), 235–264.

Muinde, C. M., Lewa, P., & Kamau, J. N. (2016). *The influence of top management support on knowledge sharing during the implementation of ERP systems in Kenya.* Academic Press.

Mungai, P. K. (2016). Challenges of Implementing Enterprise Resource Planning in Mombasa International Airport. *International Journal of Innovative Research and Development, 5*(6), 154–177.

Musyimi, N. D., & Odongo, W. O. (2015). Adoption of Enterprise Resource Planning Systems in Kenya: A Case of Selected Manufacturing Firms in Nairobi Metropolitan. *International Journal of Business Human Technology*, *5*(2), 24–32.

Njuguna, M. W. (2011). *Implementing enterprise resource planning system at Kenya Revenue Authority*. Research paper school of business University of Nairobi.

Nwankpa, J., & Roumani, Y. (2014). Understanding the link between organizational learning capability and ERP system usage: An empirical examination. *Computers in Human Behavior*, *33*, 224–234.

Nyagah, E. (2006). *An Investigation Of Critical Success Factors For Successful Implementation Of Enterprise Resource Planning (ERP) Systems in Kenya*. Research paper school of business University of Nairobi.

Nzuki, D. M., & Okelo-Odongo, W. (2015). *Adoption of Enterprise Resource Planning Systems in Kenya: A Case of Selected Manufacturing Firms in Nairobi Metropolitan*. Academic Press.

Ociepa-Kubicka, A. (2017). Advantages of using enterprise resource planning systems (ERP) in the management process. *World Scientific News*, *89*, 237–243.

Rajan, C. A., & Baral, R. (2015). Adoption of ERP system: An empirical study of factors influencing the usage of ERP and its impact on end user. *IIMB Management Review*, *27*(2), 105–117.

Rajan, C. A., & Baral, R. (2015). Adoption of ERP System: An Empirical Study of Factors Influencing the Usage of ERP and its Impact on End User. *IIMB Management Review*, *27*(2), 105–117.

Rerup Schlichter, B., & Kraemmergaard, P. (2010). A comprehensive literature review of the ERP research field over a decade. *Journal of Enterprise Information Management*, *23*(4), 486–520.

Ruivo, P., Oliveira, T., Johansson, B., & Neto, M. (2013). Differential effects on ERP post-adoption stages across Scandinavian and Iberian SMEs. *Journal of Global Information Management*, *21*(3), 1–20.

Ruivo, P., Oliveira, T., & Neto, M. (2012). ERP use and value: Portuguese and Spanish SMEs. *Industrial Management & Data Systems*, *112*(7), 1008–1025.

Shatat, A. S. (2015). Critical success factors in enterprise resource planning (ERP) system implementation: An exploratory study in Oman. *Electronic Journal of Information Systems Evaluation*, *18*(1), 36–45.

Verville, J., Palanisamy, R., Bernadas, C., & Halingten, A. (2007). ERP acquisition planning: A critical dimension for making the right choice. *Long Range Planning*, *40*(1), 45–63.

Wanyoike, F. W. (2017). *The Influence of Enterprise Resource Planning System on Organizational Performance: Case Study of Kenyan Engineering Consultancy Firms*. United States International University-Africa.

Yaghubi, S., Modiri, N., & Rafighi, M. (2014). Model Performance Indicators ERP Systems. *International Journal of Computer Science and Information Security*, *12*(1), 1–7.

Chapter 6
Evaluation of Employee Readiness for ERP Systems:
A Case of Kitale National Polytechnic

Stella Nafula Khaemba
Masinde Muliro University of Science and Technology, Kenya

ABSTRACT

Enterprise resource planning (ERP) systems are increasingly being adopted by many organizations. The cost, time, and effort of the organization need to be reflected in the uptake and use of the system by employees of the organizations in question. ERP system implementation readiness is positively associated with the ERP implementation success. It is therefore important to measure the success of such software in adopting firms which largely influenced by the readiness of the firm for ERPs. Many studies focus on other aspects of readiness leaving out the major players who are employees. This chapter discusses an effort towards extending CREM evaluation model for employee readiness with the aim of highlighting the role of their readiness in the overall success of ERP implementation. Research findings of this study help decision makers of organizations to attain a comprehensive picture about required actions to be accomplished for achieving readiness for implementing an ERP system.

DOI: 10.4018/978-1-5225-7678-5.ch006

INTRODUCTION

Enterprise Resource Planning system is a business management system that comprises integrated sets of comprehensive software and when successfully implemented, it can manage and integrate all the business functions within an organization (Shehab et al., 2004). ERP is an industry term for the broad set of activities supported by the multi-module application software that helps a manufacturer or a service provider manages the important parts of its business.

The benefits of ERP are claimed to include: significant improvements in quality and efficiency of customer service, production and distribution; cost reductions; improved decision-making; and enterprise agility (Kakouris et al., 2005). In addition, research findings shed new light on the productivity paradox associated with ERP systems and suggest that ERP adoption helps firms gain a competitive advantage over non-adopters (Hunton et al. 2003). ERP system is an important factor that enables a company to compete effectively in the global market (Rikhardson et al. 2006).

BACKGROUND

Kitale National Polytechnic is a middle-level training institution located in Kitale town in Trans Nzoia county. It has been in place since 1982 when it was initially established as a technical school that was later converted into a technical college. It has about 7 non-academic and 9 academic departments offering various courses at artisan, craft, certificate, diploma and higher diplomas. With an ICT department, the institution has various IT functions spanning from networking, database, and system management as well as ICT support services like maintenance, security among others. Kitale National Polytechnic has a student population of about 4000, 170 teaching staff Government hired and council hired as well as over 100 support staff on a permanent and casual basis.

The Institution rolled out an ERP system in 2009 called ABN developed by ABNO, a local ERPS software developer. Most of the departments rely on its 5 modules to run its daily operations. They include Admission, Examinations, Boarding, Library, and Finance. It also runs 2 stand-alone modules that link to the platform which are Timetabling and Meals Pay As You Eat (PAYE) system. Pre-implementation activities took place from 2007 to 2008. Data for this survey was collected during the post-implementation phase in June 2018 almost 9 years after the implementation phase beginning in January 2009.

Contrasted to universities, most middle-level colleges in Kenya have centralized curriculum development, examination as well as employer organizations or agencies. This creates a level of uniformity mostly in their processes and management structures. In addition, employee processes are largely similar and synchronized to academic calendars such as examination period, recruitment and student reporting, among others. Universities, on the other hand, have some independence in terms of curriculum development, staff employment and hence employee processes.

RELATED STUDIES

Several studies identify some of the advantages of ERP systems as common information access supported by a common DBMS, consistent and accurate data, and improved reports. There is reduced or no data and operations redundancy since modules access the same data from the central database and avoid multiple data inputs and update operations. Delivery and cycle time reduction is also realized by minimizing retrieving and reporting delays. Another advantage is cost reduction, Time savings, and improved control by enterprise-wide analysis of organizational decisions, easy adaptability (Kraft, 2001, Ferell, 2003, Matende, 2013, Tchokogué et al. 2005).

Nevertheless, ERPs have some disadvantages. The implementation cycle is Time-consuming, expensive where costs may vary from thousands of dollars to millions. Business process reengineering cost may be extremely high, Lack of conformity of the modules among others. The architecture and components of the selected system may at times not fully conform to the business processes, culture and strategic goals of the organization. In addition, Vendor dependence is high. Features and complexity ERP system may have too many features and modules so the user needs to consider carefully and implement the needful only. Scalability and global outreach as well as challenges of handling Extended ERP capability (Tchokogué et al. 2005).

Examining ERP implementation from a chronological process perspective aids in understanding when and how employee attitudes play an important role in determining implementation effectiveness. Herold et al. (1995) identified six phases of technology implementation. Pre-adoption is the stage at which organizations begin to consider the need to change technologies, identify technology options, and consider strategic directions. Once they have decided on an option, the result is an adoption. The adoption point marks the beginning of the pre-implementation phase.

This involves such activities as planning for the technology introduction, deciding on the role of the vendor and in-house resources in managing the introduction, providing preliminary training, planning the logistics of the change, deciding whether a pilot study will be used, and deciding whether everything will be changed at once or whether a gradual phase-in will be used. If a pilot study is used, it represents a distinct stage in the process. In the pilot study stage, employees see the technology for the first time, talk to their colleagues about it, and form impressions of how things are likely to change in the future. The next stage is the actual implementation, which may take a long period of time, and identifying when it ends may be difficult. The post-implementation stage, or ''routinization,'' represents a return to equilibrium— the new technology has been implemented, it is being used, and people are reaching whatever accommodation to it that they are likely to reach.

With time employee attitudes may suit what Goodman and Griffith (1991) describe as a ''normative consensus'', or agreement about the use and value of the new technology. Herold et al. (1995) suggest that the pre-implementation phase is very important because of its role in shaping the attitudes of those who will be charged with the implementation. They add that it may be the beginning for change in attitudes that shape future implementation phases and may be central in shaping behaviors early on (for instance, spreading of negative rumors, involvement in early planning and design phases, resistance to informational attempts, among others). In fact, factors that influence attitudes or predispositions toward an ERP system in the pre-implementation stage are important determinants of implementation behaviors. Employees who have greater levels of involvement in the pre-implementation stage are likely to have more direct experience, or first-hand learning with the new ERP system (Herold, 1995).

Existing Gaps

Studies on ERPs have been focused on Small and Medium Enterprises (SMEs). Few studies have been done in the education sector with a majority highlighting higher institutions of learning leaving out middle-level Colleges (Neilsen, 2003, Rabbai, 2009). Nevertheless, in education management, the ERP concept is quickly being embraced. Higher education institutions have implemented ERP systems in advancing their procedures and branding them more transparent and well-organized. For instance, the Information System and Application development in Albaha University have positive factors that are believed may support the improvement of the ERP systems.

According to Matende et al (2013), ERP systems for higher education development in the direction of support for key administrative and academic services. He adds that the core of such a system usually supports minimal student administration (enrolment procedures and student enrolment, financial support for students, student data), human resource management (monitoring of employees) and finance (accounting, payments, investments, budget). He further argues that it is possible to include some other programme add-ons, e.g. assets management (contracts, subsidies, grants, etc.) or for monitoring student and developmental services of institutions (Matende et al. 2013). According to ECAR organization, the main advantages of ERP for higher education institutions are, Improved information access for planning and managing the institution; improved services for the faculty, students and employees; Lower business risks; increased income and decreased expenses due to improved efficiency. Some authors describe the implementation of ERP solutions in higher education institutions as extremely difficult. Expenses and risks involved are high, whereas the return on investments is medium to long-term (Ferrell, 2003).

EMPLOYEE READINESS FOR ERPS

E-readiness assessments are useful in understanding and identifying the most key and relevant ICT based development opportunities. For example, to put ICT to effective use, a country must be 'e-ready' in terms of infrastructure, the accessibility of ICT to the population at large and the effect of the legal and regulatory framework on ICT use, benchmarking progress, collaborations, determining vision, strategy, and priorities (Docktor, 2002). An e-readiness assessment should lead to the development of a strategy and the preparation of an action plan that would address the opportunities and constraints identified in order to further the objectives of a country in the area of ICTs. Furthermore, e-readiness assessment enables governments as well as organizations to set, measure and achieve realistic goals for an information society, information-based economy, or e-government. ERP system implementation readiness is positively associated with ERP implementation Success (Bahari et al. 2013).

It is important to develop and conduct an e-readiness assessment so that the results can be leveraged to catalyze action, improve global competitiveness, and use limited resources wisely. In addition, a well-conceived assessment will map an organization's regional and global position, improve competitive strengths and promote those areas where a country has an advantage over others. Understanding other e-readiness strengths and weaknesses can also help an organization to leapfrog technologies and policy decisions to position itself ahead of its neighbors. Moreover, e-readiness assessments can help stakeholders make difficult decisions on how to use scarce resources and how to turn existing strengths into new revenues (Muketha et al, 2017). E-readiness assessments can also reveal which bottlenecks are worth the investment of time and money to be removed, and which can be worked around. Using a globally recognized e-readiness assessment methodology can be helpful in securing the necessary funding to develop an e-strategy and implement e-programs (Bahari, 2015).

EXISTING MODELS

A quick review of the literature addressing ERP systems implementation reveals that more focus has been directed to success or failure including critical success factors (CSFs), success measurement and evaluation of ERP systems. There is a paucity of studies on user participation and the contribution of users towards the successful implementation of ERP systems. (Matende et al 2013). And as such, there are several models advanced by various authors for readiness evaluation that especially emphasize the criticality of performing a deep analysis of a firm's readiness to undertake an ERP initiative.

Koh and Prybutok (2003) proposed a simple Three-Ring Model captures all Internet applications in three categories of Internet use. The categories are informational use, transactional use, and operational use. Informational use is in which organizations disseminate information to educate, entertain, influence, or reach their citizens. Transactional use is where they support a coordinated sequence of user and system activities to provide service and transfer value. Operational use is when an agency provides a new mechanism for conducting business operations by integrating IS, human intellect, and other resources into synergistic networks

A good readiness assessment should provide detailed answers to two fundamental questions: What is a firm's current ERP capability? And what changes must be in place before embarking on an ERP initiative? In addition, it should focus on the user of the ERPs. A model to assess ERP readiness is developed based upon the premise that business value should be enhanced through the alignment of complementary factors occurring along four dimensions, techno ware, human ware, info ware, and orgaware. According to researches by Somers and Nelson (2004) and Tesch, et al. (2007), the organizational readiness for ERP deployment within an organization is essential to know a readiness of an organization prior to the commence of the project and to identify as early as possible probable problems. The problems may affect the implementation outcome. Therefore, the organizational readiness is expected to meaningfully contribute to the success the ERP implementation.

CREM MODEL

Citizen Readiness Evaluation Model (CREM) is an evaluation model for an institution to assess how its users are ready to use an ERP system they intend to roll out or are already running. CREM evaluates and ranks an entity's, country or agency potential measured on the basis of four levels which are: Very Readiness, Low Readiness, High Readiness, and Very High Readiness. The CREM proposes that an assessment scope and details be stated against well-defined institutional objectives. This assessment should follow systematic criteria that reflect readiness for achieving precise objectives and requirements of the given institution.

CREM is an extension of a three-dimension evaluation framework by Yesser (2007) on the Saudi e-government program. The assessment methodology presented offers a comprehensive set of functions and principles to design the assessment, decide on evaluation criteria, conduct the assessment, obtain results, analyzing the results and finally generate the findings of the agency e-readiness status which considers the agencies clients who in this case are the employees. In this case, an ERP can be considered as a system that is accessed by clients who are the employees with the institution to get a service that enables them to carry out their mandate in within the institution.

CREM model was extended to have the following four dimensions namely; Infrastructural dimension, Architectural dimension, Process dimension, and Citizen dimension. These percentages are derived from the model where for each dimension, the calculation is done for the scores of its factors. The model proposes an average of the sum total of critical factors required to ensure certain dimension functions fully which point to its readiness. The institution's final score is calculated through the aggregation of the four dimensions.

For instance, the architectural dimension is assigned an overall score of 25%. Then each contributing aspects were broken down such that service for availability of automated service, the share of data input by database queries and availability of portals was awarded. The Layered structure of the ERP is then assessed based on the type of Operating systems used-desktop/server, the Communication system used and Data exchange standards used.

The infrastructure dimension was also assigned an overall score of 25%, with individual contributing factors such as the basic hardware/software, ratio of desktop or laptop/employee in a the institution, mainframe/server availability, percentage of departments/offices connected to Intranet, percentage of departments/offices connected to the Internet were individually scored to give an aggregate of 25%.

On process dimension, the share of service with IT support, the data and information flow where the existence or lack of data exchange among entities or agencies and the format used, the share of manual data input required in processing a service or the lack of it and the method of data notification available accumulatively gave the overall score of 25%.

Finally, user readiness was awarded 25%. Four major issues were found to be key in evaluating user readiness for most institutions. These are: service awareness, accessibility, affordability and ability to use (necessary skills), Knowledge of the existence of any given system, how to access the services or functions, the benefits of accessing the service through a given system platform as opposed to the traditional methods is key.

Accessibility to the service in question is a major factor. Awareness of staff of Service or function availability was evaluated on the basis of the number of programs, initiatives or activities for awareness creations, attitude and/or behavior change as well as encouraging adoption of online versus convention way of carrying out daily duties. The cost of service access (quantified in terms of time and effort required), as well as consumption in terms of frequency or dependency on the system, were then evaluated on the basis of overall expected costs from the citizen/user's perspective. The ICT Development index is also used to rate the individual user ability and skills to inform the citizen readiness dimension of the ability to use an ERP system.

The percentages were transformed to score as shown

0-24.9% 1 (Very Low)
25-49.9% 2 (Low)
50-74.0% 3 (High)
75-100% 4 (Very high)

ICT Development Index (IDI) was a preferred measure for the skills, access and actual use of ICT systems for the catchment areas of the citizen. IDI index is scored on a scale of 0-10, hence mapped to readiness score as follows:

Score IDI index
Very Low (1) 0-2.49
Low (2) 2.5 - 4.99
High (3) 5.0 - 7.49
Very high (4) 7.5 – 10

Critiquing the CREM Model

CREM has demonstrated some strength drawn from its inherent ability to adapt to different institutional environments. Factors that aggregate to ensure efficiency is achieved along the four dimensions vary from institution to institution. These can be added or eliminated appropriately to capture what suits the organization hence giving a true readiness picture of the institution or its employees. Secondly, the model is administered as a survey. The benefit of this is that there are higher chances of getting accurate information that can be used to accurately score the institution or its employees than if it was directly given as a scoring test where one would give inaccurate information to achieve a better score. Lastly, the survey can use a 5 point or even 7 points Linkert scale to capture accurately the opinion of the issues being surveyed.

The model weakness is that relies on a simple mean to arrive at a final score of each dimension and eventually the overall readiness score. Secondly, the dimensions have been assigned a 25% maximum score which may not be the case for all institutions. The further hypothetical test need to be done to ascertain to what extent each dimension affects the readiness for ERP in one sector say the education sector as compared to SMEs or middle-level companies

METHODOLOGY

The study employed a survey approach by administering a survey to various employees in the institution. A survey was carried out in the institution to establish the level of readiness for ERP. The study adopted a mixed design approach here both quantitative and qualitative approaches were used. Purposive stratified random sampling was done to give rise to a sample of 51 teaching staff and 30 non-teaching staff were interviewed a 21% sample size which sought to ensure a +/-3% margin of error and Confidence interval (CI) at 90%.

FINDINGS

Evaluating Employee Readiness for ERPs: Case of Kitale National Polytechnic

A survey was carried out in the institution to establish the level of readiness for ERP. Responses of around 71% were positive as the remaining percentage excused themselves or opted out from participating in the survey. The reasons given for this

Table 1.

No	Profile	Frequency	Percentage
1	Level of position: • Operational Level • Tactical Level • Strategic Level	18 52 10	22% 66% 12%
2	Number of years worked for the company • Less than 5 years • 5 – 10 years •More than 10 years	23 29 27	29% 37% 34%
3	Educational Level: • High School • Certificate/ Diploma • Degree/Professional Training • Master Degree	0 45 29 2	0% 56% 37% 1%
4	Gender: • Male • Female	36 44	45% 55%

ranged from being busy, not conversant with the system, fear of unknown especially from non-teaching staff among others. The CREM model was then applied in assessing readiness for ERP in an organization by mapping their responses on various factors onto indicators that were then used to score their level of readiness for ERP system in the college as well as the institution's readiness score.

A survey instrument, an interview schedule was used to collect data from the employees. The researcher conducted a one on one interview where information. The researcher in conjunction with organization officials identified units to survey: library (and support functions), registrar (admissions) operations (and support functions), examination and boarding operations. These units were selected because they were believed to be more directly affected by the introduction of the new ERP system. In addition, a detailed interview was held with the system developer support staff, the institutions MIS officer as well as key administrative staff for the purposes of providing background information about the system such as a history of the ERP, the technical details as well as administrative details of the same.

Summary of the sample profile of the study

The survey administered question that aided in scoring the readiness of the institution for ERP as well as individual employees on various dimensions proposed by the CREM model. The schedule used a 7 point Linkert scale that aided in capturing the opinions of respondents on varying degrees. Sample of the questions administered was;

How would you describe your level of ICT literacy skills, 83% agree to be ICT literate catering for extremely satisfied and very satisfied and just satisfied

Do you think that ABN is beneficial in your work? 88% agreed that the system was beneficial to their work,

Have you used ABN before? 28% reported to have used an ERP before, 68% said were not sure while 4% had never used any. Those that had used identified systems such as POS systems in SME, hospital billing systems, secondary school management system and industrial MISs such as ......

Were you inducted on using the system before or after deployment - 78% confirmed that they were inducted on using the system before deployment. Most of the induction was done by fellow staff mates.

What support do you get from the ICT support staff – system upgrades were reportedly done annually by the system vendors while most of the daily support and assistance is given by ICT staff as well as the institution's MIS officer.

*The rating of the system's ability on a scale of 1 to 7(**7 =extremely satisfied, 6=very satisfied, 5=satisfied, 4= neutral, 3 =dissatisfied, 2= very dissatisfied, 1= extremely dissatisfied** for the following ease of access to required service or function:*

Customer satisfaction after serving them using ABN,

Other aspects such as the speed of performing a given task using the system,

Frequency of system downtimes

The level of support for the ICT help desk were averagely rated.

DISCUSSION

The survey revealed that 68% of the respondents who most frequently interacted with the system were tactical level employees. 71% had worked at the institution for over 5years which gave the researcher more confidence with their level of experience with the ERP system. 56% had an average education level of certificate and diplomas while 38% had degrees and masters. 6% could not clearly confirm their educational status. The gender distribution was 45% male and 55% female. This was further disaggregated to reveal 56% male and 44%female from the teaching staff while 72% female and 28% male in from the non-teaching staff were involved in the survey.

From the findings, it was found that staff both teaching and non-teaching scored a low readiness for the ERP. It was also found that staff can be motivated to embrace the use of ERP once the system demonstrates the efficiency it provides to their carrying out their mandates. Additionally, workers tend to learn best from peers drawing from their experiences better than when inducted by the vendor or ICT experts. Furthermore, the non-teaching staff was found to be more conversant with the system as compared to the teaching staff. This could be attributed to the fact that very few teaching staff interact with other modules of the system besides the examination module. 71% of the lecturers agreed that they used the system once or twice a term. In comparison, 86% of the non-teaching staff respondents reported using the system on a daily basis. This gives them more experience and exposure to the system due to their nature of work

Using the model, the institution readiness score for ERP was found to be 2.5. On scoring individual employee sampled, the other three dimensions being constant, the study expanded the citizen readiness dimension to cater for other aspects of ERP use: This included easy of navigating the ABN system, awareness of all functions in the modules they use, awareness on other function and modules available in the ERP besides what they use, ability to perform minor system troubleshoot, level of dependency on ICT Help Desk support, ability to operate with back up mechanism or system bypasses in the event of system downtimes or hitches as well as relevant aptitude tests. The findings revealed that more than 52% would be rated as lowly ready for ERP. The individual score has been left out for confidentiality purposes but the findings point to the fact that the greatest ERP post-implementation challenges could be attributed to the system users' readiness for the ERP.

At inception, a few key staff drawn from both the teaching and non-teaching staff were trained on the ABN system. Further new employees are often inducted on how to use the system. Due to high turnover, some new employees not inducted in time and are forced to learn on the job or from the personal experience of others with the system. This leads to challenges such as a lack of exploiting some functions of the system. In addition, the assumption that ICT skills are adequate for an employee to use any system was found to be a great misconception. Another challenge mentioned was the high-level vendor and ICT support staff dependency for even very minor system configurations problem. Very few employees admitted to being able to perform minor troubleshooting in the event of the system downtimes or errors. In addition, the need to add or include more functionalities to the system such as adding as Small Text Messaging Service could take a long time since the system is rigid and highly controlled by the vendor. However, this also is a plus for the securing of the system.

CONCLUSION AND RECOMMENDATION

It is a fact that ERP systems are increasingly being adopted by many organizations. The cost implication of rolling out such initiatives, the time and effort of the organization need to be reflected in the uptake and use of the same by employees of the organizations in question. Besides an institution being ready for ERP implementation, its employees new and old should be brought along the implementation journey. Their readiness for the system is equally important. CREM model advocates for the consideration of four dimensions of readiness namely architectural, infrastructure, process, and user readiness.

Major ERP post-implementation challenges can be addressed if employee readiness is assessed in time. This can be done periodically since as it is with many organizations, employee turnover is expected and even with induction done at inception, new employees, as well as the old ones, need to keep abreast of the new aspects on a system. With the high rate of changes in trends in market demands, the nature of clientele and ICT Technology, in particular, an institution's attempt to adjust to suit such changes should bear in mind the system users who are the employees. Frequent retraining, system drills, and workshops should be encouraged. Furthermore, team teaching and sharing of best practices should be encouraged among employees while striving to wean the institution from high vendor or ERP developer's dependency.

The study recommends that further studies be done in this area to ascertain to what extent the user readiness, as well as other dimensions, affects the overall institution readiness for ERP systems. Comparative studies can be done to assess the level of ERP adoption and use in middle-level colleges, areas that little has been done; many pieces of research have a focus on SMEs and institutions of higher learning such as universities. The CREM model should be tried on various institutions other than those in education sectors to further strengthen and critique its applicability in evaluating employee readiness for ICT systems.

REFERENCES

Bahari, A., & Baharuddin, K. (2013). Enterprise Resource Planning (ERP) System Implementation Readiness: Institution Of Higher Learning In Malaysia. *International Journal Of Multidisciplinary Thought, 3*(4), 157–166.

Docktor, R. (2002). *E-readiness in 2002: Defining and achieving your e-fitness goals.* Available at http://www.ip3.org/pub/docktor.html

Ferrell, G. (2003). *Enterprise Systems in Universities: Panacea or Can of Worms?* JISC infoNet Publication.

Goodman, P. S., & Griffith, T. L. (1991). A process approach to the implementation of new technology. *Journal of Engineering and Technology Management, 8*(3-4), 261–285. doi:10.1016/0923-4748(91)90014-I

Hawking & Stein. (2004) Hawking, P. and Stein, A. 2004. Revisiting ERP Systems: Benefits Realization. *Proceedings of the 37th Hawaii International Conference on System Sciences.*

Herold, D. M., Farmer, S. M., & Mobley, M. I. (1995). Pre-implementation attitudes toward the introduction of robots in a unionized environment. *Journal of Engineering and Technology Management, 12*(3), 155–173. doi:10.1016/0923-4748(95)00008-7

Hunton, J. E., Lippincott, B., & Reck, J. L. (2003). Enterprise resource planning systems: Comparing the firm performance of adopters and nonadopters. *International Journal of Accounting Information Systems, 4*(3), 165–184. doi:10.1016/S1467-0895(03)00008-3

Kakouris, A. P., & Polychronopoulios, G. (2005). Enterprise Resource Planning (ERP) system: An Effective Tool for Production Management. *Management Research News, 28*(6), 66–78. doi:10.1108/01409170510784878

King, P. (2002). *The promise and Performance of Enterprise Systems in Higher Education, Respondent Summary.* ECAR Respondent Summary. Retrieved from http://www.educause.edu/ir/library/pdf/ecar _so/ers/ers0202/EKF0204.pdf

Koh & Prybutok. (2003). *The three-ring model and development of an instrument.* Academic Press.

Kraft, C. L. (2001). *Executive ERP.* Retrieved from http://www.oracle.com/oramag/profit/ 99-May/index.html?p29ind.html

Matende, S., & Ogao, P. (2013). Enterprise Resource Planning (ERP) System Implementation: A Case for User Participation. *Procedia Technology, 9*, 518–526. doi:10.1016/j.protcy.2013.12.058

Muketha, G. M., Matoke, N., & Khaemba, S. N. (n.d.). Factors affecting citizen readiness for E-government Systems in Kenya. *Journal of Research in Engineering and Applied Science.*

Muscatello, J., & Chen, I. (2008). A Case Analysis of ERP Post-Implementation Issues Vis-À-Vis Muscatello and Parente's Propositions. *International Journal of Enterprise Information Systems.*

Muscatello, J., & Chen, I. (2008). Enterprise Resource Planning (ERP) Implementations: Theory and Practice.‖. *International Journal of Enterprise Information Systems, 4*, 63–78. doi:10.4018/jeis.2008010105

Nielsen, J. L., Beekhuyzen, J., & Goodwin, M. (2005). The Evolution of Enterprise Wide Systems within Australian Higher Education. In L. von Hellens, S. Nielsen, & J. Beekhuyzen (Eds.), *Qualitative Case Studies on Implementation of Enterprise Wide Systems*. Hershey, PA: Idea Group Publishing.

PricewaterhouseCoopers. (2005). ERP Implementation in the Mid-Market Segment. PricewaterhouseCoopers (P) Ltd.

Shehab, E. M., Sharp, M. W., Supramaniam, L., & Spedding, T. A. (2004). Enterprise Resource Planning: An Integrative Review. *Business Process Management*, *10*(4), 359–386. doi:10.1108/14637150410548056

Somers, T. M., & Nelson, K. G. (2004). A taxonomy of players and activities across the ERP project life cycle. *Information & Management*, *41*(3), 257–278. doi:10.1016/S0378-7206(03)00023-5

Umble, E. J., Haft, R. R., & Umble, M. M. (2003). Enterprise Resource Planning: Implementation Procedures and Critical Success Factors. *European Journal of Operational Research*, *146*(2), 241–257. doi:10.1016/S0377-2217(02)00547-7

Wu, J.-H., & Wang, Y.-M. (2003). Enterprise resource planning experience in Taiwan: an empirical study and comparative analysis. In R. H. Sprague Jr. (Ed.), *Proceedings of the 36th. Hawaii International Conference on Systems Sciences*. IEEE Computer Society Press.

Wu & Wang. (2005). Measuring ERP success: The key-users' viewpoint of the ERP to produce a viable IS in the organization. *Computers in Human Behavior*.

Yesser, The Saudi e-Government Program. (2007). *IT Readiness Assessment for government institutions*. Safar.

APPENDIX

Figure 1. A screenshot of the Kitale National Polytechnic ABN system

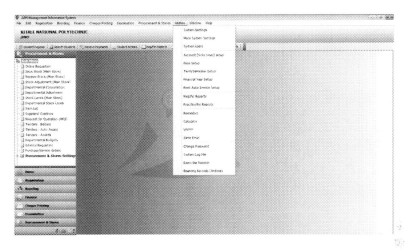

Section 2
User Perceptions and Usability Evaluation

Chapter 7
ERP User Perceptions and Service Delivery Challenges

Amos Chege Kirongo
Meru University of Science and Technology, Kenya

Guyo Sarr Huka
Meru University of Science and Technology, Kenya

ABSTRACT

This chapter introduces the service delivery challenges experienced by users of enterprise resource planning systems (ERP) by discussing the user perceptions. The authors administered questionnaires to users of ERP systems and user perception of ERPs was found to affect them in service delivery. Software complexity, software usability, and user resistance were found out as challenges contributing the challenge of service delivery. Attribution theory, diffusion of innovation theory, and compatibility maturity model are discussed; existing theories are discussed in the chapter. Findings are outlined and conclusion made based on the questionnaires addressed to the respondents.

DOI: 10.4018/978-1-5225-7678-5.ch007

INTRODUCTION

Generally, individuals tend to interpret their sensory impression in order to give meaning to their environments thus influencing groups and organizations at large to think in certain way regarding their daily works. Application of Enterprise Resource Planning (ERP) software in a business function forms important part of such environment which is perceived to aid in enhancing efficiency and effectiveness of academic and support service activities, support decision making and further meant to improve their Return on Investments (ROI). Realization of these objectives is largely dependent on the perceivers of ERP. The programme developers, academia, support service staff in universities and university students hold certain attitudes, motives, interests, experience and expectation of the ERP to deliver expected result. On the other hand, ERP programme is viewed to be the solution to complex data management and source of competent decision making by managers. Reliability of this view is subject to novelty of the programme, past successes associated with the programme, size and complexity of the functions in an organization. However, the overriding determinant will be the situation in organizations that embrace application of the ERP, including appropriate timing for introduction, work setting, organizational structure and socio-technical environment prevailing. Thus, analysis of ERP effectiveness and efficiency necessarily have to employ multi-faceted approach encompassing the synergy and integration of human, technical, social, structural and leadership variables of an organization.

Features that have made ERP systems attractive for adoption and implementation within universities include: a common data set, standardized data definitions, adaptability of the system and external systems intercommunication (Basir, Khoumbati, Ismaili, & Nizamani, 2014). Functional processes within a university context include and are not limited to student management, faculty management, human resource, finance, procurement, assets management, library services and research. In the adoption and use of Enterprise Resource Planning systems (ERPs), some of the benefits enjoyed by Universities include easier and fast access of information for better planning and management of the institution; improved services to students, faculty and other administration staff; better ways of risk management and improved data management for better decision making (Robert Kvavik, 2003).

Service delivery management in ERP faces a myriad of challenges in the quest towards automation of manual processes. It affects the areas of customers, projects, resources and programs. The challenges surround the areas of communication, relationship, problem identification and solution, planning, 24/7 support, technology, implementation, quality and integration (Sanjay, 2003). However, these challenges are both real and perceived. Therefore, management of ERPs service delivery, ought to functionally discriminate between perceived challenges and real challenges that hinders effective development and implementation of ERP.

Economic Success perception of ERP systems have a direct impact on productivity, fulfillment of industry specific requirements for documentation and traceability of business processes, quality, and customer satisfaction. In addition, it will significantly contribute towards enhancing quality work life, thus promoting conducive work environment.

With the growing complex business environment having different functional areas and requiring more inter-functional communication through sharing of enterprise data across the organization, Enterprise Resource Planning systems (ERPs) have become the obvious choice in managing organizational data and business practices (Perera & Withanage, 2008). Enterprise Resource Planning Systems (ERPs) are tools that integrate functional processes within an organization or institution to enable greater efficiencies to be achieved (Izamani, Khoumbati, Ismaili, & Amani, 2013). Just like corporate businesses, Universities are facing similar challenges in achieving operational excellence, reducing costs and creating a competitive edge for her. To increase on their efficiencies and competitiveness, Universities have replaced and /or integrated their existing information systems with ERPs.

Challenges faced in implementing the ERP systems include complexity of the system, lack of user training, low number of technical staff, poor support from consultancy / vendors, and poor support from management (Omuono, 2015). Much of the literature available on ERPs is on the adoption and implementation stages (Chian-Son Yu, 2005) and hence the need for the researchers to conduct and add to literature, research on issues surrounding post implementation success of ERPs.

Measuring success of information systems has been widely researched and various models developed over the years. Some of them include the Technology Acceptance Model (TAM) developed in 1989 by Davis, the DeLone and McLean (D&M) model developed in 1992 and reviewed ten years later, and many other researchers who have reviewed the D&M model for different contexts. The D&M Model has been used widely in analyzing the success of an information system (Petter, DeLone & McLean, 2008) and therefore can be applied to measuring the success of ERPs, which are integrated information systems. It measures project success in the following six dimensions: system quality, information quality, service quality, system use, user satisfaction and net benefits.

CHALLENGES OF SOFTWARE COMPLEXITY, USABILITY AND USER RESISTANCE

This chapter introduces software complexity, software usability and user resistance challenges and discusses them here below.

Software Complexity: the complexity of an ERP Software results from information load. Information load is affected by the data amount and the complexity of tasks as affected by the quantity of different repeated dimensions (Mittelstädt, Brauner, Blum, & Ziefle, 2015).

Software Usability: user experience and cognitive abilities affects users' ability to process information presented in an ERP system hence affecting the quality of their decisions. This is mostly interpreted by implementers as user resistance (Weerakkody, Irani, Kapoor, Sivarajah, & Dwivedi, 2016).

User Resistance: User resistance arising from fear of the unknown, structural inertia, as well as organizational culture of resistance to adoption of new culture and new innovations (Somers & Nelson, 2004) would certainly affect the rate of technological adoption. Challenges caused by lack of experience and learning curving occasionally discourages uptake of ERP, thus energizing chances of unintended resistance to new idea uptake.

LITERATURE REVIEW

Attribution theory, diffusion of innovation theory and compatibility maturity model are broadly discussed in this section based on relevant literature.

Attribution Theory

In order to understand the roles of perception in ERP application in organization, Attribution Theory (Sandra Graham, 2014) is proposed. In a work environment, individuals tend to observe behaviour and attempt to determine whether the behaviours is internally or externally caused. Internally caused behaviours are those that an individual can control and modify, while externally caused behaviours are those that individuals cannot control and modify (Aswathappa, 2008). Thus, ERP programme developers, trainers and champions as well as users of the programme would ideally have explanation for the success or failure of the programme. However, the theory further explains discriminating criterion for ascertaining the sources of individual behaviours as influenced by perception. The assessment mainly uses behaviourial characteristics that is distinctive (whether individuals display different behaviuor in different situation), consensus (degree of replicability by others) and consistency (degree of repeat behaviours). Knowing the source of behaviour whether external or internal is important for managers and users in an organization so that appropriate enablers, both human and non-human are designed to enhance successful implementation of an ERP programme. Therefore, implementers of ERP programmes and users in organization needed to be cognizant of these behavioural dispositions which could be managed through Human Resource Development (HRD) interventions.

Diffusion of Innovations Theory (DOI)

This is a theory that is widely used in the social science field. It is a theory that seeks to explain how an idea or a product gains momentum and spreads through a specific population or social system as used in understanding technology diffusion and adoption (Sahin, 2006). This process is termed as "an uncertainty reduction process" with five attributes of innovation that comprise of relative advantage, compatibility, complexity, triability, and observability, and as Rogers (2003) states that "individuals' perception of these characteristics predict the rate of adoption of innovation."

Compatibility Maturity Model (CMM)

In this theory, (Schniederjans & Yadav, 2013) suggests the maturity level of an IT innovation can only be achieved after going through six levels; level 0 to level 5. Level 0 meaning no IT architecture of maturity exists, Level 1 is where the software process is chaotic and few processes have been defined hence the success of the implementation depends on individual effort. Level 2 (repeatable level) is where the project process has been established in line with cost, schedule and functionality. Level 3 (defined software level), is where management and engineering activities are documented, standardized and integrated into a standard software process. Level 4 (the managed level), is detailed measures of product quality and software processes, which are understood and controlled. Finally, level 5 (the optimizing level) is where there is continuous process improvement as a result of quantitative feedback using innovative ideas and technologies. Other theories that support this knowledge include the strategic choice theory and contingency theory. Successful transition of the six stages is a function of the developer and the user perception in

Figure 1. The research methodology (Khaleel, 2012)

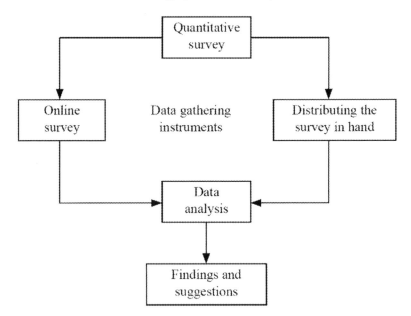

the larger environment of the organization that either promotes or dissuades uptake of a new idea. ERP implementers need to be conscious of challenges that come with stage transition as well as perceptions adduced out of beneficiaries' cognitive ability and attitude towards the functionality of the ERP program.

Several research studies have been carried out to identify the critical success factors (Ağaoğlu, Yurtkoru, & Ekmekçi, 2015) associated to the implementation, and usage of ERP. However the perception of the users is not considered in most of the studies yet in order to ensure successful implementation of the ERP it is vital to consider the users concerned during the implementation.

METHODOLOGY

Descriptive survey research design was used to capture ERP user perceptions in institutions of higher learning as proposed by (Bryman, 2008, Saunders, Lewia, & Thornbill, 2009). In particular the perceptions regarding ERP development, management and usage was studied in retrospect with Universities that are already using ERP as samples. The target population was staff, students and ERP managers in the sample Universities (Meru University of Science and Technology (MUST), Kenya

Figure 2. How users rated the level of complexity of the ERP system in their organization

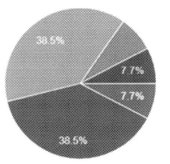 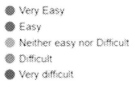

Methodist University, Karatina University and Muranga University of Technology). Purposive sampling was used to select ERP managers and simple random sampling to select staff and student's ERP users totaling to 120 samples.

Online survey questionnaires capturing ERP users and managers perception and service delivery challenges was posted to the sample respondents. Descriptive statistics (frequencies, means and percentages) and inferential statistics (ANNOVA) was employed to interpret the data. The online survey questionnaire was piloted using twenty (20) respondents from IT department in MUST. Validity and reliability test was conducted as recommended by (Kasomo, 2006). Research permit was obtained from National Council for Science, Technology and innovation (NACOSTI) and adherence to ethical research practices was guided by Meru University of Science and Technology Institutional Research Ethical Committee procedure (MIREC, 2017).

Steps for conducting the online survey exercise was carried out as guided by (Khaleel, 2012).

ERP USER PERCEPTIONS

Questionnaires addressed to respondents sought to find out the user perception with regards to complexity of the ERP systems they use in their organization. 38.5% indicated that the system is easy, neither easy nor difficult respectively while 7.7% indicated that the ERP system is very difficult to use while another 7.7% indicated that it is very easy to use. The findings above show the perception of the users about the systems enabled using ERPs is that it is an easy to use system and can be utilized by any user interested in adoption of this solution. However there still exists users that find it difficult while others find it neither easy nor hard to use.

Figure 3. How users would rate usability levels of the ERP system

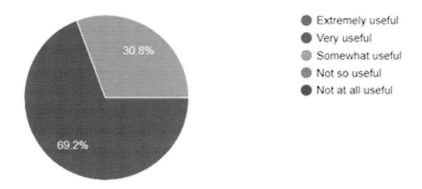

Consequently 69.2% of respondents indicated that ERP systems are very useful where as 30.8% indicated that the ERP systems are somewhat useful. The users further indicate that it is easy to use this kind of systems whereas others find it somewhat useful. This can be handled through constant training of the uses with regards to the usability of this systems.

Constant Training of the users results to uptake of the new technological change and a change of mindset towards usability of the system. Complexity of the system can be unmasked through adoption of better methods of delivery of user manuals through video tutorials and manuals. Identification of champions in each section results to user acceptance of the system as a result of receiving guidance from existing expert users.

Figure 4. How users rated the degree of user resistance to the adoption of the ERP system

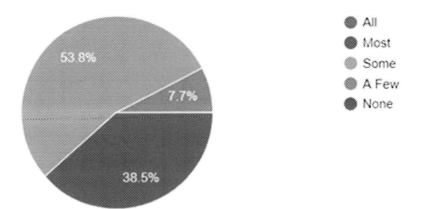

Figure 5. Degree of diffusion of the ERP with relation to the level of uptake

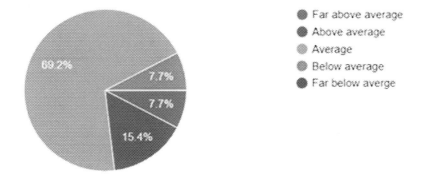

As per the above results, the 38.5% users that rate the complexity as neither easy nor difficult can be reduced through ensuring that users constantly interact with the system at different intervals and also through motivating the users to ensure that they are able to utilize the possibilities of the system.

When asked about their perception on user resistance to adoption of the ERP system, 53.8% of the respondents indicated that some staff resisted adoption and 38.5% indicated that most of the staff members resisted adoption of the ERP system. The findings indicate that there still exists some level of resistance to the adoption of the ERP system among users. The resistance necessitated by deliverables that need to be constantly addressed during the system implementation inorder that the resistance to the system can be minimized to a reasonable level.

Usability levels of ERP systems differ as a result of the user mindset and efficiency of the implementation team. Levels of ERP System usability can either increase or lower based on the ability of the user uptake and acceptance. Resistance to the system results to lower levels of usability as opposed to receptive users.

The 69.2% of the users that rate the usability level to be very useful can be increased through involvement of the top management in ensuring the usability levels are practiced through leadership from the top. Inclusion of all levels of users will also enhance the usability levels.

Respondents indicated that there was average degree of diffusion of the ERP at 69.2% with relation to the level of uptake. Diffusion of the technological solution is found to be wanting due to the aforementioned challenges. For the technology to diffuse efficiently measures have to be put in place to improve on the user perception of the system in order to improve the level of uptake of the technology among the users.

Figure 6. Degree of the attitude of the users in ERP uptake

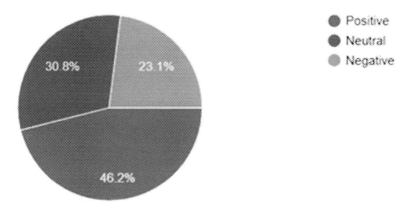

From the above statistics, the 38.5% of the users can be lowered through training for change of mindset for adoption. The 53.8% can also be lowered through change of mindset trainings and consistent user education and training, for uptake of the proposed ERP System.

The attitude of the users was tested in the questionnaire addressed to respondents and it was discovered that only 46.2% of the users had a positive attitude towards the use of the ERP system. The attitude of the users is average but can be improved by addressing the issues that are making the users not to fully enjoy the functionality of the systems as pertains to the level of attitude of users. With a positive attitude in the usage of the system, users can be able to utilize the system more efficiently and effectively, hence enabling the service delivery target.

Figure 7. Perception of the ERP implementers with regards to functionality

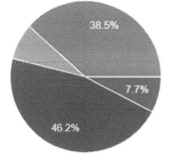
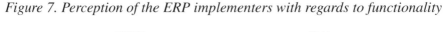

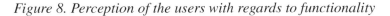

Figure 8. Perception of the users with regards to functionality

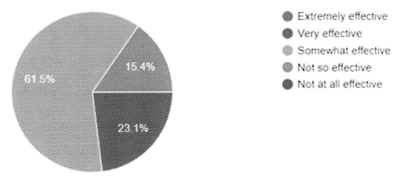

- Extremely effective
- Very effective
- Somewhat effective
- Not so effective
- Not at all effective

ERP SERVICE DELIVERY CHALLENGES

The perception of the implementers with regards to functionality was tested among the respondents and it was discovered that 38.5% of the users found it difficult to navigate through the implemented functionalities of the ERP system. Implementers mostly operate from a level of knowledge skill and over expectation of user ability to embrace anew technology based on their experience with the technology as opposed to the unforeseen challenges users have due to their preconceived perception of the ERP systems with regards to usability. Implementers have to change their perception with the aim of understanding the user anticipated experience with the system with regards to functionality and practical application on specific functionalities of the system. By interacting with users at their level of knowledge, skill, knowledge and speed of operation of the new technology, implementers can have an easy task in diffusing the usability functionalities of the ERP system among the users.

The perception of the users with regards was tested and it was discovered that 61.5% of the users were not sure of the effectiveness of the ERP systems with regards to functionality. Users find that the ERP systems are somewhat effective. Users could be right with the level of interaction knowledge and skill exposed to them by the implementers. User perception is marred with their fear of new technologies, fear of job losses and fear of the unknown in regards to the adoption of a technology that previously never existed. It is a perception that can be easily dealt with if the users can be trained and exposed to possibilities of the dew technological solution in a sequential and recurrent manner such as to enable them be able to interact with the technology more effectively.

Functionality of any new technology is key to the user acceptance if the users are well exposed to the functionalities through training. With proper and frequent trainings of the users, the technological solutions can be easily diffused and used for service delivery.

Major Challenges Associated With ERP Implementation

The respondents were further put to task to state the major challenges associated with ERP implementation and they outlined the following;

Unclear implementer instructions, inaccessible software developers to address user issues, lack of sufficient training of the users and insufficient customization of the system to fit the organizations unique needs, user resistance, unstable and unreliable data storage and retrieval, negative user attitude, poor internet connectivity, lack of training among staff, user acceptance and untimely data provided, too much data entry, too much steps for a single process, ineffective report generation, unskilled users, system failure, customization issues.

OPPORTUNITIES FOR ERP DEVELOPERS

Enterprise Resource Planning developers can get in to the following areas in order to improve service delivery as per respondents' proposals; custom made solutions for individual users, simple report generation, creation of easy to use software solutions, training users on attitude change, understand different user approach and coming up with more efficient solutions on time, dissemination of results and embracing of cloud computing.

CONCLUSION

This research finding indicated that 76.9% of the users felt that the investment made in the acquiring ERPs was worthwhile to the Return on Investment (ROI) of their organization. 92.3% of the respondents stated that ERP improve quality of work life for the users. 53.8% indicated that the ERP modules were reliable in-service delivery.

REFERENCES

Abugabah, A., & Sanzogni, L. (2010). *Enterprise Resource Planning (ERP) System in Higher Education: A literature Review and Implications.* Retrieved July 7, 2017, from https://www.researchgate.net/publication/50600909_Enterprise_Resource_Planning_ERP_System_in_Higher_Education_A_literature_Review_and_Implications

Ağaoğlu, M., Yurtkoru, E. S., & Ekmekçi, A. K. (2015). The Effect of ERP Implementation CSFs on Business Performance: An Empirical Study on Users' Perception. *Procedia: Social and Behavioral Sciences, 210*, 35–42. doi:10.1016/j.sbspro.2015.11.326

Aswathappa, K. (2008). *Human resource management: Text and cases.* MacGraw-Hill.

Bryman, A. (2008). *Social research methods.* Oxford, UK: Oxford University Press.

Chian-Son, Yu. (2005). Causes influencing the effectiveness of the post-implementation ERP system. *Industrial Management & Data Systems, 105*(1), 115–132. doi:10.1108/02635570510575225

Cue, K. (2017, March). *Commission for University Education - Home.* Retrieved July 7, 2017, from http://www.cue.or.ke/

Izamani, S., Khoumbati, K., Ismaili, A. I., & Amani, S. (2013). A Conceptual Framework for ERP Evaluation in Higher Educational Institutes of Pakistan. *Sindh University Research Journal*, 596–607.

Kasomo, D. (2006). *Research method in humanities and education.* Egerton University Press.

Khaleel, Y. (2012). Analysis of Enterprise Resource Planning System (ERP) in Small and Medium Enterprises (SME) of Malaysian Manufacturing Sectors: Current Status and Practices. *Asia-Pacific Journal of Information Technology and Multimedia, 10*(2011), 13–20.

MIREC. (2017). *Meru University of Science and Technology Institutional Research and Ethic Committee procedures.* Unpublished.

Mittelstädt, V., Brauner, P., Blum, M., & Ziefle, M. (2015). On the visual design of ERP systems – The role of information complexity, presentation and human factors. *Procedia Manufacturing, 3*, 448–455. doi:10.1016/j.promfg.2015.07.207

Omuono, G. (2015). *Presentation kenet maseno_0.pdf - Google Search*. Retrieved August 17, 2017, from https://www.google.com/search?source=hp&q=presentati on+kenet++maseno_0.pdf&oq=presentation+kenet++maseno_0.pdf&gs_l=psy-ab.3...23869.48422.0.49331.36.34.0.0.0.0.548.6421.2-7j10j1j1.19.0....0...1.1.64.psy-ab.17.15.5211.6.0j35i39k1j0i131k1j0i20k1j33i160k1j33i21k1.Tlbbu_pVY94

Perera, H., & Withanage, T. (2008). Critical Success Factors in Post ERP Implementation. Engineer. *Journal Of The Institution Of Engineers, Sri Lanka, 41*(3), 29. doi:10.4038/engineer.v41i3.7088

Petter, S., DeLone, W., & McLean, E. (2008). Measuring information systems success: Models, dimensions, measures, and interrelationships. *European Journal of Information Systems, 17*(3), 236–263. doi:10.1057/ejis.2008.15

Sahin, I. (2006, April). Detailed Review of Rogers' Diffusion of Innovations Theory and Educational Technology: Related Studies Based on Rogers' Theory. *The Turkish Online Journal of Educational Technology, 5,* 14–23. doi:10.1287/mnsc.43.7.934

Sandra Graham, V. S. F. (2014). *Attribution Theory Application to Achievement, Mental Health, and Interpersonal Conflict (2nd ed.)*. New York: Psychology Press. doi:10.4324/9781315807669

Sanjay, A. (2003). *Service Delivery Management*. Academic Press.

Saunders, M., Lewia, P., & Thornbill, A. (2009). *Research methods for business students*. London: Prentice Hall.

Schniederjans, D., & Yadav, S. (2013). Successful ERP implementation: An integrative model. *Business Process Management Journal, 19*(2), 364–398. doi:10.1108/14637151311308358

Somers, T. M., & Nelson, K. G. (2004). A taxonomy of players and activities across the ERP project life cycle. *Information & Management, 41*(3), 257–278. doi:10.1016/S0378-7206(03)00023-5

Weerakkody, V., Irani, Z., Kapoor, K., Sivarajah, U., & Dwivedi, Y. K. (2016). Open data and its usability: An empirical view from the Citizen's perspective. *Information Systems Frontiers*, 1–16. doi:10.100710796-016-9679-1

Chapter 8
Evaluating the Usability Maturity of Enterprise Resource Planning Systems

Kelvin Kabeti Omieno
Kaimosi Friends University College, Kenya

ABSTRACT

The enterprise resource planning (ERP) system is a complex and comprehensive software that integrates various enterprise functions and resources. Although ERP systems have been depicted as a solution in many organizations, there are many negative reports on ERP success, benefits, and effect on user performance. Previous research noted that there is a lack of knowledge and awareness of ERP systems and their overall value to ERP organizations. ERP systems have been widely studied during the past decade; yet they often fail to deliver the intended benefits originally expected. One notable reason for their failures is the lack of understanding in user requirements. There are many studies conducted to propose software quality models with their quality characteristics. However, there is currently no dedicated software quality model that can describe usability maturity and involve new features of ERP systems. This chapter proposes a framework for evaluating the usability maturity as a quality attribute of ERP systems.

DOI: 10.4018/978-1-5225-7678-5.ch008

INTRODUCTION

There has been a strong debate on the value of ERP systems in organizations. Enterprise Resource Planning (ERP) system is a complex and comprehensive software developed to better integrate firms' functions and resources (Ifinedo & Nahar, 2006). Today, most organizations use the ERP systems due to cost reductions, improving responsiveness to customer needs, replacement of legacy systems, and faster data transactions. Ramdani (2012) noted that the question of the ERP system's value to the end users has been a key issue in many organizations. According to Koch (2011), ERP users can influence the success or failure of the ERP system. Peslak and Boyle (2010) suggested that users play an important role in achieving success in an ERP environment. Despite the large body of literature on ERP systems, there is a need to investigate the ERP system's success from the end users' perspectives (Kwak, Park, Chung, & Ghosh, 2012). Various factors relevant to ERP success or failure have been highlighted in past research; however, the focus has been on ERP success in developed countries. Moreover, many developing countries express interest in achieving ERP success in their organizations. Talet and Alwahaishi (2011) argued that an ERP system used successfully in one region might be a failure in other regions. According to Soltani, Elkhani, and Bakri (2013), the factors that affect ERP success in developed countries need to be researched in the context of developing countries. According to Zhu, Li, Wang, and Chen (2010), ERP systems have been utilized globally, yet they have failed to deliver the intended benefits. To provide a better understanding of ERP success at the individual level of analysis, this research explored the factors that influence ERP users in an ERP environment in the Middle East. An understanding of the factors that influence end users in an ERP environment is imperative for ERP success. Following from the above, the results of this study could be used to help organizations understand the factors that influence end users in an ERP environment. Nah, Tan, and Beethe (2005) asserted that the benefit of an ERP implementation depends heavily on how the system is operated by end users. Understanding the relative importance of end users' success factors in ERP systems can help information technology (IT) managers put more emphasis on the leading issues perceived by end users (Hsu, Lai, & Weng, 2008).

Other researcher define an Enterprise Resource Planning (ERP) system as 'a highly unified, consolidated and reliable network of business systems, built on a single integrated platform' (Vaman, 2007). The removal of barriers to sharing information between functional divisions and the holistic management of processes have enabled ERP systems to increase the operational processes, profitability and productivity of organisations (Magal & Word, 2012; McGauhey & Gunasekaran, 2007). In spite of the economic recession over recent years, ERP systems are dominant in the marketplace and this trend is expected to continue (Forrester, 2011). Several studies in industry have revealed that the complexity of ERP systems has resulted in user interfaces (UIs) which suffer from poor usability (Singh & Wesson, 2009; Yeh, 2006) and user frustration (Matthews, 2008; Topi et al., 2005). The poor usability makes it difficult for users to interact with the ERP system and to complete required tasks, which further impacts the time taken to learn the system (Topi et al., 2005). Usability problems with ERP systems, similar to those reported in industry, have also been encountered by training and education institutions (Surendran & Somarajan, 2006).

With respect to the software systems quality, much work has been conducted to propose software quality models and metrics. Among these models are McCall's software quality model, Boehm's software product quality model, Dromey's quality model, FURPS quality model and ISO/IEC 9126. The metrics are qualitative indicators of system characteristics and the quality models explain the relationships between such metrics (Kumar, Grover & Kumar, 2009). Additionally, other studies have been conducted to provide guidelines for evaluating the quality of different types of software systems. However, there is a lack of studies conducted to propose ERP systems quality models and their characteristics (Thamer, Mommad & Ahmad, 2013)

BACKGROUND

Enterprise resource planning (ERP) is the most complex and largest enterprise system, providing cost effectiveness, improved operations, business growth, and support for business processes across the enterprise (Tsai, Chen, Hwang, & Hsu, 2010). The use of ERP is growing and becoming more popular; however, it is obvious that several important factors must be considered for the success of any ERP system. According to Petter, DeLone, and McLean (2008), an ERP system is a tool that manages procedures and resources; therefore, it is imperative for organizations to have this tool to facilitate the coordination of several activities within the organizations. Levi and Doron (2013) claimed that organizations consider ERP to be a vibrant tool for business success because it integrates varied business functions and enables flawless transactions and productions. Although ERP systems have been depicted as a solution in many organizations, there are many negative reports on ERP success (Levi & Doron, 2013). The ERP systems are designed to provide solutions to many different business issues and needs.

According to Amoako-Gyampah (2007), the ERP systems take advantage of a series of advanced technologies to provide transaction solutions and help different organizations share knowledge and data, reduce costs, and improve business processes. Al-Fawaz, Eldabi, and Naseer (2010) noted that various vendors provide ERP solutions to organizations in the Middle East to help them stay competitive in the global market. According to Soja and Paliwoda-Pękosz (2013), the process of information systems (IS) acceptance in developing countries is associated with different considerations as compared with acceptance observed in developed countries. In particular, IS projects conducted in developing countries struggle with lack of experience, inadequate infrastructure, and lack of strategic planning. According to Kujala (2008), despite the huge investments in ERP systems, ERP failures have been noted in many organizations. It is obvious that the benefits of ERP systems depend partially on how they are perceived by end users. ERP systems have been widely studied during the past decade, yet they fail to deliver the intended benefits originally expected. One notable reason for their failures is the lack of understanding of users' requirements at the individual and organizational level.

USABILITY FACTORS FOR QUALITY MODELS IN INFORMATION SYSTEMS

Definitions of Existing Characteristics in ERP Systems Context

The quality characteristics, functionality, reliability, usability, efficiency, maintainability, and portability have commonly been proposed in most quality models. However, scholars have different opinions while choosing sub characteristics of these characteristics. This research concentration is on the product quality rather than on quality in use. Therefore, this section defines the various characteristics and its sub-characteristics in term of ERP systems.

The *Functionality* has been defined by ISO (2001) as the capability of the software to provide functions which meet the stated and implied needs of users under specified conditions of usage. In order to evaluate such characteristic, it has been divided into four sub-characteristics, namely accuracy, suitability, interoperability, and security (Kumar, Grover and Kumar 2009). Adapting the functionality of the ERP systems reveals that the systems software should provide its functions, namely financial process, human resource management, supply chain process, manufacturing process and/ or customer service process as per the requirements when it is used under specific conditions.

The *reliability* is the capability of the software to maintain its level of performance under stated conditions for a stated period of time. Reliability has three sub-characteristics consist maturity, fault tolerance, and recoverability. In terms of ERP systems, the reliability refers to the capability of the systems to maintain its service provision under specific conditions for a specific period of time. In other words, the probability of the ERP system fails in a problem within a given period of time.

The *usability* is the capability of the software to be understood learned, used, and attractive by the users, when used under specified conditions. The usability has set of sub-characteristics, including understandability, learn ability, and operability (Kalaimagal & Srinivasan 2008). However, in the context of the ERP systems being discussed, more sub characteristics have been added to this external metrics of software quality (Omieno & Rodriguez, 2016). This characteristic is employed in this study to suggest that the ERP systems should be understood, learned, used and executed under specific conditions. Thus, the complexity has been proposed as additional sub-characteristic under this quality characteristic.

The *efficiency* refers to the capability of a system to provide performance relative to the amount of the used resources, under stated conditions. To be measured, it has also been divided into three sub-characteristics, namely time behavior, resource utilization an efficiency compliance (ISO, 2001). Adapting this characteristic to the ERP systems suggests that the systems should be concerned with the used software and hardware resources when providing the ERP systems' functions.

The *maintainability* is the capability of the software to be modified. The maintainability consists five sub-characteristics, including analyzability, changeability, stability, and testability (Al-Qutaish, 2010; ISO, 2001) in this research, any feature or part of the ERP system should be modifiable. As well as identifying a feature or part to be modified, modifying, diagnosing causes of failures, and validating the modified ERP system should not require much effort. Thus, reusability has been proposed as sub-characteristics under this quality characteristic.

Finally, the *portability* of software refers to the capability of the software to be transferred from one environment to one another (ISO, 2001) Therefore, the ERP system should be applied using different operating systems; be applied at different organizations or departments; and be applied using a variety of hardware. Similar to the previous quality characteristics, the portability has set of sub-characteristics, namely adaptability, installability, coexistence, and replace ability (Fahmy, Haslinda, Roslina, & Fariha, 2012)

ERP History

The study by Kalakota and Robinson (2001) indicate that ERP systems have their roots in Materials Requirement Planning (MRPI) systems, and Manufacturing Resource Planning (MRPII), which emerged during the 1960s. MRPI was mainly used for inventory control and managing production, while MRPII was developed to evaluate the entire production environment and to create or adjust master schedules based on feedback from current production and purchase conditions (Bedworth &

Bailey, 1987). The development of these manufacturing coordination and integration methods and tools made ERP systems possible. Companies such as SAP, Oracle, and others moved away from legacy MRPII systems and began the process of ERP implementation. An ERP system can be defined as a program that intends to provide solutions to and interface multiple corporate functions, including finance, human resources, manufacturing, materials management, and sales into a unified database system (Davenport, 2000).

ERP Benefits

ERP systems adoption comes with a number of benefits from its implementation. Zeng, Lu, and Skibniewski (2012) summarized the benefits that can be gained from the ERP system, which they classified into five different dimensions:

1. Operational benefits: ERP systems can provide benefits in terms of cost, cycle
2. time, performance, and quality.
3. Managerial benefits: ERP systems can improve decision-making and planning.
4. Strategic benefits: ERP systems can support business growth and innovations.
5. IT infrastructure benefits: ERP systems provide flexibility for current and future changes.
6. Organizational benefits: ERP systems are expected to empower workers and build a common vision.

Despite the fact that ERP systems can provide many benefits, researchers have reported that many organizations have been unable to utilize successfully their ERP systems to achieve success (Peng Nunes, 2009; Zhu et al., 2010). By using an ERP solution designed for optimum usability, organizations can achieve the following benefits:

1. **Reduce Training and Implementation Timeframes to Improve ROI:** Users can learn to use a system that's intuitive and easy to use much faster than they can with complex and confusing systems. This reduces the required training cost and time, improving system adoption rates and employee morale. In addition, the faster users begin using the system, the faster the ERP can deliver its promised benefits and provide a return on investment.
2. **Lower TCO:** An easy to use system reduces the need for users to turn to system "power users" to teach them to do something unfamiliar, thus lowering support costs.

3. **Improve Productivity:** When an ERP is intuitive and allows users to easily navigate complex business processes, users can spend more time analyzing information to make better business decisions and drive business improvements.

4. **Improve Staffing Flexibility:** With visual processes, if someone goes on vacation, another user who is unfamiliar with the system can easily cover for them without extensive additional training on the ERP module or processes applicable to their new tasks. The same is true when users wish to take on new responsibilities. In this way, an easy-to-use system makes the entire organization more flexible.

5. **Enhance Collaboration With Stakeholders:** Executives and managers can take advantage of the intuitive user interface, dashboards and drill down capabilities to directly access key information, rather than waiting for staff and managers to send reports. This improves collaboration and information sharing across the organization.

ERP Lifecycle

The success of an ERP system implementation is important to organizations as it improves their existing operations. According to Velcu (2010), the ERP system lifecycle consists of three phases, the project, shakedown, and onward and upward phases. Soja and Paliwoda-Pękosz (2013) noted that the ERP system lifecycle consisted of four phases, the chartering phase, project phase, shakedown phase, and onward and upward phase.

1. Project chartering–concerns business decisions regarding the scope of the project, budgeting, and system selection.
2. The project–the main implementation phase with the purpose of getting the system and users "up and running."
3. Shakedown–stabilizing and incorporating IS in everyday operations.
4. Onward and upward–deriving benefits from the ERP system.

The post implementation period for ERP systems begins after the implementation phase of an ERP system. The post implementation phase provides on-going support such as maintenance, training, and upgrades to help organizations sustain and prevent any disruptions to the system. To avoid an IS failure, the system requires continuous support from top management (McGinnis & Huang, 2007; Salmeron & Lopez, 2010). Many organizations upgrade and maintain their ERP systems in the post implementation phase to prevent any disruptions to the daily operations of the business (Ng, Gable, & Chan, 2002). According to Willis and Willis-Brown (2002), the post implementation stage has many challenges because the go-live phase signals a new beginning. The performance of the system continues to be challenging but necessary because the system must be extended to satisfy the current and all future business requirements (Muscatello & Chen, 2008). Other studies have also noted that one of the main challenges in ERP systems is the high cost of maintenance and support (Law, Chen, & Wu, 2010; Salmeron & Lopez, 2009). On the other hand according to Al-Mashari, Al-Mudimigh, and Zairi (2003), ERP projects can be considered successful when: (1) there is a match between the ERP system and the stated objectives, (2) the system is implemented within time and on budget, (3) users' attitudes toward the system are positive, and (4) the system matches users' expectations. Chun-Chin et al. (2008) proposed a study that adopted performance measures, such as data accuracy, output, system accuracy, and usefulness from the relevant literature. The authors noted that many organizations put their attention on selection and implementation but fail to evaluate the effectiveness of the ERP systems.

Wu and Wang (2006) identified two main types of ERP system users: (1) users that are selected from the operating department, and (2) users from where the requirements of the system were initially developed. The authors believe that users have a crucial role in the success of the ERP system. They also state that users' satisfaction is the extent to which the newly installed system meets their information requirements. It is also expected that enhanced productivity will follow. However, the authors suggest that this does not mean that satisfaction causes improved productivity. Rather, they argued that user productivity and satisfaction are caused by the extent to which the system requirements are met. Howcroft, Newell, and Wagner (2004) emphasize that it is essential for researchers to examine the way that ERP systems are shaped by individuals, organizations, and organizational culture.

Many researchers have considered end users' satisfaction and acceptance, starting with Davis' (1989) model, which explains computer usage and acceptance of information technology. Davis (1989) introduced the Technology Acceptance Model (TAM), which provides an understanding of the impact of external variables on attitudes and intentions to use of an ERP system. The effects of an IS in this model are determined by its perceived usefulness (PU) and perceived ease of use (PEU). The model argues that external variables indirectly affect attitudes toward usage, and in turn lead to an actual system use by the influence of PU and PEU.

Investigation of Usability Factors

In the study of software engineering, there are ten well-known quality models for system evaluation that can equality apply to ERP systems. Each of these models covers a part of usability factors. The researcher aim to extract usability factors from each model and then aggregate them together. In such a way, more comprehensive usability factors can be obtained for analyzing ERP systems featured with multi-functions and complex interfaces. Usability evaluation is any analysis or empirical study of the usability of a prototype or system (Foltz et al., 2008). Several studies (Costa, 2010; Singh & Wesson, 2008; Van Norren, 2009) have proposed usability criteria which can be used for usability evaluations of ERP systems. However all of these studies have taken place in industry and not in a higher education environment. The level of experience of an undergraduate student is not the same as a person in industry, therefore their perceptions of usability may differ. Existing studies of ERP adoption in the IS curricula are focused primarily on the pedagogical aspects and have not explored the usability or ease of use of the ERP system. Empirical research

Table 1. Ten quality models with usability factors

Quality Model Index	Published Year	Quality Model Name	Usability Factors
1	1977	McCall	Operability, Training, Communicativeness
2	1978	Boehm	Reliability, Efficiency, Human Engineering
3	1991	Shackel	Effectiveness, learnability, Flexibility, Attitude
4	1992	FURPS	Human Factors, Consistent in Human Interface, Online and Content Sensitive Help, Training Materials, user Documentation, Aesthetics
5	1993	Nielsen	Learnability, Efficiency, Memorability, Errors, Satisfaction
6	1998	SUMI	Efficiency, Affect, Helpfulness, Control, learnability
7	1998	ISO 9242-11 (Process)	Effectiveness, Efficiency, Satisfaction
8	2001	ISO 9126 (Product)	Understandability, learnability, operability, Attractiveness, Usability compliance
9	2006	QUIM	Productivity, Efficiency, Effectiveness, Safety, Learnability, Accessibility, Satisfaction, Truthfulness, Universality, Usefulness
10	2014	SEM	Understandabilty, Learnability, Applicability, Effectiveness/Usefulness for Future Projects, User Satisfaction

Source: (Zapha 2014)

relating to the ease of use or usability of ERP systems is required (Topi et al., 2005), particularly with regards to the evaluation of the ease of use of medium-sized ERP systems in educational environments (Hustad & Olsen, 2011)

From Table 1, there is no discussion on how we can determine maturity of implementation of ERP systems in institutions including both service industry and academic or research institutions.

Elements of Usability Maturity Based on User-Centred Design

Typically that the impact of user-centred design may vary from project to project. A capability model should recover the extent to which user-centred design is implemented in the all product development projects, throughout the organization.

In this section, the understanding is that user-centred design can achieve the position as an organisation wide routine only if usability and user-centred design are a part of business strategy. Project development managers see user-centred design typically as a new risk — meaning more cost and activities. Hakiel's (1999) conclusion is that in order to make user-centred design routine, there should be demand to it from the product owners. At a poor level of capability, the business management does not recognize need for a human-centred process and does not understand the business benefit of producing usable products. At high level of capability, the management has recognized the benefits of usability to the business, follows the competitive situation in usability in the market, and does actions to ensure the competitive level of usability of the products that the enterprise develops. Figure 1 defines elements of usability capability based on user-centered design in development projects.

Figure 1.

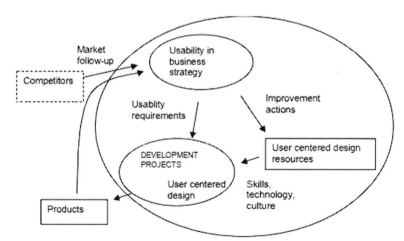

USABILITY MATURITY MODELS: USER-CENTERED APPROACH

Usability maturity models are methods for developing user-centered design processes in companies in order to facilitate usability methodologies for creating usable products. Usability maturity models help management understand the issues surrounding organizational opportunities and to improve the usability of its products. The models also benefit usability practitioners by pinpointing areas of improvement in usability processes and practices. A maturity model is composed of two main elements: First, a set of organizational areas, such as development practices, processes, infrastructure, and skills. Secondly, the capability maturity levels for rating each of the areas.

A usability maturity model can be regarded as an ideal model of user-centered design. The closer the company meets the ideal level of usability maturity, the higher rating it gets. A common method of utilizing a usability maturity model is to perform an assessment of the company's current capacity for developing usable products. In a usability maturity assessment, an assessment team analyzes organizational areas by examining documentation and interviewing key stakeholders. The team maps the findings against a usability maturity model and determines the ratings.

The researcher describe six existing usability capability models. Although they are identified by different terms (not 'usability capability model'), they all address the same theme: they try to define those characteristics of development organizations that are relevant for effective user-centered design. In this chapter the term 'usability capability model' covers all of these models. An exploration of usability capability models listed in chronological order is as presented:

1. Stages of Acceptance of User-centred Design, by Ehrlich & Rohn (1994).
2. Trillium, by Trillium (1994).
3. Usability Leadership Assessment, by IBM (Flanaghan, 1995).
4. Humanware Process Assessment, by Philips (Gupta, 1997).
5. Usability Maturity Model: Processes, by the INUSE project (Earthy, 1998b).
6. Usability Maturity Model: Human-centredness Scale, by the INUSE project (Earthy, 1998a).

Three of these usability capability models — Trillium, and Philips, INUSE Usability Maturity Model: Processes, INUSE Processes — have their origin in software process assessment models: Capability Maturity Model CMM (Paulk et al., 1995), Bootstrap (Kuvaja et al., 1994), and the international standard ISO (1998b). The rest of the models have a different approach to process assessment — the can be referred to as generic capability models. The most important background to these models is probably the quality model of (Crosby, 1978). The reader should have some knowledge about the process assessment and quality models to understand thoroughly the usability capability models.

Trillium

Trillium is a process assessment model for development of telecommunication products, developed by Bell Canada. It is a large model covering widely different processes of product development. It also includes a number of usability practices. Trillium is well documented and of public domain, and can be downloaded from the Web. Its origin is in the CMM. At the top level of the model, Trillium defines eight capability areas of product development, each of which are composed of roadmaps. One capability area is Customer Support where Usability Engineer is one roadmap, containing a number of usability practices. In addition, the roadmaps User Documentation and User Training include some more usability practices.

Trillium defines five levels of capability: from Level 1 (lowest one, unstructured) to Level 5 (highest one, fully integrated). Table 2 defines levels of capability in Trillium

IBM: Usability Management Maturity

The IBM model is quite broad; it covers organisational, skills and process aspects. There is only limited documentation available about the IBM model, without any references to other models. The only documentation publicly available is the one delivered at the CHI'95 in a special interest group session.

Table 2. Usability practices are categorized at different levels of capability in Trillium

Level of capability	Examples of usability practices
Level 2: Repeatable	- Existing competing products are assessed - Customer/ user locations are visited by designers before initiation of design - Users are involved in the design process
Level 3: defined	- Comparative analysis of competing products is performed at appropriate points in the product life cycle - Users are visited to determined how system is used - Measurable levels are specified for important usability goals - Prototyping is used to help develop all user interfaces - User documentation is developed fully - The training material is verified and validated formally
Level 4: managed	- Evolution of user needs and abilities is projected - The rationale for the user interface design is explicitly documented
Level 5: Fully integrated	- No usability practices at this level

The IBM model defines nine attributes of usability management maturity that fall into three different categories, as illustrated in Table 3. All these attributes are evaluated through benchmark statements. Examples of benchmark statements are (attribute 1):

1. Organisation accepts the value of user-centered tools and technology: Management sets a positive tone about usability and considers usability, as well as schedule and cost, to be important.
2. The organisation understands the value of measurements of and users'
3. productivity and satisfaction.
4. The organisation values HCI skills in the development team. The capability is assessed separately for each attribute with scale 1. . . 5 (1 = low, 5 = high).

Philips: Humanware Process Assessment

Another process assessment model is one developed by Philips called 'Humanware Process Assessment'. There is one position paper available about the approach. The model uses the terminology of CMM. It identifies ten key process areas. Four of these are engineering processes: 1. Understanding 2. Use. 3. Design teams 4. Develop a shared understanding of how the product is expected to be used in practice, based on information from user studies.

INUSE Usability Maturity Model (UMM): Processes

The INUSE project developed a well-documented process assessment model that is based on the format of the software process assessment model defined in ISO 15504. The model contains seven processes:

- Ensure HCD content in system strategy.
- Plan the human-centred design process.
- Specify the user and organisational requirements.
- Understand and specify the context of use.
- Produce design solutions.
- Evaluate design against requirements.
- Facilitate the human-system implementation.

The processes HCD.2–HCD.6 are derived from ISO 13407. Each process is defined with a purpose statement. In addition, there are identified a set of base practices for each process. Assessments are typically carried out through analyzing the extent and quality to which the base practices are implemented.

As an example, the purpose of the process HCD.4 is "to identify, clarify and record the characteristics of the stakeholders, their tasks and the organizational and physical environment in which the system will operate". The related base practices are:

1. Identify and document user's tasks.
2. Identify and document significant user attributes.
3. Identify and document organizational environment.
4. Identify and document technical environment.

Identify and document physical environment. Each of the processes is assessed independently, using the scale of capability that is defined in ISO 15504. The levels of capability are illustrated in Table 3.

The INUSE Processes model is the basis of the technical report TR ISO 18529, which will appear in the near future.

INUSE Usability Maturity Model (UMM): Humancentredness Scale

The INUSE Usability Maturity Model: Human-centeredness Scale, INUSE HCS, is based on the IBM model, Sherwood-Jones' Total System Maturity model (Sherwood Jones, 1995), ISO 13407, and on quality stages of Crosby (1978). The INUSE HCS model has one dimension that is "intended for use in the assessment of the human-centeredness of an organization or department". It defines five increasing levels of maturity of human-centered processes, from unrecognized to institutionalize.

Table 3. Levels of capability in the INUSE process model

Level of capability	Description
Level 0: Incomplete	- Organization is not able to carry put the process
Level 1: Performed	- The process achieves its purpose. Individuals carry put processes
Level 2: Managed	- The quality, time and resource requirements for the process are known and controlled
Level 3: Established	- The process is carried out in a manner specified by the organization and the resources are defined
Level 4: Predictable	- The performance of the process is within predicted resource and quality limits
Level 5: Optimizing	- The organization can reliably tailor the process to particular requirements

USABILITY MODEL CATEGORIES

The first usability maturity models were Trillium by Bell Canada (a general maturity model including usability engineering), Usability Leadership Maturity Model by IBM, HumanWare Process Assessment model by Philips, and User Centered Design Maturity by Loughborough University. All of these models were developed in the early 1990s. In 2000, ISO 18529 was published based on work performed by European INUSE and TRUMP research projects. This model is remarkable in the sense that its format complies with the standard processes assessment model widely used in software engineering, such as CMM (Capability Maturity Model) and its revised version CMM-I. A further extended version is ISO 18152 which includes a larger set of processes. Further developments for Usability Maturity Models include: Human-Centeredness Scale, DATech in Germany, SDOS in Japan, and KESSU in Finland. Maturity models fall into four main categories: First is Standard process assessment models (ISO 18259, ISO 18152) that use the format of the process assessment models used in software engineering. Second include Non-standard models which examine processes, but with non-standard approaches. Third is Generic models which used Standardized Usability/User-Experience and include process aspects, but also larger issues such as management awareness, skills, and organizational position on usability. Finally, we have specific models which have a limited focus.

Usability Maturity Assessment in ERPs

Quality Metrics

In comparison to other aspects of software, usability issues are more subjective in nature and hence more controversial. In some instances, a user interface (UI) element may be clearer to some users than it is to others [3]. This is not different in ERP systems. However, despite their subjective nature, usability aspects need to be tested and measured objectively. The increasing popularity of usability assessment in virtual learning systems necessitates a usability maturity evaluation methodology. From the empirical study from ERP users (the students and staff), the study has been able to identify key usability factors. From study by Omieno & Rodriguez (2016) notes that after combining several overlapping factors, such as User Requirements and User Expectations, Incremental Design Approach, Design Techniques and Knowledge of UCD Methods, and Usability Testing and Usability Assessment, ten (10) key usability practices were obtained, which are depicted in Figure 2.

Figure 2.

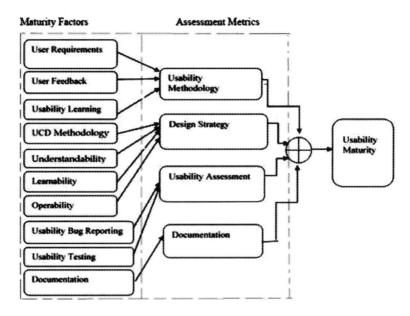

ERP Maturity Model heavily lies in Software Engineering domain and here we define four categories of assessment metrics namely: Usability Methodology (UM), Design Strategy (DS), Usability Assessment (UA) and Documentation (D). In thinking about the relationship between the four dimensions it is helpful to consider them arranged as in Figure 2 (Ten Quality Metrics Applicable for ERP Systems). The matrix of boxes used on the left to display summaries of process maturity metrics is helpful when performing comparisons within or between institutions but it can imply a hierarchical relationship that is misleading when interpreting individual process maturity results.

Description of Levels for Usability Maturity Assessment-Human Centeredness Scale

Rationale for the Scale

This scale has been developed in response to a need to measure how well organizations do the human-centered part of system development and support projects. The scale is also intended to assist those who wish to improve their organization's performance of human-centered activities. It is intended that the scale is used early in projects or process improvement activities. The scale has not been developed as part of one of the existing process models, such as the System Engineering Capability Maturity Model or ISO 15504 Software Process Assessment. This is in order to make clear the nature of organizational maturity with regard to human- centeredness and its implications for system maturity modelling. The scale uses the existence of Management Practices to assess the degree to which the organization has a human-centered approach to its work and working culture. In doing this it could be said to assess organizational attitude to human-centeredness. The most common approach to the assessment of personal attitude does not use performance of practice as the measure. However, in the case of this model the desirable measurement is not personal attitude to end-users, but the degree to which the organization implements practices which make its processes human-centered

Transition Between Levels

This section describes each of the levels in terms of the level of maturity of processes applicable to ERP systems, but the most significant aspect is that of the culture within the development team, and this is discussed here. Moving from level 1 (recognized) to level 2 (considered) is a major cultural change, from a craft-like traditional engineering outlook based on experience, to a systems approach. Usability, reliability, safety and all the other non-functional aspects become formal disciplines and do not rely on "good practice" or "engineering judgement". At level 1 design and support teams may still be actively hostile to users who don't know how to use their elegant creation. At level 2 these teams have changed and are aware that systems are made to be used by people.

Moving from 2 (considered) to 3 (implemented) is a major cultural change in a traditional systems development environment; users get thought about rather than cursed or ignored. Engineers recognize that analysts are not the same as the end users, and that what will work for the user is not necessarily what seems obvious to a technical specialist. Moving from 4 (implemented) to 5 (integrated) requires routine use of human factors expertise and human-centered methods and tools. The user is given formal recognition, and associated development processes are regarded as mainstream rather than something done by specialists for marketing or political purposes (and largely ignored). Moving from 4 (integrated) to 5 (institutionalized) requires that the systems development culture is embedded in a business (and/or safety) driven multi-disciplinary culture. The cultural and business focus is on what the customer organization will be able to do, rather than the functionality of any supporting hardware/software.

Elements to Be Included in Usability Capability

The learning curve for users is usually steep as users have to master the many menu paths within a single ERP system (Theling & Loos, 2005). Studies of ERP system adoptions have reported that medium-sized ERP systems are less complex and easier to use than large ERP systems (Hustad & Olsen, 2011; Winkelman and Matzner, 2010). However these studies have been largely qualitative. The potential benefits of ERP systems for organizations can be increased by improving the usability of ERP systems which can, in turn, reduce the length of the training time and increase employee user satisfaction. Research into improving the usability of ERP systems is required in order to address the complexity and learning curve problems of ERP systems

Different maturity models cover different organizational areas which may include:

1. *Performance of usability processes* means examination of the extent to which usability activities—such as user analysis, task analysis, usability requirements determination, and usability evaluations—are carried out. Performance of usability processes is a basic area. If there is any effective usability in an organization, it should be visible in development projects. Practically all maturity models address this to some extent. Requirements include:
    a. Existing competing products are assessed
    b. Mock-ups and prototypes are produced and evaluated
    c. Understand and specify the Context of Use
    d. The quality and impact of the activities, stating: "usability activities are carried out professionally," and "usability results have impact on design decisions."
2. *Management of usability* processes in development projects means examination of issues, such as the inclusion of usability engineering activities in a project plan, follow-up of the implementation of the plan during the project, and configuration management of the documents produced. Addressing these issues decreases the potential for problems with scheduling, resources, and document control.
3. *Usability in a quality management system* is addressed in many models. The standard process assessment models (capability level 3) examine this issue. Requirements by other models include: User documentation is developed formally, Existing procedures are extended to include Humanware activities, Integrate Human Factors processes with project processes, and Usability is part of the Quality Policy and the Quality Handbook in organizations.
4. *Systematic improvement of usability* processes examples include statements such as "Management's actions to improve the current focus on usability," and

"Systematic improvement of quality in use,". The role of usability at a strategic level is explicitly addressed in some models:

a. Activities at all organizational levels to insure a prominent focus on usability
b. A coordinator drives the policy on HumanWare throughout an organization
c. Human-system issues in business strategy (ISO 18152)

It is important to explore the impact of usability of ERP systems in relation to human-centredness. The impact of usability is also addressed: HCI skills and tasks are viewed as important, Acceptance of human-centered skills by the organization, Usability engineer is part of the design team and is responsible for design decisions, and skilled staff is involved and effective in all stages of development. Organizational culture is also covered by some models. Statements include: Awareness at all organizational levels of the importance of usability in product development and the degree to which the organization has a human-centered approach to its work and working culture. Staff members are made aware that end users' skills, background, and motivation may differ from developers or system support staff. Table 4 shows how fully each attribute should be realized in order for the level to be achieved.

The usability maturity of ERP Systems in organizations is as discussed below and is based on the maturity level as well as for each usability factor indicated in Table 2.

Level 1: Un-Recognized

Indicates that the ERP system does not have a stable and organized methodology for implementing usability. The need for a human-centred process is not recognized. If systems are received with varying degrees of satisfaction by their end users this does not cause concern. There are no positive human centred attributes at this level. There is no evidence that the ERP team practices usability to improve the software quality of their system. Additionally, there are no defined procedures for collecting user requirements and feedback, implementing usability learning, incorporating user design methodology, performing usability assessment and providing documentation.

Level 2: Recognized

University recognizes that there is a need to improve the quality in use of its systems. The organization has a development process and produces systems. Members of the organization understand the business benefit of producing usable products such as ERP. Users recognize the potential benefits of usability in ERP and accordingly, they demonstrate interest in usability. Also, users make efforts to collect user requirements and feedback, and present the same to developers where the developers acquire

Table 4. Maturity level ratings (Petter et.al 2008)

Scale	Process Attributes	Ratings
Level 1	Process recognition Performed processes	Fully or largely Fully or largely
Level 2	Problem recognition Performed processes Quality in use awareness User focus	Fully Fully Fully or largely Fully or largely
Level 3	Problem recognition Performed processes Quality in use awareness User focus User involvement Human Factory technology Human factor skills	Fully Fully Fully Fully Fully or largely Fully or largely Fully or largely
Level 4	Problem recognition Performed processes Quality in use awareness User focus User involvement Human Factory technology Human factor skills Integration Improvement Iteration	Fully Fully Fully Fully Fully Fully Fully Fully or largely Fully or largely Fully or largely
Level 5	Problem recognition Performed processes Quality in use awareness User focus User involvement Human Factory technology Human factor skills Integration Improvement Iteration Human centered leadership Organizational human-centeredness	Fully Fully Fully Fully Fully Fully Fully Fully Fully Fully Fully or largely Fully or largely

knowledge of UCD methodology. Both end users (students and staff) and developers recognize the fact that end users face difficulties in reporting usability related errors and hence understand the need for usability assessment plans. Additionally, the content developers (who in this case are staff)realize the importance of documentation at various stages of ERP content understand and recognize the importance of usability in the success of the system

Level 3: Defined

An ERP system at the "Defined" level establishes an infrastructure for implementing usability. Specifically, ERP team is able to collect and fulfil its users' requirements and expectations. Furthermore, they are able to collect feedback from users by utilizing a planned strategy for improving both software quality and usability. It is conceived that ERP managers understand, define and implement user-centered design principles. Through a systemic monitoring structure, team members (inclusive of the users) have the competency to maintain and enhance a project's satisfaction, understandability, learnability, operability and security. The team also adopts essential technical skills to provide users with a convenient usability bug reporting facility and to conduct necessary usability testing.

Level 4: Streamlined

Human-centred processes are integrated into the quality process and systems life cycle of the university. The systems and human-centred life cycles are managed to ensure that the results of the human-centred processes produce improvements in all relevant work products. The ERP team (especially the ERP providers) has acquired sufficient resources for meeting its users' requirements. Additionally, they have established a management system for recording users' feedback and taking the necessary steps to address that feedback. The users too are much aware of the steps too. Through a systemic monitoring structure, satisfaction, understandability, learnability, operability and security of ERP are regularly monitored. Moreover, quantifiable metrics are used to conduct usability assessments, and the documentation of ERP projects is regularly maintained

Level 5: Institutionalized

For virtual learning systems, the highest level for the usability maturity is referred to as "Institutionalized." The quality in use of whole ranges of ERP systems is coordinated and managed for business benefit. The culture of the organisation gains benefit from being user and human centred. Human-centred processes are used within the organisation to improve the quality in use of the processes, tools and methods used and developed by the organisation for its own use. Specifically, the ERP team has sufficient resources and skills for collecting user feedback and for understanding user expectations. Similarly, the team establishes a firm commitment to usability learning and UCD methodology, and they continuously make Assessments in the areas of satisfaction, understandability, learnability, security and operability and they constantly improve the usability bug reporting service through innovative methods and ensure the effectiveness of usability assessment by using quantitative metrics

Ways to Improve the User Experience

Modern ERP vendors are responding to user demands by implementing a wide range of capabilities that make it faster and easier for users to complete business processes and to obtain and analyze information to make more accurate and effective decisions. These capabilities include:

1. **Visual Processes:** While earlier solutions made it difficult for users to navigate work processes, new visual processes enable end users to easily see how to perform an entire process from end- to-end by providing a visual (graphical) map of a particular workflow. Users can see the entire work process at a glance to instantly determine where they are in the process and the steps necessary to complete it. Instead of navigating complex menus, users go directly to the area they need to use, click on it, and the appropriate screen appears. The screen can include ERP functions, reports, queries, requestors, statistics or other process pages. These visual processes make it very easy for new users on a system to get up to speed quickly. Pre-defined processes provided by the ERP vendor make it easy to get started using these workflows. Some systems even provide graphical tools that enable users to modify pre-defined processes or create new ones specific to their business, further improving ease of use.

2. **Graphical Dashboards:** Modernized ERP user interfaces give executives and managers across the business access to key performance indicators, which are presented in easy to interpret textual and graphical elements within a dashboard environment. Individuals that may not be familiar with the ERP software can use dashboards to gain direct access to key information - which improves information sharing (collaboration) across the business. Executives and managers no longer have to rely on spreadsheets or reports that have been compiled from multiple data sources and sent to them outside of the ERP system. They can gain direct access to the information, which creates a single source of the "truth" and facilitates faster, more accurate decisions

3. **Business Intelligence:** While graphical user portals and dashboards provide high-level information that allows users to monitor their operations and manage by exceptions, ERP solutions that offer integrated business intelligence allow users to perform more detailed analysis. With integrated business intelligence, users can analyse their business performance on-the fly and build compelling

reports using simple drag & drop of the data that is updated in real time with the flow of day-to-day operations. Systems with a built-in data warehouse further simplify set up and maintenance for system administrators.

4. **Intuitive User Interface:** Modern ERP vendors that want to make their user interfaces intuitive are taking into account user-centred design principles. When developing user-centred designs, product designers pay particular attention to the needs, wants and limitations of the product's end users throughout the design process. Designers not only try to determine how users are likely to use the product, they also test their assumptions with real users. The goal is to optimize the product around the way users want and need to use it, rather than forcing users to change the way they work to accommodate the product.

5. **Common Look and Feel:** Some ERP vendors increase the functionality of their solutions by purchasing and integrating best-of-breed products. These solutions often have inconsistent interfaces, including different commands, organizational structures and file structures for each module of the ERP system. A solution and add-ons with a common interface for the entire application is much easier for users to learn and use. Ideally, the solution should provide a global application platform - where all offices of a company share common functionalities, processes and data - that incorporates different languages, regulations and currencies so that it can be used in many different locations, countries and regions. An ERP with a global application platform makes it easy to see critical business information in real time without users having to wait for branch offices to roll up the information. For example, a single ERP deployment at a corporate headquarters in Paris should be able to connect to the branch offices around the world and handle multiple currencies, business rules and legislations.

6. **Configurability**: A system that is easily configurable, allowing users to set preferences, enable or disable a feature, or change the user look and feel allows users to work with the system the way they want to without the need for extensive programming. It also allows users to eliminate extraneous information on application screens to reduce confusion.

7. **Mobile Interface**: Users increasingly need to access their ERP solution on the road. An ERP system that provides secure browser–based and mobile dashboards makes it easy for users to access the data they need while they're out of the office from their laptop systems or mobile devices. Users should be able to query information and use application functions to perform tasks such as checking inventory or placing a purchase requisition. A mobility component to an ERP system helps broaden the user base to non-core ERP users – delivering more flexibility and improved collaboration.

SOLUTIONS AND RECOMMENDATIONS

The contribution through the proposed approach of usability maturity determination can therefore facilitate the improvement of the usability of ERP systems in any organization. ERP educators and developers can also benefit from the results presented in this chapter by taking into account the proposed criteria and guidelines when planning which ERP system to use and when evaluating potential systems. In addition they should consider the benefits of implementing a medium-sized ERP system which may be less complex than a large ERP system. The insights provided by this evaluation methodology provide important contributions to Human Computer Interaction (HCI) researchers, ERP researchers and other researchers and can assist with a deeper understanding of other similar cases or situations.

The results of this study have highlighted the need for an ERP system, and the levels of acceptability through assessment of maturity of use of such information system. This chapter also details the business impact of modern usability enhancements that include visual processes, dashboards, an intuitive user interface, a common look and feel, configurability, SOA architecture, mobile interfaces, e-Commerce integration and business intelligence. ERP solutions that incorporate these capabilities reduce training and implementation timeframes to deliver faster ROI, reduce total cost of ownership, improve productivity, improve staffing flexibility and enhance collaboration.

FUTURE RESEARCH DIRECTIONS

It will be important to explore quantitative measurement of software usability. Also, there is need to apply similar methodology to build enhanced models for evaluating other software quality attributes. This will go a long way in improving the overall. Additional research on the usability of medium-sized ERP systems is recommended which can explore the design of an ERP system that can support specific domains such as teaching, and service industry and provide improved user guidance, especially for novice users. The best ERP vendors today are meeting customer demands by upgrading their solutions with a wide range of capabilities that improve usability.

CONCLUSION

As increasing demands of ERP systems in developing countries recently, their usability evaluation has been under focused of research. ERP systems are featured with multifunctional features and complex interfaces. The popular quality evaluation models just cover partial view of usability factors. In this book chapter, the author presents an analysis of ten well known quality models and extracted their usability factors. The chapter also explores usability metrics in depth. The author then presents a usability maturity evaluation metrics for an improved model with ten factors for evaluating the usability of ERP systems based on human-centred scale. The maturity model tries to enhance acceptance of ERP systems by users. It demonstrates our model can comprehensively evaluate the usability of ERP system. In addition, it can highlight different software usability demands for different types of customers.

REFERENCES

Abugabah, A., Sanzogni, L., & Poropat, A. (2009). The impact of information systems on user performance: A critical review and theoretical model. *Proceedings of the International Conference on Information Systems (ICIS)*, 809–819.

Al-Fawaz, K., Eldabi, T., & Naseer, A. (2010). Challenges and influential factors in ERP adoption and implementation. European, *Mediterranean and Middle Eastern Conference on Information Systems*.

Al-Mashari, M., & Zairi, M. (2000). Information and business process equality: The case of SAP R/3 implementation. *The Electronic Journal on Information Systems in Developing Countries*, *1*(4), 1–15. doi:10.1002/j.1681-4835.2000.tb00011.x

Al-Qutaish, R. E. (2010). Quality Models in Software Engineering Literature: An Analytical and Comparative Study. *The Journal of American Science*, *6*, 166–175.

Amoako-Gyampah, K. (2007). Perceived usefulness, user involvement and behavioral intention: An empirical study of ERP implementation. *Computers in Human Behavior*, *23*(3), 1232–1248.

Bedworth, D. D., & Bailey, J. E. (1987). *Integrated production control systems* (2nd ed.). New York, NY: John Wiley & Sons.

Chun-Chin, W., Tian-Shy, L., & Kuo-Liang, L. (2008). An ERP performance measurement framework using a fuzzy integral approach. *Journal of Manufacturing Technology Management*, *19*(5), 607–626. doi:10.1108/17410380810877285

Crosby, P. B. (1978). *Quality is Free: The Art of Making Quality Certain*. New York: McGraw-Hill.

Davenport, T. (2000). The future of enterprise system-enabled organizations. *Information Systems Frontiers, 2*(2), 163–180. doi:10.1023/A:1026591822284

Davis, F. D. (1989). Perceived usefulness, perceived ease of use, and user acceptance of information technology. *Management Information Systems Quarterly, 13*(3), 318–340. doi:10.2307/249008

Fahmy, S., Haslinda, N., Roslina, W., & Fariha, Z. (2012). Evaluating the Quality of Software in e-Book sing the ISO 9126 Model. *International Journal of Control and Automation, 5*, 115–122.

Flanaghan, G. A. (1995). *IBM Usability Leadership Maturity model (self-assessment version)*. Distributed at CHI Workshop.

Holsapple, M. P., Burns-Naas, L. A., Hastings, K., Ladics, G. S., Lavin, A. L., Makris, S., ... Luster, M. I. (2005). A proposed testing framework for developmental immunotoxicology (DIT). *Toxicological Sciences, 83*(1), 18–24. doi:10.1093/toxsci/kfh299 PMID:15456913

Howcroft, D., Newell, S., & Wagner, E. (2004). Understanding the contextual influences on enterprise system design, implementation, use and evaluation. *The Journal of Strategic Information Systems, 13*(4), 271–277. doi:10.1016/j.jsis.2004.11.010

Hsu, L., Lai, R., & Weng, Y. (2008). Understanding the critical effect user satisfaction and impact of ERP through innovation of diffusion theory. *International Journal of Technology Management, 43*(1–3), 30–47. doi:10.1504/IJTM.2008.019405

Humphrey, W.S. (1989). *Managing the software process*. Addison-Wesley.

Ifinedo, P., & Nahar, N. (2006). Quality, Impact and Success of ERP Systems: A Study Involving Some Firms in the Nordic-Baltic Region. *Journal of Information Technology Impact, 6*, 19–46.

ISO. (2001). *ISO/IEC 9126-1: Software Engineering—Product Quality—Part 1: Quality Model*. Geneva: International Organization for Standardization.

ISO. (2004). *ISO/IEC TR 9126-4: Software Engineer in—Product Quality—Part 4: Quality in Use Metrics*. Geneva: International Organization for Standardization.

Kalaimagal, S., & Srinivasan, R. (2008). A Retrospective on Software Component Quality Models. *SIGSOFT Software Engineering, 33*(6), 1–10. doi:10.1145/1449603.1449611

Kalakota, R., & Robinson, M. (2001). *E-business 2.0: Roadmap to success.* Reading, MA: Addison-Wesley.

Koch, C. (2011). A status on enterprise resource planning (ERP) studies in information systems research. *Computer and Information Science (ICIS), IEEE/ACIS 10th International Conference,* 409–414.

Kujala, S. I. (2008). Effective user involvement in product development by improving the analysis of user needs. *Behaviour & Information Technology, 27*(6), 457–473. doi:10.1080/01449290601111051

Kumar, A., Grover, P. S., & Kumar, R. (2009). A Quantitative Evaluation of Aspect-Oriented Software Quality Model (AOSQUAMO). *Software Engineering Notes, 34,* 1–9. doi:10.1145/1598732.1598736

Kwak, Y., Park, J., Chung, B., & Ghosh, S. (2012). Understanding end-users' acceptance of enterprise resource planning (ERP) system in project-based sector. *Engineering Management. IEEE Transactions, 59*(2), 266–277.

Law, C., Chen, C., & Wu, B. (2010). Managing the full ERP life cycle: Considerations of maintenance and support requirements and IT governance practice as integral elements of the formula for successful ERP adoption. *Computers in Industry, 61*(3), 297–308. doi:10.1016/j.compind.2009.10.004

Levi, S., & Doron, T. (2013). Critical success factors in enterprise resource planning systems: Review of the last decade. *Communications of the ACM, 45*(4).

McGinnis, T., & Huang, Z. (2007). Rethinking ERP success: A new perspective from knowledge management and continuous improvement. *Information & Management, 44*(7), 626–634. doi:10.1016/j.im.2007.05.006

Muscatello, J., & Chen, I. (2008). Enterprise resource planning (ERP) implementations: Theory and practice. *International Journal of Enterprise Information Systems, 4*(1), 63–77. doi:10.4018/jeis.2008010105

Nah, F. F.-H., Tan, X., & Beethe, M. (2005). An emergent model of end users' acceptance of enterprise resource planning systems: a grounded theory research. *Proceedings of the Americas Conference on Information Systems,* 2053–2057.

Ng, C., Gable, G., & Chan, T. (2002). An ERP-client benefit-oriented maintenance taxonomy. *Journal of Systems and Software, 64*(2), 87–109. doi:10.1016/S0164-1212(02)00029-8

Omieno, K., & Rodriguez, A. (2016). Usability Maturity Model and Assessment Tool for Virtual Learning Systems. *International Journal of Advanced Research in Computer and Communication Engineering, 5*(12), 78-84. DOI doi:10.17148/IJARCCE.2016.51217

Peng, G. C., & Nunes, M. B. (2009). Surfacing ERP exploitation risks through a risk ontology. *Industrial Management & Data Systems, 109*(7), 926–942. doi:10.1108/02635570910982283

Petter, S., DeLone, W., & McLean, E. (2008). Measuring information systems success: Models, dimensions, measures, and interrelationships. *European Journal of Information Systems, 17*(3), 236–263. doi:10.1057/ejis.2008.15

Ramdani, B. (2012). Information technology and organisational performance: Reviewing the business value of IT literature. In *Information Systems Theory* (pp. 283–301). New York, NY: Springer. doi:10.1007/978-1-4419-6108-2_15

Sherwood-Jones, B. (1995). *Total Systems Maturity. Internal report, version 2.* BAeSEMA.

Soja, P., & Paliwoda-Pękosz, G. (2013). Impediments to enterprise system implementation over the system lifecycle: Contrasting transition and developed economies. *The Electronic Journal on Information Systems in Developing Countries, 57*(1), 1–13. doi:10.1002/j.1681-4835.2013.tb00403.x

Talet, N., & Alwahaishi, S. (2011). The relevance cultural dimensions on the success adoption and use of IT. In *Third International Conference on Advanced Management Science*. Singapore: IACSIT Press.

Thamer, A., Mommad, I., & Ahmad, A. (2013). Software Quality Model of ERP System in Higher Education Institutions. *European Journal of Scientific Research, 99*, 15–21.

Wu, J.-H., & Wang, Y.-M. (2007, May). the ERP to produce a viable IS in the organization. *Computers in Human Behavior, 23*(3), 1582–1596. doi:10.1016/j.chb.2005.07.005

Zhu, Y., Li, Y., Wang, W., & Chen, J. (2010). What leads to post implementation success of ERP? An empirical study of the Chinese retail industry. *International Journal of Information Management, 30*(3), 265–276. doi:10.1016/j.ijinfomgt.2009.09.007

KEY TERMS AND DEFINITIONS

Human-Centered Scale: Is an approach and management framework that develops solutions to problems by involving the human perspective in all steps of the problem-solving process.

Human-Computer Interaction: Means of interaction between a computer and human being.

Information System: An integrated set of components for collecting, storing, and processing data and for delivering information, knowledge, and digital products.

Learnability: Refers to the capability of a software product to enable the user to learn how to use it.

Metrics: Refers to a quantifiable measure that is used to track and assess the status of a specific process.

Operability: The extent to which a system or device is able to keep in a functioning condition.

Understandability: The capability of software solution being understood or comprehensible.

Usability: Is the capability of the software to be understood learned, used, and attractive by the users, when used under specified conditions.

Usability Maturity Models: Includes models that help management understand the issues surrounding organizational opportunities and to improve the usability of its products.

Chapter 9
Evaluating the Learnability of ERP Software in Universities

Masese Bogomba Nelson
Kabarak University, Kenya

ABSTRACT

The technological innovation depends on learnability of the software used in terms of user interface design, program complexity of products that match the end user requirements, program complexity deals with commands used in the given ERP software, and training needs so that the ERP user can learn all required features and commands. Learnability signifies how quickly and comfortably a new user can begin efficient and error-free interaction. The main purpose of this chapter is to evaluate software learnability and performance of ERP software. Primary data was collected using survey through the use of questionnaires. Purposive sampling was used to collect data. The collected data focused on the software complexity, user interfaces analysis, ERP performance, challenges, efficiency, and training needs of ERP. Data analysis was done by inferential and descriptive statistics. The results indicated that there exists a positive and statistically significant relationship between the variables used.

DOI: 10.4018/978-1-5225-7678-5.ch009

INTRODUCTION

Over the past three decades, researchers in the software engineering field have considered learnability attribute in software applications. A number of learnability definitions have been introduced to provide a stronger foundation to the learnability concept in software engineering (Alcalá-Fdez & Alonso, 2016). ISO/IEC 9126 introduces a standard definition of learnability that is, "the capability of a software product to enable its users to learn how to use it" (Haaksma, *et al.*, 2018). Good learnability will lead to reasonable learning times, adequate productivity during the learning phase, and thus better satisfaction in new users. Improving learnability has a significant effect on the success of the ERP software, but improvement first requires identifying and understanding learnability issues. Learnability issues can only be identified by clearly defining, and then evaluating them in a systematic and consistent way (Haritos, 2017).

Successful organizations have today recognized the need for integrated systems that can improve their quality, client satisfaction and performance, Organizations can make this vision through enterprise resource planning. ERP is accounting oriented software, relational database based, multi-module but integrated, software system for identifying and planning the resource needs of an enterprise resource (Awa, 2018). ERP provides single user-interface for the entire organization to manage product planning, materials and parts purchasing, inventory control, distribution and logistics, scheduling, capacity utilization, order tracking, as well as planning for finance and human. (Singh, *et al.*,2017).In addition, it allows automation and integration of business process by enabling data and information sharing to reach best practices in managing the business process (Wang, *et al.*, 2018). The metrics used to measure learnability are discussed as follows:

1. Memorability describes when users return to ERP after a period of not using it and how easily they can reestablish proficiency. If a user has spent some time away from ERP application and then returns to it, how quickly can they reestablish proficiency (Yuniarto, *et al.*,2018). Command prompts have a low memorability factor this is because the user has to remember every command in order to navigate the application while simple graphical user interface can lead to high memorability for a common user because the user can see images and recall the flow of the system (Tulaskar, 2018)

2. User interface design refers to the visual layout of the elements that a user might interact within an ERP or technological product. This could be the control buttons of a radio or the visual layout of an ERP. User interface designs must not only be attractive to potential users but must also be functional and created with users in mind (Mahut, *et al.*,2018)

3. Program complexity encompasses numerous properties of a piece of software, all of which affect internal interactions, complicated implies being difficult to understand but with time and effort, ultimately becomes knowable and less complex (Ajami, *et al.*,2019).

PROBLEM STATEMENT

learnable software systems offer a number of benefits that include easy to learn, easy to remember steps used to execute a given task and few errors expected (Novak, 2014). A number of studies indicate that there are many factors affecting learnability ERP that include program complexity of the program, the user interface of the program and memorability of the user to recall the various commands used (Nelson, *et al.*, 2017). Existing metrics concentrate on satisfaction, correctness maintainability and security of the mobile social software. these metrics do not generally address the learnability of the ERP software, and users are generally hesitant to use these services due to poor learnability of the applications (Pretorius *et al.*, 2015). Therefore the problem at hand is that while ERP systems have the potential to help many organizations to increase the efficiency of today's organizations, these technologies appear to be difficult to learn, to use, adapt and to benefit from. ERP that is easier to learn and use are needed today and in the future, despite the fact that there is lack of structured training of different functionalities in the ERP system, lack of sufficient documentation for users to learn these systems, lack of a valid metrics model to evaluate these ERP systems before they are used in any organization. In this chapter mobile social software learnability prediction tool designed by Nelson, *et al.*, (2017) will be used to aid in the analysis of the learnability.

The objective of this chapter is to evaluate software learnability of ERP software in Universities focusing on software complexity, memorability, user interface, performance, challenges, the efficiency and training needs of ERP systems.

The chapter will provide insights to assist software designers, software developers, and open source owners to improve their software products in a way that best supports easy learnability of the users

RELATED WORKS

ERP is an industry term for Enterprise Resource Planning. ERP is an information system software that integrates departments and functions across an organization into one computer system. ERP runs off a single database, enabling various departments to share information and communicate with each other. ERP systems comprise function specific modules, designed to interact with the other modules. A properly planned ERP solution can facilitate zero redundancy, helping you to increase your organization's efficiency and productivity (Bhattacherjee, *et al.*, 2018)

ERP has evolved from the system known as MRPII (Manufacturing Requirement planning) system with the integration of information between Vendor, Customer and Manufacturer using networks such as LAN, wan and internet, MRPII had a number of drawbacks that made it not able to effectively integrate the different functional areas to share the resources effectively (Yildirim & Kusakci, 2018).

ERP Enterprise resource planning is the glue that binds together the different computer systems for a large organization. Generally, each department would have its own system optimized for that division's particular tasks. With ERP, each department still has its own system, but it can communicate and share information easier with the rest of the university(Odell, *et al.,* 2012). ERP connects different technologies used by each individual part of a university, eliminating duplicate and incompatible technology that is costly to the university. This involves integrating accounts payable, stock-control systems, order-monitoring systems and students and employee databases into one system (Seo, 2013).

to respond to the changing needs of an enterprise, The client-server technology enables ERP to run across various database back ends through Open Database Connectivity secondly modular and open, ERP system has to have open system architecture this means that any module can be interfaced or detached whenever required without affecting the other modules, It should support multiple hardware platforms for the companies having heterogeneous collection of systems. It must support some third party additions (Naedele, *et al.,* 2015).

The ERP system usually starts with a needs assessment and requirements analysis and ends in the first cycle with training and phased implementation. The continuous circle of development shown in the diagram below suggests that soon after completion of the first phase or cycle of an ERP project, we're back to planning the next phase. Each successive round of development arises from the need to add functionality and the rapidity of upgrades to ERP software (Cram & Marabelli, 2018).

WEB-BASED ERP ARCHITECTURE

A web-based ERP system has the capabilities of Internet access, real-time information and more accurate business solutions. In this respect, ERP is a proven asset if integrated properly and used to enhance the decision-making abilities and information flow of the university (Atzori *et al.*, 2010).

Figure 1.

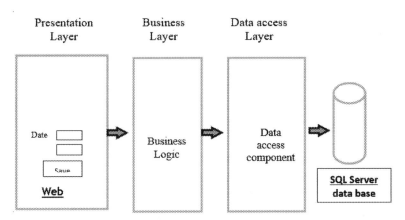

Internet-based ERP offers an entirely new outlook on the competition with the flexibility to meet the needs of clients quicker and with better accuracy. Universities are looking at ways to extend to the internet existing translation processes hosted on an ERP software package and to complement them with new functionality (Parthasarathy, 2013). Decision making and overall managerial improvements are produced through the Web's capacity to provide all the necessary information and ability to tighten relationships with students, employees, management and suppliers(Poister, 2010).

Integrating the internet with the ERP system offers access to all necessary information as well as the flexibility to coordinate these individually functioning modules constructing a complete and competitive tool for universities to use (Azeroual & Theel, 2019). ERP's role in today's perspective is to enable universities to be in touch with various university departments and the university community. ERP must gather all available information in the university departments and make this relevant data available to those who need it (VanDerSchaaf & Daim, 2018).

- **Presentation Tier:** Occupies the top level and displays information related to services available on a website. This tier communicates with other tiers by sending results to the browser and other tiers in the network, the user interacts the application using this presentation tier using a browser (Dobre & Xhafa, 2014).
- **Business Logic Tier:** this tier is pulled from the presentation tier. It controls application functionality by performing detailed processing and confirming all rules of the application are followed before the execution is done, this tier is kept independent of application servers or business logic (Han *et al* ., 2014)

- **Data Tier:** It contains the database servers where information is stored and retrieved. It provides a single unit for authoring, deploying and managing the data-tier objects instead of having to manage them separately (Bronson, 2013).

ERP MODEL

ERP Model has been designed to cover the in-depth functionalities of a University, from the perspective of various users carrying different roles and responsibilities such as Students, lecturers, Management, and subordinate staff. All the data is managed in a time sensitive manner along with the rules and policies applicable at that time, so whenever required, the exact information can be reproduced as it is (Deja & Próchnicka, 2019) this is shown in Figure 2.

The ERP has been developed after an in-depth analysis of the requirements of various departments and in close coordination with activities taking place, to help you to run all your university-related functions in the more efficient, productive and comfortable manner (Teoh, 2012). The primary purpose of the ERP is to provide mechanisms for automated processing and management of the entire institution. It reduces data error and ensures that information is managed efficiently and is always up-to-date. Complete student histories for all academic years can easily be searched, viewed and reported on the press of a button with the help of our solution (Grabski, *et al.*, 2011)

Figure 2.

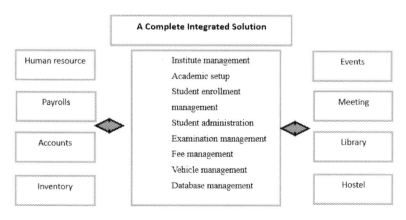

ERP FEATURES

End-to-End Solution

Whether it's the enrollment of a new student or calculation of salary for the staff, the ERP solution provides you a fully integrated end-to-end solution to manage all the functions and activities required for your education institution. It ensures that offices, faculty and students have access to timely and up-to-date information. It manages high volumes of critical information with hundred percent of accuracy helping you to run your institution more smoothly and efficiently. It creates a foundation for new processes that can yield significant returns on investment (Chen, *et al.*, 2015).

N-Tier Architecture

The ERP solution is designed on an N-Tier architecture allowing multiple users to work simultaneously from multiple locations on a single database. This helps in sharing information between different departments and users on a real-time basis (Oluwatosin, 2014).

Streamlines Educational Process

The ERP solution often prompts significant process reengineering and could breathe life into ineffective and inefficient departments or processes. It helps in proper documentation and standardization of education process by setting up protocols for each and every process. Our solution also provides you an opportunity to correct broken processes and replace them with modern, system-enabled, state-of-the-art business practices (Bell & Orzen, 2016).

Completely Organizes Data With No Redundancy

The ERP solution offers zero redundancy of data for managing the various aspects of your educational business needs. For example, you just need to add the name of a student only once and it will automatically appear in rest of the modules like Fee, Courses, Examination, Promotion for employees (Helo *et al.,* 2014).

Comprehensive Reporting System

Universities around the world consider an effective reporting system as a vehicle for evaluating and enhancing the performance of the entire system. Thus reports have become the most vital part of any application software. What so ever new features there may be in an application, the end user evaluates the quality of software by its quality of reports (Fuggetta & Di Nitto, 2014).

The ERP solution offers a powerful mechanism to generate accurate and robust reports with a great deal of flexibility. Whether you want a report for a single student or for the entire institute, it gives you plenty of options and flexibility to generate reports at multiple levels helping you to enhance the performance and productivity of your institution(Mukherjee & Das, 2017).

Easy Centralized Backup Options

Database Backup is the most critical part of any ERP solution. Our ERP comes with easy to manage the database-backup system. The database backup and restoration processes both are simple and easy and don't require any database expert to perform these activities (Bass, *et al.*, 2015)

LEARNABILITY OF ERP SYSTEMS

Learnability is the criterion used to determine the degree of effort required to learn how to use the system efficiently and effectively and can be used as one criterion to evaluate ERP system learnability(Adewumi *et al.,* 2019)

Learnability is one of the most important criteria of usability and refers to the capability of the system to enable the user to learn to use the application, Customization relates to the ability of the ERP system to be customized according to the specific needs of an organization depending on the user functions and tasks performed (Turetken, *et al.,* 2019).

Customizability is a measure of the extent which the system can be adapted, either by the user or by the system. Appropriateness of task support aims to establish if there is an accurate alignment between the system and the real world, in order to ensure effective task support and efficient task completion (Subramaniam & Nakkeeran, 2019)

TRENDS IN ERP SYSTEMS

To keep your ERP relevant or upgrading university ERP the following will be critical while are essential for the new ERP system, it includes:

1.   **Use the Cloud as the Key to Transformation:** The cloud is not only a platform or a deployment option also Develop a cloud strategy that includes your ERP and other core systems (Nieuwenhuis, *et al.,* 2018)
2.   **Extend With AI, Machine Learning, and Analytics:** Part of the university plan should be to invest in intelligence and automation. Traditionally, ERP users would look for add-on products, but that's no longer necessary. These capabilities are part of today's and future ERP systems, allowing you to grow and scale in your own way and in real-time (Pramanik, *et al.,* 2018).
3.   **Security:** Data security should be paramount and should not to be taken lightly or you pay the consequences. While ERP alone can't cover all your security requirements, it is imperative that your ERP offers controls to protect the data it contains and make it easy for you to monitor and audit (Michelman, 2018).

LEARNABILITY METRICS THAT AFFECT ERP SOFTWARE

Software metric has been defined as a measure of some property of a piece of software or its specifications (Grossman, 2012). The following are metrics that will affect ERP learnability.

Program Load Time

a loader is the part of an operating system that is responsible for loading programs and libraries. It is one of the essential stages in the process of starting a program, as it places programs into memory and prepares them for execution (Cozzi, *et al.*, 2018).

Loading a program involves reading the contents of the executable file containing the program instructions into memory, and then carrying out other required preparatory tasks to prepare the executable for running. Once loading is complete, the operating system starts the program by passing control to the loaded program code (Kuesel, *et al.*,2014).

To calculate time taken by a process, the clock() function which is available in the library the system calls the clock function at the beginning and end of the code for which we measure time, subtract the values, and then divide by clocks_per_sec that indicates the number of clock ticks per second, to get processor time, the following program is used to demonstrate the loader time (Roemer, *et al.*, 2012).

Example

```
#include <time.h>
clock_t start, end;
double cpu_time_used;
```

```
start = clock();
end = clock();
cpu_time_used = ((double) (end - start)) / CLOCKS_PER_SEC;
```

Source Lines of Code

source lines of code have been defined as a software metric used to measure the size of a computer program by counting the number of source lines in the text of the program's source code(Zhang, *et al.,* 2013). Source Lines of code metric can be used to predict the amount of effort that will be required to develop, learn and maintain the software once the software is produced (Bennin, *et al.,* 2018).

Logical lines of code attempt to measure the number of statements, physical lines of code measures are sensitive to logically irrelevant formatting and style conventions, while logical lines of code are less sensitive to formatting and style conventions (Souley & Bata, 2013).

Example

```
for (i = 0; i < 50; i += 1)
{
printf("hello");
} /* Now how many lines of code is this? */
```

In this example we have: 4 Physical Lines of Code, 2 Logical Lines of Code and 1 comment line.

The advantages of lines of code include the physical entity, manual counting effort can be easily eliminated by automating the counting process (Bhatt, *et* al.,2012). Small utilities may be developed for counting the lines of code in a program also it is an intuitive metric for measuring the size of software due to the fact that it can be seen and the effect of it can be visualized (Allamanis, & Sutton, 2013)

Software Bugs

software bugs have been defined as errors, flaws, failures or faults in a computer program or system that causes it to produce an incorrect or unexpected result, or to behave in unintended ways (Gayathri & Sudha, 2014).

Most bugs arise from mistakes and errors made in either a program's source code or its design, or in components and operating systems used by such programs. A few are caused by compilers producing incorrect codes (Ogheneovo, 2014).

Erp program that contains a large number of bugs, it seriously interferes with its functionality and is said to be defective, bugs trigger errors that may have ripple effects (Prechelt & Pepper, 2014).

Bugs may have subtle effects or cause the program to crash or freeze the computer. Others qualify as security bugs and might, for example, enable a malicious user to bypass access controls in order to obtain unauthorized privileges(Ganeshkumar & Kalaivani, 2015).

Defect density has been defined as the degree of compactness of a substance it compactness of defects in the application (Barb, *et al* ., 2014). It is calculated using the following formula: the

the average number of defects/ Functional area or KLOC(Thousand Lines of code)
Example

there are 30 defects for 15KLOC. It would then be:
Total no. of defects/KLOC = 30/15 = 0.5 = Density is 1 Defect for every 2 KLOC.

ERP FEATURES INFLUENCE LEARNABILITY

In order to influence the learnability of a system, a general understanding of the factors affecting learnability is needed. The following are major factors that will influence mobile social software learnability.

Graphical Icons

The first approach is to improve the initial learnability of ERP graphical icons for naive users will be crucial to easy learnability of the ERP software. It is well known that difficulties in interacting with the interface greatly decrease an application's overall learnability (Alshehri & Freeman, 2014).

Correctly interpreting icons is particularly important in learning to perform tasks on ERP. they have a wide variety of functionality that is not commonly available on laptop or desktop computers, such as a number of text entry methods and data connectivity options like Wi-Fi, Bluetooth, infrared and cellular (Laurillard, 2013).

Many of these functions can only be accessed through unique icons and generic buttons as opposed to dedicated buttons and other controls also there are many more operating systems for ERP such as Android, Windows and embedded Linux than desktop operating systems like Windows, MacOS, and Linux, in most cases each system typically uses its own unique set of icons(Mathôt *et al.*, 2011).

Multi-Layered Interfaces

Multi-Layered interfaces can be designed to support learning such that novices first learn to perform basic tasks by working in a reduced-functionality, simplified layer of the interface (Fan & Truong, 2018).

Once users have mastered this layer or require more advanced functionality, they can transition to increasingly complex layers and learn to perform more advanced tasks (Van & Kirschner, 2012).

multi-layered interfaces focus on improving initial learning of software applications using the multi-layered interface approach. It can be designed to support learning such that novices first learn to perform basic tasks by working in a reduced-functionality. A simplified layer allows the users who have mastered this a given layer or require more advanced functionality to transition to increasingly complex layers and learn to perform more advanced tasks (Lafreniere, & Grossman, 2018).

Thus Multi-Layered interfaces can provide a form of intrinsic scaffolding. Specifically, Multi-Layered interfaces reduce an application's complexity of functions and content during the learning process, thereby helping learners focus on key elements to begin performing tasks. Functionality reduced layers are likely to place fewer demands on the user's working memory, which may enhance learnability (Levingstone, *et al,* 2016).

Augmenting the Mobile Device's Display

ERP users already have access to a number of supportive scaffolding resources such as manuals, information on the Internet and people in their social circle. However, given the difficulties, users have with learning to use mobile devices it is not clear how effective current resources are in helping them and whether users actually use or want to use them (Waizenegger *et al.,* 2016).

These resources are generally not closely integrated with the tool being learned, and interactivity is often limited, this extra larger display can provide guidance and feedback like overlays that indicate which button to press next on, encouraging feedback after a subtask is successfully completed in a variety of media and formats such as text help, demonstration videos and real-time access to domain experts. This design approach appears to have much potential for creating a resource that can help naive users while they learn to use mobile devices (Terantino, 2011).

ERP INTERFACE FEATURES

In order to achieve learnability the ERP software should always aim to achieve the following features:

Simplicity

ERP applications are rather simple in terms of color scheme and graphics. The color scheme usually consists of a few colors along with slight monochromatic variations, the background is generally white, updates are often highlighted with a light color as well, usually green or yellow, alerts are usually highlighted with a red background color (Tella & Akinboro, 2015).

The graphics are always very simple and are used very sparingly. There are multiple reasons for this. The most important reason is the simple fact that vivid visual design isn't really useful on social networking sites (Herout *et al.*, 2011).

ERP applications are supposed to provide a shared environment where the content can be easily produced and where conversations can take place and a strong visual design would create unnecessary noise and make it harder for users to focus on their conversations (Murray, 2011).

The colors on ERP are always calm and supportive, rather than bright and unbearable. features do not fight for attention, many of them remain invisible most of the time, in fact, most social media interfaces are context-sensitive, displaying many features only on demand, with such a large amount of data and functions, bright colors would simply get in the way and distract the user (Akaichi, 2014)

Prominent and Functional Search

Good search functionality is undoubtedly the pinnacle of good usability and good user interface. in the ERP a search functionality is a must simply because of the vast amount of available information (Miroshnichenko, 2015). A common feature in ERP applications is the use of live search results and filtering, When you type into the box, the results are filtered out in a drop-down style. The filtering helps users to quickly find the content they are looking for and get rid of any content that isn't relevant to them. You want the experience to be fine-tuned to each individual user and filtering searches do just this, the search results page is even more crucial than a user-friendly design of a search box (Ghatage & Gaikwad, 2014).

Prominent Call to Action Buttons

ERP applications contain many functions that need to be communicated in some way, Consequently, buttons and links need to be placed almost on every page except a sign-up form is probably the only reasonable exception some links related to navigation and some let the user adjust specific application function. (Uncel, 2011).

Buttons are often used to animate users to actions, while links are often more passive and subtle, buttons are also often larger, more vivid and more memorable, despite the task the button performs, it needs to be large and clickable, Often ERP application has only a few call-to-action-buttons that are supposed to motivate users to actions, these buttons are usually designed and placed prominently, while other design elements remain very subtle and simple(Tella & Akinboro, 2015).

PROGRAM COMPLEXITY

Program complexity encompasses numerous properties of a piece of software, all of which affect internal interactions, complicated implies being difficult to understand but with time and effort, ultimately becomes knowable and complex (Wolf-Branigin, 2013). while the term complex, describes the interactions between a number of entities as the number of entities increases, the number of interactions between them would increase exponentially, and it would get to a point where it would be impossible to know and understand all of them (Mbonimpa, 2012).

Similarly, higher levels of program complexity in software increase the risk of unintentionally interfering with interactions and so increases the chance of introducing defects when making changes, but in more extreme cases, it can make modifying the software virtually impossible (kim, *et al*, 2014). Some of the more commonly used measures include:

Cyclomatic Complexity

Cyclomatic complexityMcCabe(1976), it is a software metric used to measure the complexity of a program. This metric measures independent paths through program source code an independent path is defined as a path that has at least one edge which has not been traversed before in any other paths(shepperd, 1988).

Cyclomatic complexity can be calculated with respect to functions, modules, methods or classes within a program, the cyclomatic complexity is more in the classes/methods where there are a lot of conditional operators. They provide insight into the overall code complexity of functions or software components by quantifying the number of linearly independent paths or decision logic(Baggen, *et al.*,2012).

Cyclomatic complexity metrics are an important indicator of readability, maintainability, and portability(Tomas et al.,2012).Cyclomatic complexity is defined as follows:

$$CC = E - N + P$$

where E = the number of edges of the graph, N = the number of nodes of the graph, P = the number of connected components

The following example illustrates how cyclomatic complexity is computed:

```
IF Z = 10 THEN
IF Y > W THEN
Z = Y
ELSE
Z = W
ENDIF
ENDIF
Print Z, Print Y, Print W
```

Explanation

The Cyclomatic complexity is calculated using the above control flow diagram that shows seven nodes(shapes) and eight edges (lines), hence the cyclomatic complexity is 8 - 7 + 2 = 3. It can be represented in Figure 3.

program module having cyclomatic complexity less than is considered to be a simple program without much risk and if the cyclomatic complexity is greater than 10 considered complexes. The overly complex module reduces maintainability and testability (Fenton & Bieman, 2014).

Cyclomatic complexity helps us by measuring the code complexity. The higher the code complexity, the more complex is the code. The number of the Cyclomatic complexity depends on how many different execution paths or control flow of your code can execute depending on various inputs. Depending on the level of complexity it may affect the quality and effectiveness of erp software(Panichella, *et al.,* 2018)

METHODOLOGY

This section describes how the data was collected, sampling method and data analysis techniques. A sample size of 90 users was sampled, drawn from a public

214

Figure 3.

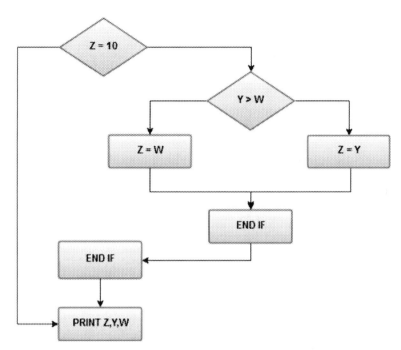

university and private university egerton and Kabarak were selected respectively. purposive sampling was used as sampling technique, the research design adopted was mixed method further the theoretical research framework was used because it provides a large, overarching structure of ideas that the researcher can then draw from in beginning to analyze a phenomenon.

Data collection tools included questionnaires that were used to collect data from the lecturers, nonteaching staff and students using the ERP system in Egerton university and Kabarak university the questionnaires were distributed equally and the interview was done to the top management, ict manager, system administrators and Network administrators to validate the collected data. the experiment was used to evaluate the memorability of the erp users through assigning them a task to execute.

learnability prediction tool designed by Nelson, Muchiri & Mbuguah (2017) was used to evaluate learnability of ERP program and it focused on the following user interface features, program complexity, memorability of ERP performance, challenges. In the end, the tool presents the learnability percentage of the user which informs the training needs of the particular user. Data analysis was done by inferential and descriptive statistics. Lastly, results were analyzed and appropriate conclusions and recommendations made.

RESULTS PRESENTATION AND DISCUSSION

This section presents the findings of the study that include demographic data, erp performance, efficiency, challenges, software complexity, and user interface features.

Demographic Information

It was noted that 66.7% were students while 33.3% were staffs. It was illustrious that there were 20% more females than males in the sampled population. Results are presented as follows in Table 1.

Cross-Tabulation Showing Age and Level of Education

According to Table 2, it was noted that 56.7% were diploma holders while Ph.D. was constituted by 3.3. % of the total population sampled. Equally, a majority were

Table 1. Respondent category and gender

		Male	**Female**	**Total**
Students	Frequency	15	45	60
Staffs	Frequency	21	9	30
Total		36	54	90
Percentage		40.0%	60.0%	100.0%

Source: (research data, 2018)

Table 2. Age and level of education

		Certificate	**Diploma**	**Degree**	**Masters**	**Doctor**	**Total**
18-25 Years	**Frequency**	2	21	29	0	0	52
	Percentage %	2.2	23.3	32.2	0.0	0.0	57.8
26-33 Years	**Frequency**	2	4	20	5	0	31
	Percentage %	2.2	4.4	22.2	5.6	0.0	34.4
34-41 Years	**Frequency**	0	2	2	0	3	7
	Percentage %	0.0	2.2	2.2	0.0	3.3	7.8
	Total Frequency	4	27	51	5	3	90
	Total percentage	4.4	30.0	56.7	5.6	3.3	100.0

Source: (research data, 2018)

between the ages of 18-33 years 92.2% while 7.8% with the advanced age of up to 41 years. The findings of cross-tabulation between age and education level are presented in table 2.

Duration of ERP Utilization

An analysis of the utilization period of ERP revealed that 80% had used ERP for up to 4 years, 15.6% have used it up to 6 years. The minority have used it for one year(4.4%). Findings are presented in Figure 4.

EVALUATING THE LEARNABILITY OF ERP SOFTWARE

This section deals with a description of the respondents' behavior to various attributes of the ERP software.

Performance

As regards to performance, up to 70% of respondents significantly agreed that ERP system has great processing speed and that The ERP system provides more than one way to filter records while at least 10% differed significantly. Additionally, at most 90% agreed that The ERP system Throughput is fast and that its response time is relatively good with chi-square =55.80;p<0.05 respectively. This view was upheld by 90% who affirm that the ERP system enhances effectiveness in their task. It was observed that all respondents 100% maintain that the ERP system has a

Figure 4.

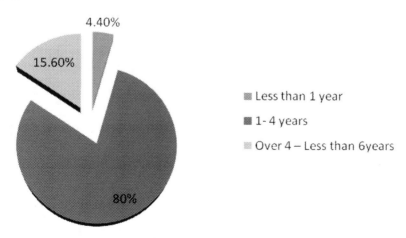

positive impact on the productivity of various tasks. The findings indicated that the performance of the ERP essential in the learnability of any ERP system. Findings are presented in Table 3.

Efficiency

majority of respondents 75.6% significantly agreed that ERP system reduces data Redundancy as it will better resource utilization 88.9%. Similarly, 78.9% agreed that ERP system combines data from units/ departments of the organization while 62.2% affirm that the ERP system of the University is timely and reliable. However, 21.1% were not decided whether an ERP system enhances more accountability while 41.1% disagreed that the ERP system allows for customization. findings imply efficiency is the key feature in enhancing performance and learnability of the ERP systems. The findings are presented in table 4.

Table 3. Performance

ERP Feature	Strongly disagree	Disagree	Neither agree/ disagree	Agree	Strongly Agree	Total
	Percent %	Percent %	Percent %	Percent %	Percent %	Percent %
ERP system has great processing speed	0.0	10.0	20.0	60.0	10.0	100
The ERP system provides more than one way to filter records	0.0	10.0	10.0	60.0	20.0	100
The ERP system enhances the effectiveness in my task	0.0	0.0	10.0	50.0	40.0	100
The ERP system Throughput is fast	0.0	0.0	20.0	70.0	10.0	100
The ERP system response time is relatively good	0.0	0.0	10.0	70.0	20.0	100
The ERP system has positive impact on the productivity of various tasks	0.0	0.0	0.0	40.0	60.0	100

Source: (research data, 2018)

Table 4. Efficiency

ERP Feature	Strongly Disagree	Disagree	Neither agree/ disagree	Agree	Strongly Agree	Total
	percent %	percent %	Percent %	percent %	Percent %	Percent %
ERP system combines data from units/ departments of the organization	0.0	1.1	20.0	48.9	30.0	100
ERP system allows for customization.	30.0	11.1	30.0	20.0	8.9	100
ERP system enhances more accountability	0.0	3.3	21.1	36.7	38.9	100
ERP will better resource utilization	0.0	1.1	10.0	50.0	38.9	100
ERP system reduce data Redundancy	0.0	2.2	22.2	57.8	17.8	100
The ERP system provides timely and reliable	0.0	0.0	37.8	43.3	18.9	100

Source: (research data, 2018)

Correlation Analysis

The results indicated that there exists a positive and significant relationship between Efficiency and ERP Performance($r=0.565$; $p<0.01$).This suggests that when ERP Software becomes more consistent, its performance increases. However, in the lack of reliability of ERP, it reduces its performance considerably. The findings are presented in Table 5.

Training

Regarding training, the findings indicate that 11.1% significantly disagreed that employees are tracked to ensure that they have received the appropriate ERP system

Table 5. Correlation between efficiency and ERP performance

		Performance	Efficiency
Performance	Pearson Correlation	1	0.565**
	Sig. (2-tailed)		.000
	N	90	90

**. Correlation is significant at the 0.01 level (2-tailed).

training. This finding also indicated 22.2% disagreed that specific user training needs were identified early in the implementation. Additionally, respondents disagreed that ERP system training review sessions are scheduled and that a formal training program has been developed to meet the requirements of ERP system users as represented by 48.9% and 42.2% respectively. It was evident that they also disagreed that training materials target the entire business task, not just the ERP screens and reports 42.2%. finally, nearly half of the respondents 26.7% agreed that training is conducted by consultants while 32.2% disagreed. By and large, training concerning ERP software needs to be fast-tracked in institutions in order to allow stakeholders to utilize this software appropriately. The findings imply that good training increases the performance of the ERP system and users are comfortable with the software if they had been trained properly. The findings are presented in Table 6.

Correlation Analysis

The results showed that there exist a positive and significant relationship between Training and ERP Performance (r=0.613; p<0.01). This implies that when the people are well trained on ERP Software, its performance increases and vice versa. The findings are presented in Table 7.

Table 6. Descriptive on training

erp Feature	Strongly Disagree	Disagree	Neither agree/ disagree	Agree	Strongly Agree	Total
	Percent %	Percent %	Percent %	Percent %	Percent %	Percent %
Training is conducted by consultants	0.0	32.2	41.1	26.7	0.0	100
ERP system training review sessions are scheduled	10.0	38.9	30.0	11.1	10.0	100
Employees are tracked to ensure that they have received ERP system training.	0.0	11.1	67.8	11.1	10.0	100
Training materials are extensive in all aspects of the ERP screens and reports	10.0	32.2	36.7	21.1	0.0	100
training/s are user tailored	10.0	32.2	36.7	11.1	10.0	100
Specific user training needs were identified early in the implementation	1.1	21.1	37.8	40.0	0.0	100

Source: (research data, 2018)

Table 7. Correlation between training and ERP performance

		Performance	Training
Performance	Pearson Correlation	1	0.613**
	Sig. (2-tailed)		0.000
	N	90	90

**. Correlation is significant at the 0.01 level (2-tailed).

Table 8. ERP challenges

ERP Feature	Strongly Disagree	Disagree	Neither agree/ disagree	Agree	Strongly Agree	Total
	Percent %	percent %	Percent %	percent %	Percent %	percent %
Quality of ERP is not up standard.	44.4	40.0	0.0	15.6	0.0	100
Security of the system easily compromised.	33.3	41.1	17.8	7.8	0.0	100
Vendors' unreliability during major trouble shooting.	11.1	41.1	30.0	17.8	0.0	100
The system is not well validated to avoid minor errors.	22.2	33.3	25.6	18.9	0.0	100
License constraints	11.1	33.3	55.6	0.0	0.0	100
Lack of skills for utilization of the ERP	11.1	55.6	10.0	23.3	0.0	100

Source: (research data, 2018)

ERP Challenges

The study findings indicated that majority of respondents 33.3% affirmed significantly that lack of skills for utilization of the ERP coupled with vendors' unreliability during major troubleshooting 17.8%, system validation 18.9% and Quality of ERP 15.6% were the major ERP Challenges. However, Security of the system and License constraints were regarded to be least of challenges affecting ERP software. the findings indicate that challenges greatly hinder the performance of the ERP software as users struggle to utilize the system. The findings are presented in Table 8.

Correlation Analysis

The results showed that there exist a negative and significant relationship between ERP Challenges and its Performance (r=-0.344; p<0.01). This implies that when ERP Challenges increases, its performance decreases while when these challenges are resolved, performance improves significantly. The findings are presented in Table 9.

Assessment of Program Complexity

Descriptive statistics were computed in order to determine the respondent's behavior concerning program complexity of the ERP. The findings revealed that 75.6% of the respondents agreed that the program includes security features. The findings were consistent with 65% of the who agreed that the program is consistent for various operations. Similarly,53.9% of the respondents agreed that the program is efficient in execution. However, respondents disagreed that the program manages well errors during data entry. The similar perception was asserted by 42.9% of the respondents who disagreed that the program maintenance is cheap, like upgrades. Further that the program supports compatibility with other applications 27.8%.

This findings, therefore, concluded that when the program of the ERP is complicated, it may affect performance. This finding implies that the program complexity of the ERP has an effect on performance in that program which is easy and manageable by users will ultimately influence positively its learnability. The results are tabulated in Table 10.

Correlation Analysis

The results showed that there exist a negative and significant relationship between ERP program complexity and its Performance (r=-0.666; p<0.01). This implies that when ERP program complexity increases, it's performance decreases while when these program complexities are resolved, performance improves significantly. The findings are presented in Table 11.

Table 9. Correlation between training and ERP performance

		Performance	**ERP Challenges**
	Pearson Correlation	1	-0.344**
Performance	Sig. (2-tailed)		.001
	N	90	90

**. Correlation is significant at the 0.01 level (2-tailed).

Table 10. Program complexity

ERP Feature	Strongly Disagree	Disagree	Neither agree/ disagree	Agree	StronglyAgree	total
	percent %	percent %	Percent %	percent %	Percent %	percent %
The program is consistent for various operations.	4.1	16.8	14.2	58.0	7.0	100
The program manages well errors.		9.9	25.5	30	8.7	100
The program includes security features.	2.3	2.9	19.1	56.5	19.1	100
The program is Efficient in execution.	2.6	18.8	24.6	37.7	16.2	100
The program supports compatibility		11.9	15.9	58.8	13.3	100
Program maintaince is cheap	8.4	34.5	19.1	23.8	14.2	100

Source: (research data, 2018)

Table 11. Correlation between program complexity and ERP performance

		Performance	Program complexity
	Pearson Correlation	1	-0.666**
Performance	Sig. (2-tailed)		.001
	N	90	90

**. Correlation is significant at the 0.01 level (2-tailed).

Assessment of User Interface Features

The findings indicated that the majority of the respondents agreed that the interface includes mechanisms that allow users to recover from the error of 76.3%. These findings are supported by the chi-square results ($\chi^2 =331.4$;p<0.01). it was observed that 61.4% agreed that the interface is clear for some operations in addition respondents averred that the icons or commands in the interface are clear. it was noted that 43.5% of the respondents agreed that the interface is well designed to enable easy navigation and that customizing some features is easy in the interface. It was realized that respondents avowed that user interface provides the user with enough suggestions and prompt towards the right usage of 55.03%. This finding was supported by 54.5% of the respondents who acknowledged that the interface provides the feedback when errors occur and provide user help facilities. However, 43.3% of the respondents disagreed that there is a clear understanding of the hierarchical of the interface throughout the program. These findings are supported by the chi-square results ($\chi^2 = 71.88$; p<0.01). The findings are tabulated in table 12.

This means that as the interface allow users to recover from errors, icons or commands becoming clear and liked to the specific functions, provides the user enough suggestions and prompt towards the right usage, provides the feedback when errors occur and provide user help facilities, the tendency of learnability increases

Correlation Analysis

The results showed that there exists a strong and significant relationship between ERP user interface and its Performance (r=0.732; p<0.01). This implies that when an ERP user interface increases the performance increases while when user interface challenges are resolved, performance improves significantly. The findings are presented in Table 13.

Table 12. User interface features

ERP Feature	Strongly Disagree	Disagree	Neither agree/ disagree	Agree	StronglyAgree	total
	Percent %	Percent %	Percent %	Percent %	Percent %	Percent %
The interface is under stable for the same operations		11.9	26.7	53.6	7.8	100
The interface has error recovery mechanisms	3.2	3.2	8.7	58.0	18.3	100
The interface provides the feedback when errors occur	2.6	17.4	25.5	38.8	15.7	100
The interface is well designed to enable easy navigation	5.2	20.9	30.4	38.3	5.2	100
the hierarchical of the interface is uniform throughout the program	8.7	33.6	16.8	27.2	13.6	100
To customize some features is easy in the interface	5.2	20.9	30.4	38.3	5.2	100

Source: (research data, 2018)

224

Table 13. Correlation between user interface and ERP performance

		Performance	User interface
	Pearson Correlation	1	0.732**
Performance	Sig. (2-tailed)		.001
	N	90	90

**. Correlation is significant at the 0.01 level (2-tailed).

MEMORABILITY INDICATORS

The experiment was performed to assess the memorability level for the ERP the main objective for the experiment was to attempt to find out the relationship between memorability and learnability attributes. it is significant noting that latter part of descriptive findings is in line with the primary data collected and then transformed to a 3-point scale of easy, moderate and difficult for easy interpretation. Easy indicates the user can be able to accomplish the task in a specific time frame, moderate indicates the user can so some steps but eventually seek help to complete the task and difficult the user has to seek help from the start to complete the task

The findings revealed that regarding memorability of changing settings for security and privacy 39,5 it was found to be easy, 50.5 percentage of respondents indicated it was moderate while 10 percentage indicated it was difficult in regard to blocking the user account 54.5 percentage of the respondents showed it was difficult to effectively complete the task on other hand 60.5 of the respondents demonstrated tacking approval of the claim was easy to perform, 11 percentage indicated applying for the imprest was difficult to perform it was observed that to modify user information and to navigate to a specific function was noted to be easy Table 14 shows the findings of the analysis.

CONCLUSION

The chapter endeavored to investigate learnability of the ERP software in universities to achieve this goal, the chapter sought to determine the main factors that affect learnability that include efficiency, training needs, challenges facing ERP, program complexity and user interface design.

The results indicated that there exists a positive and statistically significant relationship between efficiency and ERP Performance This suggests that when the ERP Software becomes more consistent, its performance increases. The results showed that there exist a positive and statistically significant relationship between

Table 14. Memorability of social software

erpfeature	Percentage %			Total (%)
	Easy	Moderate	Difficult	
Change settings for security and privacy	39.5	50.5	10.0	**100**
Block account	20.0	25.5	54.5	**100**
Tack approval of a claim	60.5	25.5	14.0	**100**
Apply for imprest	48.5	40.5	11.0	**100**
Request for a service	42.7	47.3	10.0	**100**
Modify user information	53.3	40.3	6.4	**100**
Navigate to a specific function	67.8	25.2	7.0	**100**

Source: (research data, 2018)

Training and ERP Performance This indicates that when the people are well trained on ERP Software, its performance increases and vice versa.

The results showed that there exist a negative and significant relationship between ERP Challenges and its Performance. This means that when ERP Challenges increases, its performance decreases while when these challenges are resolved, performance improves significantly, similarly to program complexity. The results showed that there exists a strong and significant relationship between ERP user interface and its Performance. This implies that when ERP user interface increases the performance increases while when user interface and memorability challenges are resolved, performance improves significantly.

RECOMMENDATION

The chapter recommends that there should be ERP model that can be used to test the developed ERP systems before they are implemented to ascertain if they comply with ERP standards, further the ERP systems should use easy user interfaces and commands that are easily understood by all end users.

REFERENCES

Adewumi, A., Misra, S., Omoregbe, N., & Sanz, L. F. (2019). FOSSES: Framework for open-source software evaluation and selection. *Software, Practice & Experience, 49*(5), 780–812. doi:10.1002pe.2682

Ajami, S., Woodbridge, Y., & Feitelson, D. G. (2019). Syntax, predicates, idioms—What really affects code complexity? *Empirical Software Engineering, 24*(1), 287–328. doi:10.100710664-018-9628-3

Akaichi, J. (2014). A medical social network for physicians' annotations posting and summarization. *Social Network Analysis and Mining, 4*(1), 1–8. doi:10.100713278-014-0225-1

Alcalá-Fdez, J., & Alonso, J. M. (2016). A survey of fuzzy systems software: Taxonomy, current research trends, and prospects. *IEEE Transactions on Fuzzy Systems, 24*(1), 40–56. doi:10.1109/TFUZZ.2015.2426212

Appel, A. P., de Cerqueira Gatti, M. A., Neto, S. M. B., Pinhanez, C. S., & Dos Santos, C. N. (2013). *U.S. Patent Application No. 13/887,354.* Washington, DC: US Patent Office.

Atzori, L., Iera, A., & Morabito, G. (2010). The internet of things: A survey. *Computer Networks, 54*(15), 2787–2805. doi:10.1016/j.comnet.2010.05.010

Awa, H. O. (2018). Some antecedent factors that shape actors' adoption of enterprise systems. *Enterprise Information Systems,* 1–25.

Azeroual, O., & Theel, H. (2019). *The effects of using business intelligence systems on excellence management and decision-making process by start-up companies: A case study.* arXiv preprint arXiv:1901.10555

Baggen, R., Correia, J. P., Schill, K., & Visser, J. (2012). Standardized code quality benchmarking for improving software maintainability. *Software Quality Journal, 20*(2), 287–307. doi:10.100711219-011-9144-9

Barb, A. S., Neill, C. J., Sangwan, R. S., & Piovoso, M. J. (2014). A statistical study of the relevance of lines of code measures in software projects. *Innovations in Systems and Software Engineering, 10*(4), 243–260. doi:10.100711334-014-0231-5

Bass, L., Weber, I., & Zhu, L. (2015). *DevOps: A Software Architect's Perspective.* Addison-Wesley Professional.

Bell, S. C., & Orzen, M. A. (2016). *Lean IT: Enabling and sustaining your lean transformation.* CRC Press.

Bennin, K. E., Keung, J., Phannachitta, P., Monden, A., & Mensah, S. (2018). Mahakil: Diversity based oversampling approach to alleviate the class imbalance issue in software defect prediction. *IEEE Transactions on Software Engineering*, *44*(6), 534–550. doi:10.1109/TSE.2017.2731766

Bhatt, K., Tarey, V., Patel, P., Mits, K. B., & Ujjain, D. (2012). Analysis of source lines of code (SLOC) metric. *International Journal of Emerging Technology and Advanced Engineering*, *2*(5), 150–154.

Bhattacherjee, A., Davis, C. J., Connolly, A. J., & Hikmet, N. (2018). User response to mandatory IT use: A Coping Theory perspective. *European Journal of Information Systems*, *27*(4), 395–414. doi:10.105741303-017-0047-0

Bronson, N., Amsden, Z., Cabrera, G., Chakka, P., Dimov, P., Ding, H., & Marchukov, M. (2013). TAO: Facebook's Distributed Data Store for the Social Graph. In *USENIX Annual Technical Conference* (pp. 49-60). USENIX.

Chen, C. S., Liang, W. Y., & Hsu, H. Y. (2015). A cloud computing platform for ERP applications. *Applied Soft Computing*, *27*, 127–136. doi:10.1016/j.asoc.2014.11.009

Colborne, G. (2010). *Simple and usable web, mobile, and interaction design*. New Riders.

Coursaris, C. K., & Kim, D. J. (2011). A meta-analytical review of empirical mobile usability studies. *Journal of Usability Studies*, *6*(3), 117–171.

Cozzi, E., Graziano, M., Fratantonio, Y., & Balzarotti, D. (2018). Understanding Linux malware. In *2018 IEEE Symposium on Security and Privacy (SP)* (pp. 161-175). IEEE. 10.1109/SP.2018.00054

Cram, W. A., & Marabelli, M. (2018). Have your cake and eat it too? Simultaneously pursuing the knowledge-sharing benefits of agile and traditional development approaches. *Information & Management*, *55*(3), 322–339. doi:10.1016/j.im.2017.08.005

Deja, M., & Próchnicka, M. (2018). Metadata as a normalizing mechanism for information-transfer behaviour in higher education institutions: The information culture perspective. *Information Research, 23*(4).

Dobre, C., & Xhafa, F. (2014). Intelligent services for big data science. *Future Generation Computer Systems*, *37*, 267–281. doi:10.1016/j.future.2013.07.014

Fan, M., & Truong, K. N. (2018). Guidelines for Creating Senior-Friendly Product Instructions. *ACM Transactions on Accessible Computing*, *11*(2), 9. doi:10.1145/3209882

Feizi, A., & Wong, C. Y. (2012, June).*Usability of user interface styles for learning a graphical software application*. In *Computer & Information Science (ICCIS), 2012 International Conference on* (Vol. 2, pp. 1089-1094). IEEE. 10.1109/ICCISci.2012.6297188

Fuggetta, A., & Di Nitto, E. (2014, May). Software process. In *Proceedings of the on Future of Software Engineering* (pp. 1-12). ACM.

Ganeshkumar, P., & Kalaivani, S. (2015). *Prediction of Software Defect Using Linear Twin Core Vector Machine Model*. Academic Press.

Garzonis, S., Jones, S., Jay, T., & O'Neill, E. (2009). Auditory icon and earcon mobile service notifications: intuitiveness, learnability, memorability and preference. In *Proceedings of the SIGCHI Conference on Human Factors in Computing Systems* (pp. 1513-1522). ACM. 10.1145/1518701.1518932

Gayathri, M., & Sudha, A. (2014). Software defect prediction system using multilayer perceptron neural network with data mining. *International Journal of Recent Technology and Engineering*, *3*(2), 54–59.

Ghatage, S. M., & Gaikwad, S. K. (2014). Sherpa–Expert's Social Network. *International Journal of Science and Research*, *3*(2), 1384–1390.

Grabski, S. V., Leech, S. A., & Schmidt, P. J. (2011). A review of ERP research: A future agenda for accounting information systems. *Journal of Information Systems*, *25*(1), 37–78. doi:10.2308/jis.2011.25.1.37

Grossman, K. W. (2012). *Careers in Cloud Computing and Mobile Technology. In Tech Job Hunt Handbook* (pp. 215–225). Apress. doi:10.1007/978-1-4302-4549-0_18

Haaksma, T. R., de Jong, M. D., & Karreman, J. (2018). Users' Personal Conceptions of Usability and User Experience of Electronic and Software Products. *IEEE Transactions on Professional Communication*, *61*(2), 116–132. doi:10.1109/TPC.2018.2795398

Han, R., Ghanem, M. M., Guo, L., Guo, Y., & Osmond, M. (2014). Enabling cost-aware and adaptive elasticity of multi-tier cloud applications. *Future Generation Computer Systems*, *32*, 82–98. doi:10.1016/j.future.2012.05.018

Haritos, T. (2017). *A Study of Human-Machine Interface (HMI) Learnability for Unmanned Aircraft Systems Command and Control* (Doctoral dissertation). Nova Southeastern University.

Helo, P., Suorsa, M., Hao, Y., & Anussornnitisarn, P. (2014). Toward a cloud-based manufacturing execution system for distributed manufacturing. *Computers in Industry, 65*(4), 646–656. doi:10.1016/j.compind.2014.01.015

Herout, A., Jošth, R., Juránek, R., Havel, J., Hradiš, M., & Zemčík, P. (2011). Real-time object detection on CUDA. *Journal of Real-Time Image Processing, 6*(3), 159–170. doi:10.100711554-010-0179-0

Kim, Y., Choi, J. S., & Shin, Y. (2014). *A decision model for optimizing the service portfolio in SOA governance.* In *Information and Communication Technologies (WICT)*, 2014 Fourth World Congress on (pp. 57-62). IEEE. 10.1109/WICT.2014.7077302

Kuesel, J. R., Kupferschmidt, M. G., Schardt, P. E., & Shearer, R. A. (2014). *U.S. Patent No. 8,776,035.* Washington, DC: U.S. Patent and Trademark Office.

Lafreniere, B., & Grossman, T. (2018, October). Blocks-to-CAD: A Cross-Application Bridge from Minecraft to 3D Modeling. In *The 31st Annual ACM Symposium on User Interface Software and Technology* (pp. 637-648). ACM.

Laurillard, D. (2013). *Rethinking university teaching: A conversational framework for the effective use of learning technologies.* Routledge. doi:10.4324/9781315012940

Levingstone, T. J., Thompson, E., Matsiko, A., Schepens, A., Gleeson, J. P., & O'Brien, F. J. (2016). Multi-layered collagen-based scaffolds for osteochondral defect repair in rabbits. *Acta Biomaterialia, 32,* 149–160. doi:10.1016/j.actbio.2015.12.034 PMID:26724503

Mahut, T., Bouchard, C., Omhover, J. F., Favart, C., & Esquivel, D. (2018). Interdependency between user experience and interaction: A kansei design approach. *International Journal on Interactive Design and Manufacturing, 12*(1), 105–132. doi:10.100712008-017-0381-4

Marenzi, I., Demidova, E., Nejdl, W., & Zerr, S. (2008). *Social software for lifelong competence development: challenges and infrastructure.* International Journal of Emerging Over Time to Infer Shared Interests. In Proc. Human Factors in Computing Systems.

Masese, Muketha, & Mbuguah. (2017). Interface Features, Program Complexity, and Memorability as Indicators of Learnability of Mobile Social Software. *International Journal of Science and Research, 6*(10).

Mathôt, S., Schreij, D., & Theeuwes, J. (2012). OpenSesame: An open-source, graphical experiment builder for the social sciences. *Behavior Research Methods, 44*(2), 314–324. doi:10.375813428-011-0168-7 PMID:22083660

Mbonimpa, J. C. (2012). Contribution of Computerised Financial Management Systems. The Functions Of Supreme Court Of Rwanda.

McCabe. (1976). A Complexity Measure. *IEEE Transactions On Software Engineering*, 308-320.

Michelman, P. (2018). *What the Digital Future Holds: 20 Groundbreaking Essays on How Technology Is Reshaping the Practice of Management*. MIT Press.

Miroshnichenko, A. (2015). Media Ecology as Ecology Contrariwise: Protecting Humans from an Environment. *Systema: Connecting Matter, Life, Culture and Technology, 3*(1), 89-104.

Mukherjee, S., & Das, S. M. (2017). Why Use SAP MII in Manufacturing Industries. In *SAP MII* (pp. 31–52). Berkeley, CA: Apress. doi:10.1007/978-1-4842-2814-2_2

Murray, J. H. (2011).*Inventing the medium: principles of interaction design as a cultural practice*. MIT Press.

Nacenta, M. A., Kamber, Y., Qiang, Y., & Kristensson, P. O. (2013). Memorability of pre-designed and user-defined gesture sets. In *Proceedings of the SIGCHI Conference on Human Factors in Computing Systems* (pp. 1099-1108). ACM. 10.1145/2470654.2466142

Naedele, M., Chen, H. M., Kazman, R., Cai, Y., Xiao, L., & Silva, C. V. (2015). Manufacturing execution systems: A vision for managing software development. *Journal of Systems and Software, 101*, 59–68. doi:10.1016/j.jss.2014.11.015

Nieuwenhuis, L. J., Ehrenhard, M. L., & Prause, L. (2018). The shift to Cloud Computing: The impact of disruptive technology on the enterprise software business ecosystem. *Technological Forecasting and Social Change, 129*, 308–313. doi:10.1016/j.techfore.2017.09.037

Novak, G. (2014). *Developing a usability method for assessment of M-Commerce systems: a case study at Ericsson*. Academic Press.

Odell, L. A., Farrar-Foley, B. T., Kinkel, J. R., Moorthy, R. S., & Schultz, J. A. (2012). *Beyond Enterprise Resource Planning (ERP): The Next Generation Enterprise Resource Planning Environment* (No. IDA/HQ-P-4852). Academic Press.

Ogheneovo, E. E. (2014). Software Dysfunction: Why Do Software Fail? *Journal of Computer and Communications*, *2*(06), 25–35. doi:10.4236/jcc.2014.26004

Oluwatosin, H. S. (2014). Client-server model. *IOSRJ Comput. Eng*, *16*(1), 2278–8727.

Panichella, A., Kifetew, F. M., & Tonella, P. (2018). A large scale empirical comparison of state-of-the-art search-based test case generators. *Information and Software Technology*, *104*, 236–256. doi:10.1016/j.infsof.2018.08.009

Parthasarathy, S. (2013). Potential concerns and common benefits of cloud-based enterprise resource planning (ERP). In *Cloud Computing* (pp. 177–195). London: Springer. doi:10.1007/978-1-4471-5107-4_9

Poister, T. H. (2010). The future of strategic planning in the public sector: Linking strategic management and performance. *Public Administration Review*, *70*(s1), s246–s254. doi:10.1111/j.1540-6210.2010.02284.x

Pramanik, P. K. D., Pal, S., & Choudhury, P. (2018). Beyond Automation: The Cognitive IoT. Artificial Intelligence Brings Sense to the Internet of Things. In *Cognitive Computing for Big Data Systems Over IoT* (pp. 1–37). Cham: Springer. doi:10.1007/978-3-319-70688-7_1

Prechelt, L., & Pepper, A. (2014). Why software repositories are not used for defect-insertion circumstance analysis more often: A case study. *Information and Software Technology*, *56*(10), 1377–1389. doi:10.1016/j.infsof.2014.05.001

Pretorius, M., Gelderblom, H. J., & Chimbo, B. (2010). Using Eye-Tracking to compare how adults and children learn to use an unfamiliar computer game. In *SAICSIT*. Bela Bela, South Africa: ACM Press. doi:10.1145/1899503.1899534

Roemer, R., Buchanan, E., Shacham, H., & Savage, S. (2012). Return-oriented programming: Systems, languages, and applications. *ACM Transactions on Information and System Security*, *15*(1), 2. doi:10.1145/2133375.2133377

Seo, G. (2013). *Challenges in implementing enterprise resource planning (ERP) system in large organizations: similarities and differences between corporate and university environment* (Doctoral dissertation). Massachusetts Institute of Technology.

Shepperd, M. (1988). A critique of cyclomatic complexity as a software metric. *Software Engineering Journal*, *3*(2), 30–36. doi:10.1049ej.1988.0003

Singh, C. D., Singh, R., & Kaur, H. (2017). *Critical appraisal for implementation of ERP in the manufacturing industry*. LAP LAMBERT Academic Publishing.

Singh, J. (2014). To Study the Quality Assurance & Control of Products in Industries. *International Journal of Research*, *1*(11), 1337–1353.

Souley, B., & Bata, B. (2013). A class coupling analyzer for Java programs. *West African Journal of Industrial and Academic Research*, *7*(1), 3–13.

Subramaniam, R., & Nakkeeran, S. (2019). Impact of Corporate E-Learning Systems in Enhancing the Team Performance in Virtual Software Teams. In *Smart Technologies and Innovation for a Sustainable Future* (pp. 195–204). Cham: Springer. doi:10.1007/978-3-030-01659-3_22

Targowski, A. (2011). The enterprise systems approach. In Enterprise Information Systems: Concepts, Methodologies, Tools, and Applications (pp. 397-426). IGI Global. doi:10.4018/978-1-61692-852-0.ch206

Tella, A., & Akinboro, E. O. (2015). The impact of social media on library services in the digital environment. *Social Media Strategies for Dynamic Library Service Development*, 279-295.

Teoh, S. Y., Pan, S. L., & Ramchand, A. M. (2012). Resource management activities in healthcare information systems: A process perspective. *Information Systems Frontiers*, *14*(3), 585–600. doi:10.100710796-010-9280-y

Terantino, J. M. (2011). Emerging technologies YouTube for foreign languages: You have to see this video. *Language Learning & Technology*, *15*(1), 10–16.

Tulaskar, R. (2018). Evolution of Embedded User Assistance: Considering Usability and Aesthetics. In *Companion Proceedings of the 2018 ACM International Conference on Interactive Surfaces and Spaces* (pp. 69-76). ACM.

Turetken, O., Ondracek, J., & Ijsselsteijn, W. (2019). Influential characteristics of enterprise information system user interfaces. *Journal of Computer Information Systems*, *59*(3), 243–255. doi:10.1080/08874417.2017.1339367

Uncel, M. (2011). "Facebook Is Now Friends with the Court": Current Federal Rules and Social Media Evidence. *Jurimetrics*, 43-69.

Van Merriënboer, J. J., & Kirschner, P. A. (2012). *Ten steps to complex learning: A systematic approach to four-component instructional design*. Routledge.

VanDerSchaaf, H., & Daim, T. (2018). Evaluating Technologies for Higher Education: E-Services. In 2018 IEEE Technology and Engineering Management Conference (TEMSCON) (pp. 1-6). IEEE.

Waizenegger, L., Thalmann, S., Sarigianni, C., Eckhardt, A., Kolb, D., Maier, R., & Remus, U. (2016). from isolation to collaboration-how the increasing diffusion of mobile devices has changed practices of knowledge sharing in non-office settings. *Social Behavior and Personality*, *36*(1), 41–42.

Wang, P. (2014). *Is a multi-touch gesture interface based on a tablet better than a smartphone for elderly users?* (Doctoral dissertation). Auckland University of Technology.

Wang, Y., Kung, L., Wang, W. Y. C., & Cegielski, C. G. (2018). An integrated big data analytics-enabled transformation model: Application to health care. *Information & Management*, *55*(1), 64–79. doi:10.1016/j.im.2017.04.001

Wolf-Branigin, M. (2013). *Using complexity theory for research and program evaluation.* Oxford University Press. doi:10.1093/acprof:oso/9780199829460.001.0001

Yildirim, V., & Kuşakcı, A. O. (2018). The Critical Success Factors of Erp Selection and Implementation: A Case Study in the Logistics Sector. *Journal of International Trade, Logistics, and Law*, *4*(1), 138–146.

Yuniarto, D., Suryadi, M., Firmansyah, E., Herdiana, D., & Rahman, A. B. A. (2018). Integrating the Readiness and Usability Models for Assessing the Information System Use. In *2018 6th International Conference on Cyber and IT Service Management (CITSM)* (pp. 1-6). IEEE.

Zhang, F., Hassan, A. E., McIntosh, S., & Zou, Y. (2017). The use of summation to aggregate software metrics hinders the performance of defect prediction models. *IEEE Transactions on Software Engineering*, *43*(5), 476–491. doi:10.1109/TSE.2016.2599161

Section 3
Implementation and Maintenance Evaluation

Chapter 10
Enterprise Resource Planning System Implementation in Higher Education Institutions:
A Theoretical Review

Stephen Kahara Wanjau
Murang'a University of Technology, Kenya

ABSTRACT

The world over, higher education institutions have resorted to the use of ERP system to automate operations on a standardized platform in line with their strategic plans. This is because ERP system supports a "do-it-all" approach to organizational management in addition to education managers' quest to improve quality of service to their students and the need to meet regional as well as global standards. In most institutions, operational areas such as student admission, finance, procurement, examination management, staffing, and alumni management can now be done through the ERP system. This chapter examines the issues associated with implementation of ERP system in higher education institutions. After studying this chapter, you should be able to: appreciate the various strategies for ERP system implementation, identify the factors leading to successful implementation of ERP system in higher education institutions, distinguish between the different models for successful ERP system implementation, and understand the metrics for measuring success rate of ERP system implementation.

DOI: 10.4018/978-1-5225-7678-5.ch010

CHOICE OF AN ERP SYSTEM FOR HIGHER EDUCATION INSTITUTIONS

The selection of an ERP system might be complicated as it is affected by various factors. These factors influence an ERP implementation success both technical and non-technical. Alanbay (2005) posited that long-term business strategy of the organization will form the basis of the selection criteria of an ERP system. He identified fifteen factors and prioritized them as follows: Customization, Real Time Changes, Implementability, Maintenance, Flexibility, User Friendliness, Cost, Systems, Requirements, After Sales Support & Training, Internet Integration, Reporting & Analysis Features, Vendor Credentials, Integration with Other Software, Back-up System and Financing Options.

Hasibua and Dantes (2012) explained twenty key success factors. These are Team Work, User Involvement, Use of Consultant, Clear Goal and Objective, Top Management Support, Project Budget, Project Time, Organization Maturity Level, Culture Readiness, ERP Implementation Strategy, ERP Implementation Methodology, Project Management, Change Management, Risk Management, Business Process Reengineering, Data analysis and migration, Communication, Training, Technology Infrastructure and Strong ERP product. These factors also have a bearing on the choice of the implementation strategy to be used. The following section discusses the choice of the implementation strategy to be used.

CHOICE OF ERP SYSTEM IMPLEMENTATION STRATEGY

The rising stakeholders' expectations (particularly from students and governments), quality and performance requirements, and competitive education environments, along with decreasing governmental support, have pressured universities to adopt new strategies in order to improve their performance. Consequently, the higher education sector has turned to Enterprise Resource Planning (ERP) systems in the hope of helping them to cope with the changing environment. For these institutions, ERP system implementation can be a daunting task, often taking a number of months to complete and costing more than the price of the hardware and system involved. However, if you are prepared, and the proper resources are applied, ERP system implementation can be completed on time, within budget, and delivering excellent return on investment (ROI). In most cases, the choice of the strategy for the implementation is important. The prospect can be set for the successful implementation of an ERP system by controlling and minimizing the major risks at the initial stage by selecting the appropriate strategy that determines how the ERP system should be deployed. The feasibility of strategy is based on a number of factors, among them include: the impact on the organization, the complexity of the institution, the duration, risk and the available budget. The following section describes the different strategies, advantages and disadvantages for each of the strategy.

Phased Strategy

A phased approach describes a scenario where elements or modules of the ERP system are introduced in a planned sequence, replacing the old systems gradually as shown in figure 1. The phased approach, implements one practical element at a time, in chronological order as shown in figure 1. Autonomous modules of ERP systems are installed in each unit, while integration of ERP modules is done at later stage of the project. This has been the most commonly used method of ERP implementation. Each business unit may have its own "instances" of ERP and database. Modular (phased) implementation reduces the risk of the installation, customization and operation of ERP systems by reducing the scope of the implementation. The unbeaten implementation of one module can help the overall success of an ERP project. The interface programs that are used in this strategy bridge the gap between the inheritance ERP system and the new ERP system until the new ERP system becomes fully purposeful. This strategy is often used in situations that do not have strong centralized synchronization in the ERP project. Some of the advantages of this

Figure 1. Phased ERP system implementation

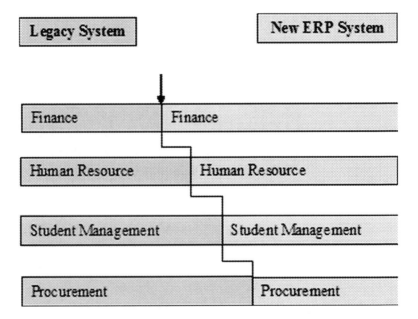

strategy are: the strategy is more user-friendly. Since the new system is implemented in one department at a time, the implementers are able to draw their attention to training one department effectively to using the new system before moving to the next. Again, as the system is tested at every stage, there is very little chance of error. The main drawback of this strategy is that it takes a lot of time to implement the whole new system to the entire organization.

Big Bang Strategy

Big bang strategy is the one where all of the main modules of an ERP system go live at the same time. The big bang approach is also called 'Direct cutover'. In this strategy, the installation of the ERP system of all modules happens across the entire organization at once, with the changeover from the old system to the new system occurring immediately the new system becomes operational as shown in Figure 2. This approach may be used if the operating environment cannot support both the legacy and new systems or they are incompatible. This strategy promised to reduce the integration cost in the condition of thorough and careful execution. It is not very time consuming as once the old system has stopped being used the new system is immediately being set up. The strategy dominated early ERP implementations and it partially contributed to the higher failure rate in ERP implementations. However, in recent years, higher education institutions are hesitant to use big bang approach as it consumes too many resources to support the go-live of the ERP system. It is also very difficult to detect small errors in the new system. In addition, if the system has not been implemented properly the new system may fail to work and this will affect the whole organization. Success in using the big bang approach comes with careful preparation and planning. But many struggle to decide whether the big bang approach is the right selection or not for their endeavor.

Figure 2. Big bang ERP system implementation

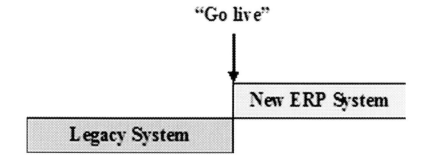

Parallel Strategy

In the Parallel implementation strategy, both the legacy system and the new ERP system are kept active for a length of time until everyone is assured that the new system is running smoothly (Vermaat, 2016) as shown in Figure 3.

The amount of time for which both systems are in operation ranges from one day to several months and may even span to several years. In this approach, portions of the same functional areas (including software) such as finance, procurement, examinations, human resource etc. operate at the same time for both the legacy system and the ERP system. One of the advantages of the parallel strategy is that it has good improvement options in case something goes off-center. By using the parallel method, small minor errors can be easily seen. Organizations are able to fix any problems with the new system before ending the previous system. Since both the legacy system and the new ERP system are in function at the same time for a particular module, the institution's business processes will not be broken up if the new ERP system breakdowns. The parallel approach also provides the most reasonable number-to-number comparisons to authenticate that the new ERP system is performing the necessary business process flows. This strategy is ideally suited for mission critical situations that cannot survive a major break down of an ERP system. One of the drawbacks of this strategy is that it is very expensive and requires a huge resource outlay. In addition, operating two systems simultaneously is also very time consuming and stressful as there is more work involved, such as creating more reports.

Pilot Strategy

The pilot strategy is carried out in one isolated part of the institution, for example, a department mainly for testing the new system in different environments. The pilot strategy is very helpful for organizations which have several locations. If the implementation works, then the system may be implemented in the rest of the

Figure 3. Parallel ERP system implementation

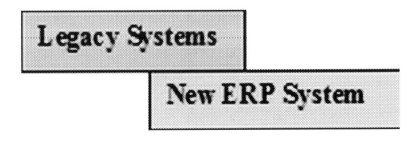

organization simultaneously or in stages. Pilot implementation allows an organization to validate its approach for full application deployment. Executing an application pilot can uncover operability issues associated with production-like conditions and provide an opportunity to address these issues before full application roll out. To effectively prepare for a pilot implementation, an organization should develop a detailed pilot approach, identify appropriate participants, plan the pilot environment, and determine how to monitor the pilot. According to O'Brien and Marakas (2006) the pilot strategy help in reducing risks compared to the direct cutover strategy. The strategy also allows the organization to see whether the new system will meet the organization's needs in one department/location before using it throughout the entire organization. One of the drawbacks of this strategy is that too much time is involved while testing the system in one location. There is also increased development and labor costs.

Hybrid Strategy

The Hybrid strategy is the combination of any of the above implementation strategies such as, phasing and parallel implementation strategy. The hybrid strategy tends to evolve into the needed agreement as ERP team members study and consider information. The complexity of a hybrid strategy varies tremendously depending upon the state. Small single-site ERP implementations tend to have simpler hybrid strategies than those used by large institutions with many dissimilar environmental locations. Many implementations use hybrid strategies because they are flexible in adapting to the specific needs of the situation. With the hybrid strategy, industries can exclusively adjust implementations for their needs.

FACTORS IN THE CHOICE OF THE STRATEGY

Migration from one system to another system occurs in almost every organization. In most cases, each of the implementation strategies discussed above may require the organization to alter hardware or operating systems. Therefore, it is important for organizations to identify the best strategy to adopt that matches the organizations purpose. If an unsuitable strategy is chosen, the organization may potentially cause risk to the future of the organization. It is advisable that an organization starts with the use of a costs-benefit analysis determining whether to implement an ERP system before making a decision on which strategy to use while implementing an ERP system. The choice of strategy depends mainly on organizational characteristics such as its size, structure, complexity and controls within the organization. More often than not, smaller and less complex organizations use the Big Bang approach whereas the larger and more complex organizations often use a phased strategy. A smaller organization using the Big-Bang strategy bears little risk whereas it is more appropriate for a larger organization to use a phased strategy. This is because risks of failure and no fallback are minimal. According to Welti (1999) the implementation strategy should be adopted on the basis of available people, expertise, financing and time which would impact on the objectives of the project and the costs.

The final decision to change to the new system is arrived at by ensuring broad consultations among the various stakeholders and with due regard to the nature of the business and the degree of acceptable risk. While investigating the factors influencing ERP implementation strategies in three countries with over 200 companies Johansson and Sudzina (2008) saw some indication that the factors influencing the choice of implementation strategy include: Chief information officer; Country; IS/IT Strategy; Organization Size and Growth.

SUCCESS FACTORS IN ERP SYSTEM IMPLEMENTATION

Many researchers have identified factors that affect the implementation of ERP systems. In the literature, researchers (Ramaprasad & Williams, 2000; Kuang, Lau, & Nah, 2001; Kumar, Kumar, & Maheshwari, 2003; Garg, 2010; Ziemba & Obłąk, 2013; Alsabaawi, 2015) have talked about Critical Success Factors (CSFs) and Critical Failure Factors (CFFs). They concluded that ERP can be identified when the business organization can achieve its objectives at the most desired duration and according to the most specific budget. Higher education institutions are of different sizes and scales. Whether these institutions have already implemented or are in the process of implementing ERP systems, the aim is to gain the benefit of integration and competitiveness advantages. In markets, reports show that 75% of the ERP projects are classified as failures (Garg, 2010). Among these factors include top management support, team work, communication, project management, change management, education and training, and user involvement. Table 1 presents a Summary of Critical Success Factors in ERP System Implementation as identified from the literature.

The following section discusses these factors and how they affect ERP system implementation in Higher Education Institutions.

Table 1. Summary of critical success factors in ERP system implementation

	Category	Factors
1	**User Factors**	User participation and involvement
		User Attitude
		Computer Self Efficacy
2	**Organizational Factors**	Top Management Support and commitment
		User Education and Training
		Clear Change Management
		Effective Communication
		Business Process Re-engineering
		Effective Project Management
3	**Technological Factors**	Technological Complexity
		Technological Compatibility
		Technical Support
		System Reliability
		Suitability of the software package

User Factors

User Participation and Involvement

End users are the people who have direct contact with the ERP system. User involvement can help increase employees' commitment to their job, as well as help build trust and loyalty to the institution. This participation and involvement of users is encouraged to ensure that user requirements are met, to gain user commitment, and to avoid user resistance. In addition, it helps employees to feel as if they are running their own institution leading them to provide the best of what they have to offer. User involvement is effective because it restores or enhances perceived control through participating the whole project plan. In implementing ERP systems, Zhang et al. (2003) finds that there are two areas for user involvement: (1) user involvement in the stage of definition of the institution's ERP system needs, and (2) during the implementation of ERP systems. Often, institutions do not recognize the impact of choosing the right internal employees with the right skill set. The internal resources should not only be experts in the institutional processes but also knowledgeable of information systems application in the industry. Involving the users in the stage of defining organizational information system needs can help reduce their resistance to the potential ERP systems, since they feel that they are the ones who choose and made the decision.

User Attitude

The attitude towards ERP system use is the behavioral tendency of users to like or dislike the usage of the implemented information systems (Hwang, 2005). Users with positive attitude and morale towards an ERP system make its implementation a success. Where users of a system are motivated to use the ERP system, they are more likely to try out any new information technology applications. Therefore, user preparedness before the implementation of an ERP system is essential to obtain a positive attitude. Positive attitude towards an ERP system frequently generate positive behavior. When system user does not adopt a positive attitude, he/she tends to follow practices that will ultimately affect their performance in the medium and long term. ERP System users will be willing to use the system to do their work if they feel the system assists them attain their interests and personal goals.

Computer Self Efficacy

Self-efficacy is a measure of a user's confidence in his/her ability to use a technology (Taylor & Todd, 1995). It is not concerned with the skills one has, but with the judgments of what one can do with whatever skills one possesses. In the context of using technology, computer self-efficacy, therefore, can be described as a judgement of one's capability to use a computer and the applications thereof, and is an important precursor of perceived usefulness. In the study by Agarwal and Karahanna (2000), computer self-efficacy was found to play an important role in explaining usage intention through perceived usefulness in a voluntary context. Venkatesh (2003) modelled and empirically tested the determinants of perceived ease of use and found that an individual's computer self-efficacy is a strong determinant of perceived ease of use and behavioral intention. Therefore, users who are computer savvy are more likely to use an ERP system since they feel being more capable of using technology.

Organizational Factors

Top Management Support and Commitment

Many studies have stressed the importance of top management support as a necessary ingredient in successful ERP implementation (Ziemba & Obłąk, 2013; Rajan & Baral, 2015; Yaşar & Gökhan, 2016). The mission of top management is to create a favorable environment for the implementation of ERP systems and attaining of desired results. Top management is necessary for ERP implementation due to the fact that it is a highly integrated information system that requires the complete cooperation of employees from all departments of the institution. Top management support can play a useful role in settling disputes and in providing clear signals to any doubts. Top management must create an environment for implementing an ERP system and obtained results and must be seen as a participant in the implementation.

According to Zhang, et al. (2003) top management support in ERP system implementation has two main facets: (1) providing leadership; and (2) providing the necessary resources. To implement an ERP system smoothly and successfully, higher education institutions require a steering committee to participate in team meetings and monitor the implementation efforts, spend time with people and provide clear directions of the project. Willingness to provide the necessary resources is another indicator of top management commitment to the ERP project. The implementation could be seriously handicapped if some of the critical resources (e.g., people, funds and equipment) are not available.

User Education and Training

Education and training refers to the process of providing management and employees with the logic and overall concepts of ERP system. ERP education and training increases the level of proficiency since it affects the shared beliefs about the benefits of the ERP system. Training also makes the users comfortable with the system and increases their expertise and knowledge level. At the end of training, users get rid of the worries about the system and they become a part of it. Through education and training; users get a better understanding of how their jobs are related to other functional areas within the institution. The user is the person who produce results and should be held accountable for making the system perform to expectations. The main reason for education and training is to increase the expertise and knowledge level of the people within the institution. According to Zhang, et al. (2003) the three aspects concerning the contents of training are: (1) logic and concepts of ERP; (2) Features of the ERP system software; and (3) hands-on training. Each of these aspects plays a vital role in the implementation of an ERP system such as providing an understanding of the processes as well as decreasing the fear that users might have towards the new systems.

Clear Change Management

Introducing new software such as ERP in an institution changes the way jobs are done. User resistance has been associated with information system change like ERP systems. ERP systems introduce a large-scale change that can cause resistance, confusion, redundancies, and errors that make the change management essential. In most cases, users resist a new system because they are worried that their job might be eliminated or be changed from their usual way of doing things. Managing change within the organization includes creating some balance of the forces that stand behind change against those forces that reject change. The success of ERP implementation can be said to be directly proportionate to an organization's determination to undergo changes. As such, an effective change management strategy can help the organization change and improve its analysis capabilities as well as helping the implementation processes to be carried out smoothly and effectively.

Effective Project Management

Project Management has evolved over the years in order to plan, coordinate and control the complex and diverse activities of modern industrial and commercial projects. Every institution should have an effective project management strategy to control the implementation process, avoiding overrun of budget and ensuring the implementation within schedule. One of the important things that management of higher education institutions should take note of is the project scope. Since ERP systems implementation is very complex, and often involves all business functions as well as requires anywhere between one and two years of effort, a project scope should be clearly defined and should identify the modules selected for implementation Zhang, et al. (2003) suggests that there are five major parts of project management: (1) having a formal implementation plan, (2) a realistic time frame, (3) having periodic project status meetings, (4) having an effective project leader who is also a champion, and (5) having project team members who are stakeholders. The formal project implementation plan defines project activities, commits personnel to those activities, and promotes organizational support by organizing the implementation process (Sum, Ang, & Yeo, 1997). Having a realistic time frame is very important. If the target completion time schedule were unrealistically short, the pressure to rush through would result in the implementation being carried out in a haphazard manner. Conversely, if the implementation is delayed for too long, people would tend to lose faith and/or patience with the system, which also will result in low morale and resistance. Conducting periodic project status meetings in which each team member reports progress and problems is an invaluable means for evaluating the progress of the ERP implementation. Similarly, selecting the right project leader is also important for the project implementation success.

Effective Communication

Effective communication is an essential factor in implementing ERP systems. In fact, the lack of communication has been linked to many project failures. Communication provides the path through which users from different functional areas share important information that can lead to successful implementation of ERP systems. Since an ERP system is an integrated information system, its design, installation and use require close co-operation of all users. A full and open communication influences success and facilitates the education within the institution. In addition, communication can be a key driver in knowledge management. It helps distribute the knowledge among employees in an institution so that everyone remains knowledgeable about any particular task. Given the benefits mentioned above, communication can be considered the glue that holds the whole institution as well as the teams together. It builds strong social relationships that help system users to cross over the hard time that they face during implementation as well as the development of trust and exchange of information needed.

Business Process Reengineering

The implementation of an ERP system in an organization is often accompanied by substantial changes in organizational structure and ways of working (Kallunki, Laitinen, & Silvola, 2011). This is called Business process re-engineering (BPR). According to Hammer and Champy (2001) business process re-engineering is "the fundamental rethinking and radical redesign of business processes to achieve dramatic improvements in critical, contemporary measures of performance, such as cost, quality, service and speed". A fairly serious problem of ERP implementation lies in a system's incompatibility with an organization's business processes and its information provision needs. Thus, implementing an ERP system involves reengineering the existing business processes to the best business process standard.

When selecting an ERP system, organizations usually consult specialists, who recommend the systems that best meet their needs. However, irrespective of the suitability of a system, there is no universal ERP system that exists that is suitable for all institutions. In the course of ERP implementation, an institution almost always needs to decide whether to reorganize her business processes according to the logic proposed by a system or to modify the system by adapting it for existing business processes. An ERP system in itself cannot improve an institution's work until it restructures its business processes. In order to obtain tangible benefits provided by an ERP system, it is necessary to reorganize institution's business processes according to the logic proposed by a system. Therefore, an institution must be prepared to accept the best practice contained in an ERP system and model its business processes accordingly.

Technological Factors

Technological Complexity

The implementation of ERP systems is a complex technological undertaking. Technological complexity is the extent to which a new technology is more complicated for its users than the previous technology used for the same or similar work, and represents an increase in the number of things the user must do at once (Aiman-Smith & Green, 2002). The complex nature of ERP systems limits the amount of knowledge that users can absorb before actual usage. The higher the complexity of the system, the higher mental workload and stress (Rajan & Baral, 2015). The complexity of the ERP system can negatively affect user's attitudes towards using it. This eventually affects its successful implementation in an institution.

Technological Compatibility

Technological compatibility is the compatibility rate between an organization's present technology and systems and new system (Yaşar & Gökhan, 2016). Technological compatibility is considered as one of the technological characteristics that affects the usage of ERP. In technological compatibility, the knowledge gained from past and present experiences with technology are considered (Rajan & Baral, 2015). Common problems in adopting ERP systems are widely recognized to be rooted in the poor fit between ERP systems and business process. If the ERP system is compatible with present business practices and user needs, then an institution can adapt more easily.

In ERP implementation in higher education institutions, systems are developed to support business processes such as, student admissions, examinations processing, fees collection and reconciliation, and so ERP implementation and business process should be closely connected.

According to Soh, Kien, & Tay-Yap (2000) procedural and data compatibility are crucial to the acceptance of the system by the employee. Enterprise resource planning packages are only compatible with the databases and operation systems of some institutions, and procedural and data compatibility are crucial to the acceptance of the system by the employees (Rajan & Baral, 2015). Technology incompatibility can therefore negatively affect system productivity, efficiency, employees' satisfaction, commitment, and motivation. The greater the compatibility of the ERP system with the existing technical systems, operating practices, and the value and belief systems of the institution, the better for its adoption and use.

Technical Support

Having available and qualified vendor support is a substantial advantage in implementing the ERP system. Zhang, Matthew, Zhang, and Banerjee (2003) identified three dimensions of vendor support as follows: (1) Service response time of the software vendor; (2) Qualified consultants with knowledgeability in both enterprises' business processes and information technology including vendors' ERP systems; and (3) Participation of vendor in ERP implementation. It's important for the vendor's staffs to be knowledgeable in both business processes and ERP system functions to ensure successful implementation. Moreover, the ERP consultants should possess good interpersonal skills and be able to work with people in the institution. ERP software vendors should be carefully selected since they play a crucial part in shaping the ultimate outcome of the implementation.

System Reliability

The reliability of a product can be defined as the probability that the product will not fail throughout a defined operating period and prescribed environment (Rajan & Baral, 2015). ERP systems are made up of a number of components or modules. The reliability of each component or module and the configuration of the system consisting of these components or modules determines the system reliability. System reliability is a major challenge for higher education institutions since unreliable systems can have dual bad effects for them. First, unreliable ERP system can frustrate users because they are the ones who are in direct contact with the ERP system. Secondly, it can be so expensive for the institution. In order to avoid these problems and the system unreliability, institutions must understand what makes a system unreliable and then fix it.

Suitability of a Software Package

The choice of an ERP software package that best matches the institution's information needs is essential to guarantee minimal customization. An erroneous decision in choosing the ERP package may lead to a commitment of architecture and applications that do not fit the institution's business processes. To ensure that this does not happen

Johansson and Sudzina (2008) argues that the decision process should entail the following considerations: (1) budgets, (2) timeframes, (3) goals, and (4) benefits. Institutions differ from each other, so not all ERP software packages are compatible with all institutions. ERP vendors use different hardware platforms, databases, and operation systems and certain ERP packages are only compatible with some databases and operation systems. Thus, institutions should conduct requirements analysis in order to confirm what problems need to be solved and select the appropriate ERP systems. ERP packages are provided as generic off-the-shelf (proprietary) or open source software. Serrano and Sarriegi (2006) posit that the benefits of applying open source software are greater for ERPs than for other kinds of software applications. The authors identify three main reasons:

1. **Increased Adaptability:** ERP software are not plug-and-play. They always need an implementation project to match the business processes and local regulations. Having full access to the ERP source code can facilitate this unavoidable customization.
2. **Decreased Reliance on a Single Supplier:** Institutions that acquire proprietary ERP software are highly dependent on the product builders and distributors – that is, ERP systems and the source code's owners. If one, or even both, of these agents disappears, upgrading and maintaining the ERP can pose significant problems.
3. **Reduced Costs:** Proprietary ERP licenses are expensive. A rule of thumb puts them at between one-sixth and one-third of the implementation project costs. Open source ERPs avoid this cost. Furthermore, they usually do not need expensive hardware to run.

Theoretical Models for Successful ERP System Implementation

A number of theoretical models have been developed to help explain user adoption of new technologies. These models introduce factors that can affect the user acceptance of technology such as Theory of Reasoned Action (Fishbein & Ajzen, 1975), Theory of Planned Behavior (Ajzen, 1985), Technology Acceptance Model (Davis,1989; (Davis, Bagozzi, & Warshaw, 1989), and the Diffusion of Innovation theory (Rogers, 2003). Therefore, an overview on available general adoption models is necessary in determining successful ERP implementation. In this section, we discuss these theoretical models to give an overview for better understanding of successful ERP Systems implementation.

Theory of Reasoned Action

The Theory of Reasoned Action (TRA) as postulated by Fishbein and Ajzen (1975) is one of the most popular theories used. The theory is about one factor that determines behavioral intention of the person's attitudes toward that behavior. The TRA theory proposes that individual beliefs influence attitudes, hence creating intentions that will generate behavior. In this sense, the intention to accept or reject an ERP system is based on a series of tradeoffs between the perceived benefits of the system to the user and the complexity of learning or using the ERP system. Therefore, a person's attitude towards the ERP system together with the subjective norm concerning the behavior, determines the behavioral intention as depicted by figure 4.

Generally, attitudes are affective and are based upon a set of beliefs about the object of behavior. For example, the ERP system makes work easier. The second factor is the person's subjective norms of what he or she perceives the immediate community's attitude to certain behavior. For example, my peers are using the ERP system to are productive in their areas of work).

Theory of Planned Behavior

The Theory of Planned Behavior (TPB) can be comprehended as an extension of the Theory of Reasoned Action. TPB proposes that a combination of attitude toward the behavior, subjective norm may lead to the formation of a behavioral intention to perform the behavior. The TPB postulates intention to act as the best predictor of behavior. The intention is itself an outcome of the combination of attitudes towards a behavior. That is, the positive or negative evaluation of the behavior and its expected outcomes and subjective norms are the social pressures exerted on an individual resulting from their perceptions of what others think they should do and their inclination to comply with these (Al-Mamary, et al., 2016). Figure 5 illustrates a description of Taylor and Todd (1995) combined TAM-TPB Model. The authors suggested that when organizations design and implement an IT system, they should take into account the user's level of experience since less experienced users will

Figure 4. Theory of reasoned action adapted from Madden et al., 1992

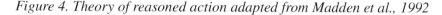

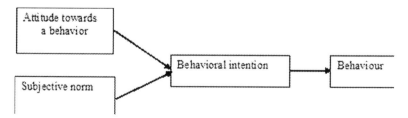

Figure 5. Combined TAM-TPB model
Source, Taylor and Todd (1995)

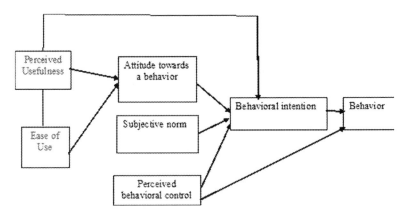

tend to rely on different factors (e.g. perceived usefulness) than experienced ones in order to start using the system.

The Combined model assumes that individuals are rational in considering their actions and the implications of their actions. That is, individuals will make a rational choice to use the ERP system. But in some cases the use of the ERP system is compulsory. The users don't have options to use the ERP system or not. This theory therefore is more suited as an optional choice only.

Diffusion of Innovations Model

Rogers (1983) proposed the first process model, a five-stage model of the implementation and adoption of innovation in organizations. The Diffusion of Innovations (DOI) model examines a diversity of innovations by introducing four factors (innovation itself, communication channels, time, and a social system) which influence the spread of a new idea. DOI model suggests a number of attributes of innovation that were perceived to assist the diffusion of technological innovation. The DOI model integrates three major components: adopter characteristics, characteristics of an innovation, and innovation decision process. In innovation decision step, five steps namely confirmation, knowledge, implementation, decision, and persuasion have taken place through a series of communication channels among the members of a similar social system over a period of time. In characteristics of an innovation step, five main constructs namely; relative advantage, compatibility, complexity, trialability, and observability have been proposed as effective factors on any innovation acceptance. In adopter characteristics step, five categories; early adopters, innovators, laggards, late majority, and early majority are defined.

Technology Acceptance Model

Developed by Davis et al. (1989), Technology Acceptance Model (TAM) is one of the most influential research models to determinate the level of information system adoption. Davis used TAM to explain the general determinants of computer acceptance that lead to explaining users' behavior across a broad range of end-user computing technologies and user populations. TAM uses the Theory of Reasoned Action (TRA) as a theoretical basis for specifying the causal linkages between two key beliefs: perceived usefulness and perceived ease of use, and users' attitudes, intentions and actual computer adoption behavior. The goal of TAM is to explain and predict determinants of computer acceptance in a broad sense, while being a justified and prudent model. The final version of Technology Acceptance Model was formed by Venkatesh and Davis (1996) as shown in Figure 6.

TAM explains the motivation of users by three factors; perceived usefulness, perceived ease of use, and attitude toward use. Therefore, not only behavioral intention would be contained in TAM but also, two chief beliefs like perceived usefulness and ease of use have considerable impact on attitude of the ERP system user. These can be determined as favorableness and unfavorable toward the ERP system. Sometimes, other factors identified as external variables (system characteristics, user training, and user participation in system design) are considered in TAM model.

Information Systems Success Model

DeLone and McLean (1992) presented a model for measuring the "complex dependent variable" in information Systems (IS) research. The authors tried to bring some awareness and structure to this dependent variable, "IS success" in IS research, and proposed taxonomy and an interactive model as frameworks. This model has gone through reviews with the more recent model presented by the authors in the year 2003 inspired by the response they received since the publication of their original

Figure 6. Technology Acceptance Model (TAM)
Source: Venkatesh and Davis, 1996)

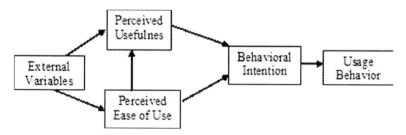

paper of 1992. The IS success model has six variables or dimensions: Information quality, System quality, Service quality, (Intention to) use, User satisfaction and the resulting Net benefits (DeLone & McLean, 2016). These variables are proposed to be more interrelated than independent as shown in Figure 7.

Information Quality

According to DeLone and McLean, the information quality dimension refers to the desirable characteristics of the system outputs; for example, management reports. Among them include, relevance, understandability, accuracy, conciseness, completeness, understandability, currency, timeliness, and usability.

System Quality

The system quality dimension is the desirable characteristics of an information system. For example, ease of use, system flexibility, system reliability, and ease of learning, as well as system features of intuitiveness, sophistication, flexibility, and response times.

Service Quality

The service quality dimension refers to the quality of the support that system users receive from the information systems, organization and IT support personnel. For example, responsiveness, accuracy, reliability, technical competence, and empathy of the IT personnel staff.

Figure 7. Updated IS success model
Source: DeLone & McLean (2003)

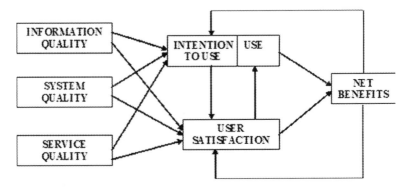

Use

The Use dimension refers to the degree and manner in which employees and customers utilize the capabilities of an information system. For example, amount of use, frequency of use, nature of use, appropriateness of use, extent of use, and purpose of use.

User Satisfaction

The User satisfaction attribute refers to users' level of satisfaction with reports, Web sites, and support services.

Net Impacts

The net impacts dimension refers to the extent to which information systems are contributing (or not contributing) to the success of individuals, groups, organizations, industries, and nations. For example: improved decision-making, improved productivity, increased sales, cost reductions, improved profits, market efficiency, consumer welfare, creation of jobs, and economic development.

In summary, DeLone and McLean, argued that the selection of the particular success dimensions are dependent on the nature and purpose of the system(s) being evaluated. For example, an e-commerce application, in contrast to an enterprise resource planning system application, would have some similar success measures and some different success measures. Both systems would measure information accuracy, while the e-commerce system is more likely to measure the personalization of information presentation than an ERP system that uses standard report formats. Similar differences in measures and metrics would be encountered in attempting to measure the success of IS systems in healthcare or government applications.

Metrics for Measuring Success Rate of ERP Systems Implementation

In the recent years, higher education institutions have spent substantial amounts of money in ERP investment with a goal to provide enhanced ability for research and teaching at reasonable or low cost. Successful ERP System implementation is a multidimensional, dynamic and relative concept. Although success is complex and difficult to measure, researchers are making efforts in doing so. Most of the practical measurements focus on delivering a functional information system product within certain economic and temporal constraints. A system must first be accepted to be used and that should increase the probability of system success. Markus and Tanis (2000) argued that there are different phases characterized by key players, typical activities, characteristic problems, appropriate performance metrics and a range of possible outcomes. Each experience made with ERP system, is unique, and experiences may differ from organization to organization and from the specific point of view. The success measurement model of Markus and Tanis (2000) can be used for multiple success measurement approaches at different stages of an ERP Systems Implementation. Based on their observations of enterprise systems projects, the authors argued that there are three main categories of success metrics. These are:

- **Project Metrics:** The project metrics measure the performance of the ERP systems project team against the planned schedule, budget and functional scope
- **Early Operational Metrics:** These metrics measures how the business operations perform in the period after the system becomes operational until "normal operation" is achieved (for example, labor costs, Cycle time, Demand forecast accuracy), and
- **Longer Term Business Results Metrics:** These metrics measures how the organization performs at various times after normal business operation has been achieved. This usually involves attaining the strategic goal behind the system implementation (for example, Rate on Investment (ROI)).

There is a common consensus that ERP systems implementation, given it is managed carefully, provide substantial intangible (nonfinancial) results as well as tangible (financial) results. Bartholomew (1999) claims that in a typical business environment, 80% of the organization's value is in intangible assets. This intangibility of assets has made it difficult for organizations to demonstrate whether they have received the benefits of an ERP system or not. There are other approaches to the measurement of system success rate. However, in this chapter we discuss the balanced score card approach to measuring the success rate of ERP system implementation in higher education institutions.

The Balanced Scorecard Approach

The Balanced Scorecard (BSC) is a technique developed by Kaplan and Norton (1992) that helps organizational decision makers to navigate the organization towards success. Researchers (Bruggeman, 1999; Rosemann & Wiese, 1999; Reo, 1999)

Figure 8. Balanced scorecard for measuring ERP performance

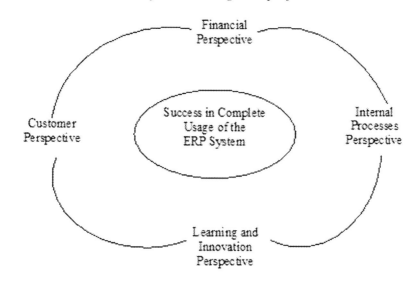

have suggested that the Balanced Scorecard approach may also help to evaluate the performance of an Information System (IS) and to evaluate IS investments in a holistic manner. The intention of the Balanced Scorecard is the supplementation of traditional financial measures with three additional perspectives – the customer perspective, the internal business process perspective and the learning and growth perspective (Kaplan & Norton, 1996).

The BSC approach complements past performance measures (financial measures) with the drivers of future performance indicators (customers, suppliers, processes, employees, technologies and innovation). The fundamental concept of the Balanced Scorecard is to derive the objectives and measures from the overall organization vision and strategy and to use the four perspectives as a "balanced" framework to monitor and achieve these objectives. The following section presents a discussion on the appropriateness of the Balanced Scorecard for measuring success rate of ERP systems implementation.

Measuring ERP Systems Success Rate Using the Balanced Scorecard

A fundamental feature of the Balanced Scorecard approach is that it requires that each measure should relate to the organizational strategies and to each other in a cause and effect relationship. Therefore, identifying the organizational goals and strategies in relation to the core perspectives is a critical preliminary step in a Balanced Scorecard approach. In a nutshell, the balanced scorecard has four perspectives. The

Learning & Growth Perspective looks at what an organization should do to achieve its vision. The Business Process perspective refers to internal business processes and what should be done so as to satisfy customers and stakeholders. The customer perspective shows an increasing realization of the importance of customer focus and customer satisfaction in any business because if customers are not satisfied, they will find other suppliers who will meet their needs, and The financial perspective looks at what should be done for the organization to succeed financially (Kaplan and Norton, 2001).

Rosemann and Wiese (1999) presented two approaches to the Balanced Scorecard that can be used for ERP success measurement. The first BSC approach is measuring the project performance and in addition to the classical perspectives (financial/cost, customer, internal process and innovation and learning). The authors added the project perspective to this BSC, a fifth perspective, which represents the typical project management tasks. The second BSC approach was the operational BSC, which measures the business performance and can be used for (continuous) controlling of the ERP software. In this chapter we consider the second approach, operational BSC.

Financial Perspective

An ERP system represents a capital investment which causes expenses as well as revenues. It is a common practice to measure the performance of any business on a financial scale. The Return on Investment (ROI) and Return on Capital Employed (ROCE) are the most common methods of measuring the financial success of a business (Kaplan & Norton, Translating Strategy in to action: The Balanced Scorecard, 1996). The Return on Investment is a ratio between the net profit and cost of investment resulting from an investment of some resource whereby high ROI means the investment's gains compare favorably to its cost. The return on capital employed is a profitability ratio that measures how efficiently an organization can generate profits from its capital employed by comparing net operating profit to capital employed. ROCE is a long-term profitability ratio because it shows how effectively assets are performing while taking into consideration long-term financing (Kaplan & Norton, 1996). Obviously, a higher ratio would be more favorable because it means that more dollars of profits are generated by each dollar of capital employed. According to Rosemann and Wiese (1999) the results of the financial perspective can help to identify poor performance. For example, negative deviations of actual training costs versus budgeted costs may indicate that the system's functions are not efficiently used by staff members. A continuous increase in external consulting expenses may point to deficiencies in the internal training staff's competence.

Customer Perspective

Higher Education Institutions are realizing the importance of a customer centered approach to survival in the face of increased domestic competition and the globalization of higher education. They have recognized that an unsatisfied customer can easily switch to another supplier that meets the same need with a lower price or a better service. This recognition has led these institutions to set targets like "Customer Satisfaction" and "Customer Retention". As customer expectations are rising, Higher Education Institutions are looking to trim budgets and increase efficiency. In higher education institutions, the direct customers are the employees and students who directly deal with the system and external business partners like suppliers, subcontractors and customers who are indirectly working with the system. For the purpose of measuring performance, concentrating on internal users seems more adequate, since the system's effects on external partners are rather remote and indirect. In light of all this, many institutions have started to use ERP system, to offer programs and courses that students feel their needs and wants are met and get an edge over the competition. In the Balanced Scorecard framework, the measures used to evaluate performance for external users include for example, the Cycle time, which is a measure of how fast the institution is responding to customer needs/orders. In essence, cycle time measures the length of time it takes to produce a good and deliver it to the customer from the moment the invoice is received. Faster cycle time demonstrates more effective processes and a higher customer satisfaction rate. Similarly, an effective ERP system should be able to accurately predict future demands based on historical numbers. The more accurate the ERP system can monitor the forecast and then keep track of the progress of reaching the predicted numbers, the more successful it is.

Internal Process Perspective

The internal process perspective focuses on the internal conditions for satisfying the customer expectations (Rosemann & Wiese, 1999). These conditions can be grouped into processes needed for operating the system on the one hand and those for improving and enhancing its capabilities on the other hand. Regarding the day-to-day operation of an ERP system, some of the essential measures for evaluating its internal processes are the number and type of trends in user complaints. An analysis of these measures should lead to a ranking of system defects by disutility to users and these are tackled accordingly. ERP systems play an important role in helping managers disaggregate the summary measures. In the Balanced Scorecard Framework, the measures in this perspective are also leading indicators of future performance. For instance, when an unexpected signal appears on the balanced scorecard, managers can query the ERP system to find the source of the trouble. If the aggregate measure for on-time delivery is poor, for example, managers can quickly look behind the aggregate measure until they can identify late deliveries, day-by-day, by a particular unit to an individual customer.

Innovation and Learning Perspective

In today's rapidly changing and competitive world, Higher Education Institutions cannot catch up with the continuously evolving technological initiatives unless they support continuous learning and improvement and invest considerable amount of resources in new technologies. The innovation and learning perspective is devoted to an assessment of the institution's ability to effectively utilize the ERP system's functions as well as to enhance and improve it. An institution's ability to innovate, improve, and learn ties directly to its value. That is, only through the ability to launch new products, create more value for customers, and improve operating efficiencies continually can an institution penetrate new markets and increase revenues and margins—in short, grow and thereby increase shareholder value. Therefore, in order to ensure long term growth and improvement, an institution should set targets such as "Improved Employee Capabilities", which can be attained by continuous learning and sharing of information among employees. A useful indicator in this case is the level of training courses, measured by the amount of time or expenses spent. Specifically, for system developers, their type of formal qualification can additionally be assessed. In the Balanced Scorecard framework, the measures in this perspective are also leading indicators of future performance since an effectively learning enterprise will easily follow the new technologies and be successful in the future.

REFERENCES

Aiman-Smith, L., & Green, S. G. (2002). Implementing new manufacturing technology: The related effects of technologycharacteristics and user learning activities. *Academy of Management Journal, 45*(2), 421–430.

Ajzen, I. (1985). From intentions to actions: A theory of planned behavior. In J. Kuhl & J. Beckmann (Eds.), *Action Control: From Cognition to Behaviour* (pp. 11–39). New York: Springer-Verlag. doi:10.1007/978-3-642-69746-3_2

Al-Mamary, Y. H., Al-nashmi, M., Ghaffar, Y. A., & Shamsuddin, A. (2016). A Critical Review of Models and Theories in Field of Individual Acceptance of Technology. *International Journal of Hybrid Information Technology*, 143-158.

Alanbay, O. (2005). ERP Selection Using Expert Choice Software. *Conference Proceeding, ISAHP 2005.*

Alsabaawi, M. (2015). Critical success factors for enterprise resource planning implementation success. *International Journal of Advances in Engineering and Technology, 8*(4), 496–506.

Bartholomew, D. (1999). *Process is back.* Cleveland. *Industry Week.*

Bruggeman, W. (1999, March). The Balanced Scorecard: Functional, Business Unit and Corporate Level Application. *Symposium on IT Based Scorecard.*

Davenport, T. H. (1998). *Putting the Enterprise into the Enterprise system.* Harvard Business Review.

Davis, F. (1986). *Technology Acceptance Model for Empirically Testing New End-User Information Systems: Theory and Results, in MIT Sloan School of Management.* MIT.

Davis, F. (1989). Perceived usefulness, perceived ease of use and user acceptance of information technology. *Management Information Systems Quarterly, 13*(3), 319–340. doi:10.2307/249008

Davis, F., Bagozzi, P., & Warshaw, P. (1989). User Acceptance of Computer Technology: A Comparison of two Theoretical models. *Management Science, 35*(8), 982–1003. doi:10.1287/mnsc.35.8.982

DeLone, W., & McLean, E. (2016). Information Systems Success Measurement. *Foundations and Trends in Information Systems, 2*(1), 1–116. doi:10.1561/2900000005

Fishbein, M., & Ajzen, I. (1975). *Belief, Attitude, Intention and Behaavior: An introduction to theory and Research.* Addison-Wesley.

Garg, P. (2010). Critical Failure Factors For Enterprise Resource Planning Implementations In Indian Retail Organizations: An Exploratory Study. *Journal of Information Technology Impact, 10*(1), 35–44.

Hammer, M., & Champy, J. (2001). *Reengineering the Corporation.* New York: Harpercollins.

Hasibua, Z. A., & Dantes, G. R. (2012). Priority of Key Success Factors (KSFS) on Enterprise Resource Planning (ERP) System Implementation Life Cycle. *Journal of Enterprise Resource Planning Studies, 2012,* 1–15. doi:10.5171/2011.122627

Holland, P., Light, B., & Gibson, N. (1999). A critical success factors model for enterprise resource planning implementation. *Proceedings of the 7th European Conference on Information Systems, 1,* 273-297.

Hwang, Y. (2005). Investigating enterprise systems adoption: Uncertainty avoidance, intrinsic motivation, and the technology aceeptance model. *European Journal of Information Systems, 14*(5), 150–161. doi:10.1057/palgrave.ejis.3000532

Johansson, B., & Sudzina, F. (2008). ERP systems and open source: An initial review and some implications for SMEs. *Journal of Enterprise Information Management, 21*(6), 649–658. doi:10.1108/17410390810911230

Kallunki, J., Laitinen, E. K., & Silvola, H. (2011). Impact of enterprise resource planning systems on management control systems and firm performance. *International Journal of Accounting Information Systems, 12*(1), 20–39. doi:10.1016/j.accinf.2010.02.001

Kaplan, R., & Norton, D. (1992, January-February). The Balanced Scorecard - Measures that drive performance. *Harvard Business Review*. PMID:10119714

Kaplan, R., & Norton, D. (1996). *Translating Strategy in to action: The Balanced Scorecard*. Boston: Harvard Business School Press.

Karande, S., Jain, V., & Ghatule, A. (2012). ERP implementation: Critical success factors for Indian Universities and higher educational institutions. *Pragyaan Journal of Information Technology, 10*(2), 24–29.

Kuang, J., Lau, J., & Nah, F. F. (2001). Critical factors for successful implementation of enterprise systems. *Business Process Management Journal, 7*(3), 285–296. doi:10.1108/14637150110392782

Kumar, U., Kumar, V., & Maheshwari, B. (2003). An investigation of critical management issues in ERP implementation: Emperical evidence from Canadian organizations. *Technovation Journal, 23*(10), 793–807. doi:10.1016/S0166-4972(02)00015-9

Leon, A. (2009). *Enterprise Resource Planning*. McGraw-Hill.

Madden, T., Ellen, P., & Ajzen, I. (1992). A comparison of the theory of planned behavior and the theory of reasoned action. *Personality and Social Psychology Bulletin, 18*(1), 3–9. doi:10.1177/0146167292181001

Markus, M., Axline, S., Petrie, D., & Tanis, C. (2000). Learning from Adopters' Experiences with ERP: Problems Encountered and Success Achieved. *Journal of Information Technology, 15*, 245–265.

Mehlinger, L. (2006). *Indicators of successful enterprise technology implementations in higher education business*. Morgan State University.

Nielsen, J. (2002). *Critical success factors for implementing an ERP system in a university environment: A case study from the Australian HES.* Brisbane: Griffith University.

O'Brien, J., & Marakas, G. (2006). *Management Information Systems* (7th ed.). McGraw-Hill Irwin.

Rajan, C., & Baral, R. (2015). Adoption of ERP system: An empirical study of factors influencing the usage of ERP andits impact on end user. *IIMB Management Review, 27*(2), 105–117. doi:10.1016/j.iimb.2015.04.008

Ramaprasad, A., & Williams, J. J. (2000). A taxonomy of critical success factors. *European Journal of Information Systems, 5*, 250–260.

Reo, D. (1999, March). The Balanced IT Scorecard for software intensive organisations: benefits and lessons learnt through industry applications. *Symposium on IT Balanced Scorecard.*

Rogers, E. (2003). *Diffusion of innovations* (5th ed.). Free Press.

Rosemann, M., & Wiese, J. (1999). Measuring the Performance of ERP Software – a Balanced Scorecard Approach. *Conference Proceeding, the 10th Australian Conference on Information Systems, 8.*

Serrano, N., & Sarriegi, J. (2006). Open source software ERPs: A new alternative for an old need. *IEEE Software, 23*(3), 94–97. doi:10.1109/MS.2006.78

Soh, C., Kien, S. S., & Tay-Yap, J. (2000). Cultural fits and misfits: Is ERP a universal solution? *Communications of the ACM, 43*(4), 47–51. doi:10.1145/332051.332070

Sum, C., Ang, J., & Yeo, L. (1997). Contextual Elements of Critical Success Factors in MRP Implementation. *Production and Inventory Management Journal, 3*, 77–83.

Taylor, S., & Todd, P. (1995). Assessing it usage: The role of prior experience. *Management Information Systems Quarterly, 19*(4), 561–570. doi:10.2307/249633

Thompson, R., Higgins, C., & Howell, J. (1991). Personal computing: Toward a conceptual model of utilization. *Management Information Systems Quarterly, 15*(1), 124–143. doi:10.2307/249443

Venkatesh, V. e., Morris, Davis, & Davis. (2003). User acceptance of information technology: Towards a unified view. *Management Information Systems Quarterly, 27*(3), 425–478. doi:10.2307/30036540

Vermaat, M. (2016). *Enhanced Discovering Computers.* Cengage Learning.

Welti, N. (1999). *Successful SAP R/3 Implementation: Practical Management of ERP Projects*. Addison-Wesley.

Yaşar, A., & Gökhan, Ö. (2016). Determination the Factors that Affect the Use of Enterprise Resource Planning Information System through Technology Acceptance Model. *International Journal of Business and Management, 11*(10), 91–108. doi:10.5539/ijbm.v11n10p91

Zhang, L., Matthew, K., Zhang, Z., & Banerjee, P. (2003). Critical Success Factors of Enterprise Resource Planning Systems Implementation Success in China. In *Proceedings of the 36th Hawaii International Conference on System Sciences (HICSS'03)*. IEEE Computer Society. 10.1109/HICSS.2003.1174613

Ziemba, E., & Obłąk, I. (2013). Critical Success Factors for ERP Systems Implementation in Public Administration. *Interdisciplinary Journal of Information, Knowledge, and Management, 8*.

Chapter 11
Implementation Evaluation Metrics for ERP Solution:
A Case of Kibabii University

Samwel Mungai Mbuguah
Kibabii University, Kenya

Franklin Wabwoba
Kibabii University, Kenya

Chrispus Kimingichi Wanjala
Kibabii University, Kenya

ABSTRACT

Most institution of higher learning are implementing enterprise resource planning (ERP) in automating various activities. The architecture of most of the ERP is based on the service-oriented architecture (SOA) where each module can be called as service. In most of the contracts signed between the vendor and the university, payment is tied to the level of implementation. The question is how to then measure the level of implementation. This chapter proposes a metric that could be used. The metric was derived based on an acceptance test on each of functionality of module as per terms of reference. The result of a test was rated as a fail; the result was then coded such that a fail was assigned a zero (0), pass one (1), and query a half (½), from which a metric was derived which measures the level implementation.

DOI: 10.4018/978-1-5225-7678-5.ch011

ORGANIZATION BACKGROUND

Kibabii University was granted a charter in 24 November 2015 with his Excellency President Uhuru Muigai Kenyatta becoming the first Chancellor of the University (Webmaster, 2018).

Kibabii University Strategic Directions are (DICT 2019)

1. To promote and maintain excellence in teaching and learning;
2. Support and sustain advancement in consultancy, Research and Extension;
3. Enhanced Administrative, Financial and Human Resource Management systems;
4. Invest in marketing, public relations and linkages;
5. Expand, maintain and improve physical facilities and infrastructure;
6. Develop and implement policies on Health services

Management Structure

The University is managed through a Council, Senate and University management board. The each are defined University Statute, 2017 and the Kibabii University Charter

Setting the Stage

On inception in 2012, the University had incomplete, unfurnished classrooms; laboratories and offices. The ICT infrastructure had been laid in the Administration block and University Library only. Several computers were purchased for student and staff on which basic Microsoft application was installed. The Finance department used Quick Books and payroll software. The University subcontracted for website development that was hosted at DeepAfrica.

The ICT infrastructure was later enhanced by the last mile radio link was to provide internet to the organization at 10Mbs. This was enhanced to 21Mbs then 66Mbs, 82Mbs, then 110 and the present speed is 264 Mbs. The University now receives internet bandwidth through a last mile fibre link. The Campus network continues to be enhanced with campus fibre backbone in place. The radio link is now used as backup. Several hotspots have been installed to allow the students and member of staff access the net. The University has a Directorate of ICT whose mandate are to (Mbuguah SM 2018):

- Establish and maintain ICT infrastructure and services.
- To advance the intellectual and human resource capacity through use of E-resources.

- To publicize University programmers, activities and promote its public image.
- Automate University wide services

The Directorate has purposed continue automating most services through the use of an Enterprise Resource Planning (ERP) solution.

Enterprise Resource Planning System

An Enterprise resource planning system is a fully integrated business management system covering functional areas of an enterprise like Student management, Procurement, Finance, Accounting and Human Resources. It organizes and integrates operation processes and information flows to make optimum use of resources such as men, material, money and machine. Enterprise resource planning uses single database, single application and single user interface for the entire enterprise, where once discrete systems (Rohit R.(ud))

The ERP should be flexible, module based to allow of integration from more module. The architecture should be open like in service-oriented architecture such the module called be called as services. These will lead to reduced coupling among the modules, leading software system which are not easy to attack.

The objective of the chapter is to identify challenges that could be encountered as one implements an ERP system, using Kibabii University as case Study. Then suggests solution to these challenges.

CURRENT CHALLENGES FACING THE ORGANIZATION

The ERP implementation is largely complete, and now is in the support phase. Three of the major challenges facing the organization are:

1. **Attitude Change**: The ERP forces people to adopt a certain workflow. The acceptance that there is a system is in place, that it is not business as usual, has been constant source of friction.
2. **Training of Users:** Initially users took training casually and hence took too long to adopt the system and continue making errors as they use the system. Also, because there are many concurrent activities happening at the University, then training within campus has not been very effective.
3. **Lack of Metrics for Measuring the Level of Implementations**: There is need to assess the degree of implementation for modules. There were no metrics in place to solve this problem, looking at available Service oriented metrics (Mbuguah & Wabwoba, 2014). Yet the University management requires an

absolute figure to enable them to determine the payment. The metric has to be sufficiently objective satisfy both the vendor and the client. The vendor had prepared a questionnaire on user acceptance. But had not provided an objective transformation of the questionnaire into a metric.

RELATED STUDIES

CGN (2006) carried out a research on ERP project measurements where they found out that the most successful projects were those where there was a high degree of Political and Operational achievement. On the contrary, the ones that had high Technical and Economic achievement, but low Political and Operational achievements were perceived as less successful in the long term.

They argued that to determine the true success of an ERP project, firms must make a paradigm shift that, incorporates a holistic approach and multi-dimensional view that includes targets, constituents, and a sequence of measurements over a long-range time frame. Only by transcending the traditional, singular financial view of return of investment (ROI) can one truly identify and differentiate successful ERP programs that provide long-term strategic value.

On technical aspect the rating was on whether the implementation is:

- Fully achieved
- Mostly achieved
- Partially achieved
- Failed to achieve

Siriku (2017) presented a paper titled measuring implementation success with a balanced Scorecard. He argued that Large Scale ERP implementation success factors consists of project management competence, knowledge sharing, ERP system quality, understanding, user involvement, business process engineering, user involvement, top management support and organization support.

Ahad et al. (2018) have written on ERP Post implementation Success Assessment: An Extended Framework. In the paper they emphasis the importance of post implementation success assessment and propose an extended model based on the original model by Ifinedo et al. (2010). That did encompass service quality, system quality, information quality, individual impact, and workgroup impact and organization impact surrogates.

There are many more authors who have highlighted various other aspects of ERP and metrics but none has attempted to measure the level of implementation of degree of implementation which is the key contribution of this chapter (Mbuguah et al. 2019).

SOLUTIONS AND RECOMMENDATIONS

This section seeks to provide possible solution to identified challenges.

Attitude

Moutaz and Henrik (2017) did carry out a research on user resistance. They identified factors that cause people to resist a new system. The factors authors: people, system, interaction approaches, perceived risk and habit. They also identified strategies that can be used reducing user resistance such as participative training and top management commitment. Authors are in support of these finding and continue to state that change of altitude will take time to be realized but as staff continue to use the system they will gradually buy into the system and their attitude will gradually change. Also continues enforcement of the workflow by the senior management will force those who are reluctant to adopt to do so ((Mbuguah et al. 2019):

It has also been recommended that most the services be automated and integrated within the ERP. Top management has discouraged any process being undertaken outside the ERP that involves service already included in the modules.

Training of Users

Derek (2017) argues that training must be implemented in the right way, and it must be tailored to staff in order to maximize its effectiveness. The authors concur with the above since the errors being experienced in the system are user based, and this could be tied up to effectiveness of the training. Generally, most of the users are demanding for more training. This should be done either formally or informally by the vendor and ICT staff. It has also been recommended by users that future training been done away from campus to allow the participants to fully concentrate (Mbuguah et al. 2019).

Lack of Metrics

To determine the level implementation Directorate of ICT (DICT), the ABNO team and the internal auditor, visited the various users in the various departments for user acceptance tests. The question then was how to evaluate the level implementation in face of nonexistent metrics. The solution then was to come up implementation metrics.

ERP Implementation Metrics

The team was to carry out an acceptance test based on each of functionality of module as per terms of reference (TOR) which informs the contract. The result of the test was then rated as Fail, Query or pass. Fail if it failed outright, query if the user was not completely satisfied and pass if a given functionality performed as required (Mbuguah et al. 2019).

The result was then coded such that a fail is assigned a zero (0), a query (½) and pass one(1) . The ½ assigned to query which the arithmetic mean of 0, and 1.

The concept was adopted from the Tristate logic in Digital logic where authors have high (1), low (0) and high impedance (Z) states. (Citation)

The metric for implementation was then defined as

Implementation % = { ((no pass +½ (no of queries))/(total number of tests))*100}

Validation of Metrics

Validation of metrics can be done both theoretically and empirically. Muketha et al.,(2011) posits that main goal of theoretical validation is to establish the theoretical soundness of the metrics. Several researches such Fenton et al. (1998), Weyuker (1988) and Briand et al. (1998) have studied the metrics for quite some time.

The metric is size metric because the level implementation increases from 0% when there is no implementation to 100% for full implementation. Theoretical validation shows that it may not be possible for implementation to be below zero (0) % or above 100% (Mbuguah et al. 2019):

Considering zero case then

Implementation % = { ((no pass +½ (no of queries))/(total number of tests))*100}

No of passes = 0
No of queries = 0

Substituting into the equation

Implementation % = { ((0 +½ (0))/(total number of tests))*100}

= 0

Considering the case of complete successful implementation

No of passes = total number of tests
No of queries = zero (0)

Substituting into equation

Implementation % = {((no pass +½ (no of queries))/(total number of tests))*100}

Implementation % = { ((total number of tests +½ (0))/(total number of tests))*100}

= total number of tests/total number of tests *100

= 1*100 = 100%

Empirical tests can also be based on Weyukker criteria and /or the Lionel Briand criteria.

But as has been, argued by Muketha (2011) and others Weyukker criteria is best for complexity metrics. Since the proposed metrics are size then Weyukker criteria may not apply here.

Briand et al. (1998) postulates that a size metric can be assessed based on, non-negative, null and additive. For non-negativity it means that the size of metric should ≥ 0, and this applies to the proposed metrics. The metric null value for an empty set and the metrics from the modules are additive. Hence authors may conclude that the metrics are empirically sound.

An Application of Metrics and Certain Instance in the Implementation

Table 1 gives the results for application of the metrics where serial no 8 -18 represents the sub-modules in the integrated finance module.

From Table 1 the total numbers of tests were 331 of which 200 were passes while 25 were queries and 106 were fails.

From these data the percentage user acceptance $=((25*1/2)+200)/331)*100 = 64.2\%$ The Implication of this is at time of assessment the University should have paid an amount not greater than the Quoted tender sum. The Vendor could use the metric to evaluate is performance.

Table 1. ERP user acceptance results

S/NO	Module name	Fail	Query	Pass	Total no Functionalities
1	Student Management	2	0	13	15
2	Student academics	2	0	20	22
3	Student Portal	2	3	6	11
4	Hostel And Accommodations	3	0	14	17
5	Human Resource	0	5	30	35
6	Procurement and Inventory	14	3	31	48
7	Time tabling	1	0	15	16
8	Finance -student finance	0	1	24	25
9	IGA	12	0	0	12
10	Account payable	0	1	17	18
11	Imprest management	2	0	10	12
12	Cash management	3	2	10	15
13	Bank Reconciliation	2	3	1	6
14	Projects	4	0	0	4
15	Budgeting modules	3	0	7	10
16	Fixed assets	24	0	0	24
17	Payroll	31	0	0	31
18	Finance -Reports	1	7	2	10
19	Total	106	25	200	331

(Source Mbuguah et al. 2019)

Application of the Metrics to Sampled Specific Modules

The metric was applied to each module.

Student Academics

In this module 22 functionalities were tested out of which 2 failed. The tests that failed were

- Capture class attendance by lecturers
- Generating departmental mark sheets
- The users acceptance from module was **(20/22)*100 =90.9%**

Should enhance control on the student unit registration so that units to be registered once.

Student Portal

In this module 11 functionalities were tested out of which 2 failed. The tests that failed were

- Students can view their attendance records online
- Students can view......

The users acceptance from module was **(7.5/11)*100 =68.2%**
In this module, the following had not been utilized

- Viewing exam results online and printing of unofficial transcript online
- View class and exam time tables online.

Hostel and Accommodations

A total of 17 functionalities were tested of which three failed. These were:

- Capture damages caused by students and invoice appropriately
- Occupancy rate
- Accommodations fees collected per hostel/campus/school etc

Online booking and room rates are had not been used.
The users acceptance for this module was **(14/17)*100 =82.4%**

Human Resource

A total of 35 functionalities were tested out which 5 had queries.

- Employee service history
- Monitoring employee suspension, discharge and disciplinary actions
- Keep record of employee training awards and appraisals
- Track employees performance reviews
- List of employees due for appraisal

The users acceptance for this module was **(32.5/35)*100 =92.9%**
The users acceptance for this module was **(15/16)*100 =93.8%**

Student Finance

A total of 25 functionalities were tested with one query. The query was ability to generate invoices to eligible students only.
The users acceptance for this module was **(24.5/25)*100 =98%.**
It takes time to generate reports.
Configuration of emailing demand notices to student not configured.

Finance IGA

In this module none of the 12 functionalities were tested.
The users acceptance for this module was **(0/12)*100 =0%**

Accounts Payable

A total of 18 functionalities were tested with only one query and no fail. The query was ability to vote and stop payment of cheques especially where there exists:

- Double entries on suppliers names.
- List of suppliers contact is not complete.
- No separation of capital and recurrent creditors.

The users acceptance for this module was **(17.5/18)*100 =97.2%**

Bank Reconciliation

A total of 6 functionalities were tested with 2 fails and 3 queries. These were

- Full bank and cash reconciliations including deposits disbursement and adjustments.
- Flexibility to import transaction from various banks systems

The users acceptance for this module was **(2.5/6)*100 =41.7%**

Projects

In this module none of the 4 functionalities were tested. There was no user.
The users acceptance for this module was **(0/4)*100 =0%**

Fixed Assets

In this module none of the 24 functionalities were tested. There was no user.
The users acceptance for this module was **(0/24)*100 =0%**

Payroll

In this module none of the 31 functionalities were tested because the user requested for more time before assessment of module could be done.
The users acceptance for this module was **(0/31)*100 =0%**

Finance Reports

A total 10 functionalities were tested with one fail and seven queries. The fail was notes to the financial statement with comparative figures
The users acceptance for this module was **(5.5/10)*100 =55%**

EVALUATION OF METRICS

The office of Auditor General in Kenya has the mandate to audit within six months after end of each financial year, any entity funded by public funds OAG (2018). Kibabii University is one such organization. In September 2018 officers from the Auditor general visited Kibabii University to exercise their mandate. In their audit they wanted to find out what criteria was used in payment of ERP. Authors informed that the payment was based on the application of the above define metrics, which determined the percentage of implementation. This percentage of implementation was then used to determine the percentage of payment. They sampled several payment vouchers and authors showed them the metric used in computation of the level of implementation and corresponding payment. The officers were satisfied that metrics were valid. They also did not raise any audit query. Hence confirming and evaluating the metrics (Mbuguah et al. 2019).

CONCLUSION

In conclusion the authors set out to identify the key challenges that are experience during ERP implementation and these were mainly altitude, training of the users and lack of implementation metrics.

On altitude authors proposed ways to win over users and borrowed from what other authors have found out on overcoming resistance. On training authors also found out what were effective strategies and authors proposed further training and if possible away from the University to allow for the participant to be fully engaged.

On metrics authors found out metrics that measured the level implementation and tied it to the payment for work done were missing. Authors defined new metrics, theoretically and empirically validated them. The office of Auditor General did not raise any audit query on the way authors applied out metrics to decide on amount to be paid to the vendor. Authors believe this is an evaluation of the metrics and that metrics were found fit for purpose. Authors believe this metric will go a long way in assessing the level implementation and tying it to payment to vendor.

Nevertheless, authors are aware that the measure of query was all rounded up to half, irrespective of how near or far from implementation the query was, this is a limitation of the metric. This could be area for future research.

REFERENCES

Ahad, Z. R., Ali, Z., & Seyed, M. H. B. (2018). *ERP Implementation Success Assessment: An extended framework*. IGI Global.

Briand, L. C., Morasca, S., & Basilli, V. R. (1996). Property-based software engineering measurement. *IEEE Transactions on Software Engineering*, *22*(1), 68–86. doi:10.1109/32.481535

CGN. (2006). *Measuring ERP*. CGN Business Performance Consulting.

Charter. (2015). *Kibabii University Charter 2015*.

Derek, L. (2017). *Eight Common mistakes organization Make with ERP in Enterprise Technology Adoption*. Academic Press.

Fenton, N. E., & Pfleeger, S. L. (1997). *Software Metrics: A Rigorous and Practical, Approach*. Boston, MA: PWS Publishing Co.

Ifinedo, P., Rapp, B., Ifinedo, A., & Sundberg, K. (2010). *Relationship among ERP Post-Implementation success constructs: Analysis at organization level*. Computers in Human Behaviour.

Kurt, W. (2017). *Introduction to Digital Logic*. Morga & Claypool Publishers.

Mbuguah, S., & Wabwoba, F. (2014). *Attackability Metrics Model for Secure Service Oriented Architecture*. Lambert Academic Publishing.

Mbuguah, S. M. (2018). *ICT-Directorate*. Retrieved from https://kibu.ac.ke/ict-directorate/

Mbuguah, S. M., Wabwoba, F., & Wanjala, C. (2019) Implementation Evaluation Metrics for Enterprise Resource Planning Solution Current. *Journal of Applied Science and Technology, 32*(3).

Moutaz, H., & Henriek, M. (2017). *User Resistance in ERP implementation: A literature review*. ScienceDirect Elsevier.

Muketha, G. M. (2011). *Size And Complexity Metrics as Indicators of Maintainability, of Business Process Execution Language Process Models* (PhD Thesis). University Putra Malaysia.

OAG. (2018). *Mandate*. Retrieved on 13/12/2018 from https://www.oagkenya.go.ke/index.php/about-us/mandate

Rohit, R. (n.d.). *An Overview of Enterprise Resource Planning ERP*. Retrieved from https://www.academia.edu/7095803/Chapter_7_An_Overview_of_Enterprise_Resource_Planning_ERP

Siriluck. (2017). Measuring ERP Implementation Success with balanced Scorecard. *The 23rd Journal Americas conference on Information System*.

Stackify. (2017). *What are software metrics and how can authors track them*. Retrieved 14/12/2018 at https://satackify.com/track-software-metrics/

Statues. (2017). *Kibabii University statutes 2017*.

UAT. (2018). *A complete guide user acceptance test*. Retrieved from https://www.softwaretestinghelp.com/

Webmaster. (2018). *History of Kibabii University*. Retrieved from https://kibu.ac.ke/history/

Weyuker, E. J. (1998). Evaluating Software complexity measures. *IEEE Transactions on Software Engineering*.

APPENDIX 1: REQUEST FOR EXPRESSION OF INTEREST FOR THE SUPPLY, INSTALLATION, COMMISSIONING OF AN ENTERPRISE RESOURCE PLANNING (ERP) FOR KIBABII UNIVERSITY COLLEGE

Introduction

Kibabii University College (KIBUCO) was established by Legal Notice No.115 of August 2011 as a constituent college of Masinde Muliro University of Science and Technology. The University College was established with two faculties: Faculty of Science and the Faculty of Education and Social Sciences (FESS). It admitted 368 studenst in its first intake in March 2012. Since the establishment of Kibabii University College, additional School of Computing and Informatics and a School of Business and Economics and School of Graduate studies have been established. The student population has increased to 4000.

These faculties and schools offer various courses in; Education, Social Sciences, Natural Sciences, Business Studies, Economics, Commerce, Computer Science, Information Technology and Criminology Studies among others. The courses are offered at the Certificate, Diploma, Undergraduate, Masters and Doctoral levels.

The present number of both teaching and non teaching staff is 251 and the figure is expected to grow to about 450 by 2016.

The present number of University owned computers 250 and this expected to increase to about 450 in near future. There several laptop and smart phones for members of staff and student that connect into the University Network.

The operating system are Windows and Linux operating system. Most of application software Microsoft office suite. The Library uses KOHA. Quick books are used in the Finance section. There other application and programming languages specifically used for teaching.

The servers are seven in number with Windows server 2012 and Linux server operating system. The expected database for the university process should be Oracle.

The university college is currently connected to the internet at a speed of 20 Mbps. The staff and students are served through structured cabling and WIFI.

Brief Operations of the University Current Processes

The processes from various departments with some of the key input/outputs from each of the process.

Call for Expression of Interest

Kibabii University College invites Expressions of Interest (EOI) from competent firms to supply,

Install, train users and commission an Enterprise Resource Planning (ERP).

Firms will be shortlisted for participation based on their demonstration of technical and financial capability in response to this request.

In addition to the information requested in the questionnaire downloadable from our website www.kibabiiuniversity.ac.ke, interested firms must provide an updated copy of their company profile demonstrating their experience in similar assignments along with the names of at least three (3) referees with contact information (physical address, e-mail address and telephone).

Please read through this document carefully and provide the requested information together with ALL required support documents.

Submission Instructions

This Expression of Interest document can be downloaded from www.kibabiiuniversity. ac.ke free of charge.

Expressions of interest letters together with all completed documents in a plain sealed envelope

clearly marked "EXPRESSION OF INTEREST TO TENDER FOR THE SUPPLY, INSTALLATION, TRAINING OF USERS AND COMMISSIONING OF AN ENTERPRISE RESOURCE PLANNING SOFTWARE" should be addressed to:-

The Principal
Kibabii University College
P.O. Box 1699 - 50200
Bungoma

And should be deposited in the tender box situated at the entance to the Administration Block at Kibabii University College in Bungoma off Bungoma - Chwele road.

Mandatory Requirements

You shall be required to attach the following mandatory documents where applicable;

1. Certificate of Incorporation, Partnership or Business registration
2. Trading Certificate

Table 2. Process and inputs

	DEPARTMENT/UNIT	PROCESS/PROCEDURE	INPUT/OUTPUTS OF THE PROCESS
1.	Procurement	Procurement	LPOs, Contracts etc
		Stores & Inventory	Stock, SRN, updates and Reports
2.	Finance	General Ledger	Transaction, reports
		Student Finance	Invoice,Fees Deposit, reports
		Income Generating Activities	Products & Sevices Sales, Reports,
		Fixed assets	Asset, Value, depreciation rate, reports
		Account Payable	PRN, LPO, Cheque, reports
		Imprest Management	Imprest request, Reports
		Part- time lecturers	Loading, hour rate, Reports
		Cash Office	Cash flow inputs, reports
		Bank reconciliation	Deposits, disbursements, charges, interest and Reports
		Payroll	Remuneration, taxes,deductions, pay slips and Reports
		Budgeting	Estimates per vote &department, update, report
		Project	Project details, budget, duration and reports
2	Academic Division	Admission & Registration	Applicants,schools, department, programmes, campuses, Status Reports
		Examination	Lectures, courses, Curriculum, units,marks, reports
		Time Tabling	Lecture room & capacity, time, Event & calendar, allocation reports.
		Student portal(Online services)	Student registration number, Reports,
3	Human resource	Personnel Management	Personal details, department, dependence, job description, reports.
		Time and Attendance	
		Leave Management	Type of leave, Duration, Address, reports
		Employee self-service	PF Number, reports
4	Library	Circulation	Check outs & check ins, Reservation, Renewals, fines, Reports
		Maintenance	Library members, Categories Durations, Charges
		Patron management	Member records, reports
		Cataloguing	Items details, OPAC, reports
		Administration	System setting, reports
5	Hostel & Accommodation	Hostel & Accommodation	Rooms, charges, room rates, allocation, reports

3. Tax compliance certificate
4. PIN certificate
5. List of Directors, telephone, postal and email address
6. CVs of Senior Staff and others as it may have been requested.
7. Organogram
8. Evidence of physical registered office (Attach miscellaneous receipt)
9. Audited financial reports for the last three years i.e. 2012, 2013 and 2014.
10. Bank statements for a period of One (1) year.

Questionnaire: Supply and Installation of an ERP

Part A: General Information

Information about the company was sought including physical location.

Part B: Eligibility

The information on this section was on legal status of company including insolvency, tax payments and integrity. It has been abridged.

Part C: Financial Information

The information sought was on the financial status of company

NB: attach firm's audited accounts and certified bank statements for the three years together with reference letters from the bankers on the firm's Credit position.

Part D: Trade References

Provide contact details for at least three referees for previous/current work that is similar or same as to the work applied for. Note that the referees may be contacted without further references to you. (Attach documentary evidence of existence of the contracts

Part E: Industry Information

1. Project history

    a. Completed Projects: List the information on projects completed over the last three (3) years in the following format and attach evidences.

    b.   **On-going Projects:** List the information on on-going projects in the following format and attach evidences.

NB: A separate sheet of paper can be attached if space provided is not enough.

2.   Experience

    a.   Describe the core business of your firm.

    b.   How many years has your firm been engaged in the business of supply and installation of ERP?...
....

    c.   State the Minimum and the Maximum labor force engaged at any one time by your firm.

Maximum ....
Minimum ....

3.   Proposed solution/System (Software/ERP)

Describe the type of ERP you wish to deploy and the features of each module, customization, installation, applicable licenses and training among other details. You are free to attach brochures on the features of the solution.

4.   Training

Describe the methodology of carrying out the training for the staff.

Part G: Certification

I/we do hereby certify that the above information is correct in all respects.

Full name:
Designation/Position:
Signature:
Date:
Company Stamp

APPENDIX 2: TERMS OF REFERENCE (TOR) FOR ERP

1.1 General Features

1.1.1 Dash Board

The system should have a dashboard that clearly indicates the student population at a glance. Other details to be shown include breakdown of the student population per school and the availability of accommodation space.

1.1.2 Concurrency

The system must be able to support 5,000 or more concurrent users regardless of the geographical locations. These clients should maintain autonomy to allow distributed processing.

1.1.3 Workflow Management

The system must support document movement within the system. The users must be notified through the push technology whenever there is a document to be worked on.

1.1.4 Importing /Exporting Data

The system should be able to import and export data to other applications especially MS Excel, MS Word, PDF, RTF, among other applications.

1.1.5 Access Points

It is envisaged that there shall be a centralized site where the database will reside. All end users (in various colleges, schools/campuses, departments and any other units of the University) must be able to access that system from any point within the University and outside.

1.1.6 Data Migration

The system should provide capabilities of **AUTOMATICALLY** migrating data from other systems currently in use.

1.2 Other Expectations

1.2.1 Number of Licenses

It is expected that the vendor will supply at least **50 LICENSES**.

1.2.2 Training

Thorough training is expected to be conducted for Senior Management, Middle level managers, Technical Staff and Operational Staff/users.

1.2.3 Implementation Schedule

The implementation schedule should be monitored in order to control unnecessary delays, implementation cost and monitor overall project progress. Clear time line of activities shall need to be outlined, observed and reported.

1.2.4 Acceptance Test

It is expected that the details of acceptance tests and testing procedures to be undertaken during user acceptance will be recorded and well documented.

1.2.5 Documentation

During implementation, technical and user manuals for the ERP shall be provided containing sufficient details to allow the relevant university staff to operate the system.

1.3 Integrated Financial Management Module

The system must be integrated and support both managerial and financial functions.

1.3.1 General Ledger

All modules must be fully integrated with the general ledger to enhance reliability of data processing.

Expected Reports

The system should be able to generate a GL report. The GL report **MUST** contain all the transactions for a given period listed by account. Other features that must be supported by the GL include the following.

1. Condensed Trial Balance
2. GL report
3. Expanded Trial Balance
4. The system should be able to produce the following Financial Statements that must comply with the *IPSAS* **Format** iStatement of Financial Performance Income with comparative figures
   a. Statement of Financial Position with comparative figures
   b. Statement of cash flows with comparative figures
   c. Statement of Budget Comparison
   d. Statement of changes in equity with comparative figures
   e. Notes to the Financial statements with comparative figures

   N/B you must illustrate to support features in (d) above.

1.3.2 Students Finance

Expected Features

1. Ability to integrate all the transactions related to students with GL
2. Ability to set fees structure.
3. Ability to integrate with Admissions Department
4. Ability to track mandatory fees for students joining from second year of study.
5. Ability to generate invoices to eligible students only. Clearly demonstrate how this is done.
6. Ability to generate receipts on every payment and allocate to specific line items e.g. Tuition, Accommodation, Supervision, Activity, Field Attachment etc.
7. Ability to handle fee refunds.
8. Ability to accommodate University Fees policy.
9. Illustrate the ability of capturing the overpayments by students and subsequently do a fair reporting. Illustrate how the overpayments are used.
10. Ability to trail all transactions of the students as they occur.
11. Illustrate the ability to handle sponsor's funds.
12. Illustrate the ability to upload data from the bank statement directly into the system and update the student accounts appropriately.

13. Illustrate the ability to cancel an erroneous receipt.
14. Illustrate the ability to do students' fees adjustment in case of an error during fees structure set up.
15. Illustrate the ability to reverse a single invoice for a student.
16. Illustrate ability to integrate to examinations department and controls put in place to ensure that only eligible students get exam cards.

Expected Reports

Ability to generate the following reports:-

1. Ability to generate daily fee collection report (Global)
2. Ability to generate daily fee collection report
3. Student fees balance summary (Global)
4. Students fees balance for various categories /departments /prpgrammes.
5. Demand letters to students with outstanding fees balance by a defined criterion. The demand letters can be e-mailed to the corporate e-mail accounts of students.
6. List of students who have overpaid fees.
7. Students with zero balance
8. Drilling of students' balances with user set criteria e.g students whose balance is greater than KShs 100,000.
9. List of Students who have paid to votes like Field Trips/ Teaching Practice.
10. Print exam cards for students who meet the minimum fees balance as may be set by the University.
11. Student fees collection summary per vote head.
12. Students Fees balance summary per vote head.
13. Periodic fees collection report e.g Monthly, Quarterly, Annually etc.
14. Ability to produce ad hoc reports.

1.3.3 Income Generating Activities (IGA)

The University operates income generating units like farm, book shop and staff catering.

Expected Features

1. Ability to capture products and services
2. Classification of products as per the IGA
3. Creating of price list
4. Ability to use credit and debit memos

5. Tracking of stock levels
6. Ability to adjust stock levels after stock taking.
7. Ability to create customers
8. Ability to generate cash sale receipts.
9. Ability to generate an invoice for a customer
10. Ability to integrate with ETR machine.

Expected Reports

1. Inventory reports by stock and Value
2. Ability to report on fast moving items.
3. Income & Expenditure for IGA.

1.3.4 Fixed Assets

Expected Features

This module must maintain records of all fixed assets and compute depreciation costs. The module must also allow for posting of asset values, depreciation and disposal. It must have but not limited to the following features.

Fixed Assets register

1. Unique asset identification
2. Comprehensive facilities to deal with all aspects of depreciation
3. Sale and purchase of assets fully integrated with the rest of the accounting system.
4. Fully integrated with general ledger accounts receivable, and accounts payable modules.
5. Records person and department responsible for the asset
6. Asset classification
7. Bar coding.
8. Valuation reports
9. Asset listings & transactions
10. Assets Disposals.
11. Warranty expiry date.
12. Insurance/Tax rate
13. Fully depreciated asset listing
14. The system has a provision for transfer of assets.
15. Asset coding;
16. Depreciation / revaluation;

17. Location tracking;
18. Service schedules;
19. Maintenance details (incidents and costs);
20. Disposal records;
21. Handling of intangible assets, e.g. computer software.
22. Unlimited asset categories
23. Generation of custom asset numbers

Expected Reports

The module should have the capability to generate the following reports:-

1. Fixed Assets Register/report
2. Fixed Asset history report
3. Fixed assets Depreciation report
4. Fixed Assets acquisition and Transfers report.
5. Valuation reports
6. Asset listings
7. Assets Disposals.
8. Warranty expiry date.

1.3.5 Accounts Payable

The system must provide for a full cycle of vendor transactions from the Purchase Requisition Note, (PRN), and Local Purchase Order (LPO) to cheque disbursements. It should on minimum meet the following features.

Expected Features

1. Ability to integrate fully with Procurement
2. Ability to capture supplier invoice
3. Ability to allocate a supplier invoice to a cost centre.
4. Ability to define default payment terms
5. Ability to control payments as per the stipulated terms.
6. Ability to hold disputed supplier invoice and payment.
7. Ability to generate Payment Vouchers
8. Ability to automatically assign voucher numbers.
9. Ability to allocate payments to suppliers' invoice.
10. Ability to pay suppler invoice in part

11. Ability for multiple invoices from a single vendor to be paid on one cheque with supporting detail on cheque stub or remittance advice.
12. Ability to void a payment voucher.
13. Ability to void and stop payment of cheques.
14. Both vendors and payment vouchers can be put on hold to prevent processing of requisitions, orders, invoices and payments.
15. Recovery and accumulation of Retention for settlement.
16. Recovery and accumulation of Withholding Tax for settlement

Expected Reports

Ability to generate the following reports:-

1. Accounts payable balances as at a given date
2. Creditors ageing summary & detail reports.
3. List of capital creditors.
4. List of recurrent creditors.
5. Supplier Ledger.
6. Supplier contact list.

1.3.6 Imprest Management

The system is expected to control and manage the issuance of imprests to staff, the accounting of imprests and the recovery of unaccounted for imprests from salaries of involved staff.

Expected Features

The system should among others expectations include the following: -

1. Generate imprests forms and automatically number them serially
2. Specify the envisaged accounting date
3. Automatic alerts for overdue unaccounted for imprests
4. Linked to the Payroll module for recovery of unaccounted for imprests
5. Embedded controls to stop issuance of further imprests to staff with an existing unaccounted imprest
6. Online approvals

Expected Reports

1. Age analysis of unaccounted imprests/ Imprest debtors
2. Imprest recovery reports
3. Automatically generate payroll recoveries
4. Auto-Generate under spent receipts analysis
5. Imprest ledger by staff.

1.3.7 Internal and External Part-Timers Module

The system is expected to control and manage payments to internal and external part timers.

Expected Features

1. Control to ensure appointment of part time lecturers before being allocated classes
2. Integrate with the approved timetable to track attendance dates.
3. Generate the teaching work load per lecturer
4. No lecturer can claim what he/she never taught/invigilated unless there is an approval from a higher authority.
5. Computation of payments based on hours worked. The computation will conform to the University system.
6. Put controls to qualify an internal lecturer as a part-timer.
7. Put controls in place to stop a lecturer from claiming twice.
8. Put controls in place to limit the number of courses a lecturer can handle.

Expected Reports

1. List of part timers
2. Work load per lecturer
3. Lecturer payment history
4. Outstanding claims for part timers by school, department, campus etc
5. Statement of tax for each part timer for purposes of making tax returns

1.3.8 Cash Office Module

The CASH Office operates as a central point for cash flows and is thus an agent for all sections.

Expected Features

1. Support for unlimited number of bank accounts
2. On line drilldown account analysis from various Banks/ Bank Statements all the way to the source transaction in the general-ledger and to migrate information to the Spread Sheets.
3. Create alarm features for a pre-determined amount payable at a time in each bank account
4. Support cheque printing both for Kalamazoo type of cheque and ordinary cheque and posting direct to the general ledger.
5. Record transfers between bank accounts
6. Allow for automatic reversal of erroneous entry
7. Returned (bounced) customer cheques
8. Disbursement of Petty Cash to various departments. Give a brief description of how the system handles beginning year float.
9. Ability to print cheques.
10. Notification of suppliers when cheques are due for collection.
11. Ability to keep cheque disbursement register. Indicate date when cheque is collected, person collecting and his ID number & telephone number etc.

Expected Reports

1. Cash Book
2. Petty cash Report
3. Cash flow movement report on daily, monthly, YTD, Annual basis.
4. Cash reconciliation report
5. Payment voucher listings and the status
6. Payments on hold report
7. Cheque payment register
8. List of voided cheques
9. List of voided vouchers
10. Uncollected cheques list
11. Daily Cheque disbursement report.
12. Receipts and Payments analysis indicating
    a. Transaction type
    b. Date
    c. Number
    d. Payee
    e. Description

f.   Clearance status

g.   GL

h.   Dr (Receipt)

i.   Cr (Payment)

j.   Cumulative Balance

1.3.9 Bank Reconciliation

Expected Features

1.   The System must support bank reconciliations across multiple banks
2.   Full bank and Cash reconciliations including deposits, disbursements and adjustments.
3.   Flexibility to import transactions from various banks systems.
4.   Post bank charges, interest charged and interest earned.

Expected Reports

1.   Bank reconciliation Summary.
2.   Bank Reconciliation by detail.

1.3.10 Payroll Module

The payroll Module should automate the employees salary and other benefits payments process by gathering data on employee remuneration, calculating various deductions and taxes and generating periodic pay cheques and pay slips.

Expected Features

1.   Ability to electronically integrate with the GL, Cash Book and other third party soft ware e.g. e-banking.
2.   Ability to automatically process employee salary and benefits
3.   Ability to calculate various employee deductions and taxes.
4.   Ability to run real-time data communication between human resource and finance sections.
5.   Ability to electronically integrate/export employee information to Microsoft excel, word or PDF.
6.   Ability to document all salary and job changes, view salary history of each employee online

7.   including salary, bonus and all deductions etc.
8.   Ability to generate a detailed Audit Trail of payroll transactions/changes.
9.   Link job scales to salary and allowances payable to each grade
10. Automatically post annual increments on the due dates.
11. Supports unlimited number of employees and staff classifications
12. Employee banking details e.g. bank, branch, account number, account type
13. Unlimited number of user definable tables e.g. PAYE, NSSF, NHIF, Pensions, Unions,
14. User defined rounding system
15. Bonus and arrears payments
16. Direct electronic salary remittance to banks
17. Tracking of loans and amounts due to financial institutions
18. Maintain historical information for unlimited number of years
19. Ability to automatically send payslips to employees through the e-mail.

Expected Reports

The system should allow the user to select fields to extract data and generate reports with various formats such as tables, graphs, bar charts etc. The system should be flexible such that it can pick relevant data from various tables in the database and generate any ad hoc report that may be required by the management from time to time. Among the reports the system is expected to provide are:-

1.   Report on Salary Payments on monthly, YTD, Annual basis.
2.   Report on tax payments, pension payments etc.
3.   Reports on payroll costs as defined by user e.g. in terms of basic pay, house allowance and other financial benefits on the basis of cost centre-department, school as may be defined by the user.
4.   User defined payslip format
5.   Bank remittances list
6.   Bank registers
7.   Payroll journal
8.   Company totals
9.   Employee details
10. User specified transaction reports
11. Cost centre reports
12. Statutory reports e.g. P9, P9A, P10, P10A etc
13. Audit trail reports
14. Exceptional reports e.g. staff earning salaries beyond their grades

1.3.11 Projects Accounts

Expected Features

1.   Creation of project details
2.   Setting up specific project budgets and expected duration

Expected Reports

1.   Budget vs. Actual reports
2.   Project progress report (Disbursement vs. Expenditure)
3.   Project completion status inform of percentage

1.3.12 Budgeting Module

Expected Features

1.   Store Approved annual estimates by vote and department
2.   Capture supplementary/virement vote allocations.
3.   Effect an inter-vote funds transfer.
4.   Update vote balance upon PRN entry
5.   Put controls to limit over expenditure
6.   Send alerts to vote holders whose balances are significantly low

Expected Features

1.   Print a vote holder's statement.
2.   Vote expenditure summary.
3.   Vote Balances report.
4.   Compare actual vs budgetary allocation at any given time.

1.4 Procurement, Stores and Inventory Management

1.4.1 Procurement

This module should provide the tools required to help procurement managers adhere to the rules and regulations guiding public procurement.

Expected Features

1. Fully integrated with finance module.
2. **Pre-qualified Suppliers**: The system should be able to capture and store all records of pre-qualified of suppliers of various items with the price list in every financial year.
3. **Tender Award**: The system should be able award automatically by use of predefined criteria. However, manual awarding should also be allowed so that the tender committee can award to the supplier of their choice.
4. **Request for Quotation (RFQ)**: Ability to generate Request for Quotations from the system.
5. **Purchase Requisition Note (PRN)**: The system should be furnished with tools to enable auto generation of PRNs
6. **Local Purchase Orders (LPO)**: The system should allow easy and efficient ordering by automatically generating LPOs.
7. **Goods Received Note (GRN):** The system should be able to generate GRN for received items.
8. **Track LPO Status**: The system should allow users to be able to track status of orders from the time they are raised to the time they are completed.
9. **Departmental Budgets**: The system should give an option to restrict ordering within departmental budgets in any given financial year or any defined budget periods (such as quarters).
10. Enable departments to Develop procurement plans
11. Ability to consolidate departmental procurement plans and link it to the university budgets.
12. Ability to link PRN to the LPO
13. The system should allow the different types of costing methods for inventory
14. The system should allow creation and display of the procurement plan for departments and the corporate plan.
15. The system should allow supplier management in terms of ratings, appraisals, assessments and evaluations etc
16. The system should be able to show rejected or goods returned records.
17. Ability to track partial delivery
18. Online approvals

Expected Reports

1. List of prequalified suppliers per item category
2. Purchase history per supplier

3. Price list and price updates per supplier
4. Outstanding PRNs
5. Outstanding LPOs
6. LPOs partially supplied
7. Cancelled PRNs
8. Cancelled LPOs
9. GRN reports
10. Rejected or Goods returned.
11. Supplier management in terms of ratings, appraisals, assessments and evaluations etc

1.4.2 Stores and Inventory Management

This module should allow the stores department to distribute and track stock levels of all items in the University ranging from stationery required in administration to food stuffs required in the kitchen.

Expected Features

This module should have the following features:

1. Ability to generate Stores Requisition Note (SRN) by the user department.
2. **Maximum Stock Level**: The system should allow the user to define the maximum stock leve per item
3. **Re-order level**: The system should alert the users when reorder level falls due.
4. **Minimum Stock Level**: The system should alert the user whenever stock levels hit the minimum threshold.
5. Maintain Stock ledgers per item
6. Have full audit trail of all stock movements
7. Stock history
8. Serial Number tracking
9. Bin Locations
10. Unit of measure configurable
11. Expiry date tracking in case of perishables
12. Update stock by goods received notes
13. Inventory counts changes and adjustments

Expected Reports

1. Issue/Receiving analysis
2. Transaction history per inventory item
3. Inventory level listings
4. Inventory movement
5. Stocktaking report
6. Inventory status by location
7. Inventory valuation summary & detail

1.5 Hostels and Accommodation Management

The system must provide features for the allocation of rooms to students and the collection of accommodation fees from students. The collection and refund of room deposit must also be incorporated.

Expected Features

1. Capture list of hostels and their respective capacities
2. List of rooms and their respective capacities
3. Room rates
4. Fees can vary per Hostel Block and even a room within that Block. The variation should also consider PSSP and GSSP who will be charged differently.
5. Allocate rooms to students who have paid fees only
6. Put controls in place to limit students allocation to specific gender
7. Put controls to limit allocation to students in session only
8. Hostel item(s) allocation
9. Reserved rooms for students with disability
10. Capture damages caused by students and invoice appropriately.
11. Online booking

Expected Reports

1. Allocated Room
2. Occupancy Rate
3. Beds space available per hostel by gender
4. Accommodation fees collected per hostel, campus, school etc
5. Hostel bed capacity status
6. Occupants by Student Type i.e PSSP and GSSP

1.6 Academic and Student Management

1.6.1 Admissions and Registration Module

Expected Features

1. Illustrate the ability to capture applicants
2. Ability to upload JAB students directly from the spread sheets.
3. Ability to capture list of campuses
4. Ability to capture list of Schools, Departments and programmes and areas of specialization.
5. Ability to store cohorts.
6. Ability to capture students status e.g teaching practice, holiday etc
7. Ability to store modes of study e.g Evening/Regular
8. Illustrate how a new student is admitted into a programme.
9. Illustrate how a continuing student reports.

Expected Reports

1. Generate admission / registration reports & forms
2. Generate Admission/Regret letters
3. List of students with the following conditions
   a. Per campus
   b. Per school
   c. Per department
   d. Per specialization
   e. Per year of study
   f. Per class
   g. Per student type i.e PSSP or GSSP
   h. Per study mode
   i. Per students status
   j. Per gender
   k. Per stay status i.e resident or non resident
   l. Per source
   m. Per county
   n. Deferred students
   o. Discontinued students
   p. Combination of different conditions to achieve a desired report.

1.6.2 Academic and Examination Module

The academic module should store comprehensive School/faculty data including lecturers, courses,

Curriculum, unit registration, marks among others. It integrates all academic data to produce various reports like transcript, student performance analysis and many more. Among the many requirements that will facilitate its application include the following.

Expected Features

1. The system should be able to store lecturers' details
2. Capture class attendance by students and enforce the 80% rule
3. Capture class attendance by lecturers
4. The system should be able to store course details
5. The system should be able to store curriculum details.
6. The system should be able to store unit registration details.
7. A lecturer should enter marks once and lock it. Once entered and saved, the system should not allow for any alteration of exams by the Lecturer.
8. Allow for only published results to be available on the student online portal.
9. Automatically maintain a historical audit trail of all grade entries or changes to a transcript.
10. Automatically calculate Dean's List and other academic standings
11. Perform grade distribution and class analysis reports
12. Track Academic performance of students by class, programme, or campus, mode of study among others.
13. Tracking students who have applied for graduation
14. The system should allow for attaching of notes to students results data to help with tracking examination results issues.
15. Archive student examination records for future reference
16. Academic record for graduating students
17. Illustrate the following practices.
    a. Unit Creation.
    b. Curriculum Set-Up
    c. Unit Registration
    d. Marks Entry
    e. Generation of Transcripts
    f. Performance analysis

Expected Reports

To produce a variety of reports to be presented and discussed in a variety of forums

1.   Departmental Mark sheets
2.   Consolidated Mark sheets per programme per class
3.   School board reports
4.   Senate reports
5.   Exam cards
6.   Generate the final academic transcript
7.   List of graduating applicants.
8.   Generation of lists for:
    a.   Graduation Students
    b.   Dean's List
    c.   Students on the prize list

1.6.3 Time Tabling Module

This system should enable Academic staff to easily schedule classes and efficiently use the available spaces for teaching at various campuses. The following functionalities are expected:

1.   Lecture rooms and their capacity
2.   Labs category and their capacity
3.   Demonstration Units
4.   Handling of blocks
5.   The system should allow updating time table.
6.   The module should be totally self-checking and should not allow for any conflicts. It should allow for both manual and automatic resolution of room allocation conflicts
7.   Event calendar: The system should maintain different type of upcoming events date and time.
8.   Room allocation based on size

Expected Reports

1.   Produce time table reports based on

    a.   Room
    b.   Class

c. Course
d. Labs
e. Lecturer
f. Master timetable
g. Enable online query of timetable schedules

1.6.4 Students Portal

The student portal will provide online services to students and will have the following features.

2. Online course registration / enrollment.
3. Students can view exam results online and print an unofficial transcript online.
4. Allow students to view their fee balance online.
5. Students can view their attendance records online.
6. Students can view academic holds online and receive instruction to resolve holds.
7. System should provide alerts to students on their fee balance status, exam results, etc.
8. Students can manage an online profile.
9. Students can update contact information and addresses online.
10. Students can communicate with institutional departments online.
11. Students can view class and exam timetables online
12. Digital Notice Board where students can be informed of the latest updates.

1.6.4 Cohort Management

Expected Features

1. Demonstrate how your system handles class management at different levels.
2. Demonstrate how the system stops students who are on holiday from being invoiced.
3. Demonstrate how your system will handle for various scenarios
4. How to control Holidays/ Field attachment sessions.
5. Managing Deferrals and repetitions/ promotions

1.7 Human Resources Management

The system should address all aspects regarding personnel management for the entire life of an employee.

Expected Features

The Human Resource module should contain on minimum the following features.

1. Employee details & photo capturing
2. Section or department the employee belongs.
3. Employee service history.
4. Leave and absence management.
5. Carefully monitors employee suspension, discharge, disciplinary action.
6. Keeps record of employee training, awards and appraisals.
7. Track employee attendance with the use of either fingerprints or smartcard.
8. Gives alerts and keeps record of personal in-formation including license, VISA and other cards expiry dates.
9. Documents can be scanned and stored electronically.
10. Provide the easiest way to organize employee files. Store all your confidential information in one place.
11. Schedule reminders for performance reviews, benefit eligibility, probation periods, birthdays, anniversaries, training, reports and other events.
12. Track all employee's performance reviews including past reviews. Create management's comments under each employee. Automatically schedule the next performance or disciplinary review.
13. Document all salary and job changes. View the salary history of each employee online including salary, bonuses and all deductions. Quickly view work history such as promotions and length of employment in a position.
14. ***Track vacation and leaves*** – Input institution's vacation and leave policies and the system should track the number of days available based on years of service.
15. Store and view all employee documents. View scanned images like resumes, applications, and accident reports stored by employee. One should also be able to link to Word, Excel and PDF files.
16. Track individual skills; store required courses, certifications and grades received. Document all awards, accomplishments and recognition each employee has received over the years.
17. Maintain an accurate history of all incidents and accidents. Enter all medical assessments per-formed for regulations.

18. Control confidential information with various security levels for different users.
19. Document all written and verbal warnings. Capture employee and supervisor comments plus disciplinary actions.
20. Store job descriptions, minimum skill requirements and salary grade levels by position.
21. Access to contact information quickly in a medical emergency.
22. Track union membership status, start and end dates, contract expiry dates and seniority.
23. Know which employee has what tool or equipment.
24. Easily export employee information to Microsoft Word, Excel or PDF.
25. ***Time & Attendance*** – Track employee attendance with the use of either fingerprints or smart-card

Expected Reports

1. List of all employees by gender, region, district, county and tribe.
2. List of employees on leave
3. List of employees due for appraisal
4. List of employees who have left the organization
5. Skills inventory report
6. Staff turnover report
7. Alerts on staff member's birthday
8. Employees trained in a given year
9. List of employees/dependants on tuition fee waiver.
10. List of employees nearing retirement

1.8 Library Management

Expected Features

The library module should contain the following features.

1. **Circulation**: The system should provide support for issues (check-outs), returns (check-ins), reservations, renewals, reminders (to those with borrowed items), barcode reader, fines (calculations and payments) user profiles and issuance of notification letters. Other features for circulation will include:
    a. Taking statistics on issues and borrowers visiting the library.
    b. Preparing overdue and recall notes.
    c. Renewals of books.

    d.   Collection of fines.

    e.   Compilation of list of defaulters and daily financial collection by individual users plus accumulatively collected.

    f.   The system should be able to provide information to answer queries from users.

    g.   The system support for e-mail communication between library staff and the users, e.g. posting of overdue item notices to affected users.

    h.   The system should be able to provide for recall, overdue and fine notices.

    i.   The system should be able to generate reports on certain activities to be used by library management for decision making e.g. number of loan items, defaulters and financial transactions on daily and monthly basis.

2.   Maintenance File:

    a.   The system should be able to maintain a list of the members of the library with different groups.

    b.   The system should be able to allow creation of unlimited number of categories of users with different maximum number of items to borrow, maximum number of days to stay with the borrowed item(s) and the fine charges for those who overstays with the item(s).

3.   **Patrons Management:** The module is should be furnished with tools to enable changing the information about members or viewing their details.

    a.   Creating and editing member records

    b.   Finding and Viewing patron records

    c.   Printing patron cards

    d.   Collecting fees and dues

4.   **Cataloguing:** the system should capture and store details of all the items in the library (catalogued).

    The system should allow definition of types of items and loaning categories (e.g. short loans). The catalogue module is equipped with the Z39.50 standard such that if you are connected to the internet, you only need to enter the ISBN number and the software will query the internet servers such as Library of Congress. Apart from the main catalogue, the system should provide an Online Public Access Catalogue (OPAC) that is used by library users to search the library.

5.   Administration:

   a.   The system should have an option where overall system settings are done. This include creating staff (librarian accounts), database maintenance, log file, departments, barcode generation and other tools like internet browser and email facilities.

   b.   OPAC: The system should enable a user to determine the availability of materials in the library through many access points such as use of keywords, author, subject and title, Keyword, ISBN/ISSN.

Chapter 12
ERP Software Maintenance

Elyjoy Muthoni Micheni
Technical University of Kenya, Kenya

ABSTRACT

This chapter will explain ERP software maintenance and the effort required to locate and fix errors in the ERP software. Software maintenance is defined as the totality of activities required to provide cost-effective support to a software system. The purpose of software maintenance is to modify and update software application after delivery to correct faults and to improve performance. The chapter will highlight activities performed during the pre-delivery stage, including planning for post-delivery operations, supportability, and logistics determination, and also activities performed during the post-delivery stage, including software modification, training, and operating a help desk. The chapter will discuss the types of maintenance and highlight the ERP process support activities and the ERP system maintainability framework. The chapter will explain the maintenance of ERP software and will also discuss the ISO/IEC 9126 and IEEE Standard 1219-1998 for software maintenance. Issues in ERP software maintenance are also presented and discussed.

DOI: 10.4018/978-1-5225-7678-5.ch012

INTRODUCTION

Software maintenance has historically not received the same degree of attention as the other phases of the software development phases despite being an integral part of a software life cycle. This has however changed in recent years because organizations are keen to obtain the most out of such investments by keeping the software operating as long as possible. It is difficult to keep software systems up and running as they age, without proper maintenance because software deteriorates as it ages even if it is well maintained. Changes over the lifetime of ERP software systems are inevitable, even if the software initially met all its design requirements because changes may be necessitated by need to adapt to increased functional requirements, business processes re-engineering and different system configurations brought about by these changes. Generally, maintenance plays an important role in software products because a significant proportion of most software's is unstructured, patched and not well documented, and maintenance can help alleviate some of these problems. There is a need to know the characteristics of ERP software and how they affect maintainability. Factors known to affect maintainability include system size, system age, number of input/output data items, application type, programming language, and the structure of controls in the system. For instance, larger systems may require more maintenance effort than smaller systems, because there is a greater learning curve associated with larger systems, and also larger systems may be more complex in terms of the variety of functions they perform. The purpose of maintenance for ERP software is to preserve the value of the software over time since without its maintenance, it may not be possible to change the problems within the product after its release, and many disasters can happen because of problems arising after its release. Enterprise Resource system is a complex and comprehensive software that integrates an organization's functions and resources, and therefore many organizations lack experience and expertise in managing ERP maintenance and upgrade effectively. The work of Poi Ng et al, (2002) showed that ERP maintenance and upgrade activities were attracting increasing attention in ERP-using organizations because annual maintenance costs approximate were approximately 25% of initial ERP implementation costs while upgrade costs were in the range of 25-33% of the initial ERP implementation. Maintainability of ERP software is its environment changes including user requirements. There should be a plan to allow the structure to capability to be modified, and consists five sub-characteristics, including analyzability, changeability, stability, and testability. The maintenance is done when there is released of the product, it allows to adapt to be modified during design phase. Similarly, the code should be clear, understandable and changed during implementation phase. When other phases are conducted well, structured code, system sufficient knowledge of system and up to date documentation the Maintenance can be done more efficiently and successful (Erdil, et al, 2003). The maintenance enables the products meets requirement of the users. It is recommended for ERP software product to adapt to change and evolved. As the ERP software is used some defects are detected, its environment changes as well as new requirement reappear. The maintenance life cycle start up after post implementation. The maintenance is part of life cycle in development of software. The maintenance of ERP software refers to changes and modification involved after the release of product to users to detect errors, correct them to improve its performance well as to adapt changes in environment. After installation and running of ERP software product within environment soon a novel requirement transpire. Hence for system to be relevant there is need to modify or incorporate new functionalities and requirements. The IEEE terms software maintenance as the modification conducted to ERP software product once it's release in order to removed faults, enhanced performance and attributes to product adaptability to environment (Jansson, 2007).ERP software maintenance is important because, when it is not conducted regularly with time it becomes uneasy run the system. The essence maintenance is the modification of the current ERP software to enhanced integrity. International standards stipulate need of conducting maintenance before final ERP software release (Erdil, et al, 2003)

THE NEED FOR ERP MAINTENANCE

Software maintenance is an integral part of software life cycle. Organizations cannot achieve excellence with unreliable software. The Lehman's laws of evolution state that successful software systems are condemned to change over time, whereby a proportion of the changes is to meet ever changing user needs. The first law of Lehman (Lehman, 1984), states that a program that is used in a real-world environment necessarily must change or become progressively less useful in that environment. Significant changes are also derived from the need to adapt software to interact with external entities, including people, organizations, and artificial systems. In fact, software is infinitely malleable and, therefore, it is often perceived as the easiest part to change in a system (Canfora & Cimitile, 2000). The achievement of excellence in ERP software demands good quality in the software. Enterprise resource planning (ERP) maintenance and upgrade activities are receiving much attention in ERP-using organizations. This is because annual maintenance costs approximate 25% of initial ERP implementation costs (Ng et al, 2003). In order to help organizations in ERP software maintenance, a number of model standards exist to guide ERP maintenance and upgrade processes and their scope in terms of size, costs, and time required, and to assess the criticality of such maintenance.

TYPES OF SOFTWARE MAINTENANCE

There are four types of ERP software maintenance define by ISO/IEC 14764 (Erdil, et al, 2003):

- **Corrective Maintenance:** These entails the changes mandated as a result of errors actualize in ERP software product as well as non-conformity of to the requirements of the user. It involved fixing the bugs within the code. The defects that requires to be fixed can include logic, coding and design errors.
- **Adaptive Maintenance:** It involved changing the ERP software. The changes essential for the product cope with changes in the environment such as adopting novel requirement on system, hardware or interface. The environment refers to the entirety of surrounding that influence the system for instance government guidelines, policies, work structure, business rules and system operating platforms. The changes were excluded during ERP software release or at design specification.
- **Perfective Maintenance:** It involved updates of the ERP software to meet user requirements, enhance performance, documentation alteration and novel or enhancement of functionality. Example -modification of payroll program for it to integrate a novel union settlement, embedding new report on sales system, improving user-interface, inclusion of online HELP facility.
- **Preventive Maintenance:** This entail the changes required to discover likely errors within a software product. It's done to hinder life loss anticipated or for safety purposes. It necessitate for documentation updates for ease software maintainability.

The ISO14764 categorizes both the perfective as well as adaptive maintenance to be enhancements while preventive and corrective maintenance as corrections.

PROCESS OF MAINTENANCE AND ACTIVITIES

The software maintenance process refers to action's sequences engaged in an ERP software product in order to amend changes (Jansson, 2007). It encompasses the maintainer's task and activities; the aims are to transform the system existing while integrity is being preserved (Singh, 1995). ERP software maintenance focuses on maintaining control over the system's day today functions and control of any system modifications, enhancing and perfecting existing acceptable functions and preventing system performance from degrading to unacceptable levels. The required inputs, outputs and operations are enhanced by process models. The maintenance standards of software are stipulates the various maintenance processes. This involved ISO/ IEC 14764 and IEEE 1219 (Pigoski, 2001). The activities of maintenance process are conducted by the maintainer and involve modification of the existing software product as well as preserving its integrity. The International Standard delivers stepwise the task done to implement maintenance process. The planning for maintenance should be conducted to ensure necessary resources are allotted before activation of the process. When the ERP software product has been delivered modification of documentation and codes are done by maintainer based on problem reports.

THE PROCESS SUPPORT ACTIVITIES

The processes that support ERP software development and maintenance include planning, configuration management, personnel training, documentation and resource analysis (ISO/IEC14764, 2006; Singh, 1995).

Maintenance Planning

Planning is very essential part of ERP software maintenance. In order to come up with reliable and accurate resource estimations such as costs. The first consideration in planning is to realize a quality novel system and followed by maintenance plans. The Issues such as scope and post-delivery during maintenance process need be addressed (Pigoski, 2001). The planning of resources is important for quality and success maintenance process such as personnel, cost, procedural requirements and documentation.

Configuration Management

The changes to any software products needs be controlled by carrying out the stipulated software configuration management procedures. It facilitates maintainer's tasks. The maintainer decides the time of migration of the software after problem solution has been achieved and enhancement stopped (Pigoski, 2001). Configuration management enables successful interaction and customization of ERP software thus enhancing integrity throughout maintenance process. This includes activities such as configuration: identification, control, evaluation, release, and product delivery (ISO/IEC14764, 2006; Singh, 1995) .

Training

The training helps in establishing all training requirement or needs for ERP system users and maintainer. The process should be well plan to gather materials and training plan (ISO/IEC14764, 2006).

Documentation

There is need to keep quality documentation for ease fault and errors identifications. They record and explain the various activities for planning,designing, creating,coding and maintaing those documents required by maintainers,users and system managers. It save cost of maintenance.

Resource Analysis

The various resources as financial, personnel and environment where maintenance will be conducted need to be analyses to ascertain all the software maintenance resource and requirements. It enables effective support for the maintainer to handle issues as training, staffing and testing throughout maintenance activities. The maintenance activities are categorized as pre-delivery and post-delivery of the software product where the maintainer plays different roles (ISO/IEC 14764).

The Pre-Delivery activities are as follows: (1) Process Implementation; (2) Establish Infrastructure; (3) Establish Training Process; (4) Establish the Maintenance Process.

The Post-Delivery activities area as follows: (1) Process Implementation; (2) Problem and Modification Analysis; (3) Modification Implementation; (4) Maintenance Review/Acceptance; (5) Migration; (6) Retirement.

ISO/IEC 12207 identifies the Maintenance Process activities depicted IEEE 14764 (Ekera & Aytaçb, 2017; Pigoski, 2001; Esteves & Pastor, 1999) as shown in Figure 1 below. These activities are briefly described below

Process Implementation

The role of maintainer in this process is to institutes the guidelines or plans to be implemented throughout the entire process of maintenance. Both the maintenance and development plans should be established concurrently. The process implementation inputs involved system documentation; problem report; appropriate baselines or

Figure 1. Process maintenance

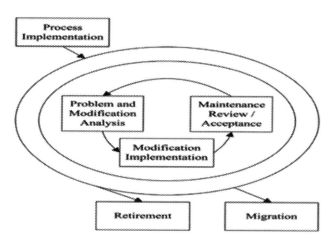

modification request. Outputs activities include plans on training, maintenance, measurement, transitions, configuration management, user feedback, maintainability assessment and or problem resolution. Based on ISO/IEC 12207 the configuration management processes is required to be accomplished by a maintainer in order to manage the existing system modification (ISO/IEC 14764).

Problem and Modification Analysis

The problem and modification analysis inputs activities is based on problem report or modification request, documentation requirement or system documentation. In this process the maintainer perform task as modification request or problem reports analysis; problem verification; modification options development; modification options approval; documentation of modification request or problem reports, execution options as well as results.

Modification Implementation

The maintainer in this process performs activities as ERP software product testing and alterations.

Maintenance Review/Acceptance

The activity of this process certifies and validates modifications of the system in accordance to approved standards and methodology. Its activity inputs include software and test results modification. The outputs activities are new-fangled baseline; established modifications incorporation and overruled modifications; test report; reports on audit and review.

Migration

Due to the changes in the environments it's essential to modify the system to adapt the new environment. Therefore, maintainer as to come up with the actions and document plans required to modify the system such as migration requirements analyses; migration effects; migration schedules; migration tools; data collection plans; conversion; migration verification and standardization and modularity.

Retirement

The ERP software requires to be retired immediately it stretched to the expiration of its worthwhile life. An inquiry need be done to help decision making such as actual cost incurred on novel technology migration; firsthand software product development or retaining of outdated software. The retiring and acquisition of novel software product operations needs to be conducted in parallel to ensure the transition are smoothly done in adopting new system where the users of the ERP software are trained. The maintainer task includes site survey; installation; preliminary tests; data collection on old and new system; data reduction and new ERP software running with old system. The retirement inputs activities include baseline of old and new ERP software product; its outputs activity involved plan for retirement; people trained; notification of intent and completion as well as retirement results.

ERP System Maintainability Framework

Närman et al., 2007; Robert, 2007 terms system maintainability as the easiness ERP software modification towards faults correction, performance advancement and attributes in addition to environment changes. The factors believed to affect system maintainability include maturity of personnel in system development, maturity maintenance processes; quality documentation, quality system's architectural, quality platform's for system execution and quality source code. The maturity maintenance personnel are appraised based on level of staff experience and knowledge of the system.

It's essential to understand the ERP product properties as durability, reliability and, functionality as well some questions on such details such as (Knezevic, 1997): (1) which task is required for maintenance purposes? (2) When will the identified task be done? (3) What challenges are likely to be encountered during maintenance? (4) What precautionary measures should be taken in tasks maintenance?(5)What amount of effort is needed for task accomplishment? (6) What period will take to complete the maintenance task? (7) What cost will be incurred during maintenance of activities? (8) What tools is necessary? (9) What personnel skills are required accomplishing recommended task activities?

The importance of maintainability is to better processes of maintenance to effects effectives of operationally, system availability, safety and cost usage.

ENTERPRISE ARCHITECTURE MODEL

The aspect of enterprise architecture models is to facilitate the making of rational decisions about informational decision making in such of alternative. It's a model established to ease resolve complexities perceived in real world to design, document, support maintainers activities and decision in ERP software systems. Närman et al., 2007; Robert, 2007 recommended on the use of enterprise architecture models in system maintainability and extended influence diagrams that model goals such as maintainability aimed at enterprise architecture analysis. It comprises of attributes that influenced maintainability. The extended relation between influence diagram and enterprise architecture models is by the model entities and attributes which facilitate diverse analyses scenarios to decide on. The influence diagram is one of expansion of Bayesian networks which utilized graphical elements to depict causal interaction among various nodes that covers a certain variable each with a given states. in addition, Bayesian network demonstrate causal relations of uncertainty by employing probabilistic rational. The extended influence diagrams make use of designated symbols to represent a set of decision problems with combination of probabilistic engine for inference. It provides a comprehensive support and intuitive depiction of various decision problems while maintaining together the desired output as well as options accessible. It is realized by using two novel nodes. The decision node which depicts the decision alternatives and utility node that represents the consequence of the decision made after exhaustive assessment. The extended influence diagram being a demonstration of real world and its functionality perceived, thus providing solution for decision makers on the paramount alternative solutions desired in an existence of feasibility constraint. The role of extended influence diagrams is to seize the definitions and fundamental determinants attributes of system quality (Pontus Johnson, Narman, & Simonsson, 2007). The steps of conducting architecture analysis involved:(1) Setting the goals for the analysis such as cost prediction of maintenance; (2) Identify the appropriate software architecture; (3) draw the various scenarios; (4) evaluate effects of each established scenario; (5) results interpretation.

ISO/IEC 9126

The maintainability is an essential activity in ERP software. A number of quality models proposed include ISO 9126, Boehm, and McCall in which each depict key attributes of maintainability (Al-Rawashdeh et al, 2014; Sharma & Baliyan, 2011; Bengtsson, Lassing, Bosch, & Vliet, 2000). The main use of this model is to streamline quality of software through the life cycle phase's software development process. It emphases on post development of software product based on end-user.

This can include performance, maintainability and interoperability. Some of other attributes represented in enterprise architecture models are stability, testability, modifiability, analyzability, understandability, conciseness and changeability. The aspect of maintainability constitutes ease of modification of the ERP software. The constituent characteristics of maintainability include stability, analyzability, testability and changeability (Alrawashdeh et al, 2013). There should easiness in modifying the ERP system through identification of any part that requires changes, causal of failure as well as validation of modified system part. These include:

- **Testability:** The validation of ERP system should be a task to be undertaken easily. This is an attribute that defined if test goal has been achieved. The degree of testability influences the ease identification of errors resulting to ERP quality. The magnitude at which a given software product institute the acceptance criterion for maintenance and performance supports.
- **Analyzability:** The process of troubleshooting the problem of the fault and identifying the part of ERP system should not be a big deal. The ISO/9126 terms it as eases of identification of causal and diagnosis of deficiencies in any software product.
- **Understandability:** This is where users are rationalizing and applying the ERP software product with ease. The proper documentation enables users to clearly use and infer system outputs. The software role should be clearer to users.
- **Modifiability:** It allows the ERP software product to adapt to the new user requirement. It's the degree of software product to expedite the integration of any alterations.
- **Modularity:** This involved the separation of system to smaller and manageable parts which increases the maintainability. Nonetheless, an ERP

system compose of a collection of modules that each one implements certain functionality.

- **Stability:** This is where any changes of the software component do not have any effect to the rest part of the system. There is need to asses if the ERP system will operate normally after its modification.

- **Changeability:** The aspect of ERP software to allow ease of modification when demand. There should be ease of ERP system modification. A good software product should allow sustainability as a result of any changes.

- **Reusability:** The characteristic relates how fit for component based software can be reuse again on new platforms. It is an important aspect of usability aimed at sufficiently allowing gaining of ERP software product benefits. It's vital to understand end users for ease usability during entire software life cycle as in coding, design, testing, maintenance and the software release. It facilitates fashioning of usable systems.

- **Tailorability:** This is where the ERP product can be customized based the customer's preferences. There should be an environment that allows component-based software's to be tailored or integrated with functionalities and user interfaces to support users' interactivity.

- **Compliance:** The characteristic defines if the ERP software product is in compliance by conforming to certification or international standard. Nevertheless, utmost systems are unable to meet compliance requirements.

- **Simplicity:** The understandability of an ERP software product is defined by minimally complex which thus more maintainable, implementable, and reliable in addition to faults reduction. The characteristic implies the software product is concise, without unnecessary information.

- **Portability:** This is when an ERP software product allows ease usage at any of the environments. Once a software product is release for similar functionality in a numerous computing platform, its essential for portability be considered to enhance reduction of cost. It addresses questions as: will ERP modules be relocated to fit new environment? Can the installation of ERP software modules have done with ease? Are there possible ways of ERP software replacement?

There are two existing popular standards models use to define the process of ERP software maintenance. This includes IEEE Standard 1219-1998 and ISO/IEC 12207. The two standards define the various activities executed in software process maintenance stipulated as appendices (Chan et al, 2002; Robert, L., 2007)

IEEE Standard 1219-1998

These standards are developed by Institute of Electrical and Electronics Engineers (IEEE). The standards focus on maintenance activities once the ERP software has been delivered. There are various maintenance process activities based on the IEEE Standard 1219-1998, and these include: (i) problem or modification identification, classification, and prioritization; (ii) analysis; (iii) design; (iv) implementation; (v) regression/system testing; (vi) acceptance testing; (vii) delivery.

ISO/IEC 12207

These standards are from International Organization for Standardization (ISO) and International Electro- technical Commission (IEC), thus terms ISO/IEC 12207. The software maintenance process involves maintainers activities conducted either when ERP software is delivered (pre-delivery), after delivery (post- delivery) or when ERP software is retired. The maintenance process activities based on ISO/ IEC 12207 are: (i) process implementation; (ii) problem and modification analysis; (iii) modification implementation; (iv) maintenance review and acceptance; (v) migration; (vi) retirement.

IEEE/EIA 12207.2-1997

This is one of the standards realized from adoption of ISO/IEC 12207 and IEEE 1219-1998 by IEEE Computer Society. The changes were established by IEEE and Electronic Industries Association (EIA) and thus term IEEE/EIA 12207.2-1997. They give a broad description of all the process maintenance activities itemizing both characteristics and metrics attributes considered throughout the entire processes.

Software Maintainability Metrics

Software maturity index is one of the suggested methods used to measure the software maintainability where it consider either that modified, added or removed on the concern modules. The various combination of characteristics measures such as source code readability, quality of documentation and software understandability (Aggarwal, Singh, & Chhabra, 2002).

Factors Influencing Software Maintainability Measurement

1. Source code readability-Most maintenance will end up modifying the source code which is a cumbersome task to undertake especially if the source code were written by a different programmer and not well organize. The percentage of source code readability is achieved by looking on the number of comments line from the total code. The ratio of comments is derived from the division of comment lines by total line codes. If the ratio is low maintainability the code is more readable.

2. Quality of Documentation-the gunning fox index is a model that measure the document quality .it calculates how readable the words in a text are. The fox index is determined by complexity of the words as well as its length. The better documentation quality is realized when fox index is a bit lower buts the higher it is quality of documentation is poorer.

3. Software understandability-This involved mixture of both documents as well as source code. The synergy of this contributes in the quality of maintainability. Otherwise the maintainability flawed and problematic to conduct. The proposed a tool for measurement was the symbols that can be incorporated within the documents as well as source code. The method was term as language software entailing the entire symbols to be used without source language and key words. The coupling and interrelationship of source code language and document language define high understandability (Aggarwal, Singh, & Chhabra, 2002).

The Fuzzy Models

The stated measures depict various software maintenance properties. The three aspects compute totally varied feature in same software. Therefore the parameters is said to be subjective hence a tool is necessary to integrate the parameters. The integrated approach model suggested which incorporates the various measures of ERP software maintainability is the fuzzy model which considers the three extents of source code readability, quality of documentation and software understandability. The fuzzy model is organized into fuzzification, knowledge base, inference engines and defuzzification modules. The transformation of inputs to fuzzy values are through fuzzification module. The processing and inferences is established by inference engine which is as a result of production rules programmed by domain expert that can be fired within the knowledge based and fuzzy inputs. There after the defuzzification module will give decisive domain information from fuzzy domain (Aggarwal, Singh, & Chhabra, 2002).

ERP SOFTWARE MAINTENANCE TOOLS

The ERP software maintenance tools are techniques that are used to facilitate the activities of ERP software modification and improvements (Grubb & Takang, 2003). The tools are categories based on the task they are executed. This consists of:

Program Comprehension and Reverse Engineering Tools

The program comprehension entails tools that facilitate the overall familiarity of the program functionality, correlations to the environs; pinpointing modifiable parts of the system and how the task should be accomplish. The reverse engineering involved tools give the detail analysis and demonstrations of system in order to support comprehension. The activities enhancing maintainability include re-documentation, reengineering, visualization, design and specification recovery. These tools consist of:

Program Slicer

To clearly understand the source code during software maintenance, the maintainer has to highlight and view only some source code which is to be changed among other unaffected codes. This is quite cumbersome due to large size of program codes. This can be solved by using slicing process which allows selection of a specific part of the program. The slicing process is realized through program slicer tool where it shows to the maintainer the data links with the associated features for ease changes tracking.

Static Analyser

The static analyser lets the programmer to extract key information about the program such as data, modules, procedures, classes etc. It enables one to create summary contents as well as chosen program text aspect relevant for modification.

Dynamic Analyser

The dynamic analyser is a tool that aids the maintainer in tracing system execution's channel thus able to point out areas to be modified. This provides the maintainer analysis and control of program that is being executed hence more information that will support software maintainability than provided through static analyser.

Cross Referencer

These are tools used in indexing of various program objects by giving information like variable that has been declared. It enables maintainer to emphasize and confine program parts that have experience modification and enhancement.

Data Flow Analyser

This tool helps maintainer to trace the entire data flows of a program as well as restoring of any changes made if necessary. It's a type of static analytic tool that can be used during the impact analysis to identify any influence as a result of ERP system component changes or modification. Consequently, it is essential tool to a maintainer since support in the fundamental logics, interdependent and analysis of a given program under exploration.

Dependency Analyser

The tools assist software maintainers in identifying relationships that exist among the varied program entities. The dependencies information allows recognize consequences of the effected change as well as duplicated relationships amid entities. It can enable visualization of the various dependencies by used of nodes to imply program entity as well as arc to shows dependencies within the graph.

Transformation Tool

These include tools that change the programs into varied state of visualization and formats as text or graphics. It enables maintainer to edit program and comprehend the ERP system parts in the most simplified view.

Software Testing Tools

These are tools that facilitate software maintenance in identification of the various system parts that demands changes or detect bugs. This involved tools as:

Test Simulator

This tool enabled testing environments to mimic a real system functionality. It helps the maintainer ascertain impact of ERP software change within environment that is control prior to real system changes.

Test Paths Generators

The tool supports the maintainers to recognize control and data flows that could be influence as a result of enhancement. The applicable test scenarios can be done allow maintainer ascertain if required changes as been realize.

Test Case Generators

This involved a collection of test data that is used to examine the existing system functionalities experiencing reformation. They allow generation of test data cases that support maintainer activities.

Software Configuration and Management Tools

There are automated tools that enhanced software configuration management. It is providing development and configuration environment that play as a warehouse of a number of codes or source file constituting ERP system software.

The Source Code Control System

The tool involved program utilities which enable maintainer traced the various files history with information of files already undergone changes.

Tools Selection Criterion

The elements that are accounted before acquiring a given tool that will support maintenance include: *(1) Usability:* The acceptability of the tools by maintainer and its user are depended on its ease of use; *(2) capability:* The tool should do/support the functionality intended to be accomplish; *(3) vendor stability*: The reputation of the vendor play a role before considering a given maintenance tool. The company's tool popularity depends on their tools features, uniqueness, and capability as well as based on customers need; *(4) features:* The selections of a tool depend on the rich features availability; *(5) programming language:* The tools obtain needs supported the programming languages that were used to create source code. This will facilitate the software maintainability; *(6) platform:* There should be consideration of maintenance tool base on the architecture and environments such as operating system it will run. These enhanced software portability and solved incompatibility and maintenance quality issues; *(7) cost and benefits analysis:* There should be a relation between the cost of a tool and its benefits.

ISSUES IN ERP SOFTWARE MAINTENANCE

A number of studies conducted have revealed issues encountered in ERP software maintenance (Sokappadu,et al, 2016; Kaur & Singh, 2015;Pigoski, 2001):

- **Maintenance Cost:** The estimation of cost is essential during planning of which maintainers has known all types of maintenance, required to be addressed. The maintenance cost is believed to spend main share of entire life cycle costs. It leads to escalations of development budget. The cost and risk of maintenance will increase since a small number of people do comprehend or perform customization (Light, 2001). The systems whose additional resources have been allocated for maintenance is believe to experience fewer problems (Kumar & Parul, 2014).
- **Limited Understanding:** A small number of personnel will be able do comprehend or perform customization (Light, 2001). Pigoski (2001) pointed out that around 40-60%of maintenance is efforts to understand and accept the software to be changed.
- **Quality of Product/Documentation:** These denote both the design specification and programming quality. The quality of product is hindered by inaccessibility of updated documentation. However, poor documentation makes problems and fault identification both costly difficult. Therefore, the quality of documentation influenced the maintainability.
- **Impact/Work Analysis:** The impact analysis is essential to determine complexity of a program through estimation of equation. It ascertains the entire ERP systems that are of concerned of which requires modification and established resources required. The IEEE 14764highlighted tasks conducted during impact analysis, this include to create modification implementation strategies; evaluates the modification request or problem reports; endorsement modification choice; developed documentation for the modification request or problem reports and reproduce or authenticate the problem.
- **Maintenance Staff Experience and Size:** The more the staff experience in system development and the fewer the problems realize as a results of quality programming and productivity. Also, the size of staff size needed to identify the personnel's required in the software development and implementation process. Subsequently, when product has been released to customers some modification may be required. Thus, additional activities will be dedicated to development staff since new team will not be assign task due to their unawareness of project to be under maintenance.

- **Process Issues:** The various maintenance activities are essential but unavailable or insufficient documentation during development of software such as online or help support.
- **Organizational Objectives Alignment:** The objectives of the organization pronounce ways to realize the returns from software maintenance accomplishments venture. The focal importance software development is to ensure users receipt the product based on their needs as per plan time frame and reasonable cost. But the software maintenance boosts and lengthens the software lifetime receded by users request for enhancement, modification and upgrades. The maintenance activities should be able to yields returns or add value the process activities otherwise they might be consuming lots of effort, time and cost.
- **Legacy Software:** This are ERP software centered on technologies which have become obsolete and past computer programming language that are nonetheless operating and important to the organization's day to day service delivery. These systems are costly and difficult to maintain.
- **Outsourcing:** The software development and testing entail identification of requirement and verification of artifacts. Most firms do outsource maintenance of which mostly are peripheral software and reluctant to release core business software applications. The outsourcing depends on the effort of the company.
- **Restructuring for Change:** Throughout the process of maintenance, the modification sometime necessitates overhaul or reorganization be carried out, as result of incompatibility of existing architecture and environment the system is operating which thus unable to reinforce any changes required.

Solutions to Software Maintenance Issues

A number of ways suggested that can lessen effort experience during maintenance of ERP software system includes (Sokappadu, et al, 2016; Kaur& Singh, 2015;Grubb & Takang, 2003):

- **Testing Quality:** A good testing techniques and approaches need to be applied for an effective error checking and thus effort used in maintenance is reduced tremendously.
- **Understandability:** To realize a good testing process, there must be a good understanding of the system such as operationality, structural and behavioral aspect. The rich information of the system enables maintainer to: (1)comprehend the various interrelationship and dependencies among various components;(2) organized, precise and accurate documentation; (3)

understand the design of the system easily; (4)easily access the technical documentation; (5) effectively communicate the changes to the design.

- **Software Reengineering:** The software Re-engineering is essential in maintaining and understanding of the ERP software system. It is used to: minimize emerging risk in software maintenance; Improves CASE tools capabilities; comprehend more insights of the software; facilitates software reusability, enhancement and maintainability; enables ease modification of software. The success factors of re-engineering involved the good planning, proper estimation of cost, noble contracting and cost benefit analysis (CBA). The software reengineering process institutes the reverse engineering as well as forward engineering. The reverse engineering is term as the analyzing of a core system in an effort to establish the interrelationships of the varied components to fashion system while reverse engineering involving tools that obtain key design information from current program (Grubb & Takang, 2003.

- **Bugs Elimination:** An automated tool is necessary to ensure frequent checks, detections as well as bugs fixing within the system.

- **Reduce Complexity:** There should be occasional monitoring and improvement the technical aspect of the system to enhanced maintenance quality and reduced the costs incurred as a result of complexities of the ERP software.

- **Re-Documentation:** The cost of maintenance is believed to escalate as a result of poor-quality documentation. This can be tremendously minimized through re-documentation. Approximately 21.5% of effort is just consumed to only comprehend the source code. The maintenance cost of at least 12% is saved with presence of a good documentation.

- **Dead Code Removal:** Those codes that are redundant which are not essential are term as a dead code. It requires that any code that is removed should not affect in any way to the system thus code size reduction. Nevertheless, 30% of codes within that system are regarded dead and thus need to eradicate. The documentation can be automated with Computer Aided Software Engineering techniques to facilitate maintenance process. The CASE techniques and tools supports maintenance through fast defect or bugs detection; substantial savings in resources for maintenance; minimizes resources that are required in software development and maintenance; and significant reusability;

- **Software Refactoring**: The software refactoring involves continuous enhancement of software for minimal degradation and boosting of non-functional aspects excluding any changes on external capabilities. These facilitate ease understandability, usability and simplification of system and program codes. Thus, ease maintainability of the ERP system software.

CHAPTER SUMMARY

The ERP Software maintenance was identified as an integral part of a software life cycle that plays an important role in ERP software products to alleviate problems. The planning activities for example; personnel's, cost, documentation and support is necessary to facilitate maintainability define by various qualities as analyzability, changeability, stability, and testability. The maintenance is conducted after released of the product to detect errors, correct them to improve its performance and to adapt changes in environment. The ISO14764 categorizes both the perfective as well as adaptive maintenance to be enhancements while preventive and corrective maintenance as corrections. The software maintenance activities and task are performed by maintainers. The enterprise architecture models in system maintainability and extended influence diagrams were used to analyses attribute that influenced maintainability. The quality models as ISO 9126, Boehm, and McCall explored to show key attributes of maintainability. The existing standards models use to define the process of ERP software maintenance included IEEE Standard 1219-1998 and ISO/IEC 12207. The software maturity index was describe as methods used to measure the software maintainability involving combination of characteristics measures such as source code readability, quality of documentation and software understandability. The integrated approach model suggested which incorporates the various measures of software maintainability is the fuzzy model which considers the three extents of source code readability, quality of documentation and software understandability. The ERP software maintenance tools discussed include program comprehension and reverse engineering tools; Software Testing Tools and software configuration and management tools. The various issues were identified during ERP software maintenance such as maintenance cost, limited understanding, and quality of product, impact/work analysis, maintenance staff experience, process issues and outsourcing. A number of ways suggested solutions to ERP software maintenance issues: testing quality; understandability; software reengineering; Bugs elimination; reduce complexity; re-documentation; dead code removal and software refactoring.

REFERENCES

Aggarwal, K. K., Singh, Y., & Chhabra, K. (2002). An Integrated Measure of Sofware Maintainability. In *2002 Proceedings Annual Reliability and Maintainability Symposium* (pp. 235-241). Delhi: IEEE. 10.1109/RAMS.2002.981648

Al-Rawashdeh, T. A., Al'azzeh, F. M., & Al-Qatawneh, S. M. (2014). Evaluation of ERP Systems Quality Model Using Analytic Hierarchy Process (AHP)Technique. *Journal of Software Engineering and Applications*, 225-232.

Alrawashdeh, T. A., Muhairat, M., & Althunibat, A. (2013). Evaluating the Quality of Software in ERP Systems Using the ISO 9126 Model. *International Journal of Ambient Systems and Applications*, *1*(1), 1–9.

Bengtsson, P., Lassing, N., Bosch, J., & Vliet, H. V. (2000). *Analyzing Software Architecture for Modifiability*. Academic Press.

Canfora, G., & Cimitile, A. (2000). *Software Maintenance*. Benevento, Italy: University of Sannio, Faculty of Engineering at Benevento.

Ekera, M., & Aytaçb, A. (2017). The Role of ERP in Advanced Managerial Accounting Techniques: A Conceptual Framework. *Business and Economics Research Journal*, *8*(1), 83–100. doi:10.20409/berj.2017126246

Erdil, K., Finn, E., Keating, K., Meattle, J., Park, S., & Yoon, D. (2003). *Software Maintenance As Part of the Software Life Cycle*. Unpublished.

Esteves, J. M., & Pastor, J. A. (1999). *An ERP Life-cycle-based Research Agenda*. Academic Press.

Grubb, P., & Takang, A. A. (2003). *Software Maintenance: Concepts and Practice* (2nd ed.). World Scientific Publishing Co. Pte. Ltd.

International Organisation for Standardization. (2017). ISO/IEC/IEEE 12207. IEEE.

ISO/IEC-12207. (2008). *Software Implementation and Support Processes*. ISO/IEC 12207:2008.

ISO/IEC14764. (2006). *Software Engineering - Software Life Cycle Processes - Maintenance*. Geneva: IEEE Std 14764-2006.

Jansson, A.-S. (2007). *Software Maintenance and Process Improvement by CMMI.* UPTEC.

Kaur, U., & Singh, G. (2015). A Review on Software Maintenance Issues and How to Reduce Maintenance Efforts. *International Journal of Computers and Applications, 118*(1), 6–11. doi:10.5120/20707-3021

Knezevic, J. (1997). *System Maintainability.* London: Springer Science & Business Media.

Light, B. (2001). The maintenance implications of the customization of ERP software. *Journal of Software Maintenance and Evolution: Research and Practice,* 415–429.

Lehman, M. M. (1980). Lifecycles and the Laws of Software Evolution. In *Proceedings of the IEEE, Special Issue on Software Engineering.* IEEE.

Lehman, M. M. (1984). Program Evolution. *Journal of Information Processing and Management, 19*(1), 19–36. doi:10.1016/0306-4573(84)90037-2

Närman, P., Johnson, P., & Nordström, L. (2007). Enterprise Architecture: A Framework Supporting System Quality Analysis. In *11th IEEE International Enterprise Distributed Object Computing Conference (EDOC 2007)* (pp. 130-130). Annapolis, MD: IEEE. 10.1109/EDOC.2007.39

Ng, C. S., Gable, G., & Chan, T. (2002). An ERP Maintenance Model. In *Proceedings of the 36th Hawaii International Conference on System Sciences (HICSS'03).* IEEE.

Pigoski, T. M. (2001). *Software Maintenance.* IEEE.

Pontus Johnson, R. L., Narman, P., & Simonsson, M. (2007). Extended Influence Diagrams for System Quality Analysis. *Journal of Software, 2*(3), 30–42.

Pui Ng, C. S., Gable, G., & Chan, T. (2002). An ERP Maintenance Model. In *Proceedings of the 36th Hawaii International Conference on System Sciences.* IEEE.

Robert, L. (2007). *Analyzing System Maintainability Using Enterprise Architecture Models.* Royal Institute of Technology.

Sharma, V., & Baliyan, P. (2011). Maintainability Analysis of Component Based Systems. *International Journal of Software Engineering and Its Applications, 5*(3), 107–118.

Singh, R. (1995). *International Standard ISO/IEC 12207 Software Life Cycle Processes*. Washington, DC: Federal Aviation Administration.

Sokappadu, G. M., Paavan, R., & Devi, R. V. (2016). Review of Software Maintenance Problems and Proposed Solutions in IT consulting firms in Mauritius. *International Journal of Computer Applications, 156*(4), 12-20.

Chapter 13
ERP Software Inspections and Audits

Julius Murumba
Technical University of Kenya, Kenya

Jackson Kipchirchir Machii
Technical University of Kenya, Kenya

ABSTRACT

The role of software inspections, product reviews, walk-troughs, and audits in ERP software is analyzed in this chapter. Software inspections are a disciplined engineering practice for detecting and correcting defects in software artifacts with the aim of correcting them. Walkthroughs involve software peer review mechanism in which a programmer leads peers through a software product, in a process in which participants ask questions and make comments about possible errors, violation of development standards, and other problems. This chapter also discusses ERP systems audit and control risks and seeks to help understand key risks and control issues surrounding ERP systems.

INTRODUCTION

Enterprise resource planning software's standardize, streamline, and integrate business processes across all departments of an organization, for example finance, human resources, procurement and distribution. Enterprise Resource Planning software usually operates on an integrated software platform using common data definitions operating on a single database, and provides several separate but integrated modules that can be installed as a package for any organization (Bae &

DOI: 10.4018/978-1-5225-7678-5.ch013

Ashcroft, 2004; Wailgum & Perkins, 2018). ERP systems help organizations track information across all departments and business functions (Hawari & Heeks, 2010). ERP software reviews are done to find defects or errors and correct them before the software is released to customers. A defect is an instance of non-conformance with the initiating software requirements or standards. Software errors can be classified into a number of general categories. These include: (1) Faulty or erroneous definition of requirements and inclusion of unnecessary requirements or functions that may not be needed in the software's future. (2) Misunderstandings resulting from defective client and developer communication may lead to errors that undermine the development process (3) Deliberate deviations from software requirements that may occur when a developer reuses software module taken from previously done projects without sufficient analysis and understanding of the changes and adaptations needed to correctly fulfill all the new requirements. This may be due to time or financial limitations, that may lead to the developer deciding to omit some functions that are required in an attempt to cope with these pressures arising out of the limitations (4) Logical design errors (5) Coding errors (6) Non-compliance with documentation and coding instructions (7) Shortcomings of the testing process (8) Procedure errors (9) Documentation errors.

ERP SOFTWARE INSPECTIONS

Software inspection is a process carried out manually in the early stages of the software development cycle by a group of peers on code and software artifacts developed by other developers. Software inspection requires human effort and is deemed to be very cost-effective, since it leads to defects being removed before they enter the phases of implementation or maintenance. The regular application and success of inspections in the software industry have led to suggestions for its introduction to ERP software. Barhate (2012) states that software inspection was first invented by M. Fagan at IBM in 1976 and has since been improved and adapted by many major software companies. ERP software inspection is a technique that can be used to achieve quality control for the source code and for identifying associated process improvements. It is part of quality assurance in the software development process performed by people i.e. reviewers and complements automatic checking tools. ERP software inspections involve careful examination of its code and other software artefacts, checking them for characteristics that are known to be problematic from past experiences. It is a formal process involving labour intensive and manual analysis techniques that are applied to code documents in the early stages of the software development. Inspections are non-execution-based meaning that the inspector does not have to compile or execute the code during the examination; and such inspections are carried out at the beginning of the development cycle of the ERP projects to identify and remove potential problems since fixing them in these early stages is least expensive. Inspections are recommended to be carried out before the first compile or test in order to ensure quality ERP products (Harjumaa, 2005).

ERP software inspections or reviews are meetings, either face to face or virtual, during which designs and code are reviewed by people other than the original developer. Software inspection is a proven method in quality assurance and is widely known to enable the detection and removal of defects in software artifacts in the early stages of their development cycles. Inspections usually involve activities in which a team of qualified personnel determines whether the created artifact is of sufficient quality. Quality deficiencies when detected are subsequently corrected, such that the inspection contributes towards software quality improvement, while at the same time leading to significant budget and time benefits (Laitenberger, 2001). Inspections reduce the amount of rework typically experienced in the development processes, increase productivity and reduce costs (Barhate, 2012). The formal steps of inspection are

1. An overview of document is given to participants
2. Participants prepare for inspection, aided with lists of fault types previously found
3. Inspection - Every piece of logic is covered at least once, and every branch is taken at least once. A written report is inspection is produce
4. Rework - Resolves all faults and problems noted in written report
5. Follow-up ensure that every single issue raised has been satisfactorily resolved

Inspection is a necessary activity in the verification and validation of a software product. Verification and validation is part of the software testing process of ERP software. Verification and validation is the process of checking whether a software system meets specifications and whether it fulfills its intended purpose. According to the Capability Maturity Model, cited in Barhate (2012), Verification is the process of evaluating software with the objective of determining whether the product of a given development phase satisfies the conditions imposed at the start of that phase, while validation is the process of evaluating software during or at the end of the development process to determine whether it satisfies requirements specified at the beginning of the process

ERP software attributes that are well-handled by inspections rather than testing include the following:

1. Fuzzy non-functional properties. And these include

a.   Maintainability; referring to the degree to which an application is understood, repaired, or enhanced.

b.   Evolve-ability; referring to a multifaceted quality attribute that describes a software's ability to easily accommodate future changes.

c.   Software reusability; referring to the process of creating software systems from existing software components rather than building them from scratch

2.   Other properties that may be tough to test such as

a.   Scalability, efficiency

b.   Security, integrity

c.   Robustness, reliability, exception handling

d.   Other requirements such as architecture and design documents because these cannot be executed and tested

Software Inspection Methods

Software inspections are important because they detect errors in the early stages of software development cycle, when those errors are least expensive to correct. Inspection provide opportunities for developers to improve their skills when they participate in such inspections and technical reviews, and this potentially leads to reduction of occurrence of errors in future. ERP software inspections and technical reviews when properly implemented drastically reduce the time required for testing, debugging, and rework, and dramatically improves the quality of the resulting software. Therefore, software inspections and review techniques when applied to ERP software, provide developers and other participants in the ERP projects with the opportunities to learn about and experience the using of these software quality tools.

Fagan Inspection

The Fagan Inspection is the most commonly cited software inspection technique in software engineering literature. In a sense, the Fagan Inspection is a standard software inspection technique as its essence is included in the IEEE Standard for Software Reviews (1997). Developed by M. E. Fagan in 1972 at IBM, the Fagan Inspection consists of six steps: (1) Planning, (2) Overview, (3) Preparation, (4) Inspection, (5) Rework, and (6) Follow-Up. Compared with walkthroughs, which are informal and consist only of two steps, Preparation and Walkthrough, Fagan Inspections are a
more formal alternative requiring an inspection team, with each member playing a role: moderator, designer, coder, or tester

Phased Inspection

The Phased Inspection technique involves conducting an Inspection as series of tightly focused steps or phases instead of in one inspection meeting.

The Benefits of Inspections

1. Provides new perspectives on software quality since finding defects may be easier for people who haven't seen the artifact before and don't have preconceived ideas about its correctness
2. There is knowledge sharing of designs and specific software artifacts and of defect detection practices
3. Enables flaws to be found early and can therefore dramatically reduce the cost of fixing errors since these may be detected even before code is executed
4. Leads to reduction of rework and testing effort, and the overall development effort
5. Leads to reduction in user reported defects, which may in turn lead to increased end user satisfaction, and generally, increase in development productivity.
6. Leads to cross-training of developers and maintainers on new products, and continuous process improvement through removal of systemic defects.

Authors rapidly learn to avoid creating defects through participating in inspections that find defects in their own work products and in the work products of others

Types of Inspections

There are there different types of inspections. These are 1) Inspections or Formal Technical Reviews. Participation in Formal Technical Reviews defined by policy and is done by developers and other designated key individuals such as peers, Quality Assurance team, review board, etc. This type of Inspection requires advance preparation by participants, typically based on checklists

Formal meetings are held to discuss the artifact, led by a moderator not the author of the software. A documented process is followed and may be virtual or conferenced. There is also a formal follow-up process involving written deliverable from the review and appraisal of the ERP product. 2) Walkthroughs. These are unstructured meetings held by software managers to publicize design and implementation concepts, without obligation to use any feedback, alternative ideas, or suggested changes resulting from the meeting. These meetings have the following characteristics: No advance preparation; Author leads discussion in meeting; No formal follow up; are Low cost and value for education 3) Other review approaches include pass-around which is essentially a preparation part of an inspection, Peer desk check which involves examination by a single reviewer e.g. in pair programming and Ad-hoc review which involves informal feedback from a team member. There are tradeoffs among the above techniques. Formal technical reviews cost more but normally find more bugs.

ERP Software Inspection Process

The purpose of ERP Software inspections and technical is to enable the detection of errors and defects early in the software development cycle, when those errors are least expensive to correct. To eliminate defects, the following checklist or steps are used in an inspection process (Barhate, 2012)

1. Work Product: In what state of development is the source code being inspected.
2. Participants: Who are the participants in the inspection?
3. Preparing for Inspection: How much lead time should be granted to the inspectors?
4. Checklist: Preparation of the checklist.
5. Meeting: The questions meetings should seek to answer are: what are the entry criteria? In other words, what must be completed before the meeting can occur? A complete preparation log and marked source code listing from each inspector.

Who attends? Who does not attend? What is the purpose? What is the time limit for the meeting? What happens during the meeting? This step requires a description of the sequence of activities. What roles does each participant play during the meeting? What documentation is created and what data is gathered during the meeting? How are the documentation and data gathered and reported? To whom? When?

6. Rework: What are the acceptance criteria for the work product? What are the procedures for carrying out rework?
7. Follow up

Members of the inspection team or stakeholders have roles and responsibilities in the inspection process. These are briefly described as follows:

1. Moderator Who organizes the review. This the person who keeps discussions on track and ensures that follow-up happens. This individual requires to have the attributes of being a good facilitator, knowledgeable, Impartial and respected, and can hold participants accountable and correct inappropriate behavior
2. Recorder who captures a log of the inspection process

3. Reader who presents material for review and provides points of comparison for author and other team members, the reader also gets comments section by section of the work under review and this hastens the process
4. The Author who is not moderator or reader, and describes the rationale for work

ERP SOFTWARE REVIEWS

Software reviews are done by inspectors working alone, normally on a single technical area while authors of the artifacts supply responses to the queries of the inspectors comprehensively, all of which results in individual discussions between each inspector and the author to arrive at an agreed upon feedback that results in a rework of the product. A formal technical review is a software quality assurance activity performed by software engineers with the following objectives (Barhate, 2012):

- To detect errors in the function or logic of the software
- To verify whether the software meets its requirements
- To ensure that the software has been developed in conformance to standards
- To make such software projects manageable

Software reviews can either be formal or informal. Informal reviews are ad hoc often involving casual or hallway conversations, pair programming, or simply passing a product around, and the roles of the reviewers are not clearly defined. In formal reviews, roles of reviewers are defined and the reviews are planned and defined ahead of time, and their outcomes are used to improve development processes. The formal technical review is advantageous since it promotes backup and continuity. The use of formal technical reviews is deemed an effective means for improving software quality. This is because reviewers become familiar with the different parts of the ERP software including those that they may not have seen before. Each formal technical review is supposed to be conducted as a meeting and is considered successful only if it is properly planned, controlled and attended. In these review processes, the review roles include the presenter who is the designer or producer, the coordinator, the recorder who records events of meeting and builds paper trail and the reviewers who are representatives of users, are involved in maintenance, and are standards bearers. The review guidelines for meetings to be followed should include building reviews into the schedule of the review team, otherwise unexpected events may be viewed as intrusion. There is also need to recognize that reviews can accelerate schedule by reducing other verification and validation activities. The review team should be kept small and the general guidelines require three to seven participants. In addition, the review team should concentrate on finding problems, but not trying to solve them, meetings require advance preparation in order to provide more value and should ideally be limited to two hours' maximum since attention span may easily get lost beyond this duration. The checklists for review meetings should include benefits since this help set focus on likely sources of error, forms quality standard that aids preparers and can bring up issues specific to a product. The checklists should also focus on priority issues that are unlikely to be found other ways. These may include historical problems and issues specific to the document or software under review.

TYPES OF REVIEWS

Management Review

Management review is the systematic assessment of the software, provision, development, operation, or maintenance process of a software, carried out by management or by its representatives, that also follow-up the software evolution, determines the status of plans and deadlines, confirms requirements and their allocation in the system, and evaluates the effectiveness of the management approaches to determine their suitability for the goals. This has the following objectives: 1) To inform management of project status 2) To resolve higher-level issues especially management decisions and 3) To agree on risk mitigation strategies. The decisions in this type of review include, to identify corrective actions, change resource allocation, change project scope and change schedule

Formal Technical Review

Formal Technical review is a software quality assurance activity performed by software engineers and involves a team of qualified personnel examining the ERP software product for its suitability with respect to its intended use and identifies discrepancies from specifications and standards. This involves a work product being examined for defects by individuals other than the person who produced it. The focus of this type of review is on specification and design to determine whether the product meet specifications. Review participants often use a checklist, a series of questions or statements that define specific quality criteria. Different checklists may be developed for different work products, and the review process may be tailored to look for certain checklist items. The objectives of such a review are to uncover error in logic, function and implementation for any representation of the software and to ensure that software is represented according to predefined standards

Walkthrough

These are used to find anomalies and evaluate conformance to standards or specifications. This type of review is typically used for source code and is an effective form of education. The producer guides the review step by step throughout the presentation of the product. The walkthrough is a review process that focuses on the consensus of reviewers through which problems are removed. In this process there is a moderator responsible for the direction of ideas and a reporter responsible for the exposition of the problems found. Discussions revolve around the report produced by the reporter, while the responsibility of keeping the revision meeting's focus lies with the moderator. Walkthroughs have the advantage of members being integrated into the group such they can work together and provides learning opportunities from those who have been in the group or reviews for longer periods of time. This process is however informal and leaving room for mistakes

IEEE Standard for Software Reviews and Audits

IEEE presented a standard for software review process in 1989, that defined the software inspection process as a rigorous peer examination consisting of six steps which very closely follow Fagan's original code inspection method (IEEE Computer Society, 2008). According to the standard, a review has been explained as an evaluation of software element(s) or project status to ascertain discrepancies from planned results and to recommend improvement. The standard describes the flow of processes for an effective review or audit, and the evaluation is expected to follow a formal process. Software inspections and walkthroughs are examples of these processes.

The phases of the IEEE Standard inspection process, and their corresponding objectives (Harjumaa, 2005):

- **The Planning Phase:** The author and moderator together set up the schedule and material for the inspection iteration.
- **The Overview Phase:** Conducted by the author and moderator. The purpose is to ensure that the members of the inspection team have adequate information about the software elements that are going to be inspected.
- **The Preparation Phase:** Inspectors familiarize themselves with the artifact under inspection, using checklists, specifications and other information that was presented in the overview.
- **The Examination Phase:** Defects are identified and recorded. The examination is carried out in an inspection meeting, for which the standard provides a fixed agenda.

- **The Meeting:** The moderator leads the inspectors through the procedural issues to ensure that preparation is done carefully by each inspector, after which the document under inspection is read and defects are recorded. Before closing the meeting, the defect list is reviewed and an unambiguous exit decision is made.
- **Re-Work:** After examination, the errors discovered are fixed in the rework phase and the corrections are confirmed in the follow-up.
- **The Follow-Up:** Phase also involves reporting the inspection data

The following review guidelines are recommended for reviewers:

1. Review the product, not the author
2. Set an agenda for the review and maintain it.
3. Debate and rebuttal should be limited
4. Problem areas should be noted or highlighted, but reviewers should not attempt to solve every problem noted.
5. Written notes should be taken
6. The number of participants should be limited and advance preparation be insisted upon
7. A checklist for each product that is likely to be reviewed should be developed
8. Allocation of resources and time schedule for formal technical reviews should be done
9. Meaningful training for all reviewers be conducted.
10. Review of earlier reviews of the team be done

There are a number of pitfalls that may impact the review process negatively. These include letting reviewers lead the quality process may have a negative impact on the process since the responsibility for quality lies with author, not reviewers. Reviewing completed software may make it harder to accept suggestions for change. Using inappropriate review statistics for evaluation may also make the review process difficult. For example, using human resource review statistics such as a manager deciding that finding more than a certain number of bugs during an inspection would count against an author may simply lead to negative effects since the author may avoid submitting for inspection or submit small pieces at a time or simply avoid pointing out defects in reviews thus missing them

ERP SOFTWARE RISKS AND AUDIT

The implementations of ERP projects are different from traditional systems analysis and design projects. There are significant differences in terms of the projects costs, scale, complexity, organizational impact, and the subsequent business impact if the project does not succeed. ERP project implementations can have a huge impact on an entire organization whereas a traditional project often impacts only a limited area of the organization (Grabski et al, 2003). In addition, the implementation of ERP systems has often been problematic for many organizations, and there have been many reported substantial failures of implementation's, implying that ERP implementations and associated changes in business processes have proven not to be an easy task.

ERP systems if not carefully planned and implemented, can create substantial concerns about system and database security, business processes interruption and process interdependency risks.

One of the common risks is lack of alignment between organizational strategy, the businesses processes and the ERP application that is chosen. Even after implementation of the ERP system, there are still many ways in which organizational processes may continue to underperform. For example, the ERP system may generate an unacceptable level of errors and may be unstable and have performance that is difficult to predict, or processes may fail in unpredictable ways and be difficult to diagnose and correct (Dey, Bennett, & Clegg, 2009). There are numerous other risks associated with the successful implementation of ERP systems and these include lack of user experience or support, lack of role clarity, lack of role definitions of individuals on the project and system complexity. The loss of control over the project is another major risk, which can arise in two ways i.e. the lack of control over the project team, and the lack of control over employees once the system is operational (Grabski et al, 2003). The scope and the complexity of the project are a source of significant business risk. Lack of in house skills is another source of risk in the implementation of ERP systems. Lack of project team expertise has often been associated with software development risk (Grabski, Leech, & Lu, 2003). ERP project members and system users often use their experiences to identify risks. The most commonly used tools and techniques for risk identification in ERP system projects include: information gathering, checklists and SWOT techniques, diagramming techniques, documentation reviews, expert judgment and assumption analysis (Rostami, 2016).

In spite of their claimed advantages, ERP systems pose potentially heightened business and audit risks for organizations due to the presence of tightly linked automated interdependencies among business processes and reliance on relational databases. Auditing ERP systems is usually a very complex task since it requires deep technical knowledge of customization of systems and also settings for the internal controls in the system (Gehrke, 2010). In order to maximize the probability of success, the risks associated with various tasks must be minimized, for example many employees in various parts an organization may be authorized to enter data concerning different activities. This may increase the risk of the data entered lacking integrity because it can be difficult to assign specific responsibility to any one employee for the authenticity of all data entered. Key risks and control issues according to Hahn (1999) include 1) Technical Complexity: System may be residing on multiple computers and therefore optimum coordination becomes a challenge. 2) Security and Access: ERPs requires extensive and well thought out definition of security access capabilities and 3) Implementation Impact: ERP implementation is usually combined with business processes reengineering and controls may have to be different from traditional software's implementation. Computer assisted audit techniques are classified in three broad categories: 1) auditing around the computer, 2) auditing with the computer and 3) auditing through the computer (Kanellou & Spathis, 2009)

ERP IMPLEMENTATION CONTROLS

Alignment of the ERP System and Business Processes

Many organizations engage in business process reengineering, develop detailed requirements specifications, conduct system testing prior to the ERP system implementation and closely monitor system performance thereafter in order to minimize the risk associated with a lack of alignment of ERP systems and business processes. Business process reengineering enables an organization's operational processes to be aligned with an ERP system and allows an organization to better obtain the full benefits offered by the ERP system. A detailed specification of requirements prior to the ERP selection also increases the probability that the ERP system will meet the organization's system requirements and support the required operational processes. The testing of the ERP System testing prior to its implementation and the subsequent monitoring of the system after implementation are critical in ensuring that the ERP system operates smoothly and is able to provide adequate support for the organization's operational processes.

Project Complexity

Senior managers should be involved in ERP system implementation projects through appointment to a steering committee. The direct involvement of senior management in system implementation projects such as ERP projects often increases the projects perceived importance within the organization which in turn encourages employees, system users and the IT department to be actively involved in, and provide support for, the ERP system implementation. The formation of a steering committee, senior managers' support, the development of a detailed implementation plan, project management, a project team with adequate skills, and involvement by both consultants and internal audit if done appropriately can greatly minimize the risks associated with project complexity. The project team and consultant should also be assigned to the project on full time basis to ensure they can focus completely on the project, it is also important for the internal audit to be involved for purposes of identification of the potential project risks, managing the risks and ensuring the effectiveness of the internal controls. These controls are important in minimizing the risks associated with project complexity.

In House Skills

To compensate for lack of in house skills a close working relationship between consultants and the organization's project team when adopted can lead to a valuable skills transfer to the organizations team attached to the project and other users. Training provides a valuable resource to develop skills that may be lacking in house, and such training is conducted by the consultants or the vendor of the software. These controls are important when it comes to efforts of minimizing the risks associated with a potential lack of in house skills. Therefore, the establishment of a close working relationship between the ERP consultant and project team, and adequate training are critical factors in overcoming the business risks associated with the lack of in-house skills.

Users' Resistance

In mitigating the business risks associated with possible user resistance, top management support, managerial soft skills, user acceptance controls, training, and communication are important. ERP projects are associated with business processes re-engineering which may lead to changes in systems, and changes in systems is normally met with user resistance especially when users get worried that their job may at worst be eliminated, or at best be changed from their usual way of doing things. To take care of problems arising due to user resistance organizations should implement some risk management strategies to minimize user resistance, for instance the ERP manager's soft skills among others may be useful for a successful ERP implementation. User training is vital in enabling users to acquire the requisite skills to utilize the ERP system. In addition, many organizations develop a communication plan, and issue regular reports to keep users informed in order to ensure that users are aware of the impact the ERP project will have on their responsibilities. Users have a higher level of acceptance for ERP projects when they perceive that top management really supports it and is willing to provide adequate resources

Control Arising Out of Decentralization of Decision Making

Organizations may minimize the risk of loss of control associated with decentralization of decision-making through such measures as formulation of a steering committees, appointment of project sponsor and internal audit involvement. Senior management of an organization can directly monitor the project team's decision-making processes by having ratification and approval of all significant decisions through the steering committee and therefore can ensure that there are adequate controls over the ERP project team's decision-making processes. The involvement of an internal auditor in the ERP system is paramount since internal audit has extensive knowledge about the organization's control environment, business operational process and weakness that may be existing in the current internal control system but may not be available to the project team, managers and external auditors.

ERP Systems Audit

Auditing is an inspection or assessment activity that verifies compliance with plans, policies and procedures. ERP systems audit involves an independent evaluation of business processes or products that ensures that the recommended processes are being followed. The general objective, mission and scope of an audit do not alter the ERP system environment. The adoption of new technologies allows quality auditing, internal control of ERP system and thus impacting the entire auditing process within the organizations. Thus there is need for well-grounded knowledge in the methodological subjects to point out and review effectively what is required in the audit. This encompasses knowledge in: Latest technology like cloud computing; operating systems like UNIX and variants; customized and specialized systems; complex ERPs such as SAP; Legacy systems including mainframes; In-house developed systems and applications and Database like Oracle or SQL Server. The scope can be ascertained through understanding of the ERP environment for auditor to evaluate risks and conduct audit tests with exceptional training, proficiency and skills (Soral & Jain, 2011). The main objectives of developing audit and assurance programs are: 1) formally document audit procedures and sequential steps. 2) create procedures that are repeatable and easy to use by internal or external auditors who need to perform similar audits. 3) document the type of testing that will be used i.e whether compliance and/or substantive. 4) meet general accepted audit standards that relate to the planning phase in the audit process (ISACA, 2016). The vital

ERP auditing process task involves evidence collection, evaluation to ascertain the strengths and weaknesses using audit tests then present a reports incorporating recommendations to be done based on existing objective known by the stakeholders. The phases of audit process identified include planning, fieldwork and documentation and finally conducting a report. The audit process each involved further subdivision. The Planning Phase include: determining audit subject; Defining audit objective; setting audit scope; performing pre-audit planning; and determining procedures. The Fieldwork and Documentation Phase includes: acquiring data; testing controls; Issuing discovery and validation; and documenting results. Finally the reporting phase include: gathering report requirements; drafting report; Issuing report and follow-up based on audit standards (ISACA, 2016).

The auditing is categorized as internal and external auditing. The internal auditing involves methods that are independent, objectivity-based, consultation and validation. It improves value and operations and related processes within the organization as results of good internal audit procedures. The external auditing is performed outside the organization through outsourced external auditors to perform the service in order to achieve high precision of quality and accurate accounting information and reports (Kanellou & Spathis, 2009).

An Audit is a formal inspection and verification process that checks whether a standard or set of guidelines is being followed, records are accurate, or efficiency and effectiveness targets are being met. The audit process requires the Information Systems auditor to gather evidence, evaluate the strengths and weaknesses of internal controls based on the evidence gathered through audit tests, and prepare an audit report that presents weaknesses and recommendations for remediation in an objective manner to stakeholders. The audit process typically consists of three main phases: planning, fieldwork and reporting (Information Systems Audit and Control Association, 2016). ERP audit is important to analyze the major areas of audit (Amancei & Surcel, 2008). These areas are:

- **Evaluating access control**: Access control evaluation in an ERP is a complex exercise and therefore requires an individual with good skills with the particular ERP. Usually all the data in the ERP are in one single database, and access to the data has to be secured not only at the application level, but also at the operating system, database and network levels through suitable controls. The information systems auditor therefore has to review the network, the operating system in use and the database management system before evaluating the access controls in the application. For access control, many ERPs use the concept of roles and assign standard authorizations to the roles and attach the roles to users as per their job descriptions and the duties these users require to perform. Each role properties and the users defined for each role have to be verified during the audit.

- **User ID evaluation** - The information systems auditor obtains a list of authorized users, their privileges and the list of standard roles and the authorizations required for the roles.in order to audit access control. The information systems auditor then ascertains that all the authorized users have the appropriate privileges in line with their job responsibilities by examining the roles that have been assigned to the various users and ensure that the roles are in sync with their current job responsibilities. The information systems auditor also evaluates whether the list is aligned to the approved policies of the organization.

- **Verification and evaluation of configurations relating to business processes.** The Information systems auditor also audits the configurations that exist in processes and modules. This because the process flow in the business activities and the possible options for carrying out these activities are decided by the configurations in the system.

- **Change management.** An interface has the potential to become a weak point that can compromise security. An audit of the interfaces is an important aspect of ERP security reviews. Controls should exist to validate data before upload and verify accuracy and integrity through controls and logs

CHAPTER SUMMARY

ERP software inspections, reviews and audit are important in software quality assurance. Inspections with follow up corrective actions and evaluation of results are used by software engineers to examine the source code of the ERP system with the aim of discovering anomalies and defects Inspections can be thought of as compliance tasks with checklists. Reviews are applied at various points during the development of ERP software to serve the purpose of uncovering errors and defects that can subsequently be removed. Audits on the other hand are useful in assessing the overall compliance with all the internal policies and regulations as well as other compliance drivers. Audits allow an organization to check it self that everything is fine and are typically conducted by a third-party to the system being audited, which in many cases could be an auditor from an external company. Compliance managers in many organization's and audit program managers are constantly seeking ways to automate and improve the management of audits.

REFERENCES

Amancei, C., & Surcel, T. (2008). ERP System Audit a Control Support For Knowledge Management. *Revista Informatica Economică, 4*(48), 13–16.

Bae, B. B., & Ashcroft, P. (2004). *Implementation of ERP Systems: Accounting and Auditing Implications.* Information Systems Audit and Control Association.

Barhate, B. H. (2012). Software Inspection Improves Quality of Software Product. *Special Issue of International Journal of Computer Science & Informatics, 2*(1,2), 2231–5292.

Dey, P. K., Bennett, D., & Clegg, B. (2009). Managing risk in enterprise resource planning projects. In *16th International Annual EurOMA Conference.* Göteborg, Sweden: European Operations Management Association.

Gehrke, N. (2010). The ERP AuditLab - A prototypical Framework for Evaluating Enterprise Resource Planning System Assurance. In *Proceedings of the 43rd Hawaii International Conference on System Sciences.* IEEE. 10.1109/HICSS.2010.377

Gottesdiener, E. (2001). Reviews, Inspections, and Walkthroughs. Academic Press.

Grabski, S. V., Leech, S. A., & Lu, B. (2003). Risks and Controls in the Implementation of ERP Systems. *The International Journal of Digital Accounting Research, 1*(1), 47–68.

Hahn, J. (1999). ERP Systems: Audit and Control Risks. In *ISACA Spring Conference.* Deloitte & Touche.

Hahn, J., & Touche, D. &. (1998). ERP Systems: Audit and Control Risks. In *ISACA Spring Conference.* Deloitte Touche Tohmatsu.

Harjumaa, L. (2005). *Improving The Software Inspection Process With Patterns* (Academic Dissertation). Oulu University Press.

Hawari, A., & Heeks, R. (2010). Explaining ERP Failure in a Developing Country: A Jordanian Case Study. *Journal of Enterprise Information Management, 23*(2), 135–160. doi:10.1108/17410391011019741

IEEE Computer Society. (2008). IEEE Standard for Software Reviews and Audits. New York, NY: IEEE.

Information Systems Audit and Control Association. (2016). *Information Systems Auditing: Tools and Techniques.* ISACA.

Kanellou, A., & Spathis, C. (2009). *ERP Systems and Auditing: a Review*. *6th International Conference on Enterprise Systems, Accounting and Logistics*, Thessaloniki, Greece.

Laitenberger, O. (2001). *A Survey of Software Inspection Technologies*. *Handbook on Software Engineering and Knowledge Engineering*.

Lech, P. (2016). Implementation of an ERP system: A case study of a full-scope SAP project Implementation of an ERP system: A case study of a full-scope. *Finanse Journal of Management and Finance, 14*(1).

Rostami, A. (2016). Tools and Techniques in Risk Identification: A Research within SMEs in the UK Construction Industry. *Universal Journal of Management, 4*(4), 203–210. doi:10.13189/ujm.2016.040406

Soral, G., & Jain, M. (2011). Impact of ER P system on auditing and internal control. The International Journal's Research. *Journal of Social Sciences and Management, 1*(4), 16–23.

Wailgum, T., & Perkins, B. (2018, February 18). *What is ERP? A guide to enterprise resource planning systems*. Retrieved from CIO: https://www.cio.com/article/2439502/enterprise-resource-planning/enterprise-resource-planning-erp-definition-and-solutions.html

Compilation of References

Abdellatief, M., Sultan, A. B. M., Jabar, M. A., & Abdullah, R. (2010). Developing General View of Quality Models for E-learning from Developers Perspective (F. Baharom, M. Mahmuddin, Y. Yusof, W. H. W. Ishak, & M. A. Saip, Eds.). Sintok: Univ Utari Malaysia-Uum.

Abdellatief, M., Sultan, A. B. M., Ghani, A. A. A., & Jabar, M. A. (2013). A mapping study to investigate component-based software system metrics. *Journal of Systems and Software*, *86*(3), 587–603. doi:10.1016/j.jss.2012.10.001

Abe, S. (2010). *Feature Selection and Extraction*. Support Vector Machines for Pattern Classification. Advances in Pattern Recognition; doi:10.1007/978-1-84996-098-4_7

Abugabah, A., & Sanzogni, L. (2010). *Enterprise Resource Planning (ERP) System in Higher Education: A literature Review and Implications*. Retrieved July 7, 2017, from https://www.researchgate.net/publication/50600909_Enterprise_Resource_Planning_ERP_System_in_Higher_Education_A_literature_Review_and_Implications

Abugabah, A., Sanzogni, L., & Poropat, A. (2009). The impact of information systems on user performance: A critical review and theoretical model. *Proceedings of the International Conference on Information Systems (ICIS)*, 809–819.

Adewumi, A., Misra, S., Omoregbe, N., & Sanz, L. F. (2019). FOSSES: Framework for open-source software evaluation and selection. *Software, Practice & Experience*, *49*(5), 780–812. doi:10.1002pe.2682

Ağaoğlu, M., Yurtkoru, E. S., & Ekmekçi, A. K. (2015). The Effect of ERP Implementation CSFs on Business Performance: An Empirical Study on Users' Perception. *Procedia: Social and Behavioral Sciences*, *210*, 35–42. doi:10.1016/j.sbspro.2015.11.326

Aggarwal, K. K., Singh, Y., & Chhabra, K. (2002). An Integrated Measure of Sofware Maintainability. In *2002 Proceedings Annual Reliability and Maintainability Symposium* (pp. 235-241). Delhi: IEEE. 10.1109/RAMS.2002.981648

Ahad, Z. R., Ali, Z., & Seyed, M. H. B. (2018). *ERP Implementation Success Assessment: An extended framework*. IGI Global.

Aiman-Smith, L., & Green, S. G. (2002). Implementing new manufacturing technology: The related effects of technologycharacteristics and user learning activities. *Academy of Management Journal*, *45*(2), 421–430.

Ajami, S., Woodbridge, Y., & Feitelson, D. G. (2019). Syntax, predicates, idioms—What really affects code complexity? *Empirical Software Engineering*, *24*(1), 287–328. doi:10.100710664-018-9628-3

Ajzen, I. (1985). From intentions to actions: A theory of planned behavior. In J. Kuhl & J. Beckmann (Eds.), *Action Control: From Cognition to Behaviour* (pp. 11–39). New York: Springer-Verlag. doi:10.1007/978-3-642-69746-3_2

Akaichi, J. (2014). A medical social network for physicians' annotations posting and summarization. *Social Network Analysis and Mining*, *4*(1), 1–8. doi:10.100713278-014-0225-1

Alanbay, O. (2005). ERP Selection Using Expert Choice Software. *Conference Proceeding, ISAHP 2005*.

Alcalá-Fdez, J., & Alonso, J. M. (2016). A survey of fuzzy systems software: Taxonomy, current research trends, and prospects. *IEEE Transactions on Fuzzy Systems*, *24*(1), 40–56. doi:10.1109/TFUZZ.2015.2426212

Al-Fawaz, K., Al-Salti, Z., & Eldabi, T. (2008). *Critical Success Factors in ERP Implementation: A Review*. European and Mediterranean Conference on Information Systems 2008 (EMCIS2008), Dubai, UAE.

Al-Fawaz, K., Eldabi, T., & Naseer, A. (2010). Challenges and influential factors in ERP adoption and implementation. European, *Mediterranean and Middle Eastern Conference on Information Systems*.

AlGhamdi, J. S., & Muzaffar, Z. (2011). Metric suite for assuring the quality of ERP implementation and development. *13th International Conference on Advanced Communication Technology (ICACT2011)*, 1348–1352.

Ali, S., Abdellatief, M., Elfaki, M. A., & Wahaballa, A. (2018). Complexity Metrics for Component-based Software Systems: Developer Perspective. *Indian Journal of Science and Technology*, *11*(32). doi:10.17485/ijst/2018/v11i32/123093

Al-Johani, A., & Youssef, A. (2013). A Framework for ERP Systems in SME Based on Cloud Computing Technology. *International Journal On Cloud Computing: Services And Architecture*, *3*(3), 1–14. doi:10.5121/ijccsa.2013.3301

Al-Mamary, Y. H., Al-nashmi, M., Ghaffar, Y. A., & Shamsuddin, A. (2016). A Critical Review of Models and Theories in Field of Individual Acceptance of Technology. *International Journal of Hybrid Information Technology*, 143-158.

Al-Mashari, M., & Zairi, M. (2000). Information and business process equality: The case of SAP R/3 implementation. *The Electronic Journal on Information Systems in Developing Countries*, *1*(4), 1–15. doi:10.1002/j.1681-4835.2000.tb00011.x

Al-Qutaish, R. E. (2010). Quality Models in Software Engineering Literature: An Analytical and Comparative Study. *The Journal of American Science, 6*, 166–175.

Al-Rawashdeh, T. A., Al'azzeh, F. M., & Al-Qatawneh, S. M. (2014). Evaluation of ERP Systems Quality Model Using Analytic Hierarchy Process (AHP)Technique. *Journal of Software Engineering and Applications*, 225-232.

Al-Rawashdeh, T. A., Al'azzeh, F. M., & Al-Qatawneh, S. M. (2014). Evaluation of ERP systems quality model using analytic hierarchy process (AHP) technique. *Journal of Software Engineering and Applications, 7*(04), 225–232. doi:10.4236/jsea.2014.74024

Alrawashdeh, T. A., Muhairat, M., & Althunibat, A. (2013). Evaluating the quality of software in ERP systems using the ISO 9126 model. *International Journal of Ambient Systems and Applications, 1*(1), 1–9.

Alrawashdeh, T. A., Muhairat, M., & Althunibat, A. (2013). Evaluating the Quality of Software in ERP Systems Using the ISO 9126 Model. *International Journal of Ambient Systems and Applications, 1*(1), 1–9.

Alsabaawi, M. (2015). Critical success factors for enterprise resource planning implementation success. *International Journal of Advances in Engineering and Technology, 8*(4), 496–506.

Amancei, C., & Surcel, T. (2008). ERP System Audit a Control Support For Knowledge Management. *Revista Informatica Economică, 4*(48), 13–16.

Amoako-Gyampah, K. (2007). Perceived usefulness, user involvement and behavioral intention: An empirical study of ERP implementation. *Computers in Human Behavior, 23*(3), 1232–1248.

Anava, O., & Levy, K. (2016). k*-Nearest Neighbors: From Global to Local. *Advances In Neural Information Processing Systems, 29*, 4916–4924. Retrieved from http://papers.nips.cc/paper/6373-k-nearest-neighbors-from-global-to-local.pdf

Appel, A. P., de Cerqueira Gatti, M. A., Neto, S. M. B., Pinhanez, C. S., & Dos Santos, C. N. (2013). *U.S. Patent Application No. 13/887,354*. Washington, DC: US Patent Office.

Askham, N., Cook, D., Doyle, M., Fereday, H., Gibson, M., & Landbeck, U. … Schwarzenbach, J. (2013). *The Six Primary Dimensions for Data Quality Assessment. Group, DAMA UK Working*. Retrieved from https://www.dqglobal.com/wp-content/uploads/2013/11/DAMA-UK-DQ-Dimensions-White-Paper-R37.pdf

Aswathappa, K. (2008). *Human resource management: Text and cases*. MacGraw-Hill.

ATHENA. (2007). *Guidelines and best practices for applying the ATHENA Interoperability Framework to support SME participation in Digital Ecosystems*. Deliverable DA8.2, ATHENA IP.

Atzori, L., Iera, A., & Morabito, G. (2010). The internet of things: A survey. *Computer Networks, 54*(15), 2787–2805. doi:10.1016/j.comnet.2010.05.010

Australian Ministry of Finance and Deregulation. (2005). *Department of Finance (Finance) Governance Arrangements for Australian Government Bodies (Governance policy document).* Author.

Aversano, L., Pennino, I., & Tortorella, M. (2010). Evaluating the Quality of Free/Open Source ERP Systems. *ICEIS*, (1), 75–83.

Aversano, L., & Tortorella, M. (2013). Quality evaluation of floss projects: Application to ERP systems. *Information and Software Technology*, *55*(7), 1260–1276. doi:10.1016/j.infsof.2013.01.007

Awa, H. O. (2018). Some antecedent factors that shape actors' adoption of enterprise systems. *Enterprise Information Systems*, 1–25.

Azeroual, O., & Theel, H. (2019). *The effects of using business intelligence systems on excellence management and decision-making process by start-up companies: A case study.* arXiv preprint arXiv:1901.10555

Azevedo, P., Romão, M., & Rebelo, E. (2012). Advantages, Limitations, and Solutions in the Use of ERP Systems (Enterprise Resource Planning) – A Case Study in the Hospitality Industry. *Procedia Technology*, *5*, 264–272. doi:10.1016/j.protcy.2012.09.029

Badewi, A., & Shehab, E. (2016). The impact of organizational project benefits management governance on ERP project success: Neo-institutional theory perspective. *International Journal of Project Management*, *34*(3), 412–428.

Badewi, A., Shehab, E., Zeng, J., & Mohamad, M. (2018). ERP benefits capability framework: Orchestration theory perspective. *Business Process Management Journal*, *24*(1), 266–294. doi:10.1108/BPMJ-11-2015-0162

Bae, B. B., & Ashcroft, P. (2004). *Implementation of ERP Systems: Accounting and Auditing Implications.* Information Systems Audit and Control Association.

Baggen, R., Correia, J. P., Schill, K., & Visser, J. (2012). Standardized code quality benchmarking for improving software maintainability. *Software Quality Journal*, *20*(2), 287–307. doi:10.100711219-011-9144-9

Bahari, A., & Baharuddin, K. (2013). Enterprise Resource Planning (ERP) System Implementation Readiness: Institution Of Higher Learning In Malaysia. *International Journal Of Multidisciplinary Thought*, *3*(4), 157–166.

Baig, J. J. A., Shah, A., & Sajjad, F. (2017). Evaluation of agile methods for quality assurance and quality control in ERP implementation. Intelligent Computing and Information Systems (ICICIS). In *2017 Eighth International Conference On*, (pp. 252–257). IEEE.

Baig, J. J. A., & Fadel, M. A. A. (2017). Measuring reusability during requirement engineering of an ERP implementation. *2017 Eighth International Conference on Intelligent Computing and Information Systems (ICICIS)*, 258–262. 10.1109/INTELCIS.2017.8260056

Bansal, V., & Negi, T. (2008). A metric for ERP complexity. *International Conference on Business Information Systems*, 369–379. 10.1007/978-3-540-79396-0_32

Barb, A. S., Neill, C. J., Sangwan, R. S., & Piovoso, M. J. (2014). A statistical study of the relevance of lines of code measures in software projects. *Innovations in Systems and Software Engineering*, *10*(4), 243–260. doi:10.100711334-014-0231-5

Barhate, B. H. (2012). Software Inspection Improves Quality of Software Product. *Special Issue of International Journal of Computer Science & Informatics, 2*(1,2), 2231–5292.

Bartholomew, D. (1999). *Process is back*. Cleveland. *Industry Week*.

Bass, L., Weber, I., & Zhu, L. (2015). *DevOps: A Software Architect's Perspective*. Addison-Wesley Professional.

Batini, C., & Scannapieco, M. (2006). Data Quality. *Quality, 262*. doi:10.1007/3-540-33173-5

Bedworth, D. D., & Bailey, J. E. (1987). *Integrated production control systems* (2nd ed.). New York, NY: John Wiley & Sons.

Bell, S. C., & Orzen, M. A. (2016). *Lean IT: Enabling and sustaining your lean transformation*. CRC Press.

Bengtsson, P., Lassing, N., Bosch, J., & Vliet, H. V. (2000). *Analyzing Software Architecture for Modifiability*. Academic Press.

Bennin, K. E., Keung, J., Phannachitta, P., Monden, A., & Mensah, S. (2018). Mahakil: Diversity based oversampling approach to alleviate the class imbalance issue in software defect prediction. *IEEE Transactions on Software Engineering*, *44*(6), 534–550. doi:10.1109/TSE.2017.2731766

Bhattacharya, P., Van Stavern, R., & Madhavan, R. (2010). Automated Data Mining: An Innovative and Efficient Web-Based Approach to Maintaining Resident Case Logs. *Journal of Graduate Medical Education*, *2*(4), 566–570. doi:10.4300/JGME-D-10-00025.1 PMID:22132279

Bhattacherjee, A., Davis, C. J., Connolly, A. J., & Hikmet, N. (2018). User response to mandatory IT use: A Coping Theory perspective. *European Journal of Information Systems*, *27*(4), 395–414. doi:10.105741303-017-0047-0

Bhatt, K., Tarey, V., Patel, P., Mits, K. B., & Ujjain, D. (2012). Analysis of source lines of code (SLOC) metric. *International Journal of Emerging Technology and Advanced Engineering*, *2*(5), 150–154.

Bhogal, J., & Choksi, I. (2015). Handling Big Data Using NoSQL. In *Proceedings - IEEE 29th International Conference on Advanced Information Networking and Applications Workshops, WAINA 2015* (pp. 393–398). IEEE. 10.1109/WAINA.2015.19

Bishop, C. M. (2006). Pattern Recognition and Machine Learning. In Pattern Recognition (Vol. 4, p. 738). Springer. doi:10.1117/1.2819119

Compilation of References

Bishop, C. M. (1995). Neural networks for pattern recognition. *Journal of the American Statistical Association, 92*, 482. doi:10.2307/2965437

Bititci, U. S., Carrie, A. S., & Mcdevitt, L. (1997). Integrated performance measurement system: A development guide –. *International Journal of Operations & Production Management, 17*(5-6), 522–534. doi:10.1108/01443579710167230

Bjelland, E., & Haddara, M. (2018). Evolution of ERP Systems in the Cloud: A Study on System Updates. *Systems, 6*(2), 22. doi:10.3390ystems6020022

Board, E. (2017). SAP SE (NYSE: SAP). *Global Journal of Enterprise Information System, 9*(1), 136. doi:10.18311/gjeis/2017/15884

Bouwers, E., & Vis, R. (2009). Multidimensional software monitoring applied to erp. *Electronic Notes in Theoretical Computer Science, 233*, 161–173. doi:10.1016/j.entcs.2009.02.067

Briand, L. C., Morasca, S., & Basilli, V. R. (1996). Property-based software engineering measurement. *IEEE Transactions on Software Engineering, 22*(1), 68–86. doi:10.1109/32.481535

Bronson, N., Amsden, Z., Cabrera, G., Chakka, P., Dimov, P., Ding, H., & Marchukov, M. (2013). TAO: Facebook's Distributed Data Store for the Social Graph. In *USENIX Annual Technical Conference* (pp. 49-60). USENIX.

Bruggeman, W. (1999, March). The Balanced Scorecard: Functional, Business Unit and Corporate Level Application. *Symposium on IT Based Scorecard*.

Bryman, A. (2008). *Social research methods*. Oxford, UK: Oxford University Press.

Bukhari, A., & Liu, X. (2018). A Web service search engine for large-scale Web service discovery based on the probabilistic topic modeling and clustering. *Service Oriented Computing and Applications, 12*(2), 169–182. doi:10.100711761-018-0232-6

C4ISR. (1998). *Architecture working group (AWG), Levels of information systems interoperability (LISI)*. C4ISR.

Cai, S.-M., Zhou, P.-L., Yang, H.-J., Yang, C.-X., & Wang, B.-H. (n.d.). Diffusion entropy analysis on the scaling behavior of financial markets. *Physica A, 367*, 337–344.

Canfora, G., & Cimitile, A. (2000). *Software Maintenance*. Benevento, Italy: University of Sannio, Faculty of Engineering at Benevento.

Capaldo, G., & Rippa, P. (2008). A Methodological Proposal to Assess the Feasibility of ERP Systems Implementation Strategies. *Proceedings of the 41st Annual Hawaii International Conference on System Sciences (HICSS 2008)*, 401–401. 10.1109/HICSS.2008.30

Capaldo, G., & Rippa, P. (2015). Awareness of organisational readiness in ERP implementation process. *International Journal of Information Systems and Change Management, 7*(3), 224–241.

Capital, F. M. (2013). Kenafric Industries adopts SAP ERP Platform. *Capital News*. Retrieved from https://www.capitalfm.co.ke/business/2013/12/kenafric-industries-adopts-sap-erp-platform/

Cappiello, C., Francalanci, C., & Pernici, B. (2004). *Data Quality Assessment From the User's Perspective*. IQIS.

Caprioli, E. (2014). Commentary on digital evidence and electronic signature of a consumer credit contract in France. *Digital Evidence And Electronic Signature Law Review*, *11*(0). doi:10.14296/deeslr.v11i0.2160

CGN. (2006). *Measuring ERP*. CGN Business Performance Consulting.

Charter. (2015). *Kibabii University Charter 2015*.

Chavan, A., & Nighot, M. (2016). Secure and Cost-effective Application Layer Protocol with Authentication Interoperability for IOT. *Procedia Computer Science*, *78*, 646–651. doi:10.1016/j.procs.2016.02.112

Chen, D., & Daclin, N. (2007), Barrier driven methodology for enterprise interoperability, PROVE2007. *Proc. Establishing The foundation of Collaborative Networks,* 453-460.

Chen, C. C., Law, C. C., & Yang, S. C. (2009). Managing ERP implementation failure: A project management perspective. *IEEE Transactions on Engineering Management*, *56*(1), 157–170. doi:10.1109/TEM.2008.2009802

Chen, C. S., Liang, W. Y., & Hsu, H. Y. (2015). A cloud computing platform for ERP applications. *Applied Soft Computing*, *27*, 127–136. doi:10.1016/j.asoc.2014.11.009

Chian-Son, Yu. (2005). Causes influencing the effectiveness of the post-implementation ERP system. *Industrial Management & Data Systems*, *105*(1), 115–132. doi:10.1108/02635570510575225

Ching, L. (2010). New Governance, Old Problems: Explaining the Appeal of Third-Party Tools. *Asia Pacific Journal Of Public Administration*, *32*(2), 187–197. doi:10.1080/23276665.2010.10779374

Chun-Chin, W., Tian-Shy, L., & Kuo-Liang, L. (2008). An ERP performance measurement framework using a fuzzy integral approach. *Journal of Manufacturing Technology Management*, *19*(5), 607–626. doi:10.1108/17410380810877285

Clark & Jones. (2011). *Organisational Interoperability Maturity Model for C2*. Academic Press.

Clark, T., & Jones, R. (1999). Organisational Interoperability Maturity Model for C2. *Command and Control Research and Technology Symposium*. Retrieved March 7, 2011, from http://www.dodccrp.org/events/1999_CCRTS/pdf_files/track_5/049clark.pdf

Colborne, G. (2010). *Simple and usable web, mobile, and interaction design*. New Riders.

Cortes, C., & Vapnik, V. (1995). Support-Vector Networks. *Machine Learning*, *20*(3), 273–297. doi:10.1007/BF00994018

Costa, C. J., Ferreira, E., Bento, F., & Aparicio, M. (2016). Enterprise resource planning adoption and satisfaction determinants. *Computers in Human Behavior*, *63*, 659–671.

Coursaris, C. K., & Kim, D. J. (2011). A meta-analytical review of empirical mobile usability studies. *Journal of Usability Studies, 6*(3), 117–171.

Cozzi, E., Graziano, M., Fratantonio, Y., & Balzarotti, D. (2018). Understanding Linux malware. In *2018 IEEE Symposium on Security and Privacy (SP)* (pp. 161-175). IEEE. 10.1109/SP.2018.00054

Cram, W. A., & Marabelli, M. (2018). Have your cake and eat it too? Simultaneously pursuing the knowledge-sharing benefits of agile and traditional development approaches. *Information & Management, 55*(3), 322–339. doi:10.1016/j.im.2017.08.005

Crosby, P. B. (1978). *Quality is Free: The Art of Making Quality Certain.* New York: McGraw-Hill.

Cue, K. (2017, March). *Commission for University Education - Home.* Retrieved July 7, 2017, from http://www.cue.or.ke/

Daneva, M. (2008). Complementing approaches in ERP effort estimation practice: an industrial study. *Proceedings of the 4th International Workshop on Predictor Models in Software Engineering,* 87–92. 10.1145/1370788.1370808

Davenport, T. (2000). The future of enterprise system-enabled organizations. *Information Systems Frontiers, 2*(2), 163–180. doi:10.1023/A:1026591822284

Davenport, T. H. (1998). *Putting the Enterprise into the Enterprise system.* Harvard Business Review.

Davenport, T. H., & Harris, J. G. (2007). *Competing on analytics: The new science of winning.* Harvard Business Press.

Davis, F. (1986). *Technology Acceptance Model for Empirically Testing New End-User Information Systems: Theory and Results, in MIT Sloan School of Management.* MIT.

Davis, F. D. (1989). Perceived usefulness, perceived ease of use, and user acceptance of information technology. *Management Information Systems Quarterly, 13*(3), 318–340. doi:10.2307/249008

Davis, F., Bagozzi, P., & Warshaw, P. (1989). User Acceptance of Computer Technology: A Comparison of two Theoretical models. *Management Science, 35*(8), 982–1003. doi:10.1287/mnsc.35.8.982

De Carvalho, R. A., & Monnerat, R. M. (2008). Development support tools for enterprise resource planning. *IT Professional, 10*(5), 39–45. doi:10.1109/MITP.2008.100

Deja, M., & Próchnicka, M. (2018). Metadata as a normalizing mechanism for information-transfer behaviour in higher education institutions: The information culture perspective. *Information Research, 23*(4).

DeLone, W., & McLean, E. (2016). Information Systems Success Measurement. *Foundations and Trends in Information Systems, 2*(1), 1–116. doi:10.1561/2900000005

Derek, L. (2017). *Eight Common mistakes organization Make with ERP in Enterprise Technology Adoption.* Academic Press.

Deshmukh, P. D., Thampi, G. T., & Kalamkar, V. R. (2015). Investigation of quality benefits of ERP implementation in Indian SMEs. *Procedia Computer Science*, *49*, 220–228. doi:10.1016/j.procs.2015.04.247

Dey, P. K., Bennett, D., & Clegg, B. (2009). Managing risk in enterprise resource planning projects. In *16th International Annual EurOMA Conference*. Göteborg, Sweden: European Operations Management Association.

Dimitrova, E. S., Licona, M. P. V., McGee, J., & Laubenbacher, R. (2010). Discretization of Time Series Data. *Journal of Computational Biology*, *17*(6), 853–868. doi:10.1089/cmb.2008.0023 PMID:20583929

Dittrich, Y., Vaucouleur, S., & Giff, S. (2009). ERP customization as software engineering: Knowledge sharing and cooperation. *IEEE Software*, *26*(6), 41–47. doi:10.1109/MS.2009.173

Dobre, C., & Xhafa, F. (2014). Intelligent services for big data science. *Future Generation Computer Systems*, *37*, 267–281. doi:10.1016/j.future.2013.07.014

Docktor, R. (2002). *E-readiness in 2002: Defining and achieving your e-fitness goals*. Available at http://www.ip3.org/pub/docktor.html

Ducq, Y., & Vallespir, B. (2005). Definition and aggregation of a Performance Measurement System in three Aeronautical workshops using the ECOGRAI Method. *International Journal of Production Planning and Control*, *16*(2), 163-177.

Dutta, S., & Bhattacharya, A. (2010). Most significant substring mining based on chi-square measure. In Lecture Notes in Computer Science (Vol. 6118, pp. 319–327). Springer. doi:10.1007/978-3-642-13657-3_35

Ekera, M., & Aytaçb, A. (2017). The Role of ERP in Advanced Managerial Accounting Techniques: A Conceptual Framework. *Business and Economics Research Journal*, *8*(1), 83–100. doi:10.20409/berj.2017126246

Erdil, K., Finn, E., Keating, K., Meattle, J., Park, S., & Yoon, D. (2003). *Software Maintenance As Part of the Software Life Cycle*. Unpublished.

Ertuğrul, I., & Güneş, M. (2007). The Usage of Fuzzy Quality Control Charts to Evaluate Product Quality and an Application. In P. Melin, O. Castillo, E. G. Ramírez, J. Kacprzyk, & W. Pedrycz (Eds.), Analysis and Design of Intelligent Systems using Soft Computing Techniques (pp. 660–673). doi:10.1007/978-3-540-72432-2_67

Erturk, E., & Arora, J. K. (2017). *An Exploratory Study on the Implementation and Adoption of ERP Solutions for Businesses*. arXiv preprint arXiv:1701.08329

Esteves, J. M., & Pastor, J. A. (1999). *An ERP Life-cycle-based Research Agenda*. Academic Press.

Esteves, J., Pastor-Collado, J., & Casanovas, J. (2002). Measuring sustained management support in ERP implementation projects: a GQM approach. *AMCIS 2002 Proceedings*, 190.

European Communities. (2004). *European Interoperability Framework for Pan-European eGovernment Services.* Luxembourg: Office for Official Publications of the European Communities.

Even, A., & Shankaranarayanan, G. (2007). Utility-Driven Assessment of Data Quality. *The Data Base for Advances in Information Systems, 38*(2), 75–93. doi:10.1145/1240616.1240623

Fahmy, S., Haslinda, N., Roslina, W., & Fariha, Z. (2012). Evaluating the Quality of Software in e-Book sing the ISO 9126 Model. *International Journal of Control and Automation, 5*, 115–122.

Fan, M., & Truong, K. N. (2018). Guidelines for Creating Senior-Friendly Product Instructions. *ACM Transactions on Accessible Computing, 11*(2), 9. doi:10.1145/3209882

Feizi, A., & Wong, C. Y. (2012, June). *Usability of user interface styles for learning a graphical software application.* In *Computer & Information Science (ICCIS), 2012 International Conference on* (Vol. 2, pp. 1089-1094). IEEE. 10.1109/ICCISci.2012.6297188

Fenton, N. E., & Pfleeger, S. L. (1997). *Software Metrics: A Rigorous and Practical, Approach.* Boston, MA: PWS Publishing Co.

Ferrell, G. (2003). *Enterprise Systems in Universities: Panacea or Can of Worms?* JISC infoNet Publication.

Firouzabadi, S., & Mehrizi, S. (2015). ERP software quality assessment using fuzzy VIKOR. *Uncertain Supply Chain Management, 3*(2), 189–196. doi:10.5267/j.uscm.2014.12.001

Fishbein, M., & Ajzen, I. (1975). *Belief, Attitude, Intention and Behaavior: An introduction to theory and Research.* Addison-Wesley.

Flanaghan, G. A. (1995). *IBM Usability Leadership Maturity model (self-assessment version).* Distributed at CHI Workshop.

Fuggetta, A., & Di Nitto, E. (2014, May). Software process. In *Proceedings of the on Future of Software Engineering* (pp. 1-12). ACM.

Ganeshkumar, P., & Kalaivani, S. (2015). *Prediction of Software Defect Using Linear Twin Core Vector Machine Model.* Academic Press.

Gao, S. (2009). Manufacturing Resource Planning Technology Based on Genetic Programming Simulation. *Chinese Journal of Mechanical Engineering, 22*(02), 177. doi:10.3901/CJME.2009.02.177

García, M. A., & Rodríguez, F. (2013). Analysis of MODIS NDVI time series using quasi-periodic components. In *Proceedings of SPIE - The International Society for Optical Engineering* (Vol. 8795). 10.1117/12.2027170

Garefalakis, A., Mantalis, G., Vourgourakis, E., Spinthiropoulos, K., & Lemonakis, C. (2016). Healthcare Firms and the ERP Systems. *Journal of Engineering Science & Technology Review, 9*(1), 139–144. doi:10.25103/jestr.091.021

Garg, P. (2010). Critical Failure Factors For Enterprise Resource Planning Implementations In Indian Retail Organizations: An Exploratory Study. *Journal of Information Technology Impact*, *10*(1), 35–44.

Garzonis, S., Jones, S., Jay, T., & O'Neill, E. (2009). Auditory icon and earcon mobile service notifications: intuitiveness, learnability, memorability and preference. In *Proceedings of the SIGCHI Conference on Human Factors in Computing Systems* (pp. 1513-1522). ACM. 10.1145/1518701.1518932

Gassel, F. (2010). Robotizing housing and design. *Gerontechnology (Valkenswaard)*, *9*(2). doi:10.4017/gt.2010.09.02.128.00

Gayathri, M., & Sudha, A. (2014). Software defect prediction system using multilayer perceptron neural network with data mining. *International Journal of Recent Technology and Engineering*, *3*(2), 54–59.

Gehrke, N. (2010). The ERP AuditLab - A prototypical Framework for Evaluating Enterprise Resource Planning System Assurance. In *Proceedings of the 43rd Hawaii International Conference on System Sciences*. IEEE. 10.1109/HICSS.2010.377

Geum, Y., Kim, M., & Lee, S. (2017). Service Technology: Definition and Characteristics Based on a Patent Database. *Service Science*, *9*(2), 147–166. doi:10.1287erv.2016.0170

Ghalayini, A. M., Noble, J. S., & Crowe, T. J. (1997). An integrated dynamic performance measurement system for improving manufacturing competitiveness –. *International Journal of Production Economics*, *48*(3), 1997. doi:10.1016/S0925-5273(96)00093-X

Ghatage, S. M., & Gaikwad, S. K. (2014). Sherpa–Expert's Social Network. *International Journal of Science and Research*, *3*(2), 1384–1390.

Gleghorn, R. (2005). Enterprise application integration: A manager's perspective. *IT Professional*, *7*(6), 17–23. doi:10.1109/MITP.2005.143

González, A., Dueñas-Osorio, L., Sánchez-Silva, M., & Medaglia, A. (2015). The Interdependent Network Design Problem for Optimal Infrastructure System Restoration. *Computer-Aided Civil and Infrastructure Engineering*, *31*(5), 334–350. doi:10.1111/mice.12171

Goodman, P. S., & Griffith, T. L. (1991). A process approach to the implementation of new technology. *Journal of Engineering and Technology Management*, *8*(3-4), 261–285. doi:10.1016/0923-4748(91)90014-I

Gottesdiener, E. (2001). Reviews, Inspections, and Walkthroughs. Academic Press.

Grabski, S. V., Leech, S. A., & Lu, B. (2003). Risks and Controls in the Implementation of ERP Systems. *The International Journal of Digital Accounting Research*, *1*(1), 47–68.

Grabski, S. V., Leech, S. A., & Schmidt, P. J. (2011). A review of ERP research: A future agenda for accounting information systems. *Journal of Information Systems*, *25*(1), 37–78. doi:10.2308/jis.2011.25.1.37

Gradmann, S. (2008). *Interoperability: A key concept for large scale, persistent digital libraries.* Available: http://www.digitalpreservationeurope.eu/publications

Grossman, K. W. (2012). *Careers in Cloud Computing and Mobile Technology. In Tech Job Hunt Handbook* (pp. 215–225). Apress. doi:10.1007/978-1-4302-4549-0_18

Grubb, P., & Takang, A. A. (2003). *Software Maintenance: Concepts and Practice* (2nd ed.). World Scientific Publishing Co. Pte. Ltd.

Gupta, H., Aye, K. T., Balakrishnan, R., Rajagopal, S., & Nguwi, Y. Y. (2014). A Study of Key Critical Success Factors (CSFs) for Enterprise Resource Planning (ERP) Systems. *International Journal of Computer and Information Technology, 3*(4).

Haaksma, T. R., de Jong, M. D., & Karreman, J. (2018). Users' Personal Conceptions of Usability and User Experience of Electronic and Software Products. *IEEE Transactions on Professional Communication, 61*(2), 116–132. doi:10.1109/TPC.2018.2795398

Hahn, J. (1999). ERP Systems: Audit and Control Risks. In *ISACA Spring Conference.* Deloitte & Touche.

Hahn, J., & Touche, D. &. (1998). ERP Systems: Audit and Control Risks. In *ISACA Spring Conference.* Deloitte Touche Tohmatsu.

Hamilton & Murtagh. (2000). *Enabling Interoperability Via Software Architecture.* Technical Reports, AD Number: ADA458021. Retrieved from http://www.dtic.mil/dtic

Hammer, M., & Champy, J. (2001). *Reengineering the Corporation.* New York: Harpercollins.

Han, R., Ghanem, M. M., Guo, L., Guo, Y., & Osmond, M. (2014). Enabling cost-aware and adaptive elasticity of multi-tier cloud applications. *Future Generation Computer Systems, 32,* 82–98. doi:10.1016/j.future.2012.05.018

Haritos, T. (2017). *A Study of Human-Machine Interface (HMI) Learnability for Unmanned Aircraft Systems Command and Control* (Doctoral dissertation). Nova Southeastern University.

Harjumaa, L. (2005). *Improving The Software Inspection Process With Patterns* (Academic Dissertation). Oulu University Press.

Harris, M. A., & Weistroffer, H. R. (2008). Does User Participation Lead to System Success? *Proceedings of the Southern Association for Information Systems Conference,* Richmond, VA.

Hasibua, Z. A., & Dantes, G. R. (2012). Priority of Key Success Factors (KSFS) on Enterprise Resource Planning (ERP) System Implementation Life Cycle. *Journal of Enterprise Resource Planning Studies, 2012,* 1–15. doi:10.5171/2011.122627

Hauck, M. (2014). NoSQL Databases Explained. *MongoDB.* Retrieved from http://www.mongodb.com/nosql-explained

Hawari, A., & Heeks, R. (2010). Explaining ERP Failure in a Developing Country: A Jordanian Case Study. *Journal of Enterprise Information Management, 23*(2), 135–160. doi:10.1108/17410391011019741

Hawking & Stein. (2004) Hawking, P. and Stein, A. 2004. Revisiting ERP Systems: Benefits Realization. *Proceedings of the 37th Hawaii International Conference on System Sciences.*

Heckerman, D. (1995). A tutorial on learning with Bayesian networks. *Tutorial.* Retrieved from http://citeseerx.ist.psu.edu/viewdoc/summary?doi=10.1.1.56.1431

Helo, P., Suorsa, M., Hao, Y., & Anussornnitisarn, P. (2014). Toward a cloud-based manufacturing execution system for distributed manufacturing. *Computers in Industry, 65*(4), 646–656. doi:10.1016/j.compind.2014.01.015

Herold, D. M., Farmer, S. M., & Mobley, M. I. (1995). Pre-implementation attitudes toward the introduction of robots in a unionized environment. *Journal of Engineering and Technology Management, 12*(3), 155–173. doi:10.1016/0923-4748(95)00008-7

Herout, A., Jošth, R., Juránek, R., Havel, J., Hradiš, M., & Zemčík, P. (2011). Real-time object detection on CUDA. *Journal of Real-Time Image Processing, 6*(3), 159–170. doi:10.100711554-010-0179-0

Heubusch, K. (2006, January). Interoperability: What it Means, Why it Matters. *Journal of American Health Information Management Association, 77*(1), 26–30. PMID:16475733

Hoch, J., & Dulebohn, J. (2013). Shared leadership in enterprise resource planning and human resource management system implementation. *Human Resource Management Review, 23*(1), 114–125. doi:10.1016/j.hrmr.2012.06.007

Holland, P., Light, B., & Gibson, N. (1999). A critical success factors model for enterprise resource planning implementation. *Proceedings of the 7th European Conference on Information Systems, 1*, 273-297.

Holsapple, M. P., Burns-Naas, L. A., Hastings, K., Ladics, G. S., Lavin, A. L., Makris, S., ... Luster, M. I. (2005). A proposed testing framework for developmental immunotoxicology (DIT). *Toxicological Sciences, 83*(1), 18–24. doi:10.1093/toxsci/kfh299 PMID:15456913

Horowitz-Kraus, T. (2015). Improvement in non-linguistic executive functions following reading acceleration training in children with reading difficulties: An ERP study. *Trends in Neuroscience and Education, 4*(3), 77–86. doi:10.1016/j.tine.2015.06.002

Hossain, L., Rashid, M. A., & Patrick, J. D. (2002). A Framework for Assessing ERP Systems Functionality for the SMEs in Australia. In Enterprise Resource Planning: Solutions and Management (pp. 182–208). IGI Global.

Hostmann, B., Rayner, N., & Friedman, T. (2006). Gartner's Business Intelligence and Performance Management Framework. *Business (Atlanta, Ga.).*

Howcroft, D., Newell, S., & Wagner, E. (2004). Understanding the contextual influences on enterprise system design, implementation, use and evaluation. *The Journal of Strategic Information Systems, 13*(4), 271–277. doi:10.1016/j.jsis.2004.11.010

Hsu, L., Lai, R., & Weng, Y. (2008). Understanding the critical effect user satisfaction and impact of ERP through innovation of diffusion theory. *International Journal of Technology Management, 43*(1–3), 30–47. doi:10.1504/IJTM.2008.019405

Huang, T., & Yasuda, K. (2016). Comprehensive review of literature survey articles on ERP. *Business Process Management Journal, 22*(1), 2–32.

Huifen, W., & Chiang, D. (2010). Evaluation ERP II Application Performance from Institutional Theory View. *Software Engineering (WCSE), 2010 Second World Congress On, 1*, 89–93. 10.1109/WCSE.2010.83

Humphrey, W.S. (1989). *Managing the software process.* Addison-Wesley.

Hunton, J. E., Lippincott, B., & Reck, J. L. (2003). Enterprise resource planning systems: Comparing the firm performance of adopters and nonadopters. *International Journal of Accounting Information Systems, 4*(3), 165–184. doi:10.1016/S1467-0895(03)00008-3

Hustad, E., Haddara, M., & Kalvenes, B. (2016). ERP and Organizational Misfits: An ERP Customization Journey. *Procedia Computer Science, 100*, 429–439. doi:10.1016/j.procs.2016.09.179

Hwang, G., Han, S., Jun, S., & Park, J. (2014). Operational Performance Metrics in Manufacturing Process: Based on SCOR Model and RFID Technology. *International Journal of Innovation, Management and Technology, 5*(1). doi:10.7763/IJIMT.2014.V5.485

Hwang, Y. (2005). Investigating enterprise systems adoption: Uncertainty avoidance, intrinsic motivation, and the technology aceeptance model. *European Journal of Information Systems, 14*(5), 150–161. doi:10.1057/palgrave.ejis.3000532

Hyvärinen, A., & Oja, E. (2000). Independent component analysis: Algorithms and applications. *Neural Networks, 13*(4-5), 411–430. doi:10.1016/S0893-6080(00)00026-5 PMID:10946390

IEEE Computer Society. (2008). IEEE Standard for Software Reviews and Audits. New York, NY: IEEE.

IEEE. (1990). *IEEE Standard Computer Dictionary: A Compilation of IEEE Standard Computer Glossaries.* New York, NY: Institute of Electrical and Electronics Engineers.

Ifinedo, P., & Nahar, N. (2006). Quality, Impact and Success of ERP Systems: A Study Involving Some Firms in the Nordic-Baltic Region. *Journal of Information Technology Impact, 6*, 19–46.

Ifinedo, P., Rapp, B., Ifinedo, A., & Sundberg, K. (2010). *Relationship among ERP Post-Implementation success constructs: Analysis at organization level.* Computers in Human Behaviour.

Information Systems Audit and Control Association. (2016). *Information Systems Auditing: Tools and Techniques*. ISACA.

International Organisation for Standardization. (2017). ISO/IEC/IEEE 12207. IEEE.

ISO. (2001). *ISO/IEC 9126-1: Software Engineering—Product Quality—Part 1: Quality Model*. Geneva: International Organization for Standardization.

ISO. (2004). *ISO/IEC TR 9126-4: Software Engineer in—Product Quality—Part 4: Quality in Use Metrics*. Geneva: International Organization for Standardization.

ISO/IEC 21000-6 RDD Registration Authority. (n.d.). Retrieved from http://www.iso21000-6.net

ISO/IEC-12207. (2008). *Software Implementation and Support Processes*. ISO/IEC 12207:2008.

ISO/IEC14764. (2006). *Software Engineering - Software Life Cycle Processes - Maintenance*. Geneva: IEEE Std 14764-2006.

Izamani, S., Khoumbati, K., Ismaili, A. I., & Amani, S. (2013). A Conceptual Framework for ERP Evaluation in Higher Educational Institutes of Pakistan. *Sindh University Research Journal*, 596–607.

Jack, W., & Suri, T. (2010). *Monetary Theory and Electronic Money: Reflections on the Kenyan Experience*. Retrieved from http://www.mobilemoneyexchange.org/Files/8e31752b

Jain, A. (2011). Approach for reducing menu access time by enabling bidirectional cursor movement within the nested menu(s). *Software Engineering Notes*, *36*(5), 1. doi:10.1145/2020976.2020986

Jansson, A.-S. (2007). *Software Maintenance and Process Improvement by CMMI*. UPTEC.

Jenkins, B. (2008). *Developing Mobile Money Ecosystems*. Washington, DC: IFC and the Harvard Kennedy School. Retrieved from http://www.hks.harvard.edu/m- rcbg/CSRI/publications/report_30_MOBILEMONEY.pdf

Jiawei, H., & Micheline, K. (2006). *Data Mining: Concepts and Techniques* (2nd ed.). Morgan Kauffman.

Jin, R., Breitbart, Y., & Muoh, C. (2009). Data discretization unification. *Knowledge and Information Systems*, *19*(1), 1–29. doi:10.100710115-008-0142-6

Johansson, B., & de Carvalho, R. A. (2010). Software tools for requirements management in an ERP system context. *Proceedings of the 2010 ACM Symposium on Applied Computing*, 169–170. 10.1145/1774088.1774123

Johansson, B., & Sudzina, F. (2008). ERP systems and open source: An initial review and some implications for SMEs. *Journal of Enterprise Information Management*, *21*(6), 649–658. doi:10.1108/17410390810911230

Jolliffe, I. T. (2005). Principal component analysis. *Applied Optics*, *44*(May), 6486. doi:10.1007/SpringerReference_205537 PMID:16252661

Kakouris, A. P., & Polychronopoulios, G. (2005). Enterprise Resource Planning (ERP) system: An Effective Tool for Production Management. *Management Research News*, 28(6), 66–78. doi:10.1108/01409170510784878

Kalaimagal, S., & Srinivasan, R. (2008). A Retrospective on Software Component Quality Models. *SIGSOFT Software Engineering*, 33(6), 1–10. doi:10.1145/1449603.1449611

Kalakota, R., & Robinson, M. (2001). *E-business 2.0: Roadmap to success*. Reading, MA: Addison-Wesley.

Kallunki, J., Laitinen, E. K., & Silvola, H. (2011). Impact of enterprise resource planning systems on management control systems and firm performance. *International Journal of Accounting Information Systems*, 12(1), 20–39. doi:10.1016/j.accinf.2010.02.001

Kanellou, A., & Spathis, C. (2009). *ERP Systems and Auditing: a Review. 6th International Conference on Enterprise Systems, Accounting and Logistics*, Thessaloniki, Greece.

Kang'ethe, P. N. N. (2007). *An Evaluation of the Successful Implementation Of Enterprise Resource Planning System at HACO Industries*. Research Paper School of Business University of Nairobi.

Kaplan, R.S., & Norton, D.P. (1996). *The Balanced Scorecard*. Harvard Business School Press.

Kaplan, R., & Norton, D. (1992, January-February). The Balanced Scorecard - Measures that drive performance. *Harvard Business Review*. PMID:10119714

Kaplan, R., & Norton, D. (1996). *Translating Strategy in to action: The Balanced Scorecard*. Boston: Harvard Business School Press.

Karande, S., Jain, V., & Ghatule, A. (2012). ERP implementation: Critical success factors for Indian Universities and higher educational institutions. *Pragyaan Journal of Information Technology*, 10(2), 24–29.

Karpiuk, M. (2016). Bill of materials as a part of CAD and ERP integration. *Mechanik*, (12), 1874-1875. doi:10.17814/mechanik.2016.12.531

Karthikeyan, R., Venkatesan, K. G. S., & Chandrasekar, A. (2016). A Comparison of Strengths and Weaknesses for Analytical Hierarchy Process. *Journal of Chemical and Pharmaceutical Sciences*, 9(3), 4.

Kasomo, D. (2006). *Research method in humanities and education*. Egerton University Press.

Kasunic, M., & Anderson, W. (2004). *Measuring Systems Interoperability: Challenges and Opportunities, Software Engineering Measurement and Analysis Initiative*. Technical Note CMU/SEI-2004-TN-003. Retrieved from http://www.sei.cmu.edu/library

Kaur, U., & Singh, G. (2015). A Review on Software Maintenance Issues and How to Reduce Maintenance Efforts. *International Journal of Computers and Applications*, 118(1), 6–11. doi:10.5120/20707-3021

Khaleel, Y. (2012). Analysis of Enterprise Resource Planning System (ERP) in Small and Medium Enterprises (SME) of Malaysian Manufacturing Sectors: Current Status and Practices. *Asia-Pacific Journal of Information Technology and Multimedia, 10*(2011), 13–20.

Kilic, H. S., Zaim, S., & Delen, D. (2014). Development of a hybrid methodology for ERP system selection: The case of Turkish Airlines. *Decision Support Systems, 66*, 82–92. doi:10.1016/j. dss.2014.06.011

Kim, Y., Choi, J. S., & Shin, Y. (2014). *A decision model for optimizing the service portfolio in SOA governance.* In *Information and Communication Technologies (WICT)*, 2014 Fourth World Congress on (pp. 57-62). IEEE. 10.1109/WICT.2014.7077302

King, P. (2002). *The promise and Performance of Enterprise Systems in Higher Education, Respondent Summary.* ECAR Respondent Summary. Retrieved from http://www.educause.edu/ir/library/pdf/ecar _so/ers/ers0202/EKF0204.pdf

Kitchenham, B. (2004). Procedures for performing systematic reviews. Keele, UK: Keele University.

Kitchenham, B., Brereton, O. P., Budgen, D., Turner, M., Bailey, J., & Linkman, S. (2009). Systematic literature reviews in software engineering–a systematic literature review. *Information and Software Technology, 51*(1), 7–15. doi:10.1016/j.infsof.2008.09.009

Kitchenham, B., Pfleeger, S. L., & Fenton, N. (1995). Towards a framework for software measurement validation. *IEEE Transactions on Software Engineering, 21*(12), 929–944. doi:10.1109/32.489070

Kitchenham, B., Pretorius, R., Budgen, D., Brereton, O. P., Turner, M., Niazi, M., & Linkman, S. (2010). Systematic literature reviews in software engineering–a tertiary study. *Information and Software Technology, 52*(8), 792–805. doi:10.1016/j.infsof.2010.03.006

Knezevic, J. (1997). *System Maintainability.* London: Springer Science & Business Media.

Koch, C. (2011). A status on enterprise resource planning (ERP) studies in information systems research. *Computer and Information Science (ICIS), IEEE/ACIS 10th International Conference,* 409–414.

Koch, S. (2007). ERP implementation effort estimation using data envelopment analysis. In *Technologies for business information systems* (pp. 121–132). Springer. doi:10.1007/1-4020-5634-6_11

Koh & Prybutok. (2003). *The three-ring model and development of an instrument.* Academic Press.

Kohonen, T. (1982). Self-organized formation of topologically correct feature maps. *Biological Cybernetics, 43*(1), 59–69. doi:10.1007/BF00337288

Kraft, C. L. (2001). *Executive ERP.* Retrieved from http://www.oracle.com/oramag/profit/ 99-May/index.html?p29ind.html

Kuang, J., Lau, J., & Nah, F. F. (2001). Critical factors for successful implementation of enterprise systems. *Business Process Management Journal, 7*(3), 285–296. doi:10.1108/14637150110392782

Kuesel, J. R., Kupferschmidt, M. G., Schardt, P. E., & Shearer, R. A. (2014). *U.S. Patent No. 8,776,035*. Washington, DC: U.S. Patent and Trademark Office.

Kujala, S. I. (2008). Effective user involvement in product development by improving the analysis of user needs. *Behaviour & Information Technology, 27*(6), 457–473. doi:10.1080/01449290601111051

Kumar, A., Tadayoni, R., & Sorensen, L. T. (2015). Metric based efficiency analysis of educational ERP system usability-using fuzzy model. *Image Information Processing (ICIIP), 2015 Third International Conference On*, 382–386.

Kumar, A., Grover, P. S., & Kumar, R. (2009). A Quantitative Evaluation of Aspect-Oriented Software Quality Model (AOSQUAMO). *Software Engineering Notes, 34*, 1–9. doi:10.1145/1598732.1598736

Kumar, A., Tadayoni, R., & Sorensen, L. T. (2015). Metric based efficiency analysis of educational ERP system usability-using fuzzy model. *2015 Third International Conference on Image Information Processing (ICIIP)*, 382–386. 10.1109/ICIIP.2015.7414801

Kumar, U., Kumar, V., & Maheshwari, B. (2003). An investigation of critical management issues in ERP implementation: Emperical evidence from Canadian organizations. *Technovation Journal, 23*(10), 793–807. doi:10.1016/S0166-4972(02)00015-9

Kurt, W. (2017). *Introduction to Digital Logic*. Morga & Claypool Publishers.

Kutswa, C. E. (2011). *Challenges of Implementing Enterprise Resource Planning Strategy At The Kenya Electricity Generating Company*. Research Paper School of Business University of Nairobi.

Kwak, Y. H., Park, J., Chung, B. Y., & Ghosh, S. (2012). Understanding end-users' acceptance of enterprise resource planning (ERP) system in project-based sectors. *IEEE Transactions on Engineering Management, 59*(2), 266–277. doi:10.1109/TEM.2011.2111456

Kwak, Y., Park, J., Chung, B., & Ghosh, S. (2012). Understanding end-users' acceptance of enterprise resource planning (ERP) system in project-based sector. *Engineering Management. IEEE Transactions, 59*(2), 266–277.

Laaksonen, J., & Oja, E. (1996). Classification with learning k-nearest neighbors. *ICNN 96. The 1996 IEEE International Conference on Neural Networks, 3*, 1480–1483. 10.1109/ICNN.1996.549118

Lafreniere, B., & Grossman, T. (2018, October). Blocks-to-CAD: A Cross-Application Bridge from Minecraft to 3D Modeling. In *The 31st Annual ACM Symposium on User Interface Software and Technology* (pp. 637-648). ACM.

Laitenberger, O. (2001). *A Survey of Software Inspection Technologies. Handbook on Software Engineering and Knowledge Engineering*.

Lallana Emmanuel, C. (2008). *eGovernment Interoperability*. UNDP. Retrieved from http://www.apdip.net/projects/gif/gifeprimer

Laurillard, D. (2013). *Rethinking university teaching: A conversational framework for the effective use of learning technologies*. Routledge. doi:10.4324/9781315012940

Law, C., Chen, C., & Wu, B. (2010). Managing the full ERP life cycle: Considerations of maintenance and support requirements and IT governance practice as integral elements of the formula for successful ERP adoption. *Computers in Industry, 61*(3), 297–308. doi:10.1016/j.compind.2009.10.004

Lebreton, B., & Legner, C. (2007). Interoperability Impact Assessment Model: An Overview. In R. J. Gonçalves, J. P. Müller, K. Mertins & M. Zelm (Eds.), *Enterprise Interoperability II - New Challenges and Approaches* (pp. 725-728). Springer London. Retrieved from http://www.xml.coverpages.org/Comptia-ISC-OpenStandards.pdf

Lech, P. (2016). Implementation of an ERP system: A case study of a full-scope SAP project Implementation of an ERP system: A case study of a full-scope. *Finanse Journal of Management and Finance, 14*(1).

Lee, J. A., & Verleysen, M. (2007). Nonlinear dimensionality reduction. Advances in Neural Information Processing Systems, 5. doi:10.1007/978-0-387-39351-3

Lee, Y., Pipino, L., Funk, J., & Wang, R. (2006). *Journey to data quality. Computer* (Vol. 1). Retrieved from http://141.105.33.55/~lomov/??????????/bigdvd/dvd44/Lee.pdf

Lehman, M. M. (1980). Lifecycles and the Laws of Software Evolution. In *Proceedings of the IEEE, Special Issue on Software Engineering*. IEEE.

Lehman, M. M. (1984). Program Evolution. *Journal of Information Processing and Management, 19*(1), 19–36. doi:10.1016/0306-4573(84)90037-2

Leite, R. S., de Carvalho, R. B., & Gonçalves Filho, C. (1899). Measuring Perceived Quality and Satisfaction of ERP Systems: an Empirical Study with Customers of a Brazilian Software Company. Hicss, 1–8.

Leon, A. (2009). *Enterprise Resource Planning*. McGraw-Hill.

Leskovec, J., Rajaraman, A., & Ullman, J. (2014). Dimensionality reduction. *Mining of Massive Datasets*, 405–437. Retrieved from http://www.mmds.org/

Levingstone, T. J., Thompson, E., Matsiko, A., Schepens, A., Gleeson, J. P., & O'Brien, F. J. (2016). Multi-layered collagen-based scaffolds for osteochondral defect repair in rabbits. *Acta Biomaterialia, 32*, 149–160. doi:10.1016/j.actbio.2015.12.034 PMID:26724503

Levi, S., & Doron, T. (2013). Critical success factors in enterprise resource planning systems: Review of the last decade. *Communications of the ACM, 45*(4).

Light, B. (2001). The maintenance implications of the customization of ERP software. *Journal of Software Maintenance and Evolution: Research and Practice*, 415–429.

Li, R. F., & Wang, X. Z. (2002). Dimension reduction of process dynamic trends using independent component analysis. *Computers & Chemical Engineering*, 26(3), 467–473. doi:10.1016/S0098-1354(01)00773-6

Lloyd, S. P. (1982). Least Squares Quantization in PCM. *IEEE Transactions on Information Theory*, 28(2), 129–137. doi:10.1109/TIT.1982.1056489

Lotfy, M. A., & Halawi, L. (2015). A conceptual model to measure ERP user-value. *Issues in Information Systems*, 16(3), 54.

Luo, W., & Strong, D. M. (2004). A framework for evaluating ERP implementation choices. *IEEE Transactions on Engineering Management*, 51(3), 322–333. doi:10.1109/TEM.2004.830862

Maclachlan, G. (2011). Scandal, Spyware, and Trust. *Infosecurity*, 8(5), 45. doi:10.1016/S1754-4548(11)70071-7

Madden, T., Ellen, P., & Ajzen, I. (1992). A comparison of the theory of planned behavior and the theory of reasoned action. *Personality and Social Psychology Bulletin*, 18(1), 3–9. doi:10.1177/0146167292181001

Mahut, T., Bouchard, C., Omhover, J. F., Favart, C., & Esquivel, D. (2018). Interdependency between user experience and interaction: A kansei design approach. *International Journal on Interactive Design and Manufacturing*, 12(1), 105–132. doi:10.100712008-017-0381-4

Ma, R., Zhou, X., Peng, Z., Liu, D., Xu, H., Wang, J., & Wang, X. (2015). Data mining on correlation feature of load characteristics statistical indexes considering temperature. *Zhongguo Dianji Gongcheng Xuebao. Zhongguo Dianji Gongcheng Xuebao*, 35(1), 43–51. doi:10.13334/j.0258-8013.pcsee.2015.01.006

Marenzi, I., Demidova, E., Nejdl, W., & Zerr, S. (2008). *Social software for lifelong competence development: challenges and infrastructure.* International Journal of Emerging Over Time to Infer Shared Interests. In Proc. Human Factors in Computing Systems.

Markus, M., Axline, S., Petrie, D., & Tanis, C. (2000). Learning from Adopters' Experiences with ERP: Problems Encountered and Success Achieved. *Journal of Information Technology*, 15, 245–265.

Masese, Muketha, & Mbuguah. (2017). Interface Features, Program Complexity, and Memorability as Indicators of Learnability of Mobile Social Software. *International Journal of Science and Research, 6*(10).

Matende, S., & Ogao, P. (2013). Enterprise Resource Planning (ERP) System Implementation: A Case for User Participation. *Procedia Technology, 9*, 518–526. doi:10.1016/j.protcy.2013.12.058

Matende, S., Ogao, P., & Nabukenya, J. (2015). User participation in ERP Implementation: A Case-based Study. *International Journal of Computer Applications Technology and Research*, *4*(1), 24–29.

Mathôt, S., Schreij, D., & Theeuwes, J. (2012). OpenSesame: An open-source, graphical experiment builder for the social sciences. *Behavior Research Methods*, *44*(2), 314–324. doi:10.375813428-011-0168-7 PMID:22083660

Matsuda, M., & Wang, Q. (2010). Software Interoperability Tools. *Standardized Capability-Profiling Methodology, ISO16100*. doi:10.1007/978-3-642-15509-3_13

Mazurczyk, W., & Caviglione, L. (2015). Information Hiding as a Challenge for Malware Detection. *IEEE Security and Privacy*, *13*(2), 89–93. doi:10.1109/MSP.2015.33

Mbonimpa, J. C. (2012). Contribution of Computerised Financial Management Systems. The Functions Of Supreme Court Of Rwanda.

Mbuguah, S. M. (2018). *ICT-Directorate*. Retrieved from https://kibu.ac.ke/ict-directorate/

Mbuguah, S. M., Wabwoba, F., & Wanjala, C. (2019) Implementation Evaluation Metrics for Enterprise Resource Planning Solution Current. *Journal of Applied Science and Technology, 32*(3).

Mbuguah, S., & Wabwoba, F. (2014). *Attackability Metrics Model for Secure Service Oriented Architecture*. Lambert Academic Publishing.

McCabe. (1976). A Complexity Measure. *IEEE Transactions On Software Engineering*, 308-320.

McGinnis, T., & Huang, Z. (2007). Rethinking ERP success: A new perspective from knowledge management and continuous improvement. *Information & Management*, *44*(7), 626–634. doi:10.1016/j.im.2007.05.006

McLachlan, G. J. (2004). *Discriminant analysis and statistical pattern recognition. Wiley series in probability and statistics*. doi:10.1002/0471725293

McLaughlin, D. (2015). Assessing the fit of biotic ligand model validation data in a risk management decision context. *Integrated Environmental Assessment and Management*, *11*(4), 610–617. doi:10.1002/ieam.1634 PMID:25779880

Meghanathan, N. (2013). Source Code Analysis to Remove Security Vulnerabilities in Java Socket Programs: A Case Study. *International Journal Of Network Security & Its Applications*, *5*(1), 1–16. doi:10.5121/ijnsa.2013.5101

Mehlinger, L. (2006). *Indicators of successful enterprise technology implementations in higher education business*. Morgan State University.

Michelberger, P., & Horváth, Z. (2017). Security aspects of process resource planning. *Polish Journal Of Management Studies*, *16*(1), 142–153. doi:10.17512/pjms.2017.16.1.12

Michelman, P. (2018). *What the Digital Future Holds: 20 Groundbreaking Essays on How Technology Is Reshaping the Practice of Management*. MIT Press.

Miller, P. (2000). Interoperability: what is it and why should I want it. *Ariadne, 23*.

Miller, C., & Stuart Wells, F. (2007). Balancing Security and Privacy in the Digital Workplace. *Journal of Change Management, 7*(3-4), 315–328. doi:10.1080/14697010701779181

MIREC. (2017). *Meru University of Science and Technology Institutional Research and Ethic Committee procedures*. Unpublished.

Miroshnichenko, A. (2015). Media Ecology as Ecology Contrariwise: Protecting Humans from an Environment. *Systema: Connecting Matter, Life, Culture and Technology, 3*(1), 89-104.

Mittelstädt, V., Brauner, P., Blum, M., & Ziefle, M. (2015). On the visual design of ERP systems – The role of information complexity, presentation and human factors. *Procedia Manufacturing, 3*, 448–455. doi:10.1016/j.promfg.2015.07.207

Momoh, A., Roy, R., & Shehab, E. (2010). Challenges in enterprise resource planning implementation: State-of-the-art. *Business Process Management Journal, 16*(4), 537–565.

Montesi, M., & Owen, J. M. (2008). From conference to journal publication: How conference papers in software engineering are extended for publication in journals. *Journal of the American Society for Information Science and Technology, 59*(5), 816–829. doi:10.1002/asi.20805

Moon, Y. B. (2007). *Enterprise Resource Planning (ERP): a review of the literature*. Intern.

Moon, Y. B. (2007). Enterprise Resource Planning (ERP): A review of the literature. *International Journal of Management and Enterprise Development, 4*(3), 235–264.

Morgan, D. (2004). Network security and custom Web applications. *Network Security, 2004*(4), 15–17. doi:10.1016/S1353-4858(04)00068-6

Moutaz, H., & Henriek, M. (2017). *User Resistance in ERP implementation: A literature review*. ScienceDirect Elsevier.

Mou, Y., Zhou, L., You, X., Lu, Y., Chen, W., & Zhao, X. (2017). Multiview partial least squares. *Chemometrics and Intelligent Laboratory Systems, 160*, 13–21. doi:10.1016/j.chemolab.2016.10.013

Muinde, C. M., Lewa, P., & Kamau, J. N. (2016). *The influence of top management support on knowledge sharing during the implementation of ERP systems in Kenya*. Academic Press.

Muketha, G. M. (2011). *Size And Complexity Metrics as Indicators of Maintainability, of Business Process Execution Language Process Models* (PhD Thesis). University Putra Malaysia.

Muketha, G. M., Matoke, N., & Khaemba, S. N. (n.d.). Factors affecting citizen readiness for E-government Systems in Kenya. *Journal of Research in Engineering and Applied Science*.

Mukherjee, S., & Das, S. M. (2017). Why Use SAP MII in Manufacturing Industries. In *SAP MII* (pp. 31–52). Berkeley, CA: Apress. doi:10.1007/978-1-4842-2814-2_2

Mungai, P. K. (2016). Challenges of Implementing Enterprise Resource Planning in Mombasa International Airport. *International Journal of Innovative Research and Development, 5*(6), 154–177.

Murikipudi, A., Prakash, V., & Vigneswaran, T. (2015). Performance Analysis of Real Time Operating System with General Purpose Operating System for Mobile Robotic System. *Indian Journal of Science and Technology, 8*(19). doi:10.17485/ijst/2015/v8i19/77017

Murray, J. H. (2011).*Inventing the medium: principles of interaction design as a cultural practice.* MIT Press.

Muscatello, J., & Chen, I. (2008). A Case Analysis of ERP Post-Implementation Issues Vis-À-Vis Muscatello and Parente's Propositions. *International Journal of Enterprise Information Systems.*

Muscatello, J., & Chen, I. (2008). Enterprise Resource Planning (ERP) Implementations: Theory and Practice.‖. *International Journal of Enterprise Information Systems, 4*, 63–78. doi:10.4018/jeis.2008010105

Musyimi, N. D., & Odongo, W. O. (2015). Adoption of Enterprise Resource Planning Systems in Kenya: A Case of Selected Manufacturing Firms in Nairobi Metropolitan. *International Journal of Business Human Technology, 5*(2), 24–32.

Nacenta, M. A., Kamber, Y., Qiang, Y., & Kristensson, P. O. (2013). Memorability of pre-designed and user-defined gesture sets. In *Proceedings of the SIGCHI Conference on Human Factors in Computing Systems* (pp. 1099-1108). ACM. 10.1145/2470654.2466142

Naedele, M., Chen, H. M., Kazman, R., Cai, Y., Xiao, L., & Silva, C. V. (2015). Manufacturing execution systems: A vision for managing software development. *Journal of Systems and Software, 101*, 59–68. doi:10.1016/j.jss.2014.11.015

Nah, F. F.-H., Tan, X., & Beethe, M. (2005). An emergent model of end users' acceptance of enterprise resource planning systems: a grounded theory research. *Proceedings of the Americas Conference on Information Systems*, 2053–2057.

Närman, P., Johnson, P., & Nordström, L. (2007). Enterprise Architecture: A Framework Supporting System Quality Analysis. In *11th IEEE International Enterprise Distributed Object Computing Conference (EDOC 2007)* (pp. 130-130). Annapolis, MD: IEEE. 10.1109/EDOC.2007.39

Nedelcu, B. (2012). Business Intelligence Systems. *Database Systems Journal, 4*, 12–20. Retrieved from http://www.dbjournal.ro/archive/14/14_2.pdf

Neely, A., Adams, C., & Kennerley, M. (2002). The performance Prism – The scorecard for measuring and managing Business Success. Prentice Hall.

Ng, C. S., Gable, G., & Chan, T. (2002). An ERP Maintenance Model. In *Proceedings of the 36th Hawaii International Conference on System Sciences (HICSS'03).* IEEE.

Ng, C., Gable, G., & Chan, T. (2002). An ERP-client benefit-oriented maintenance taxonomy. *Journal of Systems and Software, 64*(2), 87–109. doi:10.1016/S0164-1212(02)00029-8

Nielsen, J. (2002). *Critical success factors for implementing an ERP system in a university environment: A case study from the Australian HES.* Brisbane: Griffith University.

Nielsen, J. L., Beekhuyzen, J., & Goodwin, M. (2005). The Evolution of Enterprise Wide Systems within Australian Higher Education. In L. von Hellens, S. Nielsen, & J. Beekhuyzen (Eds.), *Qualitative Case Studies on Implementation of Enterprise Wide Systems.* Hershey, PA: Idea Group Publishing.

Nielsen, T. D., & Jensen, F. V. (2009). *Bayesian Network and Decision Graph.* Springer Science & Business Media; doi:10.1007/978-0-387-68282-2

Nieuwenhuis, L. J., Ehrenhard, M. L., & Prause, L. (2018). The shift to Cloud Computing: The impact of disruptive technology on the enterprise software business ecosystem. *Technological Forecasting and Social Change*, *129*, 308–313. doi:10.1016/j.techfore.2017.09.037

Njuguna, M. W. (2011). *Implementing enterprise resource planning system at Kenya Revenue Authority.* Research paper school of business University of Nairobi.

Nordin, N., & Adegoke, O. (2015). Learning from ERP Implementation: A Case Study of Issues and Challenges in Technology Management. *Jurnal Teknologi*, *74*(1). doi:10.11113/jt.v74.3369

Novak, G. (2014). *Developing a usability method for assessment of M-Commerce systems: a case study at Ericsson.* Academic Press.

Nuñez-Varela, A. S., Pérez-Gonzalez, H. G., Martínez-Perez, F. E., & Soubervielle-Montalvo, C. (2017). Source code metrics: A systematic mapping study. *Journal of Systems and Software*, *128*, 164–197. doi:10.1016/j.jss.2017.03.044

Nwankpa, J., & Roumani, Y. (2014). Understanding the link between organizational learning capability and ERP system usage: An empirical examination. *Computers in Human Behavior*, *33*, 224–234.

Nyagah, E. (2006). *An Investigation Of Critical Success Factors For Successful Implementation Of Enterprise Resource Planning (ERP) Systems in Kenya.* Research paper school of business University of Nairobi.

Nylen, E. L., Wallisch, P., Nylen, E. L., & Wallisch, P. (2017). Dimensionality Reduction. In Neural Data Science (pp. 223–248). Academic Press. doi:10.1016/B978-0-12-804043-0.00008-8

Nzuki, D. M., & Okelo-Odongo, W. (2015). *Adoption of Enterprise Resource Planning Systems in Kenya: A Case of Selected Manufacturing Firms in Nairobi Metropolitan.* Academic Press.

O'Brien & Marakas. (2010). *Management Information Systems* (10th ed.). McGraw-Hill. Retrieved from http://getcollegecredit.com/assets/pdf/dsst_fact_sheets/DSST_ManagementInformationSystems.pdf

O'Brien, J., & Marakas, G. (2006). *Management Information Systems* (7th ed.). McGraw-Hill Irwin.

OAG. (2018). *Mandate*. Retrieved on 13/12/2018 from https://www.oagkenya.go.ke/index.php/about-us/mandate

Ociepa-Kubicka, A. (2017). Advantages of using enterprise resource planning systems (ERP) in the management process. *World Scientific News*, *89*, 237–243.

Odell, L. A., Farrar-Foley, B. T., Kinkel, J. R., Moorthy, R. S., & Schultz, J. A. (2012). *Beyond Enterprise Resource Planning (ERP): The Next Generation Enterprise Resource Planning Environment* (No. IDA/HQ-P-4852). Academic Press.

Ogheneovo, E. E. (2014). Software Dysfunction: Why Do Software Fail? *Journal of Computer and Communications*, *2*(06), 25–35. doi:10.4236/jcc.2014.26004

Oh, Y., Han, H., Shin, D., Kim, D., & Kim, N. (2015). The Framework for Adaptive ERP Systems Using the Ontology Model of a Manufacturing Supply Chain. *Journal Of Korean Institute Of Industrial Engineers*, *41*(4), 344–351. doi:10.7232/JKIIE.2015.41.4.344

Olson, J. E. (2003). *Data Quality: The Accuracy Dimension. Data Quality: The Accuracy Dimension*. doi:10.1016/B978-1-55860-891-7.X5000-8

Oluwatosin, H. S. (2014). Client-server model. *IOSRJ Comput. Eng*, *16*(1), 2278–8727.

Omieno, K., & Rodriguez, A. (2016). Usability Maturity Model and Assessment Tool for Virtual Learning Systems. *International Journal of Advanced Research in Computer and Communication Engineering*, *5*(12), 78-84. DOI doi:10.17148/IJARCCE.2016.51217

Omuono, G. (2015). *Presentation kenet maseno_0.pdf - Google Search*. Retrieved August 17, 2017, from https://www.google.com/search?source=hp&q=presentat ion+kenet++maseno_0.pdf&oq=presentation+kenet++maseno_0.pdf&gs_l=psy-ab.3...23869.48422.0.49331.36.34.0.0.0.0.548.6421.2-7j10j1j1.19.0....0...1.1.64.psy-ab.17.15. 5211.6.0j35i39k1j0i131k1j0i20k1j33i160k1j33i21k1.Tlbbu_pVY94

Ömüral, N. K., & Demirörs, O. (2017). Effort estimation methods for ERP projects based on function points: a case study. *Proceedings of the 27th International Workshop on Software Measurement and 12th International Conference on Software Process and Product Measurement*, 199–206. 10.1145/3143434.3143464

Oracle. (2011). *What Is Data Mining*. Retrieved from https://docs.oracle.com/cd/B28359_01/datamine.111/b28129/process.htm#CHDFGCIJ

Orougi, S. (2015). Recent advances in enterprise resource planning. *Accounting*, 37-42. doi:10.5267/j.ac.2015.11.004

Ouyang, G., Herzmann, G., Zhou, C., & Sommer, W. (2011). Residue iteration decomposition (RIDE): A new method to separate ERP components on the basis of latency variability in single trials. *Psychophysiology*, *48*(12), 1631–1647. doi:10.1111/j.1469-8986.2011.01269.x PMID:21895682

Panichella, A., Kifetew, F. M., & Tonella, P. (2018). A large scale empirical comparison of state-of-the-art search-based test case generators. *Information and Software Technology, 104*, 236–256. doi:10.1016/j.infsof.2018.08.009

Papazoglou & Ribbers. (2009). e-Business: Organisation and Technical Foundation. Wiley India Pvt, Ltd.

Parthasarathy, S. (2013). Potential concerns and common benefits of cloud-based enterprise resource planning (ERP). In *Cloud Computing* (pp. 177–195). London: Springer. doi:10.1007/978-1-4471-5107-4_9

Parthasarathy, S., & Anbazhagan, N. (2006). Significance of Software Metrics in ERP Projects. *2006 Annual IEEE India Conference*, 1–4. 10.1109/INDCON.2006.302776

Parthasarathy, S., & Anbazhagan, N. (2007). Evaluating ERP implementation choices using AHP. *International Journal of Enterprise Information Systems, 3*(3), 52–65. doi:10.4018/jeis.2007070104

Parthasarathy, S., & Sharma, S. (2016). Efficiency analysis of ERP packages—A customization perspective. *Computers in Industry, 82*, 19–27. doi:10.1016/j.compind.2016.05.004

Parthasarathy, S., & Sharma, S. (2017). Impact of customization over software quality in ERP projects: An empirical study. *Software Quality Journal, 25*(2), 581–598. doi:10.100711219-016-9314-x

Pavel, J., & Evelyn, T. (2017). An Illustrative Case Study of the Integration of Enterprise Resource Planning System. *Journal of Enterprise Resource Planning Studies*, 1-9. doi:10.5171/2017.176215

Peng, G. C., & Nunes, M. B. (2009). Surfacing ERP exploitation risks through a risk ontology. *Industrial Management & Data Systems, 109*(7), 926–942. doi:10.1108/02635570910982283

Peng, X. (2012). Efficient Construction Scheme of Software Service Outsourcing Industry. *Journal of Software, 7*(11). doi:10.4304/jsw.7.11.2583-2590

Perera, H., & Withanage, T. (2008). Critical Success Factors in Post ERP Implementation. Engineer. *Journal Of The Institution Of Engineers, Sri Lanka, 41*(3), 29. doi:10.4038/engineer.v41i3.7088

Petter, S., DeLone, W., & McLean, E. (2008). Measuring information systems success: Models, dimensions, measures, and interrelationships. *European Journal of Information Systems, 17*(3), 236–263. doi:10.1057/ejis.2008.15

Pipino, L. L., Lee, Y. W., & Wang, R. Y. (2002). Data quality assessment. *Communications of the ACM, 45*(4), 211. doi:10.1145/505248.506010

Poister, T. H. (2010). The future of strategic planning in the public sector: Linking strategic management and performance. *Public Administration Review, 70*(s1), s246–s254. doi:10.1111/j.1540-6210.2010.02284.x

Pollock, J. (2004). Adaptive Information: Improving Business through Semantic Interoperability, Grid Computing, and Enterprise Integration. John Wiley & Sons.

Pontus Johnson, R. L., Narman, P., & Simonsson, M. (2007). Extended Influence Diagrams for System Quality Analysis. *Journal of Software*, 2(3), 30–42.

Pramanik, P. K. D., Pal, S., & Choudhury, P. (2018). Beyond Automation: The Cognitive IoT. Artificial Intelligence Brings Sense to the Internet of Things. In *Cognitive Computing for Big Data Systems Over IoT* (pp. 1–37). Cham: Springer. doi:10.1007/978-3-319-70688-7_1

Prechelt, L., & Pepper, A. (2014). Why software repositories are not used for defect-insertion circumstance analysis more often: A case study. *Information and Software Technology*, 56(10), 1377–1389. doi:10.1016/j.infsof.2014.05.001

Pretorius, M., Gelderblom, H. J., & Chimbo, B. (2010). Using Eye-Tracking to compare how adults and children learn to use an unfamiliar computer game. In *SAICSIT*. Bela Bela, South Africa: ACM Press. doi:10.1145/1899503.1899534

PricewaterhouseCoopers. (2005). ERP Implementation in the Mid-Market Segment. PricewaterhouseCoopers (P) Ltd.

Pui Ng, C. S., Gable, G., & Chan, T. (2002). An ERP Maintenance Model. In *Proceedings of the 36th Hawaii International Conference on System Sciences*. IEEE.

Rajan, C. A., & Baral, R. (2015). Adoption of ERP system: An empirical study of factors influencing the usage of ERP and its impact on end user. *IIMB Management Review*, 27(2), 105–117.

Rajan, C. A., & Baral, R. (2015). Adoption of ERP System: An Empirical Study of Factors Influencing the Usage of ERP and its Impact on End User. *IIMB Management Review*, 27(2), 105–117.

Rajan, C., & Baral, R. (2015). Adoption of ERP system: An empirical study of factors influencing the usage of ERP andits impact on end user. *IIMB Management Review*, 27(2), 105–117. doi:10.1016/j.iimb.2015.04.008

Ramaprasad, A., & Williams, J. J. (2000). A taxonomy of critical success factors. *European Journal of Information Systems*, 5, 250–260.

Ramdani, B. (2012). Information technology and organisational performance: Reviewing the business value of IT literature. In *Information Systems Theory* (pp. 283–301). New York, NY: Springer. doi:10.1007/978-1-4419-6108-2_15

Ramírez-Gallego, S., García, S., Mouriño-Talín, H., Martínez-Rego, D., Bolón-Canedo, V., & Alonso-Betanzos, A., … Herrera, F. (2016). Data discretization: Taxonomy and big data challenge. *Wiley Interdisciplinary Reviews. Data Mining and Knowledge Discovery*. doi:10.1002/widm.1173

Rasmussen, C. E. (2006). Gaussian processes for machine learning. *International Journal of Neural Systems*, 14(2), 69–106. doi:10.1142/S0129065704001899 PMID:15112367

Reo, D. (1999, March). The Balanced IT Scorecard for software intensive organisations: benefits and lessons learnt through industry applications. *Symposium on IT Balanced Scorecard*.

Rerup Schlichter, B., & Kraemmergaard, P. (2010). A comprehensive literature review of the ERP research field over a decade. *Journal of Enterprise Information Management, 23*(4), 486–520.

Robert, L. (2007). *Analyzing System Maintainability Using Enterprise Architecture Models.* Royal Institute of Technology.

Roemer, R., Buchanan, E., Shacham, H., & Savage, S. (2012). Return-oriented programming: Systems, languages, and applications. *ACM Transactions on Information and System Security, 15*(1), 2. doi:10.1145/2133375.2133377

Rogers, E. (2003). *Diffusion of innovations* (5th ed.). Free Press.

Rohit, R. (n.d.). *An Overview of Enterprise Resource Planning ERP.* Retrieved from https://www.academia.edu/7095803/Chapter_7_An_Overview_of_Enterprise_Resource_Planning_ERP

Rosemann, M., & Wiese, J. (1999). Measuring the Performance of ERP Software – a Balanced Scorecard Approach. *Conference Proceeding, the 10th Australian Conference on Information Systems, 8.*

Rostami, A. (2016). Tools and Techniques in Risk Identification: A Research within SMEs in the UK Construction Industry. *Universal Journal of Management, 4*(4), 203–210. doi:10.13189/ujm.2016.040406

Rowlands. (2009). *Beyond Interoperability: A new policy framework for e-Government.* Available: http://www.cstransform.com/white_papers/BeyondInteropV1.0.pdf

Ruivo, P., Oliveira, T., Johansson, B., & Neto, M. (2013). Differential effects on ERP post-adoption stages across Scandinavian and Iberian SMEs. *Journal of Global Information Management, 21*(3), 1–20.

Ruivo, P., Oliveira, T., & Neto, M. (2012). ERP use and value: Portuguese and Spanish SMEs. *Industrial Management & Data Systems, 112*(7), 1008–1025.

Rukanova, B. D., Van Slooten, K., & Stegwee, R. A. (2006). Business Process Requirements, Modeling Technique and Standard: how to Identify Interoperability Gaps on a Process Level. In D. Konstantas, J.-P. Bourrières, M. Léonard, & N. Boudjlida (Eds.), *Interoperability of Enterprise Software and Applications* (pp. 13–23). London: Springer-Verlag. doi:10.1007/1-84628-152-0_2

Sabau, G., Munten, M., Bologa, A.-R., Bologa, R., & Surcel, T. (2009a). An evaluation framework for higher education ERP systems. *WSEAS Transactions on Computers, 8*(11), 1790–1799.

Sabau, G., Munten, M., Bologa, A.-R., Bologa, R., & Surcel, T. (2009b). An evaluation framework for higher education ERP Systems. *WSEAS Transactions on Computers, 8*(11), 1790–1799.

Saha, B., & Srivastava, D. (2014). Data quality: The other face of Big Data. In *Proceedings - International Conference on Data Engineering* (pp. 1294–1297). Academic Press. 10.1109/ICDE.2014.6816764

Sahin, I. (2006, April). Detailed Review of Rogers' Diffusion of Innovations Theory and Educational Technology: Related Studies Based on Rogers' Theory. *The Turkish Online Journal of Educational Technology, 5*, 14–23. doi:10.1287/mnsc.43.7.934

Sanchez. (2008). *Enterprise Architectures - Enabling Interoperability Between Organizations.* Academic Press.

Sandra Graham, V. S. F. (2014). *Attribution Theory Application to Achievement, Mental Health, and Interpersonal Conflict (2nd ed.).* New York: Psychology Press. doi:10.4324/9781315807669

Sanjay, A. (2003). *Service Delivery Management.* Academic Press.

Saran, C. (2007). Oracle extends sector specific ERP for SMEs. *Computer Weekly, 16*. Retrieved from http://search.ebscohost.com/login.aspx?direct=true&db=bth&AN=26259654&site=eho st-live

Saunders, L. (2014). Linking Resource Decisions to Planning. *New Directions for Community Colleges, 2014*(168), 65–75. doi:10.1002/cc.20121

Saunders, M., Lewia, P., & Thornbill, A. (2009). *Research methods for business students.* London: Prentice Hall.

Schniederjans, D., & Yadav, S. (2013). Successful ERP implementation: An integrative model. *Business Process Management Journal, 19*(2), 364–398. doi:10.1108/14637151311308358

Scholkopf, B., Smola, A. J., & Muller, K. R. (2012). Kernel Principal Component Analysis. *Computer Vision And Mathematical Methods In Medical And Biomedical Image Analysis, 1327*, 583–588. doi:10.1162/089976698300017467

Scholtz, B., Cilliers, C., & Calitz, A. (2010). Qualitative techniques for evaluating enterprise resource planning (ERP) user interfaces. *Proceedings of the 2010 Annual Research Conference of the South African Institute of Computer Scientists and Information Technologists*, 284–293. 10.1145/1899503.1899535

Seemann, L., Hua, J.-C., McCauley, J. L., & Gunaratne, G. H. (2012). Ensemble vs. time averages in financial time series analysis. *Physica A, 391*(23), 6024–6032. doi:10.1016/j.physa.2012.06.054

Selmeci, A., Orosz, I., Györök, G., & Orosz, T. (2012). Key Performance Indicators used in ERP performance measurement applications. *Intelligent Systems and Informatics (SISY), 2012 IEEE 10th Jubilee International Symposium On*, 43–48. 10.1109/SISY.2012.6339583

Seo, G. (2013). *Challenges in implementing enterprise resource planning (ERP) system in large organizations: similarities and differences between corporate and university environment* (Doctoral dissertation). Massachusetts Institute of Technology.

Serrano, N., & Sarriegi, J. (2006). Open source software ERPs: A new alternative for an old need. *IEEE Software, 23*(3), 94–97. doi:10.1109/MS.2006.78

Sharma, V., & Baliyan, P. (2011). Maintainability Analysis of Component Based Systems. *International Journal of Software Engineering and Its Applications*, *5*(3), 107–118.

Shatat, A. S. (2015). Critical success factors in enterprise resource planning (ERP) system implementation: An exploratory study in Oman. *Electronic Journal of Information Systems Evaluation*, *18*(1), 36–45.

Shehab, E. M., Sharp, M. W., Supramaniam, L., & Spedding, T. A. (2004). Enterprise Resource Planning: An Integrative Review. *Business Process Management*, *10*(4), 359–386. doi:10.1108/14637150410548056

Shepperd, M. (1988). A critique of cyclomatic complexity as a software metric. *Software Engineering Journal*, *3*(2), 30–36. doi:10.1049ej.1988.0003

Sherwood-Jones, B. (1995). *Total Systems Maturity. Internal report, version 2*. BAeSEMA.

Sheth, P. A. (1998). *Changing Focus on Interoperability in Information Systems from system, syntax, structure to semantics*. Interoperability Geographic Information System. Retrieved from http://lsdis.cs.uga.edu/library/download/S98-changing.pdf

Singh, A., & Wesson, J. (2009). Evaluation Criteria for Assessing the Usability of ERP Systems. *Proceedings of the 2009 Annual Research Conference of the South African Institute of Computer Scientists and Information Technologists*, 87–95. 10.1145/1632149.1632162

Singh, C. D., Singh, R., & Kaur, H. (2017). *Critical appraisal for implementation of ERP in the manufacturing industry*. LAP LAMBERT Academic Publishing.

Singh, J. (2014). To Study the Quality Assurance & Control of Products in Industries. *International Journal of Research*, *1*(11), 1337–1353.

Singh, R. (1995). *International Standard ISO/IEC 12207 Software Life Cycle Processes*. Washington, DC: Federal Aviation Administration.

Siriluck. (2017). Measuring ERP Implementation Success with balanced Scorecard. *The 23rd Journal Americas conference on Information System.*

Soh, C., Kien, S. S., & Tay-Yap, J. (2000). Cultural fits and misfits: Is ERP a universal solution? *Communications of the ACM*, *43*(4), 47–51. doi:10.1145/332051.332070

Soja, P., & Paliwoda-Pękosz, G. (2013). Impediments to enterprise system implementation over the system lifecycle: Contrasting transition and developed economies. *The Electronic Journal on Information Systems in Developing Countries*, *57*(1), 1–13. doi:10.1002/j.1681-4835.2013. tb00403.x

Sokappadu, G. M., Paavan, R., & Devi, R. V. (2016). Review of Software Maintenance Problems and Proposed Solutions in IT consulting firms in Mauritius. *International Journal of Computer Applications*, *156*(4), 12-20.

Somers, T. M., & Nelson, K. G. (2004). A taxonomy of players and activities across the ERP project life cycle. *Information & Management, 41*(3), 257–278. doi:10.1016/S0378-7206(03)00023-5

Soral, G., & Jain, M. (2011). Impact of ER P system on auditing and internal control. The International Journal's Research. *Journal of Social Sciences and Management, 1*(4), 16–23.

Souley, B., & Bata, B. (2013). A class coupling analyzer for Java programs. *West African Journal of Industrial and Academic Research, 7*(1), 3–13.

Stackify. (2017). *What are software metrics and how can authors track them.* Retrieved 14/12/2018 at https://satackify.com/track-software-metrics/

Statues. (2017). *Kibabii University statutes 2017.*

Stoilov, T., & Stoilova, K. (2008). Functional Analysis of Enterprise Resource Planning Systems. *Proceedings of the 9th International Conference on Computer Systems and Technologies and Workshop for PhD Students in Computing, 43*, 8–43. 10.1145/1500879.1500927

Subramaniam, R., & Nakkeeran, S. (2019). Impact of Corporate E-Learning Systems in Enhancing the Team Performance in Virtual Software Teams. In *Smart Technologies and Innovation for a Sustainable Future* (pp. 195–204). Cham: Springer. doi:10.1007/978-3-030-01659-3_22

Sum, C., Ang, J., & Yeo, L. (1997). Contextual Elements of Critical Success Factors in MRP Implementation. *Production and Inventory Management Journal, 3*, 77–83.

Surendro, K., & Olivia, O. (2016). Academic Cloud ERP Quality Assessment Model. *Iranian Journal of Electrical and Computer Engineering, 6*(3), 1038–1047.

Sutton, H. (2018). Scaling up PLA requires strong policies, planning backend processes. *The Successful Registrar, 18*(2), 1–5. doi:10.1002/tsr.30454

Tahir, T., Rasool, G., & Noman, M. (2018). A Systematic Mapping Study on Software Measurement Programs in SMEs. E-*Informatica Software Engineering Journal, 12*(1).

Talet, N., & Alwahaishi, S. (2011). The relevance cultural dimensions on the success adoption and use of IT. In *Third International Conference on Advanced Management Science*. Singapore: IACSIT Press.

Targowski, A. (2011). The enterprise systems approach. In Enterprise Information Systems: Concepts, Methodologies, Tools, and Applications (pp. 397-426). IGI Global. doi:10.4018/978-1-61692-852-0.ch206

Tax, D. M. J., & Duin, R. P. W. (2004). Support vector data description. *Machine Learning, 54*(1), 45–66. doi:10.1023/B:MACH.0000008084.60811.49

Taylor, S., & Todd, P. (1995). Assessing it usage: The role of prior experience. *Management Information Systems Quarterly, 19*(4), 561–570. doi:10.2307/249633

Tella, A., & Akinboro, E. O. (2015). The impact of social media on library services in the digital environment. *Social Media Strategies for Dynamic Library Service Development,* 279-295.

Teoh, S. Y., Pan, S. L., & Ramchand, A. M. (2012). Resource management activities in healthcare information systems: A process perspective. *Information Systems Frontiers, 14*(3), 585–600. doi:10.100710796-010-9280-y

Terantino, J. M. (2011). Emerging technologies YouTube for foreign languages: You have to see this video. *Language Learning & Technology, 15*(1), 10–16.

Terminanto, A. (2014). Forecast to Plan Cycle in Oracle E Business Suite (Case Study Automotive Company). *Advanced Science Letters, 20*(1), 203–208. doi:10.1166/asl.2014.5279

Thamer, A., Mommad, I., & Ahmad, A. (2013). Software Quality Model of ERP System in Higher Education Institutions. *European Journal of Scientific Research, 99*, 15–21.

Thompson, R., Higgins, C., & Howell, J. (1991). Personal computing: Toward a conceptual model of utilization. *Management Information Systems Quarterly, 15*(1), 124–143. doi:10.2307/249443

Tobias, R. D. (1995). An Introduction to Partial Least Squares Regression. In *Proceedings of the Twentieth Annual SAS Users Group International Conference* (pp. 1250–1257). Cary, NC: SAS Institute Inc;

Tolk, A., & Muguira, J. A. (2003). *The Levels of Conceptual Interoperability Model.* Virginia Modeling Analysis & Simulation Centre (VMASC), College of Engineering and Technology. Retrieved from http://www.Psu.edu

Tong, X., Zhang, X., Xu, X., & Qi, J. (2014). Improving Workflow Management System Implementation with Workflow Localization Method. *Applied Mechanics And Materials, 513-517*, 3859-3863. Retrieved from www.scientific.net/amm.513-517.3859

Tulaskar, R. (2018). Evolution of Embedded User Assistance: Considering Usability and Aesthetics. In *Companion Proceedings of the 2018 ACM International Conference on Interactive Surfaces and Spaces*(pp. 69-76). ACM.

Turetken, O., Ondracek, J., & Ijsselsteijn, W. (2019). Influential characteristics of enterprise information system user interfaces. *Journal of Computer Information Systems, 59*(3), 243–255. doi:10.1080/08874417.2017.1339367

UAT. (2018). *A complete guide user acceptance test.* Retrieved from https://www.softwaretestinghelp.com/

Umble, E. J., Haft, R. R., & Umble, M. M. (2003). Enterprise Resource Planning: Implementation Procedures and Critical Success Factors. *European Journal of Operational Research, 146*(2), 241–257. doi:10.1016/S0377-2217(02)00547-7

Uncel, M. (2011). "Facebook Is Now Friends with the Court": Current Federal Rules and Social Media Evidence. *Jurimetrics*, 43-69.

Valdebenito, J., & Quelopana, A. (2018). Understanding the landscape of research in Enterprise Resource Planning (ERP) systems adoption. *Proceedings of the 2018 International Conference on Computers in Management and Business*, 35–39. 10.1145/3232174.3232178

Van Merriënboer, J. J., & Kirschner, P. A. (2012). *Ten steps to complex learning: A systematic approach to four-component instructional design.* Routledge.

VanDerSchaaf, H., & Daim, T. (2018). Evaluating Technologies for Higher Education: E-Services. In 2018 IEEE Technology and Engineering Management Conference (TEMSCON) (pp. 1-6). IEEE.

Veer, H., & Wiles, A. (2008). *Achieving Technical Interoperabilty – the ETSI approach.* European Telecommunications Standards Institute. Retrieved from http://www.etsi.org

Veltman, K. H. (2001). Syntatic and semantic interoperability: New approaches to knowledge and the semantic web. *New Reviews of Information Networking, 7*(1), 159–183. doi:10.1080/13614570109516975

Venkadasalam, S. (2015). Linear Programming: An Alternative Enterprise Resource Planning (ERP) in Higher Learning Institution. *Journal Of Business And Economics, 6*(9), 1633–1637. doi:10.15341/jbe(2155-7950)/09.06.2015/010

Venkatesh, V. e., Morris, Davis, & Davis. (2003). User acceptance of information technology: Towards a unified view. *Management Information Systems Quarterly, 27*(3), 425–478. doi:10.2307/30036540

Vermaat, M. (2016). *Enhanced Discovering Computers.* Cengage Learning.

Verville, J., Palanisamy, R., Bernadas, C., & Halingten, A. (2007). ERP acquisition planning: A critical dimension for making the right choice. *Long Range Planning, 40*(1), 45–63. doi:10.1016/j.lrp.2007.02.002

Vigneau, E., Devaux, M. F., Qannari, E. M., & Robert, P. (1997). Principal component regression, ridge regression and ridge principal component regression in spectroscopy calibration. *Journal of Chemometrics, 11*(3), 239–249. doi:10.1002/(SICI)1099-128X(199705)11:3<239::AID-CEM470>3.0.CO;2-A

Wailgum, T., & Perkins, B. (2018, February 18). *What is ERP? A guide to enterprise resource planning systems.* Retrieved from CIO: https://www.cio.com/article/2439502/enterprise-resource-planning/enterprise-resource-planning-erp-definition-and-solutions.html

Waizenegger, L., Thalmann, S., Sarigianni, C., Eckhardt, A., Kolb, D., Maier, R., & Remus, U. (2016). from isolation to collaboration-how the increasing diffusion of mobile devices has changed practices of knowledge sharing in non-office settings. *Social Behavior and Personality, 36*(1), 41–42.

Wand, M. P., & Jones, M. C. (1995). Kernel Smoothing. Encyclopedia of Statistics in Behavioral Science, 60(60), 212. doi:10.2307/1268906

Wang, P. (2014). *Is a multi-touch gesture interface based on a tablet better than a smartphone for elderly users?* (Doctoral dissertation). Auckland University of Technology.

Wang, C., & Tsai, W. (2014). Elucidating How Interface Design and Cognitive Function Affect Learning Performance in the Enterprise Resource Planning (ERP) Software System. *Journal of Testing and Evaluation*, *44*(1), 20140044. doi:10.1520/JTE20140044

Wang, R. Y. (1998). Total Data Quality Management. *Communications of the ACM*, *41*(2), 58–65. doi:10.1145/269012.269022

Wang, R. Y., Kon, H. B., & Madnick, S. E. (1993). Data Quality Requirements Analysis and Modeling. *Data Engineering*, *8*(April), 670–677. doi:10.1109/ICDE.1993.344012

Wang, Y., Kung, L., Wang, W. Y. C., & Cegielski, C. G. (2018). An integrated big data analytics-enabled transformation model: Application to health care. *Information & Management*, *55*(1), 64–79. doi:10.1016/j.im.2017.04.001

Wanyoike, F. W. (2017). *The Influence of Enterprise Resource Planning System on Organizational Performance: Case Study of Kenyan Engineering Consultancy Firms*. United States International University-Africa.

Webb, N., Richter, A., & Bonsper, D. (2010). Linking Defense Planning and Resource Decisions: A Return to Systems Thinking. *Defense & Security Analysis*, *26*(4), 387–400. doi:10.1080/14751798.2010.534647

Webmaster. (2018). *History of Kibabii University*. Retrieved from https://kibu.ac.ke/history/

Weerakkody, V., Irani, Z., Kapoor, K., Sivarajah, U., & Dwivedi, Y. K. (2016). Open data and its usability: An empirical view from the Citizen's perspective. *Information Systems Frontiers*, 1–16. doi:10.100710796-016-9679-1

Welti, N. (1999). *Successful SAP R/3 Implementation: Practical Management of ERP Projects*. Addison-Wesley.

Weyuker, E. J. (1998). Evaluating Software complexity measures. *IEEE Transactions on Software Engineering*.

Winter. (2002). *Chapter on Interoperability*. European Territorial Management Information Infrastructure (ETeMII). Retrieved from http://www.ec-gis.org/etemii/reports/chapter3.pdf

Wolf-Branigin, M. (2013). *Using complexity theory for research and program evaluation*. Oxford University Press. doi:10.1093/acprof:oso/9780199829460.001.0001

Woodings, T. L., & Bundell, G. A. (2001). A framework for software project metrics. *Proc. 12th European Conference on Software Control and Metrics (ESCOM'01)*.

Woodley. (2001). *Dublin Core Metadata Initiative, Glossary*. Retrieved from http://dublincore.org/documents/2001/04/12/usageguide/glossary.shtml#S

Wu & Wang. (2005). Measuring ERP success: The key-users' viewpoint of the ERP to produce a viable IS in the organization. *Computers in Human Behavior*.

Wu, J.-H., & Wang, Y.-M. (2003). Enterprise resource planning experience in Taiwan: an empirical study and comparative analysis. In R. H. Sprague Jr. (Ed.), *Proceedings of the 36th. Hawaii International Conference on Systems Sciences*. IEEE Computer Society Press.

Wu, J.-H., & Wang, Y.-M. (2007, May). the ERP to produce a viable IS in the organization. *Computers in Human Behavior, 23*(3), 1582–1596. doi:10.1016/j.chb.2005.07.005

Xu, Y., Rahmati, N., & Lee, V. C. (2008). A review of literature on Enterprise Resource Planning systems. *Service Systems and Service Management, 2008 International Conference On*, 1–6. 10.1109/ICSSSM.2008.4598481

Xu, H. (2006). The Importance of Data Quality for SAP Implementation in Medium-sized Organizations. *Issues in Information Systems, VII*(2), 88–91. Retrieved from https://digitalcommons. butler.edu/cgi/viewcontent.cgi?article=1082&context=cob_papers

Yaghubi, S., Modiri, N., & Rafighi, M. (2014). Model Performance Indicators ERP Systems. *International Journal of Computer Science and Information Security, 12*(1), 1–7.

Yan, S. M. (2008). Principle Component Analysis and Partial Least Square: Two Dimension Reduction Techniques for Regression. *Casualty Actuarial Society*, 79–90. Retrieved from https:// www.casact.org/pubs/dpp/dpp08/08dpp76.pdf

Yaşar, A., & Gökhan, Ö. (2016). Determination the Factors that Affect the Use of Enterprise Resource Planning Information System through Technology Acceptance Model. *International Journal of Business and Management, 11*(10), 91–108. doi:10.5539/ijbm.v11n10p91

Yesser, The Saudi e-Government Program. (2007). *IT Readiness Assessment for government institutions*. Safar.

Yildirim, V., & Kuşakcı, A. O. (2018). The Critical Success Factors of Erp Selection and Implementation: A Case Study in the Logistics Sector. *Journal of International Trade, Logistics, and Law, 4*(1), 138–146.

Yin, X., Ng, B. W.-H., & Abbott, D. (2012). Feature Extraction and Selection. In Terahertz Imaging for Biomedical Applications (pp. 95–118). Academic Press. doi:10.1007/978-1-4614-1821-4_7

Yuniarto, D., Suryadi, M., Firmansyah, E., Herdiana, D., & Rahman, A. B. A. (2018). Integrating the Readiness and Usability Models for Assessing the Information System Use. In *2018 6th International Conference on Cyber and IT Service Management (CITSM)* (pp. 1-6). IEEE.

Zafar, H. (2013). Human resource information systems: Information security concerns for organizations. *Human Resource Management Review, 23*(1), 105–113. doi:10.1016/j. hrmr.2012.06.010

Zare, A., & Ravasan, A. (2014). An Extended Framework for ERP Post-Implementation Success Assessment. *Information Resources Management Journal, 27*(4), 45–65. doi:10.4018/ irmj.2014100103

Zeng, Y., & Skibniewski, M. (2013). Risk assessment for enterprise resource planning (ERP) system implementations: A fault tree analysis approach. *Enterprise Information Systems*, *7*(3), 332–353. doi:10.1080/17517575.2012.690049

Zhang, F., Hassan, A. E., McIntosh, S., & Zou, Y. (2017). The use of summation to aggregate software metrics hinders the performance of defect prediction models. *IEEE Transactions on Software Engineering*, *43*(5), 476–491. doi:10.1109/TSE.2016.2599161

Zhang, L., Matthew, K., Zhang, Z., & Banerjee, P. (2003). Critical Success Factors of Enterprise Resource Planning Systems Implementation Success in China. In *Proceedings of the 36th Hawaii International Conference on System Sciences (HICSS'03)*. IEEE Computer Society. 10.1109/HICSS.2003.1174613

Zhu, Y., Li, Y., Wang, W., & Chen, J. (2010). What leads to post implementation success of ERP? An empirical study of the Chinese retail industry. *International Journal of Information Management*, *30*(3), 265–276. doi:10.1016/j.ijinfomgt.2009.09.007

Ziemba, E., & Obłąk, I. (2013). Critical Success Factors for ERP Systems Implementation in Public Administration. *Interdisciplinary Journal of Information, Knowledge, and Management, 8*.

About the Contributors

Geoffrey Muchiri Muketha is Associate Professor and Ag. Dean of the School of Computing and Information Technology, Murang'a University of Technology, Kenya. He received his BSc. in Information Science from Moi University in 1995, his MSc. in Computer Science from Periyar University in 2004, and his Ph.D. in Software Engineering from Universiti Putra Malaysia in 2011. He has many years of experience in teaching, research, and supervision of postgraduate students. His research interests include software and business process metrics, software quality, verification and validation, empirical methods in software engineering, and component-based software engineering. He is a member of the International Association of Engineers (IAENG).

Elyjoy M. Micheni is a Senior lecturer in Information Systems in the Department of Management Science and Technology at The Technical University of Kenya. She holds a PhD (Information Technology) from Masinde Muliro University of Science and Technology, Master of Science (Computer Based Information Systems) from Sunderland University, (UK); Bachelor of Education from Kenyatta University; Post Graduate Diploma in Project Management from Kenya Institute of Management. She has taught Management Information System courses for many years at University level. She has presented papers in scientific conferences and has many publications in referred journals. She has also co-authored a book for Middle level colleges entitled: "Computerized Document Processing". Her career objective is to tap computer based knowledge as a tool to advance business activities, promote research in ICT and enhance quality service.

* * *

Ibrahim Ahmed Al-Baltah is Assistant Professor in the Department of Information Technology at Sanaa University where he has been a faculty member since 2015. He received the B.Sc. in Statistics and Computer Science (2007) from University of Gezira, Sudan, M.Sc. in Software Engineering (2009) from University Putra Malaysia, Malaysia, and Ph.D. in Software Engineering (2014) from University Putra Malaysia, Malaysia. He is a reviewer in some reputed international journals. He focused in green software engineering, resilience software engineering, cognitive software engineering, semantic web, semantic web of things, and semantic data fusion.

Raphael Angulu holds a PhD in Computer Science from the University of Kwazulu Natal, South Africa. He is an accomplished scholar who is a lecturer at Masinde Muliro University of Science and technology. He has widely published in refereed journals and conferences including IEEE. His research interests are in deep learning, data mining, image analysis and Programming Languages.

Guyo S. Huka is a senior lecturer of Human Resource Development (HRD) in the School of Business and Economics, Meru University of Science and Technology, Kenya. He received PhD-HRD from Mt. Kenya University, MBA (HRM & Marketing Management) – Bangalore University, India and B.Ed (Egerton University). Dr. Guyo was the founding Chair, Department of Business management, Dean - School of Business and Economics and currently Director - Innovation and Entrepreneurship and Acting Registrar – Research Development and Extension of Meru University of Science and Technology. His current research interests are service delivery innovations especially for special populations (youths, women & PwDs) through higher education. He has research passion for innovation adoption and utilization.

Ramgopal Kashyap's area of interest is image processing, pattern recognition and machine learning. He has published many research papers, and book chapters in international journals and conferences like Springer, Inderscience, Elsevier, ACM and IGI-Global indexed by Science Citation Index (SCI) and Scopus (Elsevier). He has Reviewed Research Papers in the Science Citation Index Expanded, Springer Journals and Editorial Board Member and conferences programme committee member of the IEEE, Springer international conferences and journals held in countries: Czech Republic, Switzerland, UAE, Australia, Hungary, Poland, Taiwan, Denmark, India, USA, UK, Austria, and Turkey. He has written many book chapters published by IGI Global, USA, Springer, and Elsevier.

Stella Khaemba is a Senior Technical Trainer at Kitale National Polytechnic. She has over 15 years of experience with technical education and sits on various committees at the institution among them, Research development and innovation. She has been an associate faculty for over 6 years at various universities. A scholar with an IT background, she is a Ph.D. student at Masinde Muliro University of Science and Technology. She has presented various papers on e-readiness in several seminars and conferences. Stella has championed for many ICT initiatives in Kenya's education institutions and remains a firm believer that information technology is a driver of change and must be brought closer to every human being in this 21st century.

Amos C. Kirongo is a Tutorial Fellow at the Department of Computer Science, In the School of Computing and Informatics, and Coordinator Innovations and Entrepreneurship in the Directorate of Research Development and Extension at Meru University of Science and Technology, Kenya. He received his BSc in Computer Information Systems from Kenya Methodist University, Kenya and his MSc in Data Communications from KCA University, Kenya, and is currently a Doctoral Student of PhD. Information Technology at The Masinde Muliro University of Science and Technology. Amos spearheaded the implementation of the ERP System in the Meru University of Science and Technology while serving as the System Administrator. His current research interests are Enterprise Resource Planning Software Adoption, Open Government Data, Assistive Technologies, Big Data Analytics, Data Mining, and Image Processing Algorithms for Precision Agriculture. Amos is a member of ACM - Association of Computing Machinery and IEEE - Institute of Electrical and Electronics Engineers and ISSUP – International Society of Substance Use Professionals.

Jackson Kipchirchir Machii is a Tutorial Fellow in Management Science and Technology, Technical University of Kenya. He received his BSc. in Computer Science from Moi University in 2011, his MBA in Management Information System from Kenyatta University in 2015 and is undergoing a Ph.D. in Strategic Information System at University of Nairobi. He has many years of experience in teaching and supervision of under graduate students. His research interests include Cloud Computing, Data Science, E-Learning, Application of Strategy and Information System in providing the Societal Solution.

Samwel Mbuguah is a PhD holder in Information Technology. A Senior Lecturer in School Computing and Informatics Kibabii University. He is also the Director in the Directorate of ICT. An author and Reviewer. An external Examiner In two Public Universities in Kenya. He also a Chartered Engineer and assessor for the engineering council.

Majdi Abdellatief is an assistant professor in the Department of Computer Science at Sudan Technological University, Ministry of Higher Education & Scientific Research, Sudan. He is also an academic member at University of Shaqra, Suadi Arabia. He holds a Doctoral degree in Software Engineering from University Putra, Malaysia, M.Sc. in Information Technology from the Faculty of Computer Science and Information Technology, Alneelain University, Sudan. He has more than 10 years of teaching experience in three different countries. His research interstates includes software measurements, Component based Software Engineering (CBSE) , ERP and Data Science and Advance Software Engineering.

Benard Muma is a Lecturer, Technical University of Kenya.

Julius Murumba is a doctoral student of Information Technology at Kibabii University, Kenya. He holds a Bsc and MSc (Information Systems), and is currently a Lecturer at the Technical University of Kenya. His research interests include software quality assurance and technology enhanced learning.

Makau Mutua holds a Ph.D in Systems Analysis & Integration from the University of Shanghai for Science and Technology, China. He has published widely in both refereed journals and conferences. His research interests are in data mining, Neural Networks, Artificial Intelligence and Complex Networks. Currently, he is a senior lecturer in the school of computing and informatics of Meru University, Kenya.

Masese Bogomba Nelson holds masters of computer applications degree from Periyar University, India and a Ph.D. from Kibabii University. He is currently a lecturer in Information Technology at Kabarak University Kenya. His research interests are mobile applications and security.

Julius Odhiambo is a Lecturer, Department of Management Science, Technical University of Kenya.

Kelvin Kabeti Omieno is a Senior Lecturer and Founding Dean, School of Computing and Information Technology (SCIT), Kaimosi Friends University College (A Constituent College of Masinde Muliro University of Science and Technology), Kenya. He holds a PhD in Business Information Systems of Jaramogi Oginga Odinga University of Science & Technology (Kenya). Besides, he has MSc in Information Technology and First Class Honors Bachelor of Science in Computer Science from Masinde Muliro University of Science and Technology (Kenya). Dr. Omieno has been involved in a number of research projects of ICTs and development, including Data Analytics, Computational Grid Project, Health Informatics, E-learning systems and E-waste management in Kenya. Besides, he has published widely in journals and conference proceedings in Information technology and ICTs for development. He is a professional member of the Association for Computing Machinery (ACM), the largest association of computing professionals globally and is a reviewer with two International Journals.

Evance Onyango has a Bachelor of Business Information Technology-Technical University of Kenya. Author of CISI Managing Cyber Security Web Programming Using Python A-Z OF HCI Ongoing Research on Nanospace-A Subset of Nano-Technology.

Amir Talib is an Assistant Professor in Information Technology Department, College of Computer and Information Sciences at Al Imam Mohammad Ibn Saud Islamic University, Riyadh, Kingdom of Saudi Arabia (KSA). He holds a B.Sc in Computer Engineering from Technological & Science University, Sudan (2006), M.Sc in Computer Science from Universiti Putra Malaysia (2009), and PhD in Software Engineering field at Faculty of Computer Science and Information System at Universiti Putra Malaysia (2012). He has more than 9 years of teaching experience and with about 3 years of system development experience as a system developer at Ejtihad Company, Malaysia. He currently teaches system analysis and design, and software engineering course at both undergraduate and graduate levels. His research interests include Knowledge Management, Information and Network Security, Software Engineering, and Cloud Computing. He has also published and wrote books, articles, and technical papers in numerous journals and conference proceedings with regards to his research interest.

Franklin Wabwoba holds a PhD in Information Technology from Masinde Muliro University of Science Technology. A Professor in School of Computing and Informatics in Kibabii University. He is the Dean of the School. He has published widely and is external Examiner In three public Universities in Kenya. He consults for the Commission of University Education in Kenya and Inter university council for East Africa.

Chripus Wanjala holds a BSc Degree in Computer Science and Master of Science In information Technology from Masinde Muliro University of Science and Technology. He has published a paper on Bluetooth information security. He is Senior Database Administrator in the Directorate of ICT at Kibabii University in Charge with the implementation, support and management of the ERP.

Stephen Kahara Wanjau currently serves as the Director of ICT at Murang'a University of Technology, Kenya. He received his BSc. degree in Information Sciences from Moi University, Kenya in 2006 and a Master of Science degree in Organizational Development from the United States International University – Africa in 2010. He received his MSc. Degree in Computer Systems from Jomo Kenyatta University of Agriculture and Technology, Kenya in June 2018. His research interests are machine learning, artificial intelligence, Knowledge management, Enterprise Resource Planning Systems and cloud computing.

Index

Ensure Quality Research is Introduced to the Academic Community

Become an IGI Global Reviewer for Authored Book Projects

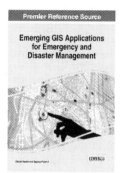

Premier Reference Source

Emerging GIS Applications for Emergency and Disaster Management

Premier Reference Source

Managerial Strategies and Green Solutions for Project Sustainability

Premier Reference Source

Comparative Approaches to Using R and Python for Statistical Data Analysis

Premier Reference Source

Solutions for High-Touch Communications in a High-Tech World

The overall success of an authored book project is dependent on quality and timely reviews.

In this competitive age of scholarly publishing, constructive and timely feedback significantly expedites the turnaround time of manuscripts from submission to acceptance, allowing the publication and discovery of forward-thinking research at a much more expeditious rate. Several IGI Global authored book projects are currently seeking highly qualified experts in the field to fill vacancies on their respective editorial review boards:

Applications may be sent to:
development@igi-global.com

Applicants must have a doctorate (or an equivalent degree) as well as publishing and reviewing experience. Reviewers are asked to write reviews in a timely, collegial, and constructive manner. All reviewers will begin their role on an ad-hoc basis for a period of one year, and upon successful completion of this term can be considered for full editorial review board status, with the potential for a subsequent promotion to Associate Editor.

If you have a colleague that may be interested in this opportunity, we encourage you to share this information with them.

Printed in the United States
By Bookmasters